UNCTAD/DTCI/30(Vol. I)

United Nations Conference on Trade and Development
Division on Transnational Corporations and Investment

International Investment Instruments: A Compendium

Volume I
Multilateral Instruments

United Nations
New York and Geneva, 1996

NOTE

The UNCTAD Division on Transnational Corporations and Investment serves as the focal point within the United Nations Secretariat for all matters related to foreign direct investment and transnational corporations. In the past, the Programme on Transnational Corporations was carried out by the United Nations Centre on Transnational Corporations (1975-1992) and the Transnational Corporations and Management Division of the United Nations Department of Economic and Social Development (1992-1993). In 1993, the Programme was transferred to the United Nations Conference on Trade and Development and became the Division on Transnational Corporations and Investment. The Division on Transnational Corporations and Investment seeks to further the understanding of the nature of transnational corporations and their contribution to development and to create an enabling environment for international investment and enterprise development. The work of the Division is carried out through intergovernmental deliberations, policy analysis and research, technical assistance activities, seminars, workshops and conferences.

The term "country", as used in the boxes added by the UNCTAD Secretariat at the beginning of the instruments reproduced in this volume, also refers, as appropriate, to territories or areas; the designations employed and the presentation of the material do not imply the expression of any opinion whatsoever on the part of the Secretariat of the United Nations concerning the legal status of any country, territory, city or area or of its authorities, or concerning the delimitation of its frontiers or boundaries. Moreover, the country or geographical terminology used in these boxes may occasionally depart from standard United Nations practice when this is made necessary by the nomenclature used at the time of negotiation, signature, ratification or accession of a given international instrument.

To preserve the integrity of the texts of the instruments reproduced in this volume, references to the sources of the instruments that are not contained in their original text are identified as "note added by the editor".

The texts of the instruments included in this volume are reproduced as they were written in one of their original languages or an official translation thereof. When an obvious linguistic mistake has been found, the word "sic" has been added in brackets.

The materials contained in this volume have been reprinted with special permission of the relevant institutions. For those materials under copyright protection, all rights are reserved by the copyright holders.

It should be further noted that this collection of instruments has been prepared for documentation purposes only, and their contents do not engage the responsibility of UNCTAD.

UNCTAD/DTCI/30. Vol. I

UNITED NATIONS PUBLICATION

Sales No. E.96.II.A.9

ISBN 92-1-104463-4

Complete set of three volumes:
ISBN 92-1-104466-9

PREFACE

This selection of international instruments relating to foreign direct investment (FDI) and the activities of transnational corporations (TNCs), presented in three volumes, is intended to fill a gap in existing publications on the topic. In spite of the proliferation in recent years of multilateral and regional instruments dealing with various aspects of FDI, there has been no collection of texts that would make them conveniently available to interested policy-makers, scholars and business executives. Lately, this *lacuna* has become particularly apparent as new initiatives are underway to negotiate a multilateral agreement on investment. In response to this need, and in pursuance of its analytical and consensus-building function, UNCTAD has designed and prepared the present *International Investment Instruments: A Compendium (I.I.I. Compendium)*.

While by necessity selective, the present collection seeks to provide a faithful record of the evolution and present status of intergovernmental cooperation concerning FDI and TNCs. While the emphasis is on relatively recent documents (more than half of the instruments reproduced date from after 1980), it was deemed useful to include important early instruments as well, with a view towards providing some indications of the historical development of international concerns over FDI in the decades since the end of the Second World War.

The core of this collection consists of legally-binding international instruments, mainly multilateral conventions and regional agreements that have entered into force. In addition, a number of "soft law" documents, such as guidelines, declarations and resolutions adopted by intergovernmental bodies, have been included since these instruments also play a role in the elaboration of an international framework for FDI. In an effort to enhance the understanding of the efforts behind the elaboration of this framework, certain draft instruments that never entered into force, or texts of instruments the negotiations of which were not concluded, are also included; and, in an annex, several prototypes of bilateral investment treaties are reproduced. Included also are a number of influential documents prepared by professional associations, business, consumer and labour organizations. It is clear from the foregoing that no implications concerning the legal status or the legal effect of an instrument can be drawn from its inclusion in this collection.

In view of the great diversity of instruments -- in terms of subject matter, approach, legal form and extent of participation of States -- the simplest possible method of presentation was deemed the most appropriate. Thus, within each subdivision, instruments are reproduced in chronological order:

- Volume I is devoted to multilateral instruments, that is to say, multilateral conventions as well as resolutions and other documents issued by multilateral organizations.

- Volume II covers interregional and regional instruments, including agreements, resolutions and other texts from regional organisations within an inclusive geographical context.

Both volumes cover international instruments widely differing in scope and coverage. A few are designed to provide an overall, general framework for FDI and cover many, although rarely all, aspects of investment operations. Most instruments deal with particular aspects and issues concerning FDI. A significant number address core FDI issues, such as investment liberalization, the promotion and protection of investment, dispute settlement and insurance and guarantees. Others cover specific issues, of direct but not exclusive relevance to FDI and TNCs, such as international trade, transfer of technology, intellectual property, avoidance of double taxation, competition and the protection of consumers and the environment. A relatively small number of instruments of this last category has been reproduced, since each of these specific issues often involves an entire system of legal regulation of its own, whose proper coverage would require an extended exposition of many kinds of instruments and arrangements.

The three annexes in volume III cover three types of instruments that differ in their context or their origin from those included in the two main parts:

- Annex A reproduces investment-related provisions in regional free trade and integration agreements. The specific function and, therefore, the effect of such provisions is largely determined by the economic integration process which they are intended to promote and in the context of which they operate.

- Annex B (the only section that departs from the chronological pattern) offers the texts of prototype bilateral treaties for the promotion and protection of foreign investments of several developed and developing countries, and a list of these treaties concluded up to July 1995. The bilateral character of these treaties differentiates them from the bulk of the instruments included in the *I.I.I. Compendium*. Over 900 such treaties had been adopted by July 1995.

- Annex C supplies the texts of documents prepared by non-governmental organizations; these give an indication of the broader environment in which the instruments collected here are prepared.

The *I.I.I. Compendium* is meant to be a collection of instruments, not an anthology of relevant provisions. Indeed, to understand a particular instrument, it is normally necessary to take into consideration its entire text. An effort has been made, therefore, to reproduce complete instruments, even though, in a number of cases, reasons of space and relevance have dictated the inclusion of excerpts.

The texts collected are not offered as models. On the contrary, an effort has been made to select instruments that reflect a broad variety of political backgrounds, forms, attitudes towards FDI, preferred approaches and policies, and effectiveness of their provisions. The collection is intended as a record of international action, not as a codification of legal prescriptions.

For the same reason, the UNCTAD Secretariat has deliberately refrained from adding its own commentaries to the texts reproduced. The only exception to this rule are the boxes added at the beginning of each instrument which provide information on some basic facts, such as its date of adoption, date of entering into force, status as of 1995 and, where appropriate, signatory countries. Moreover, to facilitate the identification of each instrument in the table of contents, additional information has been added, in brackets, next to each title, on the year of its signature and the name of the institution involved.

UNCTAD hopes that the *I.I.I. Compendium* will help policy makers, business executives and researchers to understand better past developments and the current state of the regulatory framework relating to FDI.

Rubens Ricupero
Secretary-General of UNCTAD

Geneva, March 1996

ACKNOWLEDGEMENTS

The *I.I.I. Compendium* was prepared by Victoria Aranda and Michael Gestrin, with inputs from Anna Joubin-Bret, Vincent Casim, Mohamed Fayache and Letizia Salvini, and assisted by Mario Ardiri, Eric Gill, Per Kall, Christine Jeannet, and Liane Wolly, under the direction of Karl P. Sauvant. Arghyrios A. Fatouros prepared the Introduction and provided overall guidance and advice. Secretarial support was provided by Medarde Almario, Nayana Hein, Elisabeth Mahiga and Jenifer Tacardon.

CONTENTS

Page

VOLUME I
MULTILATERAL INSTRUMENTS

PREFACE iii

INTRODUCTION: THE EVOLVING INTERNATIONAL FRAMEWORK FOR FOREIGN DIRECT INVESTMENT xvii

MULTILATERAL INSTRUMENTS

1. Havana Charter for an International Trade Organization (excerpts) (1948) 3

2. Convention on the Recognition and Enforcement of Foreign Arbitral Awards (United Nations, 1958) 15

3. United Nations General Assembly Resolution 1803 (XVII): Permanent Sovereignty over Natural Resources (1962) 21

4. Convention on the Settlement of Investment Disputes between States and Nationals of other States (International Bank for Reconstruction and Development, 1965) 25

5. United Nations General Assembly Resolution 3201 (S-VI): Declaration on the Establishment of a New International Economic Order (1974) 47
   and
   United Nations General Assembly Resolution 3202 (S-VI): Programme of Action on the Establishment of a New International Economic Order (excerpts) (1974) 52

6. United Nations General Assembly Resolution 3281 (XXIX): Charter of Economic Rights and Duties of States (1974) 57

7. Arbitration Rules of the United Nations Commission on International Trade Law (1976) 71

8. ILO Tripartite Declaration of Principles Concerning Multinational Enterprises and Social Policy (International Labour Office, 1977) 89
   and

Procedure for the Examination of Disputes Concerning the Application of the Tripartite Declaration of Principles Concerning Multinational Enterprises and Social Policy by Means of Interpretation of its Provisions (International Labour Office, 1986) 101

9. Draft International Agreement on Illicit Payments (United Nations Economic and Social Council, 1979) 103

10. United Nations Model Double Taxation Convention between Developed and Developing Countries (1979) 109

11. The Set of Multilaterally Agreed Equitable Principles and Rules for the Control of Restrictive Business Practices (United Nations Conference on Trade and Development, 1980) 133

Resolution Adopted by the Conference Strengthening the Implementation of the Set (United Nations Conference on Trade and Development, 1990) 145

12. International Code of Marketing of Breast-milk Substitutes (World Health Organization, 1981) 151

13. Draft United Nations Code of Conduct on Transnational Corporations (1983 version) 161

14. Draft International Code of Conduct on the Transfer of Technology (United Nations Conference on Trade and Development, 1985) 181

15. United Nations General Assembly Resolution 39/248: Guidelines for Consumer Protection (1985) 203

16. Convention Establishing the Multilateral Investment Guarantee Agency (International Bank for Reconstruction and Development, 1985) 213

17. Criteria for Sustainable Development Management: Towards Environmentally Sustainable Development (United Nations Centre on Transnational Corporations, 1990) 245

18. Guidelines on the Treatment of Foreign Direct Investment (The World Bank Group 1992) 247

19. Permanent Court of Arbitration Optional Rules for Arbitrating Disputes between Two Parties of which only One is a State (1993) 257

20. Marrakesh Agreement Establishing the World Trade Organization. Annex 1A: Multilateral Agreements on Trade in Goods. Agreement on Trade-Related Investment Measures (1994) 279

21. Marrakesh Agreement Establishing the World Trade Organization. Annex 1B: General Agreement on Trade in Services 285

Ministerial Decisions Relating to the General Agreement on Trade in Services (1994) 323

22. Marrakesh Agreement Establishing the World Trade Organization. Annex 1C: Agreement on Trade-Related Aspects of Intellectual Property Rights (1994) 337

VOLUME II
REGIONAL INSTRUMENTS

PREFACE iii

REGIONAL INSTRUMENTS

23. Code of Liberalisation of Capital Movements (Organisation for Economic Co-operation and Development, 1961) 3

24. Code of Liberalisation of Current Invisible Operations (Organisation for Economic Co-operation and Development, 1961) 31

25. Model Tax Convention on Income and on Capital (Organisation for Economic Co-operation and Development, 1963) 71

26. Common Convention on Investments in the States of the Customs and Economic Union of Central Africa (1965) 89

27. Revised Recommendation of the Council Concerning Co-operation Between Member Countries on Anticompetitive Practices Affecting International Trade (Organisation for Economic Co-operation and Development, 1967) . . . 103

28. Draft Convention on the Protection of Foreign Property (Organisation for Economic Co-operation and Development, 1967) . . . 113

29. Agreement on Investment and Free Movement of Arab Capital among Arab Countries (Agreement of Arab Economic Unity, 1970) . . . 121

30. Convention Establishing the Inter-Arab Investment Guarantee Corporation (1971) . . . 127

31. Joint Convention on the Freedom of Movement of Persons and the Right of Establishment in the Central African Customs and Economic Union (1972) . . . 155

32. Agreement on the Harmonisation of Fiscal Incentives to Industry (Caribbean Common Market, 1973) . . . 161

33. The Multinational Companies Code in the UDEAC (Customs and Economic Union of Central Africa, 1975) . . . 175

34. Declaration on International Investment and Multinational Enterprises (Organisation for Economic Co-operation and Development, 1976) . . . 183

35. Guidelines Governing the Protection of Privacy and Transborder Flows of Personal Data (Organisation for Economic Co-operation and Development, 1980) . . . 203

Declaration on Transborder Data Flows (Organisation for Economic Co-operation and Development, 1985) . . . 208

36. Unified Agreement for the Investment of Arab Capital in the Arab States (1980) . . . 211

37. Convention for the Protection of Individuals with Regard to Automatic Processing of Personal Data (Council of Europe, 1981) . . . 229

38. Agreement on Promotion, Protection and Guarantee of Investments among Member States of the Organisation of the Islamic Conference (1981) 241

39. Community Investment Code of the Economic Community of the Great Lakes Countries (CEPGL) (1982) 251

40. Agreement for the Establishment of a Regime for CARICOM Enterprises (1987) 267

41. Revised Basic Agreement on ASEAN Industrial Joint Ventures (1987) 281

42. An Agreement Among the Governments of Brunei Darussalam, the Republic of Indonesia, Malaysia, the Republic of the Philippines, the Republic of Singapore and the Kingdom of Thailand for the Promotion and Protection of Investments (1987) 293

43. Amended Proposal for a Council Regulation (EEC) on the Statute for a European Company (Council of the European Communities, 1989) 301

44. Fourth ACP-EEC Convention of Lomé (excerpts) (1989) 385

45. Charter on a Regime of Multinational Industrial Enterprises (MIEs) in the Preferential Trade Area for Eastern and Southern African States (1990) 427

46. Decision 291 of the Commission of the Cartagena Agreement: Common Code for the Treatment of Foreign Capital and on Trademarks, Patents, Licenses and Royalties (Andean Group, 1991) 447

Decision No. 24 of the Commission of the Cartagena Agreement: Common Regulations Governing Foreign Capital Movement, Trade Marks, Patents, Licences and Royalties (Andean Group, 1970) 454

47. Decision 292 of the Commission of the Cartagena Agreement. Uniform Code on Andean Multinational Enterprises (Andean Group, 1991) 475

48. Articles of Agreement of the Islamic Corporation for the Insurance of Investment and Export Credit (1992) 483

49. Protocolo de Colonia Para la Promoción y Protección Reciproca de Inversiones en el MERCOSUR (Intrazona) (1994) . . . 513

50. Recommendation of the Council on Bribery in International Business Transactions (Organisation for Economic Cooperation and Development, 1994) . . . 523

51. Protocolo Sobre Promoción y Protección de Inversiones Provenientes de Estados No Partes del MERCOSUR (1994) . . . 527

52. APEC Non-Binding Investment Principles (1994) . . . 535

53. Final Act of the European Energy Charter Conference, the Energy Charter Treaty, Decisions with Respect to the Energy Charter Treaty and Annexes to the Energy Charter Treaty (excerpts) (1994) . . . 539

VOLUME III
REGIONAL INTEGRATION, BILATERAL AND NON-GOVERNMENTAL INSTRUMENTS

PREFACE . . . iii

ANNEX A. INVESTMENT-RELATED PROVISIONS IN FREE TRADE AND REGIONAL ECONOMIC INTEGRATION INSTRUMENTS

54. Treaty Establishing the European Community (excerpts) (1957) . . . 3

55. Agreement on Arab Economic Unity (excerpts) (1957) . . . 25

56. Agreement on Andean Subregional Integration (excerpts) (1969) . . . 27

57. Treaty Establishing the Caribbean Community (excerpts) (1973) . . . 43

58. Treaty Establishing the Latin American Integration Association (excerpts) (1980) . . . 51

59. Treaty for the Establishment of the Economic Community of Central African States (excerpts) (1983) 61

60. North American Free Trade Agreement (excerpts) (1992) 73

61. Treaty Establishing the Common Market for Eastern and Southern Africa (excerpts) (1993) 101

Treaty for the Establishment of the Preferential Trade Area for Eastern and Southern African States (excerpts) (1981) 110

ANNEX B. PROTOTYPE BILATERAL INVESTMENT TREATIES AND LIST OF BILATERAL INVESTMENT TREATIES (1959-1995)

62. Asian-African Legal Consultative Committee Revised Draft of Model Agreements for Promotion and Protection of Investments 115

63. CARICOM Guidelines for use in the Negotiation of Bilateral Treaties 139

64. Agreement between the Government of the Republic of Chile and the Government of ________ on the Reciprocal Promotion and Protection of Investments 143

65. Agreement between the Government of the People's Republic of China and the Government of ________ Concerning the Encouragement and Reciprocal Protection of Investments 151

66. Projet d'Accord entre le Gouvernement de la Republique Française et le Gouvernement ________ sur l'Encouragement et la Protection Reciproques des Investissements 159

67. Treaty between the Federal Republic of Germany and ________ concerning the Encouragement and Reciprocal Protection of Investments 167

68. Agreement between the Swiss Confederation and ________ on the Promotion and Reciprocal Protection of Investments 177

69. Agreement between the Government of the United Kingdom of Great Britain and Northern Ireland and the Government of __________ for the Promotion and Protection of Investments 185

70. Treaty between the Government of the United States of America and the Government of __________ concerning the Encouragement and Reciprocal Protection of Investment. 195

71. Investment Incentive Agreement between the Government of the United States of America and __________ 207

Appendix: Bilateral Investment Treaties Concluded up to July 1995 213

ANNEX C. NON-GOVERNMENTAL INSTRUMENTS

72. Draft Statutes of the Arbitral Tribunal for Foreign Investment and of the Foreign Investments Court (International Law Association, 1948) 259

73. International Code of Fair Treatment for Foreign Investments (International Chamber of Commerce, 1949) 273

74. Guidelines for International Investment (International Chamber of Commerce, 1972) 279

75. Charter of Trade Union Demands for the Legislative Control of Multinational Companies (International Confederation of Free Trade Unions, 1975) 293

76. International Chamber of Commerce Rules of Conciliation and Arbitration (1975) 335

77. International Chamber of Commerce Recommendations to Combat Extortion and Bribery in Business Transactions (1977) 351

78. The Business Charter for Sustainable Development: Principles for Environmental Management (International Chamber of Commerce, 1991) 361

79. The CERES Principles (1992) 365

80. Consumer Charter for Global Business (Consumers International, 1995) 369

81. Pacific Basin Charter on International Investments (Pacific Basin Economic Council, 1995) 375

Select list of publications of the UNCTAD Division on Transnational Corporations and Investment 381

Questionnaire 387

INTRODUCTION: THE EVOLVING INTERNATIONAL FRAMEWORK FOR FOREIGN DIRECT INVESTMENT

The globalization of production has at its core the growth of foreign direct investment (FDI), in quantitative as well as qualitative terms. Its total volume has kept increasing, so that today FDI stock surpasses $ 2.5 trillion in book value. In terms of operational forms, the relatively isolated operators of the past have been replaced in the past few decades by increasingly integrated transnational corporations (TNCs). A new international actor has thus come to the fore, whose activities have been a major factor in the unprecedented degree of integration of the world economy. In fact, not only FDI, but also a good part of trade, technology transfer and financial flows are now conducted under the common governance of TNCs. Each of these activities can best be understood as one of several interwoven modalities of international production rather than as a separate, alternative form of operation.[1]

In this transformation, legal and policy changes at the national and international levels have been both cause and effect. The decrease and eventual elimination of national barriers to trade and other forms of economic exchange -- throughout the half century since the end of the Second World War, and at an increasing pace in the past decade -- have made possible close interactions across borders and have thereby facilitated international production. At the same time, the dynamic growth of the TNC has put continuing pressure on policy makers at all levels to create a legal framework to match these enterprises' needs and purposes. A major consequence has been that FDI is now increasingly accepted as a matter for international regulation. Only a few decades ago, FDI was still perceived as governed mainly by national legal rules and principles. International law was deemed to be relevant only as far as the allocation of national jurisdiction was concerned and with respect to the treatment of measures causing major disruption of investment operations. Today, the accepted role of international law rules and processes -- customary, conventional or other -- in investment matters has considerably expanded. The substance of pertinent rules is itself in the process of changing, chiefly in the direction of further liberalization.

I. The international legal framework for foreign direct investment

The legal framework for FDI, as it exists today, consists of a wide variety of national and international principles and rules, of diverse origins and forms, differing extensively in their strength and specificity. They operate at several levels, with extensive gaps in their coverage of issues and countries. In this framework, national legislation is still of paramount importance.[2] It

---

[1] For an elaboration, see UNCTAD, Division on Transnational Corporations and Investment, *World Investment Report 1993: Transnational Corporations and Integrated International Production* (New York, United Nations), United Nations publication, Sales No. E.93.II.A.14.

[2] For a collection of legal studies on the role of national regulation of TNCs, see, S. J. Rubin and D. Wallace, Jr., eds., *Transnational Corporations and National Law. United Nations Library on Transnational Corporations* (London and New York, Routledge for the United Nations, 1994), vol. 19.

establishes the relevant legal concepts and categories, creates the broader legal environment for the operation of TNCs and reflects in its diversity the prevailing currents and trends on the topic. International rules and concepts operate in constant reference to national ones. While the number and importance of international norms keep increasing, their interplay with national ones remains at the heart of the matter.

This broader "transnational" framework, which covers national and international rules and policies (as well as the processes of private law-making that are particularly active in this area), should be distinguished from the "international legal framework" properly speaking, which consists of international legal rules, principles and procedures, whether of customary, conventional, institutional or other origin.[3] The present collection addresses a major component of the international framework, namely international instruments dealing with FDI

Use of the comprehensive, nonspecific term "instrument" is meant to reflect the variety of form and effect of the international acts and documents involved, whose diversity is enhanced by their varying substantive scope and their differing policy orientations. An indicative listing of the types of instruments involved, addressing only their differing forms and membership, includes:

- international multilateral agreements, universal or quasi-universal in their membership;
- regional international agreements, in which participating countries belong to a particular group, defined geographically or otherwise;
- bilateral agreements;
- other instruments reflecting arrangements among States, such as declarations, non-binding guidelines etc.;
- resolutions of organs of international organizations, whether legally binding or not.

Existing international instruments must be seen against the background of customary international law, as manifested in rules on the exercise of domestic jurisdiction, state competence over the entry and treatment of foreign enterprises and state responsibility for injuries to aliens and their property. Depending on their form and substance, international instruments may give effect, specify, supplement, replace or derogate from customary norms.

[3] For earlier efforts to define and describe the notion of a legal framework for TNCs and FDI, see, P. Hansen and V. Aranda, "An emerging international framework for transnational corporations", *Fordham International Law Journal*, 14 (1991), pp. 881-891; K. P. Sauvant and V. Aranda, "The international legal framework for transnational corporations", in A.A. Fatouros, ed., *Transnational Corporations: The International Legal Framework. United Nations Library on Transnational Corporations* (London and New York, Routledge for the United Nations, 1994), vol. 20, pp. 83-115; A. A. Fatouros, "Introduction", ibid., pp. 1-37.

International organizations dealing with monetary matters (the International Monetary Fund), financing (the World Bank), trade (the World Trade Organization), intellectual property (the World Intellectual Property Organization) and other economic issues constitute part of the institutional basis of the framework, with a definite and sometimes direct impact on FDI matters.

International agreements of various types are of increasing importance as elements of the legal framework for FDI. At the present time, no comprehensive international treaty covers the most important issues and many countries, but efforts in this direction are underway; however, several multilateral instruments of less comprehensive scope are directly relevant. In addition, regional agreements have increasingly dealt with FDI, sometimes pioneering international trends in the field. Expanding networks of bilateral investment agreements have developed principles directly concerned with the treatment and protection of FDI.

Legal rules of other kinds, of varying normative intensity and general applicability, are also relevant. Authoritative texts with no formal binding force ("soft law"), adopted by states or international organizations on a universal or regional basis, are an important element of the framework. To the extent that they express the goals of important actors in the international community and reflect their normative expectations, they influence the development of national and international law on the subject. Transnational arbitration not only provides the indispensable procedures for dispute settlement but also, through the corpus of its awards, gradually fills in the gaps in the legal framework on FDI. Finally, the contribution of private persons and groups, scholars, professional associations and others should not be ignored. They do not provide, of course, authoritative texts and rules; but they help to construct the conceptual framework and to crystallise approaches and expectations that may eventually find expression in formal binding texts.

While the main emphasis of the present collection is on multilateral and regional agreements, it also includes in the main body of the collection or in the annexes other types of instruments, thus seeking to reflect the diversity of instruments and norms.

To introduce the international instruments contained in these volumes, it was deemed useful to place them in context by looking at the recent history of the matter and to identify briefly the main issues that they address. A full analysis of instruments and trends would require a much more thorough study than can be undertaken in this Introduction.[4]

[4] For recent attempts to provide such analysis, see M. Sornarajah, *The International Law on Foreign Investment* (Cambridge, Cambridge University Press, 1994); P. Muchlinski, *Multinational Enterprises and the Law* (Oxford, Blackwell, 1995). And for a collection of relevant legal literature, see Fatouros, op. cit.

II. International law and policy towards foreign direct investment over the past half-century

A. *The first decades*

Immediately after the end of the Second World War, an attempt was made to formulate international principles concerning FDI in the Havana Charter of 1948 (no. 1),[5] intended to establish an International Trade Organization. The Charter dealt mainly with international trade (the original General Agreement on Trade and Tariffs was in fact based on its trade provisions), but it also contained several articles on investment. While these provisions were initially proposed with a view to reaffirming the rights of investors to fair treatment and protection, in the text that emerged from the Havana Conference these rights were circumscribed with a number of qualifications. Dissatisfaction of major capital-exporting countries with these provisions was one of the reasons for the eventual failure of the Havana Charter to enter into effect.[6] A comparable effort at the regional level, the Economic Agreement of Bogota of 1948,[7] had the same fate.

Throughout the early part of the half-century after the end of the Second World War, concerns of both host countries, particularly developing ones, and foreign investors focused on FDI in natural resources and key industries. The issue was initially perceived in terms of political ideology, particularly in view of the afterwar wave of nationalizations in Western Europe and in the countries of Central and East Europe. Quite soon, however, the decolonization process that reached its height in the early 1960s imported radically new elements. For many of the countries emerging into political independence, the principal issue was regaining control over their natural wealth and their economy. They feared that foreign control over natural resources and key industries would deprive them of economic benefits and compromise their newly-found political independence. The number of cases of nationalization or expropriation of foreign property (chiefly in natural resources) kept increasing, reaching its highest level in the early 1970s.

Still, by and large, the attitude of host countries towards FDI during this period was mixed.[8] A realization of the need for and possible benefits from FDI coexisted with a conviction that national controls and limitations on it were necessary. Thus, after a series of United Nations General Assembly resolutions in the 1950s elaborated the principle of permanent sovereignty over

---

[5] Numbers in parentheses refer to the numbering of the instruments in the table of contents of the *I.I.I. Compendium*.

[6] See, C. Wilcox, *A Charter for World Trade* (New York, Macmillan, 1949), pp. 145-148; G. Bronz, "The International Trade Organization Charter", *Harvard Law Review*, 62 (1969), pp. 1089-1125; W. Diebold, *The End of the ITO* (Princeton Essays in International Finance, No. 16, Princeton 1952).

[7] Economic Agreement of Bogota, Pan American Union Law and Treaty Series no. 25 (1949); see in particular its Articles 25-27. And see S. J. Rubin, "Private foreign investment: the ITO Charter and the Bogota Economic Agreement", American Foreign Law Association, *Proceedings*, No. 31 (1948).

[8] For a survey of the attitudes and policies of the time, see, A. A. Fatouros, *Government Guarantees to Foreign Investors* (New York, Columbia University Press, 1962), pp. 29-58, 69-189.

natural wealth and resources, resolution 1803 (XVII) (no. 3), adopted in 1962, gave to the principle its definite formulation.[9] The resolution marked a watershed in the efforts to find common ground between developed and developing countries. On the one hand, it recognized the rights of peoples and nations over their natural resources, including their right to exercise control over investments in such resources and to nationalize them. On the other hand, it provided expressly that appropriate compensation should be paid for any taking of such investments and that agreements between foreign investors and governments should be observed in good faith.

Even in many developed countries, prevailing trends favoured national controls over FDI. Various proposals, by developed country governments and private investor associations, for the conclusion of a comprehensive international agreement aimed primarily at the protection of foreign investments did not materialize.[10] In the Organisation for Economic Co-operation and Development (OECD), a Draft Convention on the Protection of Foreign Property (no. 28) was approved in 1967 by the Organisation's Council but never opened for signature.[11] The few successful efforts on a world-wide basis were directed at specific aspects of FDI protection. The World Bank-sponsored Convention on the Settlement of Investment Disputes between States and Nationals of Other States (no. 4) was signed in 1965, initially with a rather limited membership, which expanded considerably in the following decades.[12]

Regional efforts at liberalization among developed countries were gradually quite effective. OECD members adopted in 1961 the Codes of Liberalisation of Capital Movements and of Current Invisible Operations (nos. 23 and 24), which established binding rules and provided effective machinery for their gradual expansion and implementation.[13] Numerous examples of regional efforts among developing countries are also available (see, for examples, nos. 26, 29, 55 and 56).

---

[9] See, inter alia, K. Gess, "Permanent sovereignty over natural resources: analytical review of the United Nations Declaration and its genesis", *International and Comparative Law Quarterly*, 13 (1964), pp. 398-449; R. Kemper, *Nationale Verfuegung ueber natuerliche Ressourcen und die neue Weltwirtschaftsordnung der Vereinten Nationen* (Berlin, Duncker und Humblot, 1976); D. Rosenberg, *Le Principe de Souveraineté des Etats sur leurs Resources Naturelles* (Paris, LGDJ, 1983).

[10] See, A.S. Miller, "Protection of private foreign investment by multilateral convention", *American Journal of International Law*, 53 (1959), pp. 371-378; "Symposium", in *Journal of Public Law*, 9 (1960), pp. 125; A. A. Fatouros, "An international code to protect private investment: proposals and perspectives", *University of Toronto Law Journal*, 14 (1961), pp. 77-102.

[11] See, G. van Hecke, "Le projet de convention de l'OCDE sur la protection des biens etrangers", *Revue Générale de Droit International Public*, 68 (1964), pp. 641-664.

[12] From the rich literature on the Convention, see in particular, A. Broches, "The Convention on the Settlement of Investment Disputes between States and Nationals of other States", *Hague Academy Recueil des Cours*, 130 (1972), pp. 331-410.

[13] The history and analysis of the Codes have recently been presented in OECD, *Introduction to the OECD Codes of Liberalisation* (OECD, Paris, 1995).

At the same time, the early 1960s saw the beginning of the process of negotiating bilateral investment promotion and protection agreements. Through them, an increasing number of developing countries subscribed to a number of standards for investment protection (see vol. III, Annex B of the *I.I.I. Compendium*).

B. The 1970s

The decade of the 1970s, after the first energy crisis, saw the developing countries gaining more influence in international fora. They determined the agenda concerning FDI. Demands for radical changes in the world trading and financial system, generally under the banner of the creation of a New International Economic Order, found formal expression in a series of United Nations General Assembly resolutions, supported and resisted to varying degrees by the developed countries. The most relevant for present purposes are the 1974 Declaration on the Establishment of a New International Economic Order and its accompanying Programme of Action (no. 5), as well as the Charter of Economic Rights and Duties of States (no. 6). In matters of FDI, attention was now focused on host country demands for economic independence and on the role of, and the modalities of national controls over, TNCs.

On the regional and national levels as well, elaborate structures for the control of the entry and operations of TNCs were established in many developing countries. Generally, they sought to ensure that TNCs would serve on a concrete and immediate basis the development needs of the host country, as determined by its government. A characteristic regional instrument that reflected national approaches and methods, was Decision 24 of the Andean Pact, adopted in 1970 (no. 46), which imposed stringent screening procedures and other controls on FDI and the transfer of technology, including a "fade-out" provision, requiring the disinvestment of foreign firms after a number of years (see also nos. 31 and 57).

At the same time, the efforts to establish standards for the conduct of TNCs led to negotiations for the adoption, albeit in legally non-binding forms, of "codes of conduct" for the activities of TNCs. The lead was once again taken on the regional level by the OECD, which adopted in 1976 a Declaration on International Investment and Multinational Enterprises that included a set of voluntary Guidelines for Multinational Enterprises (no. 34). The Guidelines are addressed to enterprises and cover both general issues and specific topics, such as employment and industrial relations and the disclosure of information. A process of review and clarification led to successive reformulations on various issues. The Declaration further included decisions addressed to governments that dealt with several aspects of TNC treatment: assurance of national treatment, problems of incentives and disincentives and conflicting requirements imposed on TNCs. Together, these instruments provided important elements of a framework on both the conduct and the treatment of TNCs in the OECD area.

Parallel efforts were undertaken at the universal level, in the framework of the United Nations system. The most comprehensive text of this kind was the draft United Nations Code of Conduct on Transnational Corporations (no. 13). Despite agreement over most of its provisions during the lengthy negotiations, the instrument was never adopted. Other codes of conduct, dealing with specific issues, were the subject of negotiations, with varying results: the International Labour Organization Governing Body adopted in 1977 the Tripartite Declaration of Principles Concerning Multinational Enterprises and Social Policy (no. 8). In 1980, the United Nations General Assembly adopted the Set of Multilaterally Agreed Equitable Principles and Rules for the Control of Restrictive Business Practices (no. 11), negotiated under the auspices of the United Nations Conference on Trade and Development. On the other hand, the negotiations on an international Code of Conduct on Transfer of Technology (no. 14) in the framework of the same organization has not led so far to the adoption of a final acceptable instrument. However, several other codes, or similar instruments, dealing with more limited aspects of TNC activity were adopted: for instance, the World Health Organization's International Code of Marketing of Breast-milk Substitutes (no. 12) and the United Nations Guidelines on Consumer Protection (no. 15). The negotiations over codes of conduct, whether ultimately successful or not, were instrumental in defining the areas of common understanding over the proper conduct of TNCs and in clarifying the standards for their treatment.[14]

C. *The past fifteen years*

By the end of the 1970s and the early 1980s, a reverse trend had set in. The ability of developing countries to determine the agenda of international economic relations decreased considerably. Their bargaining position weakened, in part because of the slackening and eventual termination of the Cold War and partly under the impact of excessive indebtedness. The debt crisis brought about a relative scarcity of financing and investment and made FDI more desirable: not only was it relatively more available but it did not burden the country with debt and it brought additional contributions to the host economy, in terms of know-how, technology skills and access to markets. The perception of the need for controlling FDI was thereby affected. In most developing countries, moreover, the process of gaining control over natural resources had considerably advanced since the immediate postwar period and was no longer a matter of prime concern. Interest therefore shifted to the need -- and competition -- for investment in other sectors.

In the developed countries, once the constraints of the energy crises had been overcome, changes in domestic policies and economic conditions affected policies towards developing countries and TNCs. Important changes in the dominant political approaches took place. Welfare-state approaches of earlier decades were redefined in many countries to the advantage of trends inimical to State intervention in economic matters.

All these developments had a significant impact on laws and policies for FDI. The past fifteen years have been a time of investment liberalization, promotion and protection. Extensive -- one might even say, radical -- changes in policies have marked national investment laws. The screening requirements and other restrictions imposed earlier have been considerably softened or

[14] On international codes of conduct, their purpose and contents, see N. Horn, ed., *Legal Problems of Codes of Conduct for Multinational Enterprises* (Deventer, Kluwer, 1980); S. Metaxas, *Entreprises Transnationales et Codes de Conduite* (Zurich, Schulthess, 1988).

eliminated. Restrictions on the entry and operations of foreign affiliates have weakened considerably; investors are increasingly allowed freely to transfer their profits and capital out of the host country; the incidence of property takings has greatly decreased; and acceptance of international arbitration for resolving conflicts between investors and host governments is expanding.

These recent changes at the national level have not been extensively reflected yet in general multilateral instruments. The scarcity of pertinent documents in Part One of the present collection attests to this. The most important multilateral instruments expressing these trends are the World Bank-sponsored Convention establishing the Multilateral Investment Guarantee Agency (MIGA) in 1985 (no. 16) and three of the 1994 Uruguay Round agreements that addressed topics directly or indirectly related to investment: the General Agreement on Trade in Services (including the Ministerial Decisions relating to it) (no. 21), the Agreement on Trade-Related Investment Measures (no. 20) and the Agreement on Trade-Related Aspects of Intellectual Property Rights (no. 22). Among non-binding texts, the 1992 Guidelines on the Treatment of Foreign Direct Investment prepared in the framework of the World Bank (no. 18) are of particular relevance. Still, one has to look at other types of instruments, primarily regional and interregional, as well as bilateral ones, to perceive the effects of current trends.

At the regional level, the liberalization trends are particularly apparent in instruments reflecting the numerous efforts (of varying degrees of intensity and success) at economic integration. It is possible to discern these trends in the provisions of the Fourth Lomé Convention between the European Community and a large group of African, Caribbean and Pacific States (no. 44), as well as in the association agreements concluded after 1989 by the European Community with countries of Central and Eastern Europe, as well as Northern Africa (see also nos. 42, 49, 51 and 61).

In the early 1990s, indeed, events have picked up pace. Perhaps the most telling case is that of the amendments in the Andean countries' instruments on foreign investment and transfer of technology (i.e., Decisions 291 and 292: nos. 46 and 47, respectively) that replaced their earlier more restrictive regulations (i.e., Decision 24, no. 46). The North American Free Trade Agreement between Canada, Mexico and the United States (no. 60) may cover three States only, but their size and overall importance, as well as the process of liberalization the agreement has set in motion, makes it particularly important. The Energy Charter Treaty (no. 53), adopted by fifty countries, including most OECD members and countries of Central and East Europe and the Commonwealth of Independent States, is limited to the energy sector but contains important provisions on investment liberalization and protection. The 1994 APEC Non-Binding Investment Principles (no. 52) and the Pacific Basin Charter on International Investments (no. 81) are also significant. Other regional instruments are also important in this respect.

Bilateral investment treaties have continued to be negotiated in increasing numbers, so that by now more than nine hundred such treaties have been concluded (see figure below and the Appendix to Annex B of Vol. III). The initiative for their conclusion was taken at the start by the major capital-exporting developed countries; most of these countries are by now at the center of extensive networks of bilateral treaties with developing countries or countries in transition. In recent years, however, a considerable number of such treaties has also been concluded by smaller

identical in their scope and language, they are by and large fairly similar in their import. Many of the developed countries have in fact elaborated model or "prototype" texts which they propose to their treaty partners. While the actual effects of the resulting treaty networks fall far short of those of a multilateral agreement, their cumulative impact may be seen as pointing in that direction.[15]

Figure. Growth of bilateral investment treaties, 1950-1995 (Culmulative totals)

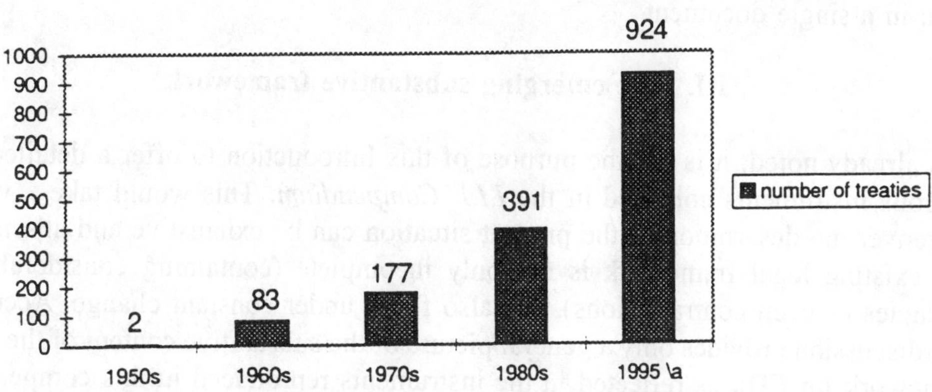

Source: UNCTAD, Division on Transnational Corporations and Investment. *World Investment Report 1995: Transnational Corporations and Competitiveness* (Geneva, United Nations, 1995), United Nations publication, Sales No. E.95.II.A.9.

a First six months of 1995 only.

D. The current picture

When describing trends, an impression of uniformity and complete certainty or full clarity would be misleading. The present international legal framework is increasingly more favourable to FDI; but it still consists of many instruments and norms at several levels, differing on many issues, and it is riddled with gaps.

Changes in the approaches to FDI are not limited to the basic attitudes of favour or mistrust. Conceptual and policy-oriented changes are also taking place. International concern over both the treatment and the effects of FDI and the operations of foreign affiliates has increased over the years. The industries in which TNCs are active have changed, and the attitudes towards them have been correspondingly affected. In the first decades after the Second World War, as already noted, most discussions on FDI dealt by implication with the exploitation of petroleum and other natural resources. In recent years, concern has shifted to investments in manufacturing, services and high technology.

---

[15] For detailed recent studies of bilateral agreements, see Rudolf Dolzer and Margrete Stevens, *Bilateral Investment Treaties* (Washington, D.C., ICSID, 1995); K. J. Vandevelde, *United States Investment Treaties: Theory and Practice* (Deventer, Kluwer, 1992); and UNCTC and ICC, *Bilateral Investment Treaties 1959-1991* (New York, United Nations, 1992), United Nations publication, Sales No. E.92.II.A.16.

The very perception of the investment process has changed as well, reflecting current realities of the world economy. As the Uruguay Round negotiations have made evident, the *problématique* of FDI and technology transfer has become more closely linked to that of international trade, in the sense that they are both increasingly perceived as part of the same process of international production. Some of these changes are reflected in varying manners in the more recent among the instruments contained in the *I.I.I. Compendium*, but a more definite comprehensive picture of the process is only now emerging and has still to find its formal expression in a single document.

III. The emerging substantive framework

As already noted, it is not the purpose of this Introduction to offer a detailed analysis of the numerous instruments collected in the *I.I.I. Compendium*. This would take a volume of its own. Moreover, no description of the present situation can be exhaustive and all-encompassing, since the existing legal framework is not only incomplete (containing considerable gaps and inconsistencies or even contradictions), but also fluid, under constant change. Accordingly, the following discussion provides only a general picture of the substantive content of the international legal framework for FDI, as reflected in the instruments reproduced in this compendium.

The structure of this part of the Introduction corresponds to the several facets of current trends in the legal regulation of FDI, even though categories of measures and policies often overlap and cannot be fully and clearly distinguished one from another. The first section deals with the preliminary question of the definition of investment. The next two sections address two major trends in investment regulation, first the liberalisation of laws and policies relating to FDI and secondly the incidence of measures concerning investment protection. The sections that follow discuss the settlement of investment-related disputes and emerging international norms relating to obligations of investors. Investment-promotion policies, as they relate to the facilitation of investment through the provision of services and information and to the offer of investment incentives, are a separate issue that falls outside the scope of the present Introduction.

A. *What is an investment ?*

In legal instruments, definitions are not neutral descriptions but form part of an instrument's normative content. Their purpose is to determine the object to which the instrument's rules or principles shall apply. As a result, the scope and purpose of the instrument determine the exact contents of the definitions in it.

As far as the definition of investment is concerned, instruments dealing with FDI fall in two broad categories:

- Those that concern the cross-border movement of capital and resources, whether in view of its control or of its liberalisation. Such instruments usually define FDI in narrow terms, insisting on control over an enterprise as a necessary element of the concept. Since different rules may apply to FDI and to other types of financial (or other) transactions, such instruments stress the differences between various types of investment of capital. A classical definition of this type is the one found in Annex A of the OECD Code of Liberalisation of Capital Movements (no. 23).

- Instruments mainly directed at the protection of FDI. Definitions found in such instruments are generally broad and comprehensive. They can cover not only the capital that has crossed borders with a view to the acquisition of control over an enterprise, but also most other kinds of assets of an enterprise or of an investor, including several types of loans and portfolio transactions. Such a definition is found, for instance, in the World Bank-sponsored Convention on the creation of MIGA (no. 16), in the NAFTA investment chapter (no. 60) and in bilateral investment treaties (nos. 62-71).

The rationale for these differing approaches is evident. Protection-oriented instruments seek to safeguard the interests of the investors (or, in a broader context, to promote FDI by safeguarding the investors' interests). Investment is understood in passive terms, as something that is already there. The older terminology, which referred to "acquired rights" or to "foreign property" (see, e.g., the 1967 OECD Draft Convention on the Protection of Foreign Property (no. 28), whose provisions have indeed served as a model for many bilateral investment treaty provisions), makes the context clear. The exact character of the particular assets is not by itself important in this case, since protection is to be extended to assets after their acquisition by the investors, when they already form part of the investors' patrimony. Definitions tend therefore to be broad, in order to cover as many as possible of the investors' assets.

Capital movement-oriented instruments, on the other hand, look at the matter in a dynamic context. They address an investment before it is made -- in the past, with a view to its control, in the current context of liberalisation, with a view to removing obstacles to its realization. Even though the resources invested may be of several kinds -- funds, technology or other elements of the package that constitutes an investment -- it is their actual movement that is of concern. The definition looks primarily to the act of investing, not the assets in which the investment becomes eventually embodied.

The two types of definitions are therefore not inconsistent. They simply serve different purposes. The broader, protection-oriented, definition appears to cover all the elements of the narrower one, but also includes elements the narrower definition leaves out. Use of a single definition in a multi-purpose instrument would require careful drafting of its provisions so as to ensure that all of the purposes involved would be properly served.

B. Liberalization measures

1. Restrictions and standards of treatment

The process of liberalization with respect to FDI may be understood as consisting in major part of (a) the removal of restrictive, and thereby market-distorting, government measures; and (b) the application of certain positive standards of treatment, primarily directed at the elimination of discrimination against foreign investors. The two types of measures are closely interconnected, but it is useful for analytical purposes to keep them distinct.[16] Restrictions and standards of treatment may apply to different phases or different aspects of an investment: to its entry and establishment, its ownership or its operations after entry.

Restrictions. Current developments must be seen against the background of the earlier restrictive trends outlined above. The rationale for the restrictions imposed on foreign affiliates, apart from the ubiquitous national security considerations, was the protection of the national economy from excessive foreign influence or domination and the support of local firms against foreign competitors deemed to be more powerful. The new directions of national and international FDI regulation reflect a reconsideration of the need for such restrictions, increased doubts as to the possibilities for their effective administration and an awareness of their impact on a country's position in the competition for FDI.

Restrictions on investment are in many instances discriminatory, that is to say they are directed specifically at foreign investors. Only in a relatively limited number of cases are restrictions directed at both domestic and foreign investors. As a result, the removal of restrictions on FDI may be effected not only by their express abolition but also by means of the adoption of non-discriminatory standards of treatment.

Standards of treatment. The most common such standards are the "most-favoured-nation" standard and the national treatment standard. The former standard ensures equality of treatment, as between investors from different (foreign) countries. The latter provides for no discrimination as between foreign and domestic investors. The two standards are relative (or "contingent"), in that they do not define expressly the contents of the treatment they accord but establish it by reference to an existing legal regime: that of other aliens in one case and that of host state nationals in the other. The legal regime to which reference is made changes over time, and the changes apply to the beneficiaries of most-favoured-nation or national treatment, as well.

Both standards originated in commercial treaties, where their international validity was originally based. Exceptions and qualifications to their application are generally contained in the pertinent treaties, whether as part of their definitions, in express provisions or in separate protocols.

Formal definitions of both standards refer not to "equal" treatment but to "treatment no less favourable" than that accorded to the "most-favoured" third nation, in the one case, and to the nationals (and products) of the host country, in the other. Illustrations may be found in a large

---

[16] For a more complete analysis of the notion of liberalization, as applied to recent trends in the legal framework for FDI, based on a broad survey of pertinent developments, see, UNCTAD-DTCI, *World Investment Report 1994: Transnational Corporations, Employment and the Workplace* (New York and Geneva, United Nations, 1994), United Nations publication, Sales No. E.94.II.A.14, pp. 286-312. To the two elements of liberalisation mentioned in the text, that analysis adds an important third element, generally not reflected in international instruments on FDI, namely, the presence of a general legal framework incorporating the rules and controls ensuring the proper functioning of the market.

number of instruments reproduced in this collection, for instance, the OECD 1976 Declaration on International Investment and Multinational Enterprises (no. 34) and the representative bilateral investment treaties (nos. 62-71). The clear implication of the formula is that privileged treatment for FDI is possible, even though, with few exceptions (see below, next section), equality of treatment may be in fact accorded. In many cases, the definitions make clear that most-favoured-nation or national treatment is to be accorded "in like situations"; this formula is sometimes construed as importing additional limitations to the application of the standard.

The most frequent among the express general exceptions refer to matters relating to national security and public order; in a number of cases, particular industries or business activities may be listed where these standards (especially, national treatment) may not apply. In current practice concerning foreign investment, the most-favoured-nation standard seems by and large generally accepted. While the national treatment standard is increasingly accepted, many governments continue to maintain explicit exceptions or broad qualifications to its application because they see national treatment as undermining their capacity to formulate national economic development policies.

2. Entry and establishment

Restrictions on FDI involve in many instances the exercise of controls over the admission of investments. Prospective investors must apply to a host country's authorities for permission to invest; the latter allow an investment when it meets the policy criteria set in the relevant laws and regulations. Certain key industries may be closed to foreign investment, or admission may be allowed only subject to conditions relating to the structure of ownership (e.g., participation of local investors) or the nature of a firm's operations (e.g., the technology used, employment of local personnel, utilization of local raw materials and supplies, emphasis on exports). As noted, restrictions relating to the protection of national security, sometimes very broadly defined, are also common. On the other hand, in countries where exchange controls are in effect, the registration or authorization of foreign investment on entry is often a precondition for allowing later transfers of funds.

Most restrictions and other requirements were and are established by national law; they are not to be found in international instruments. A major exception to that generalisation was Decision 24 of the Commission of the Cartagena Agreement (no. 46) which allowed (and in some cases required) member States to take several types of restrictive measures concerning FDI. The entire system of control was founded on the screening and registration of all inward investments and on the prohibition of certain kinds of investment transactions (e.g., purchase of shares in existing companies owned by local nationals) or of investments in certain industries. Reinvestment was subject to the same restrictions as new investments. Technology-transfer contracts were also to be registered and their contents strictly controlled. Decision 24 was amended in 1988 and eventually replaced by Decision 291 of 1991 (no. 46), which removed many of the restrictive features of the earlier provisions. The dramatic contrast between the two decisions is characteristic of the changes in policies and approaches in the twenty years that intervened.

Other instruments reflect in more distant manners past restrictive attitudes towards admission of FDI. Some of them, in fact, do so chiefly by providing expressly for the removal of existing restrictions to admission. The "liberalisation lists" in the Annexes of the OECD Code of Liberalisation of Capital Movements (no. 23) are illustrations of this process. The Code and its lists are also important as models of a process of gradual elimination of restrictions that has proven its effectiveness over the years.

By and large, however, and despite the enormous change in policies in the past decade, controls and restrictions on entry of widely varying import are still in effect in many countries, developed as well as developing, even though less in the former than in the latter. In most cases, they involve limitations on entry into particular industries (especially, natural resources and public utilities). While most of the instruments reproduced in the *I.I.I. Compendium* do not address this issue, those that do illustrate a variety of specific approaches (compare, e.g., the provisions on establishment in nos. 59 and 60).

Since entry restrictions are in most cases discriminatory, their removal may be brought about, as already noted, by the application of non-discriminatory standards of treatment, especially national treatment. An interesting development in this respect is the recent United States practice of providing in its bilateral investment treaties for national and most-favoured-nation treatment in matters of entry and establishment (no. 71). The bilateral treaties concluded by most other countries, on the other hand, while providing for a general favourable approach to FDI admission, accept that such admission is subject to the host country's laws and regulations. The position of the World Bank's Guidelines on the Treatment of Foreign Direct Investment (no. 18) is essentially similar: it accepts the host countries' right to regulate entry, while recommending "open admission, possibly subject to a restricted list of investments (which are either prohibited or require screening and licensing)". The APEC Non-Binding Investment Principles (no. 52) provide for most-favoured-nation treatment as far as admission of investments is concerned.

The case of the recently concluded Energy Charter Treaty (no. 53) is also relevant. While energy investments already made are accorded, in the Treaty, national and most-favoured-nation treatment, whichever is most favourable, only "best efforts" to that effect are provided with respect to investments to be made. It is further provided, however, that negotiations will start immediately upon the main treaty's conclusion with a view to concluding a supplementary treaty that will provide (in binding terms) for the grant of the same treatment to the admission of investments. The reason for this two-phase approach was that many of the countries parties to the Energy Charter Treaty were still developing new domestic legislation on energy resources to replace their earlier state-oriented laws. Thus, the actual contents of the national and/or most-favoured-nation treatment legislation was uncertain, and this made difficult, if not impossible, the negotiation of appropriate qualifications and exceptions.

Regional arrangements, whether directed at economic integration or at other forms of economic cooperation short of that, have often provided for special legal regimes, regarding admission as well as post-admission treatment, for enterprises from countries participating in them. Such efforts have multiplied in recent years, although the degree of their success or even of their reality, in terms of effective and extensive application, varies widely (compare, e.g., the weak treatment of admission in no. 58 with the strong treatment in no. 60).

The Andean Pact countries were the first to create, in 1971,[17] a subregional type of corporation, the "multinational enterprise". These are duly registered companies owned predominantly by nationals of participating countries (with limits on the participation of extra-regional investors). Such enterprises are to be accorded special treatment, in most cases national treatment, in each participating state. Similar entities, with extensive variations as to their specific legal status and treatment, have been created since in the framework of other economic integration or cooperation efforts: "multinational companies", in the Central African Customs and Economic Union (no. 33), "Community enterprises", in the Economic Community of the Great Lakes Countries in Central Africa (no. 39), "ASEAN industrial joint ventures", in the ASEAN framework (no. 41), "CARICOM enterprises", in the framework of the Caribbean Common Market (no. 40), the "multinational industrial enterprises", in the Preferential Trade Area for Eastern and Southern African States (no. 45). In the European Community, on the other hand, proposals for the creation of a "European company" (no. 43) with a special community status have been debated for a long time, but no agreement has been reached.

Investors from countries participating in economic cooperation or integration arrangements are sometimes accorded in member States national treatment as to admission and operation in the absence of a requirement for a common corporate form. This has been the case in the European Community, by virtue of the founding treaty's provisions on establishment (no. 54). Provisions for free admission of investments are found in other regionally oriented agreements as well, such as the Unified Agreement for the Investment of Arab Capital in the Arab States (no. 36), and the Agreement on Promotion, Protection and Guarantee of Investments among Member States of the Organisation of the Islamic Conference (no. 38) and NAFTA (no. 60).

3. *Treatment after admission*

Foreign affiliates already admitted in a country are subject to that country's jurisdiction and operate under its legal system. As a general rule, subject to specific exceptions, they are not entitled to special treatment. The main problems of international relevance that may arise in this respect concern the possibility of restrictive and/or discriminatory national measures affecting the operations of foreign affiliates.

The rules regarding post-establishment treatment have been considerably liberalised, probably more so than rules relating to entry. Of the two standards ensuring non-discrimination, namely most-favoured-nation and national treatment, the former is by now fairly generally accepted as to post-admission treatment. The latter standard, national treatment, still has a way to go, although it is found not only in bilateral investment treaties but also in important recent

[17] Decision 46 of the Commission of the Cartagena Agreement, adopted in 1971, entered in force in 1976, amended by decision 292 (1991); see, e.g., H.A. Grigera Naon, "Transnational enterprises under the Pacto Andino and national laws of Latin America", in N. Horn, ed., *Legal Problems of Codes of Conduct for Multinational Enterprises* (Deventer, Kluwer, 1980), pp. 237-273.

regional instruments, such as NAFTA (no. 60) and the Energy Charter Treaty (no. 53), as well as in "soft law" texts, such as the World Bank-sponsored Guidelines on the Treatment of Foreign Direct Investment (no. 18) and the APEC Non-Binding Investment Principles (no. 52).

A third standard of treatment found in many instruments is that of "fair and equitable" treatment. It differs from the other two in that it is an absolute (or noncontingent) standard: its contents, while not very well defined in all respects, do not depend on an external, changing legal regime. It is used in bilateral agreements as well as in several multilateral and regional ones, mainly with respect to post-admission treatment, but sometimes (as in the case, e.g., of the Energy Charter Treaty) regarding entry as well.

Treatment after admission obviously involves a broad range of topics and issues. Some of the international instruments concerning FDI and TNCs have sought to deal with all or most of these topics. This is eminently the case with the draft United Nations Code of Conduct on Transnational Corporations (no. 13). Most instruments, however, have addressed only particular issues arising with respect to investment.

Since many of these issues fall within well-established separate domains of international action, they are often regulated by general instruments -- multilateral or regional conventions, networks of bilateral treaties or decisions of international organizations -- that deal with the relevant domain as a whole, specific FDI matters being regulated incidentally along with other topics. This is the case, for instance, with taxation issues, which are of principal importance to investors, but which constitute a separate, extensive and highly technical field. Two model versions of bilateral agreements on double taxation are included in the present collection, the United Nations Model Double Taxation Convention between Developed and Developing Countries (no. 10) and the OECD Model Tax Convention on Income and on Capital (no. 25). In addition, a related agreement that points to another direction is included, the Caribbean Common Market's Agreement on the Harmonisation of Fiscal Incentives to Industry (no. 32).

Specific issues of this kind are often of major importance to investments or assume special forms in connection with them, so that they may also be dealt with, in addition to the more general instruments, in special instruments relating to FDI or related matters. This is preeminently the case with the issues relating to intellectual property, which are covered by several broader conventions on the subject, yet are also dealt with by the recently concluded Agreement on Trade-Related Aspects of Intellectual Property Rights, in the WTO framework (no. 22), as well as by several bilateral investment agreements (Annex B of Vol. III).

Transfer of technology is closely related to this issue, since many of the relevant legal issues are governed, apart from national legislation, by multilateral conventions on intellectual property. Technology transfer is in fact an important facet of FDI operations, and some current definitions of FDI cover the contractual aspects of technology transfer, such as licensing of patents, trademarks and other kinds of intellectual property rights, even when they are not associated with acquisition of control over an enterprise. In the 1970s, it was sought to prepare an international code of conduct that would establish universally acceptable norms and standards for transfer of technology transactions in response to the burgeoning growth of international technology flows and a heightened awareness of the important role played by technology in developing countries. Six sessions of the United Nations Conference on an International Code of Conduct on the Transfer of Technology were held, the last of which was in 1985 (no. 14). However, despite these efforts, no general consensus among governments has emerged. The topic has come up again in recent years, although with a different focus and emphasis. In addition to the Agreement on Trade-Related Aspects of Intellectual Property Rights mentioned in the preceding paragraph, provisions related to technology transfer are to be found in the 1994 Energy Charter Treaty (no. 53).

Performance requirements have been used by host countries over the past quarter of a century, partly as a substitute for more restrictive types of controls over FDI. The imposition on investors, usually at the time of entry and with their, however reluctant, consent of requirements concerning local content, export performance, technology transfer and other facets of their operations were meant to enhance the local economy's benefits from the investment. The market and trade-distorting effects of these requirements led the developed countries to seek their removal. Clauses to that effect have been included in bilateral investment agreements, especially those concluded by France and the United States (see nos. 66 and 70, respectively), regional agreements (e.g., NAFTA, no. 60) and, in the framework of the Uruguay Round, in the agreement banning certain "trade-related investment measures" (no. 20).

4. Transfer of funds

The problems arising in connection with transfer of funds (profits, capital, royalties and other types of payments) by foreign investors outside the host country fall within the broad area of the regulation of movement of capital and payments. Some of the relevant issues, e.g., convertibility of currencies, are covered by the Articles of Agreement of the International Monetary Fund and its decisions and acts. Among OECD members, the Liberalisation Codes (nos. 23 and 24) provide for the removal of restrictions not only on capital movements but also on current payments, including transfer of profits from investments.

Given the presence of exchange controls and restrictions in many host countries, instruments specifically concerned with investment also address this issue. In many cases, indeed, provisions on transfer of funds in pertinent national and international instruments involve something beyond the mere freedom of investors to buy foreign exchange; where exchange restrictions are in force, foreign investors may be guaranteed that exchange will be made available to them or that they will have priority access to it. In such cases, the issue may be understood as involving investment protection rather than mere treatment. Older instruments, even among developed countries, in view of the then prevailing conditions in the international economy, tended to avoid very strong provisions on fund transfers. The recommendation in this respect in the OECD 1967 Draft Convention on the Protection of Foreign Property (no. 28) is characteristic.

In national FDI legislation, provisions were common, and still continue in a number of cases, whereby investors were entitled to transfer abroad, under specified conditions, their profits and, usually under more restrictive terms, the capital invested. An early illustration of such provisions, at the subregional level, are the relevant articles of Decision 24 of the Andean Pact (no. 46).

Recent instruments have more liberal provisions on the subject, although this is true of few multilateral instruments; one important case is that of the World Bank Guidelines on the Treatment of Foreign Direct Investment (no. 18). Such provisions are more common on the regional level, as, for instance, in Decision 291 of the Andean Pact (no. 46) and in several of the regional instruments cited earlier in the section on admission. Provisions allowing the free transfer of funds are also found in the APEC Non-Binding Investment Principles (no. 52), in the Energy Charter Treaty (no. 53) and in bilateral investment treaties (nos. 62-71).

C. *Investment protection*

The contents of the broad category of issues under this general heading have been changing over the recent decades. The heading covers international rules and principles designed to protect the interests of foreign investors against host government actions detrimental to the investors' interests. In a way, these issues arise because the international legal framework is still incomplete and uncertain, and specific provisions to make general provisions effective may be needed. To the extent that the framework is gradually completed, that liberalisation progresses, so that restrictions are eliminated and positive general standards applied, and that reliable dispute settlement machinery is established, the need for measures of protection diminishes.

The government measures addressed in this context may be seen as falling in two general categories. First and foremost, measures, such as property takings and abrogations of contracts, which cause major disruptions or even put an end to an investor's operations in the host country. Secondly, other measures detrimental to the investor's interests that do not amount to major disruption, such as discriminatory taxation, disregard of industrial property rights, arbitrary refusal of licenses and similar, by definition relatively small-scale, measures. The borderline between the two categories is not watertight, because the distinction is based on the scale of the measures' impact, on the one hand, and on the intent behind the measures, on the other. Thus, the term "creeping" or "indirect" expropriation is sometimes applied to cases that do not expressly involve expropriations or property takings, where the effect is ruinous for the investor and an intent to cause major disruption is alleged.

The scope of the second class of protection issues is variable in another sense as well. The number of such issues decreases, as other norms concerning investment treatment are expanding. To the extent, e.g., that investors are entitled to non-discriminatory general treatment under a number of recent instruments, specific discriminatory measures would be considered as infringements of this general principle and would not be treated as investment-protection matters. And to the extent that the ongoing process of liberalization eliminates exchange restrictions, provisions for transfer of funds may no longer be treated as protection issues. Such changes in classification, however, do not generally affect the substance of the legal norms involved.

Finally, a number of possible assurances to investors, generally falling in the realm of investment promotion, such as those concerning special tax treatment or guarantees as to the immutability of the legal regime under which the investment was undertaken, are generally the subject of contractual or quasi-contractual arrangements between investor and host state. They are rarely covered by broader international instruments, save to the extent that the latter seek to ensure that all promises given to investors should be carried out in good faith. Some agreements, such as NAFTA (no. 60), include provisions restricting the linking of such benefits to the fulfilment of performance requirements.

1. *Takings of property*

The principal measures against which investors seek protection are expropriations, nationalizations and other major cases of deprivation of property and infringement of rights of investors. As already noted, the first postwar decades saw many instances of large-scale action of this kind, the consequences of socio-political change (in Western and Eastern Europe), of decolonization (in Asia and Africa) and of developing country efforts to assert control over their natural resources. Both the historical context and the ideological motivations have today changed. Although the not-so-distant past has left some mistrust and apprehension in its wake, the actual risk of large-scale action of this sort is considerably diminished. The possibility of arbitrary measures against individual investors, however, because of political problems or of failures in the application of laws or the administration of justice, has not yet totally disappeared.

The international law norms on deprivation of foreign property and abrogation of contracts have been the object of considerable debate in the decades since the end of the Second World War.[18] Developed countries have insisted that, for such actions to be lawful in international law, they have to meet certain requirements: the measures have to be taken in the public interest, they should not be discriminatory, and they should be accompanied by full compensation. Developing countries have asserted that the conditions for property takings within a country's territory are to be determined by the host country, in the exercise of its exclusive jurisdiction, although they have allowed that compensation should normally be paid. In practice, the requirement of compensation and the modalities for its assessment and payment have been at the centre of the debate.

The controversies just outlined are mirrored in several of the earlier instruments in the *I.I.I. Compendium*, starting with the Havana Charter (no. 1), a first, unsuccessful, effort at finding a middle ground. A more successful such effort, in specific context, was the 1962 United Nations General Assembly resolution on Permanent Sovereignty over Natural Resources (no. 3). The developed countries' positions are reflected in such texts as the 1967 OECD Draft Convention (no. 28) and the earlier International Chamber of Commerce proposals for "fair treatment" and Guidelines for Investment (nos. 73 and 74, respectively). The positions of developing countries in the 1970s may be seen in the United Nations General Assembly resolutions associated with

[18] See the recent survey of the literature in Sornarajah, op. cit. On expropriations, see R. Higgins, "The taking of property by the State", *Hague Academy Recueil des Cours*, 176 (1982), pp. 259-392; A. Mouri, *The International Law of Expropriation as Reflected in the Work of the Iran-U.S. Claims Tribunal* (Dordrecht, Nijhoff, 1994); and on state contracts, Ph. Leboulanger, *Les Contrats entre Etats et Enterprises étrangères* (Paris, Economica, 1985); and E. Paasivirta, *Participation of States in International Contracts* (Helsinki, Finnish Lawyers' Publishing Co., 1990).

a New International Economic Order, especially the Charter of Economic Rights and Duties of States (no. 6). The problems of investment protection were a major point of difference in the negotiations on the Draft United Nations Code of Conduct on Transnational Corporations (no. 13).

The current situation is not totally clear, although, once again, certain trends are unmistakeable. The most important change has been one in perspective. Concern has shifted from dealing with past situations to establishing the rules for the future. Host countries appear to be increasingly inclined to provide assurances of fair treatment to future investors (even though established investments are generally covered as well). Such assurances generally include undertakings against expropriation, promises of full compensation and acceptance of dispute-settlement procedures. The positions that thus appear to crystallize in several recent texts are closer to those that were initially supported by the developed countries and that now are increasingly accepted by developing countries and countries in transition. These are in fact positions that host countries have accepted for several decades in bilateral investment treaties (nos. 62-71), although they had generally resisted their incorporation into multilateral instruments. It is in this last respect that their attitudes appear to be changing. As a result, strong provisions on the subject are found in such recent instruments as NAFTA (no. 60), the Energy Charter Treaty (no. 53) and the World Bank Guidelines on the Treatment of Foreign Direct Investment (no. 18).

2. Other issues of investment protection

Provisions on other possible measures detrimental to the investors' interests are found in those international instruments that are specifically directed at investment protection, particularly, bilateral investment treaties. Since they cover a variety of possible situations, they are usually less specific and concrete than the provisions on protection against expropriation and they are closely related to the provisions on the general treatment of investors discussed in the preceding section (on liberalisation). To protect against discriminatory treatment (e.g., in matters of taxation), the general non-discrimination standards are invoked. In addition, absolute standards, preeminently that of "fair and equitable treatment", are utilized.

The case of the Energy Charter Treaty (no. 53) is characteristic. The first paragraph in the article dealing with investment provides a series of norms and standards regarding the appropriate treatment of investments (before and after admission). According to that paragraph, parties shall "accord at all times to investments ... fair and equitable treatment" and treatment no less favourable than "that required by international law"; investments "shall enjoy the most constant protection" and no party "shall in any way impair by unreasonable or discriminatory measures their management, maintenance, use, enjoyment or disposal."

Finally, an important aspect of investment protection is the availability, at both the national and international levels, of investment insurance against non-commercial risks, which cover measures relating to both classes of protection issues. National programmes to that effect have been operating for several decades. On the international level, the adoption in 1985 of the convention establishing the Multilateral Investment Guarantee Agency (no. 16), under the auspices of the World Bank, made possible the provision of insurance to investments that might not have been fully eligible under national programmes. At the regional level as well, several international agreements have established investment-guarantee agencies, as in the case of the Convention establishing the Inter-Arab Investment Guarantee Corporation (no. 30), and the Articles of Agreement of the Islamic Corporation for the Insurance of Investments and Export Credit (no. 48).

D. *Settlement of disputes*

The complex operations of a modern enterprise give rise to a number of possible legal problems. Proper legal planning combined with good management may succeed in resolving most of them, without their reaching the point where they become legal disputes. But it is to be expected that some problems will not be resolved through negotiations or other arrangements. With respect to the operations of a foreign affiliate in a host country, and depending on the parties concerned, three classes of disputes may be distinguished, although the borderlines between the categories are not always very clear: interstate (or State-to-State) disputes, disputes between the host State and the investor, and disputes between the investor and another private party.[19]

State-to-State arbitration or adjudication is, of course, a major procedure in traditional public international law. Older instruments, as well as the relatively recent Rules of Arbitration prepared by the Permanent Court of Arbitration (no. 19), contain relevant procedures. Many of the instruments in the *I.I.I. Compendium* provide that, with respect to any dispute concerning the interpretation or application of the instrument itself and usually after the failure of diplomatic or other efforts at resolving the dispute, recourse may be had to interstate arbitration (or adjudication before the International Court of Justice). Such provisions are of direct relevance to the topic at hand because they also cover the (equally traditional) possibility of the espousal of investors' claims by their home States, on the basis of the rules of state responsibility for the treatment of aliens. It is precisely in order to avoid elevating an investment dispute to an interstate problem that provision for investor-State arbitration is made in many of the investment-related international instruments.

Bilateral investment treaties (nos. 62-71) generally provide in some detail for both State-to-State and investor-State arbitration. Among recent regional instruments, NAFTA (no. 60) as well as the Energy Charter Treaty (no. 53) also cover in lengthy provisions these two possibilities.

The dispute-settlement method most relevant to investment disputes is arbitration between an investor and a State (usually the host State). In the past, such disputes sometimes came before special (arbitral) tribunals (often entitled Mixed Claims Commissions) on the basis of agreements between the states concerned, concluded after the dispute had arisen. A major recent instance is the operation of the Iran-United States Claims Tribunal.

---

[19] For a recent comprehensive survey of institutions, methods and possibilities, see C. Gray, *Judicial Remedies in International Law* (Oxford, Clarendon Press, 1990).

It is evident that a more orderly method is to provide for such proceedings before a dispute has arisen. This was effected in the mid-1960s by the conclusion of the Convention on the Settlement of Investment Disputes between States and Nationals of Other States (no. 4). The Convention was proposed by and negotiated under the auspices of the World Bank and is administered by the Centre for Settlement of Investment Disputes. A permanent machinery and binding procedures for arbitration (and conciliation) of investment disputes has thus been established. The Permanent Court of Arbitration has recently issued a set of optional rules for such disputes (not necessarily restricted to investment issues) (no. 19). Other instruments also provide for the possibility of such arbitration, whether in specific context (e.g., the earlier effort of the International Law Association (no. 72), and the examples mentioned in the preceding paragraph) or as part of the usual process of commercial arbitration (e.g., the ICC Rules of Conciliation and Arbitration, no. 76).

Disputes between private parties are normally left to be resolved through recourse to the host country judicial system or to arbitration between the parties ("commercial arbitration"). The presence of a properly functioning national system of administration of justice is a central element of a country's investment climate and of the general legal framework necessary for effective liberalisation. But this cannot be ensured by an international instrument. Classical international law has generally not been directly concerned with such disputes, save in exceptional cases, where some failing of state organs might be detected and the rules of the law of State responsibility invoked. International instruments have addressed this issue with a view to facilitating the execution of the eventual arbitral awards, something that initially met in many countries procedural and jurisdictional obstacles. This is the task that the New York Convention on the Recognition and Enforcement of Foreign Arbitral Awards (no. 2) has performed with considerable success.

Other instruments, some inter-governmental and others from non-governmental bodies, have sought to establish procedures and mechanisms that can be voluntarily used in such arbitrations (as well as in investor-State ones); the UNCITRAL rules of arbitration (no. 7) and those promulgated and administered by the International Chamber of Commerce (no. 76) are prime illustrations of successful efforts. Developed countries have sometimes sought to ensure that the option of private commercial arbitration is available to investors. The issue was debated during the negotiations on the United Nations draft Code of Conduct on Transnational Corporations (no. 13).

E. International obligations of foreign investors

A new dimension in the legal regulation of FDI and TNCs has emerged in the past two decades which goes beyond established legal approaches and methods. In dealing with FDI issues, one is confronted with two types of legal norms: in oversimplified terms and omitting many necessary qualifications, one has, on the one hand, the international law norms, customary or conventional, that determine the limits of national jurisdiction and of its exercise towards foreign investors, and, on the other, the national law obligations imposed by a host State on the foreign investor, within the framework of the jurisdictional norms of international law. Although international law, in its traditional manner of operation, may impose on States duties (or recognise rights and competencies) that concern investors, to their benefit or to their detriment, it does not directly address investors: foreign affiliates do not have international law duties, nor do they have direct rights in international law.

This pattern is of course modelled on the international law status of individuals and is beginning to change just as that status begins to change as well. For example, the development of international legal norms for the protection of human rights and for the suppression of international crimes and terrorism is increasingly bringing individuals within the ambit of international law by directly imposing on them duties and recognizing rights established by international law. In the FDI context, a number of international standards may be emerging which may relate and be directly applicable to the conduct of TNCs and their affiliates. The legal mechanisms by which such standards may become operative are complicated and at this moment still uncertain. The most effective avenue for lending effectiveness to them remains the traditional one of recourse to national action.

The contents of international standards for TNC activities are, however, becoming increasingly clear and definite in a number of particular areas. Protection of the environment is probably the domain in which this process is the most advanced. Relevant provisions not necessarily related to FDI are found in many recent instruments. Some of them (as in the case of maritime pollution), provide in fact for legally-binding rules. In most FDI-related cases, either the instruments themselves are not legally binding, or, when they are, the formulation of the relevant provisions tends to be relatively "soft" (see, e.g., nos. 78 and 79). An illustration of the latter case is the recent Energy Charter Treaty (no. 53). Among documents of the former type, one may cite the UNCTC Criteria for Sustainable Development Management (no. 17), and the relevant provisions of the draft United Nations Code of Conduct on Transnational Corporations (no. 13). At the regional level, the pertinent chapter of the OECD Declaration on International Investment and Multinational Enterprises (no. 34) is of particular significance. On specific issues, the series of OECD recommendations on the avoidance of transborder pollution is of immediate relevance.

Similar standards have been proposed in other areas of FDI-related activity. The codes of conduct adopted in the 1970s or early 1980s contain numerous provisions on such issues. Labour and employment issues are dealt with in the International Labour Organization Tripartite Declaration (no. 8), the OECD Declaration (no. 34) and the Charter of Trade Union Demands for the Legislative Control of Multinational Companies (no. 75). Protection of consumers is the topic of several instruments, such as the International Code of Marketing of Breast-milk Substitutes (no. 12), the United Nations Guidelines for Consumer Protection (no. 15) and the Consumer Charter for Global Business (no. 80). The topic of bribery and illicit payments has been repeatedly addressed in various instruments, such as the draft International Agreement on Illicit Payments, prepared by the United Nations Economic and Social Council (no. 9), the recent OECD Recommendation (no. 50), as well as the ICC rules of conduct on the subject (no. 77). Protection of privacy and regulation of transborder data flows have also been dealt with by a Council of Europe Convention (no. 37) and by important OECD instruments (no. 35).

Another important domain where international standards appear to be developing is that of restrictive business practices. International concern in this area dates back to the first postwar years; repeated efforts have been made since then, with limited success. The most significant of related instruments is the Set of Multilaterally Agreed Equitable Principles and Rules for the Control of Restrictive Business Practices (no. 11) and the Revised Recommendation of the Council Concerning Co-operation between Member Countries on Anticompetive Practices Affecting International Trade (no. 27), while the matter was also extensively debated in the context of the draft International Code of Conduct on Transfer of Technology (no. 14). Recently, however, the matter has come again to the foreground during the Uruguay Round negotiations on trade-related investment measures, where it was argued that "performance requirements" are sometimes necessary to counteract TNC restrictive practices. While these arguments are not reflected in the operative provisions of the relevant agreement (no. 20), the latter provides that, at the first review of related issues, the possibility of adding provisions on "competition policy" shall be considered.

It is clear that the international standards relating to TNC conduct have by no means reached the stage of legal perfection that would render them capable of being effectively invoked by States (and others, possibly non-governmental organizations) in their relations with TNCs and their affiliates. It is however significant that this is at the moment an area of active concern in international fora. Apart from providing models for national legislation, whose international legitimacy would be hard to dispute, such standards may also be contributing towards the creation of a general climate on their various subject-matters, a climate that TNCs will have increasingly to take into account in determining the manner of their operations.

IV. Conclusions

This review of the forms and content of the instruments constituting a major part of the international legal framework for FDI is too short and too summary to allow clear and definite conclusions. In the past four decades, national and international legal policies and rules concerning foreign direct investment have repeatedly changed. Foreign direct investment itself has also changed, in its form, its magnitude and its context. It is now generally admitted that FDI is a matter of international concern -- and the contents of this voluminous collection bear witness to the intensity of that concern.

In national laws and policies towards FDI, the trends towards liberalisation and increased protection have gathered strength during the past fifteen years, and at a faster pace in the 1990s. Entry controls and restrictions have been relaxed and in many cases dismantled. Non-discriminatory treatment after admission is becoming the rule rather than the exception. Guarantees of non-expropriation and for the free transfer of funds are increasingly given. These trends are gradually spreading to the international level; they are already predominant at the bilateral level; they are increasingly expanding to the regional one; and they are by now approaching the multilateral world-wide level as well.

The international legal framework for FDI, however, is still uncertain and incomplete. There is no comprehensive global agreement on the subject. Existing multilateral instruments are partial and fragmentary. Regional and bilateral agreements have in the recent past taken the lead in adapting legal rules to new conditions, but it is not self-evident that the approaches appropriate at the regional (and, even less, at the bilateral) level are also possible and proper at the world-wide level, without considerable adaptation.

The OECD Multilateral Agreement on Investment

The OECD launched its initiative to negotiate a Multilateral Agreement on Investment (MAI) at its ministerial meeting of May 1995, with actual negotiations having started in September 1995. The mandate for the negotiators of the MAI called for the negotiation of an agreement that would:

" -- provide a broad multilateral framework for international investment with high standards for the liberalisation of investment regimes and investment protection and with effective dispute settlement procedures;

-- be a free-standing international treaty open to all OECD Members and the European Communities, and to accession by non-OECD Member countries.

Close co-operation will be ensured with the appropriate OECD Committees, including the Trade Committee and the Committee on Fiscal Affairs to take account of areas of common interest.

Negotiations should commence immediately with the objective of reaching an agreement by the time of the Ministerial meeting in 1997, with a progress report to the Ministerial meeting in 1996.

Given the desirability of including non-Member countries in a MAI, arrangements will be made for consulting them as negotiations progress."*

**Source*: Organisation for Economic Co-operation and Development, *Report by the Committee on International Investment and Multinational Enterprises (CIME) and the Committee on Capital Movements and Invisible Transactions (CMIT)*, OCDE/GD(95)/65 (OECD: Paris), p. 5.

Certain fundamental features of the current situation seem worth considering at this point. To begin with, the presence of TNCs, as important and largely autonomous actors, complicates the picture. Their influence, their structures and strategies and their extensive capabilities should not be lost from sight in any international rule-making efforts. Secondly, the constant interaction between international rules and policies and national ones must also be kept in mind. The process of globalization may render desirable a degree of uniformity in the treatment of FDI, with a view to decreasing or eliminating distortions in international FDI flows; but the legal tools utilized in international arrangements (namely, the application of non-discrimination standards of national and most favoured nation treatment) do not necessarily promote uniformity. One way to achieve a degree of uniformity might be the adoption of substantive international rules concerning the conduct of the principal actors. In some domains, such as the protection of the environment or of consumers, such rules are beginning timidly to appear. In others, for instance, the protection of competition and the control of restrictive practices, the possibility of such rules is beginning to be discussed. Finally, the emphasis in this survey (as in most recent action in this domain) has been on the liberalization of inward FDI. It may be time, however, to start looking at laws and policies concerning outward FDI as well. In the absence of detailed studies, it cannot be asserted that existing structures and norms in investment-exporting countries are fully responsive to market conditions and do not cause distortions on that side of FDI flows, as there have been, and still are, on the other.

The beginning of negotiations in the framework of the OECD, with a view towards concluding a multilateral agreement on investment, represents an effort to address this lack of uniformity in the international legal framework for FDI (see box above). The OECD's negotiating mandate is ambitious in terms of both timing and contents. It provides for concluding the negotiations by early 1997; it looks to a comprehensive agreement, covering issues of admission, treatment and protection; and it envisages a "free-standing" agreement, in which non-OECD members may be able to participate.[20] The negotiations themselves, and of course their outcome, should help to clarify the regulatory framework for FDI.[21]

If discussions and negotiations on trade-related investment issues take place in the World Trade Organization, they could contribute to further clarification. UNCTAD contributes to this process by identifying and clarifying issues relevant to a multilateral framework on investment, in particular their development aspects, and stimulating a dialogue between developing and developed countries towards consensus on investment issues.

[20] For details see William H. Witherell, "The OECD Multilateral Agreement on Investment", *Transnational Corporations*, 4, 2 (Geneva, United Nations, 1995), pp. 1-14.

[21] On recent developments with respect to multilateral negotiations on investment, see Sir Leon Brittan, "Investment liberalization: the next great boost to the world economy", *Transnational Corporations*, 4, 1 (Geneva, United Nations, 1995) pp. 1-10; and Renato Ruggiero, "Foreign direct investment and the multilateral trading system", *Transnational Corporations*, forthcoming.

Multilateral Instruments

HAVANA CHARTER FOR AN INTERNATIONAL TRADE ORGANIZATION*
[excerpts]

The Havana Charter for an International Trade Organization was drawn up at the International Conference on Trade and Employment, which met at Havana from 21 November 1947 to 24 March 1948, for submission to the governments represented. The Final Act of the International Conference on Trade and Employment was signed by the representatives of Afghanistan, Australia, Austria, Belgium, Bolivia, Brazil, Burma, Canada, Ceylon, Chile, China, Colombia, Costa Rica, Cuba, Czechoslovakia, Denmark, Dominican Republic, Ecuador, Egypt, El Salvador, France, Greece, Guatemala, Haiti, India, Indonesia, Iran, Iraq, Ireland, Italy, Lebanon, Liberia, Luxembourg, Mexico, the Netherlands, New Zealand, Nicaragua, Norway, Pakistan, Panama, Peru, Philippines, Portugal, Southern Rhodesia, Sweden, Switzerland, Syria, Transjordan, South Africa, United Kingdom, United States of America, Uruguay, Venezuela, the United Nations and the United Nations Conference on Trade and Employment. The Charter never entered into force.

CHAPTER III

ECONOMIC DEVELOPMENT AND RECONSTRUCTION

Article 11
Means of Promoting Economic Development and Reconstruction

1. Progressive industrial and general economic development, as well as reconstruction, requires among other things adequate supplies of capital funds, materials, modern equipment and technology and technical and managerial skills. Accordingly, in order to stimulate and assist in the provision and exchange of these facilities:

(a) Members shall co-operate, in accordance with Article 10, in providing or arranging for the provision of such facilities within the limits of their power, and Members shall not impose unreasonable or unjustifiable impediments that would prevent other Members from obtaining on equitable terms any such facilities for their economic development or, in the case of Member countries whose economies have been devastated by war for their reconstruction;

*Source: United Nations Conference on Trade and Employment, *Final Act and Related Documents* (New York: United Nations), Sales No. 1948.II.D.4.1 [Note added by the editor].

(b) no Member shall take unreasonable or unjustifiable action within its territory injurious to the rights or interests of nationals of other Members in the enterprise, skills, capital, arts or technology which they have supplied.

2. The Organization may, in such collaboration with other inter-governmental organizations as may be appropriate:

(a) make recommendations for and promote bilateral or multilateral agreements on measures designed:

(i) to assure just and equitable treatment for the enterprise, skills, capital, arts and technology brought from one Member country to another;

(ii) to avoid international double taxation in order to stimulate foreign private investment;

(iii) to enlarge to the greatest possible extent the benefits to Members from the fulfilment of the obligations under this Article;

(b) make recommendations and promote agreements designed to facilitate an equitable distribution of skills, arts, technology, materials and equipment, with due regard to the needs of all Members;

(c) formulate and promote the adoption of a general agreement or statement of principles regarding the conduct, practices and treatment of foreign investment.

Article 12

International Investment for Economic Development and Reconstruction

1. The Members recognize that:

(a) international investment, both public and private, can be of great value in promoting economic development and reconstruction, and consequent social progress;

(b) the international flow of capital will be stimulated to the extent that Members afford nationals of other countries opportunities for investment and security for existing and future investments;

(c) without prejudice to existing international agreements to which Members are parties, a Member has the right:

(i) to take any appropriate safeguards necessary to ensure that foreign investment is not used as a basis for interference in its internal affairs or national policies;

(ii) to determine whether and to what extent and upon what terms it will allow future foreign investment;

(iii) to prescribe and give effect on just terms to requirements as to the ownership of existing and future investments;

(iv) to prescribe and give effect to other reasonable requirements with respect to existing and future investments;

(d) the interests of Members whose nationals are in a position to provide capital for international investment and of Members who desire to obtain the use of such capital to promote their economic development or reconstruction may be promoted if such Members enter into bilateral or multilateral agreements relating to the opportunities and security for investment which the Members are prepared to offer and any limitations which they are prepared to accept of the rights referred to in sub-paragraph (c).

2. Members therefore undertake:

(a) subject to the provisions of paragraph 1(c) and to any agreements entered into under paragraph 1(d),

(i) to provide reasonable opportunities for investment acceptable to them and adequate security for existing and future investments, and

(ii) to give due regard to the desirability of avoiding discrimination as between foreign investments;

(b) upon the request of any Member and without prejudice to existing international agreements to which Members are parties to enter into consultation or to participate in negotiations directed to the conclusion, if mutually acceptable, of an agreement of the kind referred to in paragraph 1(d).

3. Members shall promote co-operation between national and foreign enterprises or investors for the purpose of fostering economic development or reconstruction in cases where such co-operation appears to the Members concerned to be appropriate.

CHAPTER V
RESTRICTIVE BUSINESS PRACTICES

Article 46
General Policy towards Restrictive Business Practices

1. Each Member shall take appropriate measures and shall co-operate with the Organization to prevent, on the part of private or public commercial enterprises, business practices affecting international trade which restrain competition, limit access to markets, or foster monopolistic control, whether such practices have harmful effects on the expansion of production or trade and interfere with the achievement of any of the other objective set forth in Article 1.

2. In order that the Organization may decide in a particular instance whether a practice has or is about to have the effect indicated in paragraph 1, the Members agree, without limiting paragraph 1, that complaints regarding any of the practices listed in paragraph 6 shall be subject to investigation in accordance with the procedure regarding complaints provided for in Articles 48 and 50, whenever

(a) such a complaint is presented to the Organization, and

(b) the practice is engaged in, or made effective, by one or more private or public commercial enterprises or by any combination, agreement or other arrangement between any such enterprises, and

(c) such commercial enterprises, individually or collectively, possess effective control of trade among a number of countries in one or more products.

3. The practices referred to in paragraph 2 are the following:

(a) fixing prices, terms or conditions to be observed in dealing with others in the purchase, sale or lease of any product;

(b) excluding enterprises from, or allocating or dividing, any territorial market or field of business activity, or allocating customers, or fixing sales quotas or purchase quotas;

(c) discriminating against particular enterprises;

(d) limiting production or fixing production quotas;

(e) preventing by agreement the development or application of technology or invention whether patented or unpatented;

(f) extending the use of rights under patents, trade marks or copyrights granted by any Member to matters which, according to its laws and regulations, are not within the scope of such grants, or to products or conditions of production, use or sale which are likewise not the subjects of such grants.

(g) any similar practices which the Organization may declare, by a majority of two-thirds of the Members present and voting, to be restrictive business practices.

Article 47
Consultation Procedure

Any affected Member which considers that in any particular instance a practice exists (whether engaged in by private or public commercial enterprises) which has or is about to have the effect indicated in paragraph 1 of Article 46 may consult other Members directly or request the Organization to arrange for consultation with particular Members with a view to reaching mutually satisfactory conclusions. If requested by the Member and if it considers such action to be justified, the Organization shall arrange for and assist in such consultation. Action under this Article shall be without prejudice to the procedure provided for in Article 48.

Article 48
Investigation Procedure

1. In accordance with paragraphs 2 and 3 of Article 46, any affected Member on its own behalf or any Member on behalf of any affected person, enterprise or organization within that Member's jurisdiction, may present a written complaint to the Organization that in any particular instance a practice exists (whether engaged in by private or public commercial enterprises) which has or is about to have the effect indicated in paragraph 1 of Article 46; *Provided* that in the case of complaints against a public commercial enterprise acting independently of any other enterprise, such complaints may be presented only by a Member on its own behalf and only after the Member has resorted to the procedure of Article 47.

2. The Organization shall prescribe the minimum information to be included in complaints under this Article. This information shall give substantial indication of the nature and harmful effects of the practices.

3. The Organization shall consider each complaint presented in accordance with paragraph 1. If the Organization deems it appropriate, it shall request Members concerned to furnish supplementary information, for example, information from commercial enterprises within their jurisdiction. After reviewing the relevant information, the Organization shall decide whether an investigation is justified.

4. If the Organization decides that an investigation is justified, it shall inform all Members of the complaint, request any Member to furnish such additional information relevant to the complaint as the Organization may deem necessary, and shall conduct or arrange for hearings on the complaint. Any Member, and any person, enterprise or organization on whose behalf the

complaint has been made, as well as the commercial enterprises alleged to have engaged in the practice complained of, shall be afforded reasonable opportunity to be heard.

5. The Organization shall review all information available and decide whether the conditions specified in paragraph 2 and 3 of Article 46 are present and the practice in question has had, has or is about to have the effect indicated in paragraph 1 of that Article.

6. The Organization shall inform all Members of its decision and the reasons therefor.

7. If the Organization decides that in any particular case the conditions specified in paragraph 2 and 3 of Article 46 are present and that the practice in question has had, has or is about to have the effect indicated in paragraph 1 of that Article, it shall request each Member concerned to take every possible remedial action, and may also recommend to the Members concerned remedial measures to be carried out in accordance with their respective laws and procedures.

8. The Organization may request any Member concerned to report fully on the remedial action it has taken in any particular case.

9. As soon as possible after its proceedings in respect of any complaint under this Article have been provisionally or finally closed, the Organization shall prepare and publish a report showing fully the decisions reached, the reasons therefor and any measures recommended to the Members concerned. The Organization shall not, if a Member so requests, disclose confidential information furnished by that Member, which if disclosed would substantially damage the legitimate business interests of a commercial enterprise.

10. The Organization shall report to all Members and make public the remedial action which has been taken by the Members concerned in any particular case.

Article 49
Studies relating to Restrictive Business Practices

1. The Organization is authorized:

(a) to conduct studies, either on its own initiative or at the request of any Member or of any organ of the United Nations or of any other inter-governmental organization, relating to

(i) general aspects of restrictive business practices affecting international trade;

(ii) conventions, laws and procedures concerning, for example, incorporation, company registration, investments, securities, prices, markets, fair trade practices, trade marks, copyrights, patents and the exchange and development of technology in so far as they are relevant to restrictive business practices affecting international trade; and

(iii) the registration of restrictive business agreements and other arrangements affecting international trade; and

(b) to request information from Members in connection with such studies.

2. The Organization is authorised:

(a) to make recommendations to Members concerning such conventions, laws and procedures as are relevant to their obligations under this Chapter; and

(b) to arrange for conferences of Members to discuss any matters relating to restrictive business practices affecting international trade.

Article 50
Obligations of Members

1. Each Member shall take all possible measures by legislation or otherwise in accordance with its constitution or system of law and economic organization, to ensure, within its jurisdiction, that private and public commercial enterprises do not engage in practices which are as specified in paragraphs 2 and 3 of Article 46 and have the effect indicated in paragraph 1 of that Article and it shall assist the Organization in preventing these practices.

2. Each Member shall make adequate arrangements for presenting complaints, conducting investigations and preparing information and reports requested by the Organization.

3. Each Member shall furnish to the Organization, as promptly and as fully as possible, such information as is requested by the Organization for its consideration and investigation of complaints and for its conduct of studies under this Chapter; *Provided* that any Member on notification to the Organization may withhold information which the Member considers is not essential to the Organization in conducting an adequate investigation and which, if disclosed, would substantially damage the legitimate business interests of a commercial enterprise. In notifying the Organization that it is withholding information pursuant to this clause, the Member shall indicate the general character of the information withheld and the reason why it considers it not essential.

4. Each Member shall take full account of each request, decision and recommendation of the Organization under Article 48 and, in accordance with its constitution or system of law and economic organization, take in the particular case the action it considers appropriate having regard to its obligations under this Chapter.

5. Each Member shall report fully any action taken independently or in concert with other Members to comply with the requests and carry out the recommendations of the Organization

and, when no action has been taken, inform the Organization of the reasons therefor and discuss the matter further with the Organization if it so requests.

6. Each Member shall, at the request of the Organization, take part in consultations and conferences provided for in this Chapter with a view to reaching mutually satisfactory conclusions.

Article 51
Co-operative Remedial Arrangements

1. Members may co-operate with each other for the purpose of making more effective within their respective jurisdictions any remedial measures taken in furtherance of the objectives of this Chapter and consistent with their obligations under other provisions of this Charter.

2. Members shall keep the Organization informed of any decision to participate in any such co-operative action and of any measures taken.

Article 52
Domestic Measures against Restrictive Business Practices

No act or omission to act on the part of the Organization shall preclude any Member from enforcing any national statute or decree directed towards preventing monopoly or restraint of trade.

Article 53
Special Procedures with respect to Services

1. The Members recognize that certain services, such as transportation, telecommunications, insurance and the commercial services of banks, are substantial elements of international trade and that any restrictive business practices by enterprises engaged in these activities in international trade may have harmful effects similar to those indicated in paragraph 1 of Article 46. Such practices shall be dealt with in accordance with the following paragraphs of this Article.

2. If any Member considers that there exist restrictive business practices in relation to a service referred to in paragraph 1 which have or are about to have such harmful effects, and that its interests are thereby seriously prejudiced, the Member may submit a written statement explaining the situation to the Member or Members whose private or public enterprises are engaged in the services in question. The Member or Members concerned shall give sympathetic consideration to the statement and to such proposals as may be made and shall afford adequate opportunities for consultation with a view to effecting a satisfactory adjustment.

3. If no adjustment can be effected in accordance with the provisions of paragraph 2, and if the matter is referred to the Organization, it shall be transferred to the appropriate inter-governmental organization, if one exists, with such observations as the Organization may wish

to make. If no such inter-governmental organization exists, and if Members so request, the Organization may, in accordance with the provisions of paragraph 1 (c) of Article 72, make recommendations for, and promote international agreement on, measures designed to remedy the particular situation so far as it comes within the scope of this Charter.

4. The Organization shall, in accordance with paragraph 1 of Article 87, co-operate with other inter-governmental organizations in connection with restrictive business practices affecting any field coming within the scope of this Charter and those organizations shall be entitled to consult the Organization, to seek advice, and to ask that a study of a particular problem be made.

Article 54
Interpretation and Definition

1. The provisions of this Chapter shall be construed with due regard for the rights and obligations of Members set forth elsewhere in this Charter and shall not therefore be so interpreted as to prevent the adoption and enforcement of any measures in so far as they are specifically permitted under other Chapters of this Charter. The Organization may, however, make recommendations to Members or to any appropriate Inter-governmental organization concerning any features of these measures which may have the effect indicated in paragraph 1 of Article 46.

2. For the purposes of this Chapter

(a) the term "business practice" shall not be so construed as to include an individual contract between two parties as seller and buyer, lessor and lessee or principal and agent provided that such contract is not used to restrain competition, limit access to markets or foster monopolistic control;

(b) the term "public commercial enterprises" means

(i) agencies of governments in so far as they are engaged in trade, and

(ii) trading enterprises mainly or wholly owned by public authority, provided the Member concerned declares that for the purposes of this Chapter it has effective control over or assumes responsibility for the enterprises;

(c) the term "private commercial enterprises" means all commercial enterprises other than public commercial enterprises;

(d) the terms "decide" and "decision" as used in Article 46, 48 (except in paragraphs 3 and 4) and 50 do not determine the obligations of Members, but mean only that the Organization reaches a conclusion.

CHAPTER VII
THE INTERNATIONAL TRADE ORGANIZATION

Article 72
Functions

1. The Organization shall perform the functions attributed to it elsewhere in this Charter. In addition, the Organization shall have the following functions:

(a) to collect, analyze and publish information relating to international trade, including information relating to commercial policy, business practices, commodity problems and industrial and general economic development;

(b) to encourage and facilitate consultation among Members on all questions relating to the provisions of this Charter;

(c) to undertake studies, and, having due regard to the objectives of this Charter and the constitutional and legal systems of Members, make recommendations and promote bilateral or multilateral agreements concerning measures designed

(i) to assure just and equitable treatment for foreign nationals and enterprises;

(ii) to expand the volume and to improve the bases of international trade including measures designed to facilitate commercial arbitration and the avoidance of double taxation;

(iii) to carry out, on a regional or other basis, having due regard to the activities of existing regional or other intergovernmental organizations, the functions specified in paragraph 2 of Article 10;

(iv) to promote and encourage establishments for the technical training that is necessary for progressive industrial and economic development; and

(v) generally, to achieve any of the objectives set forth in Article 1;

(d) in collaboration with the Economic and Social Council of the United Nations and with such inter-governmental organizations as may be appropriate, to undertake studies on the relationship between world prices of primary commodities and manufactured products, to consider and where appropriate, to recommend international agreements on, measures designed to reduce progressively any unwarranted disparity in those prices;

(e) generally, to consult with and make recommendations to the Members and, as necessary, furnish advice and assistance to them regarding any matter relating to the operation of this Charter, and to take any other action necessary and appropriate to carry out the provisions of the Charter;

(f) to co-operate with the United Nations and other inter-governmental organizations in furthering the achievement of the economic and social objectives of the United Nations and the maintenance or restoration of international peace and security.

2. In the exercise of its functions the Organization shall have due regard to the economic circumstances of Members, to the factors affecting these circumstances and to the consequences of its determinations upon the interests of the Member or Members concerned.

* * *

CONVENTION[1] ON THE RECOGNITION AND ENFORCEMENT OF FOREIGN ARBITRAL AWARDS*

The Convention on the Recognition and Enforcement of Foreign Arbitral Awards was prepared and opened for signature on 10 June 1958 by the United Nations Conference on International Commercial Arbitration, held in New York from 20 May to 10 June 1958. The Convention entered into force on 7 June 1959, ninety days after the date of deposit of three instruments of ratification or accession with the Secretary-General of the United Nations. As of 14 November 1995, 106 States had ratified the Convention.

Article I

1. This Convention shall apply to the recognition and enforcement of arbitral awards made in the territory of a State other than the State where the recognition and enforcement of such awards are sought, and arising out of differences between persons, whether physical or legal. It shall also apply to arbitral awards not considered as domestic awards in the State where their recognition and enforcement are sought.

2. The term "arbitral awards" shall include not only awards made by arbitrators appointed for each case but also those made by permanent arbitral bodies to which the parties have submitted.

3. When signing, ratifying or acceding to this Convention, or notifying extension under article X hereof, any State may on the basis of reciprocity declare that it will apply the Convention to the recognition and enforcement of awards made only in the territory of another Contracting State. It may also declare that it will apply the Convention only to differences arising out of legal relationships, whether contractual or not, which are considered as commercial under the national law of the State making such declaration.

Article II

1. Each Contracting State shall recognize an agreement in writing under which the parties undertake to submit to arbitration all or any differences which have arisen or which may

[1]In accordance with article XII, the Convention came into force on 7 June 1959, the ninetieth day following the date of deposit with the Secretary-General of the United Nations of the third instrument of ratification or accession. The following States have deposited their instruments of ratification or accession (a) on the dates indicated; Israel, 5 January 1959; Morocco, 12 February 1959 (a), United Arab Republic, 9 March 1959(a).

* Source: United Nations (1959). "Convention on the Recognition and Enforcement of Foreign Arbitral Awards", *United Nations Treaty Series*, vol. 330 (New York: United Nations), pp.38-48 [Note added by the editor].

arise between them in respect of a defined legal relationship, whether contractual or not, concerning a subject matter capable of settlement by arbitration.

2. The term "agreement in writing" shall include an arbitral clause in a contract or an arbitration agreement, signed by the parties or contained in an exchange of letters or telegrams.

3. The court of a Contracting State, when seized of an action in a matter in respect of which the parties have made an agreement within the meaning of this article, at the request of one of the parties, refer the parties to arbitration, unless it finds that the said agreement is null and void, inoperative or incapable of being performed.

Article III

Each Contracting State shall recognize arbitral awards as binding and enforce them in accordance with the rules of procedure of the territory where the award is relied upon, under the conditions laid down in the following articles. There shall not be imposed substantially more onerous conditions or higher fees or charges on the recognition or enforcement of arbitral awards to which this Convention applies than are imposed on the recognition or enforcement of domestic arbitral awards.

Article IV

1. To obtain the recognition and enforcement mentioned in the preceding article, the party applying for recognition and enforcement shall, at the time of the application, supply:

(a) The duly authenticated original award or a duly certified copy thereof;

(b) The original agreement referred to in article II or a duly certified copy thereof.

2. If the said award or agreement is not made in an official language of the country in which the award is relied upon, the party applying for recognition and enforcement of the award shall produce a translation of these documents into such language. The translation shall be certified by an official or sworn translator or by a diplomatic or consular agent.

Article V

1. Recognition and enforcement of the award may be refused, at the request of the party against whom it is invoked, only if that party furnishes to the competent authority where the recognition and enforcement is sought, proof that:

(a) The parties to the agreement referred to in article II were, under the law applicable to them, under some incapacity, or the said agreement is not valid under the law to which the parties have subjected it or, failing any indication thereon, under the law of the country where the award was made; or

(b) The party against whom the award is invoked was not given proper notice of the appointment of the arbitrator or of the arbitration proceedings or was otherwise unable to present his case; or

(c) The award deals with a difference not contemplated by or not falling within the terms of the submission to arbitration, or it contains decisions on matters beyond the scope of the submission to arbitration, provided that, if the decisions on matters submitted to arbitration can be separated from those not so submitted, that part of the award which contains decisions on matters submitted to arbitration may be recognized and enforced; or

(d) The composition of the arbitral authority or the arbitral procedure was not in accordance with the agreement of the parties, or, failing such agreement, was not in accordance with the law of the country where the arbitration took place; or

(e) The award has not yet become binding on the parties, or has been set aside or suspended by a competent authority of the country in which, or under the law of which, that award was made.

2. Recognition and enforcement of an arbitral award may also be refused if the competent authority in the country where recognition and enforcement is sought finds that:

(a) The subject matter of the difference is not capable of settlement by arbitration under the law of that country; or

(b) The recognition or enforcement of the award would be contrary to the public policy of that country.

Article VI

If an application for the setting aside or suspension of the award has been made to a competent authority referred to in article V (1) *(e)*, the authority before which the award is sought to be relied upon may, if it considers it proper, adjourn the decision on the enforcement of the award and may also, on the application of the party claiming enforcement of the award, order the other party to give suitable security.

Article VII

1. The provisions of the present Convention shall not affect the validity of multilateral or bilateral agreements concerning the recognition and enforcement of arbitral awards entered into by the Contracting States nor deprive any interested party of any right he may have to avail himself of an arbitral award in the manner and to the extent allowed by the law or the treaties of the country where such award is sought to be relied upon.

2. The Geneva Protocol on Arbitration Clauses of 1923[2] and the Geneva Convention on the Execution of Foreign Arbitral Awards of 1927[3] shall cease to have effect between Contracting States on their becoming bound and to the extent that they become bound, by this Convention.

Article VIII

1. This Convention shall be open until 31 December 1958 for signature on behalf of any Member of the United Nations and also on behalf of any other State which is or hereafter becomes a member of any specialized agency of the United Nations, or which is or hereafter becomes a party to the Statute of the International Court of Justice, or any other State to which an invitation has been addressed by the General Assembly of the United Nations.

2. This Convention shall be ratified and the instrument of ratification shall be deposited with the Secretary-General of the United Nations.

Article IX

1. This Convention shall be open for accession to all States referred to in article VIII.

2. Accession shall be effected by the deposit of an instrument of accession with the Secretary-General of the United Nations.

Article X

1. Any State may, at the time of signature, ratification or accession, declare that this Convention shall extend to all or any of the territories for the international relations of which it is responsible. Such a declaration shall take effect when the Convention enters into force for the State concerned.

2. At any time thereafter any such extension shall be made by notification addressed to the Secretary-General of the United Nations and shall take effect as from the ninetieth day after the day of receipt by the Secretary-General of the United Nations of this notification, or as

---

[2]League of Nations, *Treaty Series,* Vol. XXVII, p. 157; Vol. XXXI, p. 260; Vol. XXXV, p. 314; Vol. XXXIX, p. 190; Vol. XLV, p. 116; Vol. L, p. 161; Vol. LIX, p. 355; Vol. LXIX, p. 79; Vol. LXXII, p. 452; Vol. LXXXIII, p. 393; Vol. LXXXVIII, p. 312; Vol. XCVI, p. 190; Vol. C, p. 211; Vol. CIV, p. 499; Vol. CVII, p. 470; Vol. CXI, p. 403; Vol. CXVII, p. 55; Vol. CLVI, p. 185; Vol. CLXXXI, p. 356; Vol. CLXXXV, p. 372; Vol. CXCIII, p. 268, and Vol. CC, p.500; and United Nations, *Treaty Series,* Vol. 117, p. 394; Vol. 261 p. 422, and Vol. 325.

[3]League of Nations, *Treaty Series,* Vol. XCII, p. 301; Vol. XCVI p. 205; Vol. C, p. 259; Vol. CIV, p. 526; Vol. CVII, p. 528; Vol. CXI, p. 414; Vol. CXVII, p. 303; Vol. CXXX, p. 457; Vol. CLVI, p. 210; Vol. CLXXXI, p. 389; Vol. CLXXXV, p. 391 and Vol. CXCIII, p. 269; and United Nations, *Treaty Series,* Vol. 122, p. 346; Vol. 134, p. 402; Vol. 269, p. 384, and Vol.325.

from the date of entry into force of the Convention for the State concerned, whichever is the later.

3. With respect to those territories to which this Convention is not extended at the time of signature, ratification or accession, each State concerned shall consider the possibility of taking the necessary steps in order to extend the application of this Convention to such territories, subject, where necessary for constitutional reasons, to the consent of the Governments of such territories.

Article XI

In the case of a federal or non-unitary State, the following provisions shall apply:

(a) With respect to those articles of this Convention that come within the legislative jurisdiction of the federal authority, the obligations of the federal Government shall to this extent be the same as those of Contracting States which are not federal States;

(b) With respect to those articles of this Convention that come within the legislative jurisdiction of constituent states or provinces which are not, under the constitutional system of the federation, bound to take legislative action, the federal Government shall bring such articles with a favourable recommendation to the notice of the appropriate authorities of constituent states or provinces at the earliest possible moment;

(c) A federal State Party to this Convention shall, at the request of any other Contracting State transmitted through the Secretary-General of the United Nations, supply a statement of the law and practice of the federation and its constituent units in regard to any particular provision of this Convention, showing the extent to which effect has been given to that provision by legislative or other action.

Article XII

1. This Convention shall come into force on the ninetieth day following the date of deposit of the third instrument of ratification or accession.

2. For each State ratifying or acceeding [sic] to this Convention after the deposit of the third instrument of ratification or accession, this Convention shall enter into force on the ninetieth day after deposit by such State of its instrument of ratification or accession.

Article XIII

1. Any Contracting State may denounce this Convention by a written notification to the Secretary-General of the United Nations. Denunciation shall take effect one year after the date of receipt of the notification by the Secretary-General.

2. Any State which has made a declaration or notification under article X may, at any time thereafter, by notification to the Secretary-General of the United Nations, declare that this Convention shall cease to extend to the territory concerned one year after the date of the receipt of the notification by the Secretary-General.

3. This Convention shall continue to be applicable to arbitral awards in respect of which recognition or enforcement proceedings have been instituted before the denunciation takes effect.

Article XIV

A Contracting State shall not be entitled to avail itself of the present Convention against other Contracting States except to the extent that it is itself bound to apply the Convention.

Article XV

The Secretary-General of the United Nations shall notify the States contemplated in article VIII of the following:

(a) Signatures and ratifications in accordance with article VIII;
(b) Accessions in accordance with article IX;
(c) Declarations and notifications under articles I, X and XI;
(d) The date upon which this Convention enters into force in accordance with article XII;
(e) Denunciations and notifications in accordance with article XIII.

Article XVI

1. This Convention, of which the Chinese, English, French, Russian and Spanish texts shall be equally authentic, shall be deposited in the archives of the United Nations.

2. The Secretary-General of the United Nations shall transmit a certified copy of this Convention to the States contemplated in article VIII.

* * *

UNITED NATIONS GENERAL ASSEMBLY RESOLUTION 1803 (XVII): PERMANENT SOVEREIGNTY OVER NATURAL RESOURCES*

The United Nations General Assembly resolution 1803 (XVII) on Permanent Sovereignty over Natural Resources was adopted by the General Assembly of the United Nations at its seventeenth session on 14 December 1962.

The General Assembly,

Recalling its resolutions 523 (VI) of 12 January 1952 and 626 (VII) of 21 December 1952,

Bearing in mind its resolution 1314 (XIII) of 12 December 1958, by which it established the Commission on Permanent Sovereignty over Natural Resources and instructed it to conduct a full survey of the status of permanent sovereignty over natural wealth and resources as a basic constituent of the right to self-determination, with recommendations, where necessary, for its strengthening, and decided further that, in the conduct of the full survey of the status of the permanent sovereignty of peoples and nations over their natural wealth and resources, due regard should be paid to the rights and duties of States under international law and to the importance of encouraging international co-operation in the economic development of developing countries,

Bearing in mind its resolution 1515 (XV) of 15 December 1960, in which it recommended that the sovereign right of every State to dispose of its wealth and its natural resources should be respected,

Considering that any measure in this respect must be based on the recognition of the inalienable right of all States freely to dispose of their natural wealth and resources in accordance with their national interests, and on respect for the economic independence of States,

Considering that nothing in paragraph 4 below in any way prejudices the position of any Member State on any aspect of the question of the rights and obligations of successor States and Governments in respect of property acquired before the accession to complete sovereignty of countries formerly under colonial rule,

Noting that the subject of succession of States and Governments is being examined as a matter of priority by the International Law Commission,

---

*Source: United Nations (1963). "General Assembly Resolution 1803 (XVII): Permanent sovereignty over natural resources", *Official Records of the General Assembly: Seventeenth Session,* Supplement No. 17 (A/5217) (New York: United Nations), pp. 15-16 [Note added by the editor].

Considering that it is desirable to promote international co-operation for the economic development of developing countries, and that economic and financial agreements between the developed and the developing countries must be based on the principles of equality and of the right of peoples and nations to self-determination,

Considering that the provision of economic and technical assistance, loans and increased foreign investment must not be subject to conditions which conflict with the interests of the recipient State,

Considering the benefits to be derived from exchanges of technical and scientific information likely to promote the development and use of such resources and wealth, and the important part which the United Nations and other international organizations are called upon to play in that connection,

Attaching particular importance to the question of promoting the economic development of developing countries and securing their economic independence,

Noting that the creation and strengthening of the inalienable sovereignty of States over their natural wealth and resources reinforces their economic independence,

Desiring that there should be further consideration by the United Nations of the subject of permanent sovereignty over natural resources in the spirit of international co-operation in the field of economic development, particularly that of the developing countries,

I

Declares that:

1. The right of peoples and nations to permanent sovereignty over their natural wealth and resources must be exercised in the interest of their national development and of the well-being of the people of the State concerned.

2. The exploration, development and disposition of such resources, as well as the import of the foreign capital required for these purposes, should be in conformity with the rules and conditions which the peoples and nations freely consider to be necessary or desirable with regard to the authorization, restriction or prohibition of such activities.

3. In cases where authorization is granted, the capital imported and the earnings on that capital shall be governed by the terms thereof, by the national legislation in force, and by international law. The profits derived must be shared in the proportions freely agreed upon, in each case, between the investors and the recipient State, due care being taken to ensure that there is no impairment, for any reason, of that State's sovereignty over its natural wealth and resources.

4. Nationalization, expropriation or requisitioning shall be based on grounds or reasons of public utility, security or the national interest which are recognized as overriding purely individual or private interests, both domestic and foreign. In such cases the owner shall be paid appropriate compensation, in accordance with the rules in force in the State taking such measures in the exercise of its sovereignty and in accordance with international law. In any case where the question of compensation gives rise to a controversy, the national jurisdiction of the State taking such measures shall be exhausted. However, upon agreement by sovereign States and other parties concerned, settlement of the dispute should be made through arbitration or international adjudication.

5. The free and beneficial exercise of the sovereignty of peoples and nations over their natural resources must be furthered by the mutual respect of States based on their sovereign equality.

6. International co-operation for the economic development of developing countries, whether in the form of public or private capital investments, exchange of goods and services, technical assistance, or exchange of scientific information, shall be such as to further their independent national development and shall be based upon respect for their sovereignty over their natural wealth and resources.

7. Violation of the rights of peoples and nations to sovereignty over their natural wealth and resources is contrary to the spirit and principles of the Charter of the United Nations and hinders the development of international co-operation and the maintenance of peace.

8. Foreign investment agreements freely entered into by or between sovereign States shall be observed in good faith; States and international organizations shall strictly and conscientiously respect the sovereignty of peoples and nations over their natural wealth and resources in accordance with the Charter and the principles set forth in the present resolution.

II

Welcomes the decision of the International Law Commission to speed up its work on the codification of the topic of responsibility of States for the consideration of the General Assembly;[1]

III

Requests the Secretary-General to continue the study of the various aspects of permanent sovereignty over natural resources, taking into account the desire of Member States to ensure the protection of their sovereign rights while encouraging international co-operation in the field of

[1]Official Records of the General Assembly, Seventeenth Session, Supplement No. 9 (A/5209), paras. 67-69.

economic development, and to report to the Economic and Social Council and to the General Assembly, if possible at its eighteenth session.

1194th plenary meeting,
14th December 1962.

* * *

CONVENTION ON THE SETTLEMENT OF INVESTMENT DISPUTES BETWEEN STATES AND NATIONALS OF OTHER STATES*

The Convention on the Settlement of Investment Disputes Between States and Nationals of Other States was submitted to Governments by the Executive Directors of the International Bank for Reconstruction and Development on 18 March 1965 and entered into force on 14 October 1966. As of July 1995, 136 States had signed the Convention and 122 States had ratified it. In June 1979 the "Rules Governing the Additional Facility for the Administration of Proceedings by the Secretariat of the International Center for Settlement of Investment Disputes" (Additional Facility Rules) were adopted. The "Additional Facility Rules" have not been included in this volume.

PREAMBLE

The Contracting States

Considering the need for international cooperation for economic development, and the role of private international investment therein;

Bearing in mind the possibility that from time to time disputes may arise in connection with such investment between Contracting States and nationals of other Contracting States;

Recognizing that while such disputes would usually be subject to national legal processes, international methods of settlement may be appropriate in certain cases;

Attaching particular importance to the availability of facilities for international conciliation or arbitration to which Contracting States and nationals of other Contracting States may submit such disputes if they so desire;

Desiring to establish such facilities under the auspices of the International Bank for Reconstruction and Development;

Recognizing that mutual consent by the parties to submit such disputes to conciliation or to arbitration through such facilities constitutes a binding agreement which requires in particular that due consideration be given to any recommendation of conciliators, and that any arbitral award be complied with; and

* Source: International Center for Settlement of Investment Disputes. *Convention on the Settlement of Investment Disputes between States and Nationals of Other States*, document ICSID/2 (Washington D. C.: International Centre for Settlement of Investment Disputes) [Note added by the editor].

Declaring that no Contracting State shall by the mere fact of its ratification, acceptance or approval of this Convention and without its consent be deemed to be under any obligation to submit any particular dispute to conciliation or arbitration,

Have agreed as follows:

CHAPTER I
International Centre for Settlement of Investment Disputes

SECTION 1
Establishment and Organization

Article 1

(1) There is hereby established the International Centre for Settlement of Investment Disputes (hereinafter called the Centre).

(2) The purpose of the Centre shall be to provide facilities for conciliation and arbitration of investment disputes between Contracting States and nationals of other Contracting States in accordance with the provisions of this Convention.

Article 2

The seat of the Centre shall be at the principal office of the International Bank for Reconstruction and Development (hereinafter called the Bank). The seat may be moved to another place by decision of the Administrative Council adopted by a majority of two-thirds of its members.

Article 3

The Centre shall have an Administrative Council and a Secretariat and shall maintain a Panel of Conciliators and a Panel of Arbitrators.

SECTION 2
The Administrative Council

Article 4

(1) The Administrative Council shall be composed of one representative of each Contracting State. An alternate may act as representative in case of his principal's absence from a meeting or inability to act.

(2) In the absence of a contrary designation, each governor and alternate governor of the Bank appointed by a Contracting State shall be ex officio its representative and its alternate respectively.

Article 5

The President of the Bank shall be ex officio Chairman of the Administrative Council (hereinafter called the Chairman) but shall have no vote. During his absence or inability to act and during any vacancy in the office of President of the Bank, the person for the time being acting as President shall act as Chairman of the Administrative Council.

Article 6

(1) Without prejudice to the powers and functions vested in it by other provisions of this Convention, the Administrative Council shall

(a) adopt the administrative and financial regulations of the Centre;
(b) adopt the rules of procedure for the institution of conciliation and arbitration proceedings;
(c) adopt the rules of procedure for conciliation and arbitration proceedings (hereinafter called the Conciliation Rules and the Arbitration Rules);
(d) approve arrangements with the Bank for the use of the Bank's administrative facilities and services;
(e) determine the conditions of service of the Secretary-General and of any Deputy Secretary-General;
(f) adopt the annual budget of revenues and expenditures of the Centre;
(g) approve the annual report on the operation of the Centre.

The decisions referred to in sub-paragraphs (a), (b), (c) and (f) above shall be adopted by a majority of two-thirds of the members of the Administrative Council.

(2) The Administrative Council may appoint such committees as it considers necessary.

(3) The Administrative Council shall also exercise such other powers and perform such other functions as it shall determine to be necessary for the implementation of the provisions of this Convention.

Article 7

(1) The Administrative Council shall hold an annual meeting and such other meetings as may be determined by the Council, or convened by the Chairman, or convened by the Secretary-General at the request of not less than five members of the Council.

(2) Each member of the Administrative Council shall have one vote and, except as otherwise herein provided, all matters before the Council shall be decided by a majority of the votes cast.

(3) A quorum for any meeting of the Administrative Council shall be a majority of its members.

(4) The Administrative Council may establish, by a majority of two-thirds of its members, a procedure whereby the Chairman may seek a vote of the Council without convening a meeting of the Council. The vote shall be considered valid only if the majority of the members of the Council cast their votes within the time limit fixed by the said procedure.

Article 8

Members of the Administrative Council and the Chairman shall serve without remuneration from the Centre.

SECTION 3
The Secretariat

Article 9

The Secretariat shall consist of a Secretary-General, one or more Deputy Secretaries-General and staff.

Article 10

(1) The Secretary-General and any Deputy Secretary-General shall be elected by the Administrative Council by a majority of two-thirds of its members upon the nomination of the Chairman for a term of service not exceeding six years and shall be eligible for re-election. After consulting the members of the Administrative Council, the Chairman shall propose one or more candidates for each such office.

(2) The offices of Secretary-General and Deputy Secretary-General shall be incompatible with the exercise of any political function. Neither the Secretary-General nor any Deputy Secretary-General may hold any other employment or engage in any other occupation except with the approval of the Administrative Council.

(3) During the Secretary-General's absence or inability to act, and during any vacancy of the office of Secretary-General, the Deputy Secretary-General shall act as Secretary-General. If there shall be more than one Deputy Secretary-General, the Administrative Council shall determine in advance the order in which they shall act as Secretary-General.

Article 11

The Secretary-General shall be the legal representative and the principal officer of the Centre and shall be responsible for its administration, including the appointment of staff, in accordance with the provisions of this Convention and the rules adopted by the Administrative

Council. He shall perform the function of registrar and shall have the power to authenticate arbitral awards rendered pursuant to this Convention, and to certify copies thereof.

SECTION 4
The Panels

Article 12

The Panel of Conciliators and the Panel of Arbitrators shall each consist of qualified persons, designated as hereinafter provided, who are willing to serve thereon.

Article 13

(1) Each Contracting State may designate to each Panel four persons who may but need not be its nationals.

(2) The Chairman may designate ten persons to each Panel. The persons so designated to a Panel shall each have a different nationality.

Article 14

(1) Persons designated to serve on the Panels shall be persons of high moral character and recognized competence in the fields of law, commerce, industry or finance, who may be relied upon to exercise independent judgment. Competence in the field of law shall be of particular importance in the case of persons on the Panel of Arbitrators.

(2) The Chairman, in designating persons to serve on the Panels, shall in addition pay due regard to the importance of assuring representation on the Panels of the principal legal systems of the world and of the main forms of economic activity.

Article 15

(1) Panel members shall serve for renewable periods of six years.

(2) In the case of death or resignation of a member of a Panel, the authority which designated the member shall have the right to designate another person to serve for the remainder of that member's term.

(3) Panel members shall continue in office until their successors have been designated.

Article 16

(1) A person may serve on both Panels.

(2) If a person shall have been designated to serve on the same Panel by one or more Contracting State, or by one or more Contracting States and the Chairman, he shall be deemed to have been designated by the authority which first designated him or, if one such authority is the State of which he is a national, by that State.

(3) All designations shall be notified to the Secretary-General and shall take effect from the date on which the notification is received.

SECTION 5
Financing the Centre

Article 17

If the expenditure of the Centre cannot be met out of charges for the use of its facilities, or out of other receipts, the excess shall be borne by Contracting States which are members of the Bank in proportion to their respective subscriptions to the capital stock of the Bank, and by Contracting States which are not members of the Bank in accordance with rules adopted by the Administrative Council.

SECTION 6
Status, Immunities and Privileges

Article 18

The Centre shall have full international legal personality. The legal capacity of the Centre shall include the capacity

(a) to contract;
(b) to acquire and dispose of movable and immovable property;
(c) to institute legal proceedings.

Article 19

To enable the Centre to fulfil its functions, it shall enjoy in the territories of each Contracting State the immunities and privileges set forth in this Section.

Article 20

The Centre, its property and assets shall enjoy immunity from all legal process, except when the Centre waives this immunity.

Article 21

The Chairman, the members of the Administrative Council, persons acting as conciliators or arbitrators or members of a Committee appointed pursuant to paragraph (3) of Article 52, and the officers and employees of the Secretariat

(a) shall enjoy immunity from legal process with respect to acts performed by them in the exercise of their functions, except when the Centre waives this immunity;

(b) not being local nationals, shall enjoy the same immunities from immigration restrictions, alien registration requirements and national service obligations, the same facilities as regards exchange restrictions and the same treatment in respect of travelling facilities as are accorded by Contracting States to the representatives, officials and employees of comparable rank of other Contracting States.

Article 22

The provisions of Article 21 shall apply to persons appearing in proceedings under this Convention as parties, agents, counsel, advocates, witnesses or experts; provided, however, that sub-paragraph (b) thereof shall apply only in connection with their travel to and from, and their stay at, the place where the proceedings are held.

Article 23

(1) The archives of the Centre shall be inviolable, wherever they may be.

(2) With regard to its official communications, the Centre shall be accorded by each Contracting State treatment not less favourable than that accorded to other international organizations.

Article 24

(1) The Centre, its assets, property and income, and its operations and transactions authorized by this Convention shall be exempt from all taxation and customs duties. The Centre shall also be exempt from liability for the collection or payment of any taxes or customs duties.

(2) Except in the case of local nationals, no tax shall be levied on or in respect of expense allowances paid by the Centre to the Chairman or members of the Administrative Council, or on or in respect of salaries, expense allowances or other emoluments paid by the Centre to officials or employees of the Secretariat.

(3) No tax shall be levied on or in respect of fees or expense allowances received by persons acting as conciliators, or arbitrators, or members of a Committee appointed pursuant to paragraph (3) of Article 52, in proceedings under this Convention, if the sole jurisdictional basis for such tax is the location of the Centre or the place where such proceedings are conducted or the place where such fees or allowances are paid.

CHAPTER II
Jurisdiction of the Centre

Article 25

(1) The jurisdiction of the Centre shall extend to any legal dispute arising directly out of an investment, between a Contracting State (or any constituent subdivision or agency of a Contracting State designated to the Centre by that State) and a national of another Contracting State, which the parties to the dispute consent in writing to submit to the Centre. When the parties have given their consent, no party may withdraw its consent unilaterally.

(2) "National of another Contracting State" means:

(a) any natural person who had the nationality of a Contracting State other than the State party to the dispute on the date on which the parties consented to submit such dispute to conciliation or arbitration as well as on the date on which the request was registered pursuant to paragraph (3) of Article 28 or paragraph (3) of Article 36, but does not include any person who on either date also had the nationality of the Contracting State party to the dispute; and

(b) any juridical person which had the nationality of a Contracting State other than the State party to the dispute on the date on which the parties consented to submit such dispute to conciliation or arbitration and any juridical person which had the nationality of the Contracting State party to the dispute on that date and which, because of foreign control, the parties have agreed should be treated as a national of another Contracting State for the purposes of this Convention.

(3) Consent by a constituent subdivision or agency of a Contracting State shall require the approval of that State unless that State notifies the Centre that no such approval is required.

(4) Any Contracting State may, at the time of ratification, acceptance or approval of this Convention or at any time thereafter, notify the Centre of the class or classes of disputes which it would or would not consider submitting to the jurisdiction of the Centre. The Secretary-General shall forthwith transmit such notification to all Contracting States. Such notification shall not constitute the consent required by paragraph (1).

Article 26

Consent of the parties to arbitration under this Convention shall, unless otherwise stated, be deemed consent to such arbitration to the exclusion of any other remedy. A Contracting State may require the exhaustion of local administrative or judicial remedies as a condition of its consent to arbitration under this Convention.

Article 27

(1) No Contracting State shall give diplomatic protection, or bring an international claim, in respect of a dispute which one of its nationals and another Contracting State shall have consented to submit or shall have submitted to arbitration under this Convention, unless such other Contracting State shall have failed to abide by and comply with the award rendered in such dispute.

(2) Diplomatic protection, for the purposes of paragraph (1), shall not include informal diplomatic exchanges for the sole purpose of facilitating a settlement of the dispute.

CHAPTER III
Conciliation

SECTION 1
Request for Conciliation

Article 28

(1) Any Contracting State or any national of a Contracting State wishing to institute conciliation proceedings shall address a request to that effect in writing to the Secretary-General who shall send a copy of the request to the other party.

(2) The request shall contain information concerning the issues in dispute, the identity of the parties and their consent to conciliation in accordance with the rules of procedure for the institution of conciliation and arbitration proceedings.

(3) The Secretary-General shall register the request unless he finds, on the basis of the information contained in the request, that the dispute is manifestly outside the jurisdiction of the Centre. He shall forthwith notify the parties of registration or refusal to register.

SECTION 2
Constitution of the Conciliation Commission

Article 29

(1) The Conciliation Commission (hereinafter called the Commission) shall be constituted as soon as possible after registration of a request pursuant to Article 28.

(2) (a) The Commission shall consist of a sole conciliator or any uneven number of conciliators appointed as the parties shall agree.

(b) Where the parties do not agree upon the number of conciliators and the method of their appointment, the Commission shall consist of three conciliators, one conciliator appointed by each party and the third, who shall be the president of the Commission, appointed by agreement of the parties.

Article 30

If the Commission shall not have been constituted within 90 days after notice of registration of the request has been dispatched by the Secretary-General in accordance with paragraph (3) of Article 28, or such other period as the parties may agree, the Chairman shall, at the request of either party and after consulting both parties as far as possible, appoint the conciliator or conciliators not yet appointed.

Article 31

(1) Conciliators may be appointed from outside the Panel of Conciliators, except in the case of appointments by the Chairman pursuant to Article 30.

(2) Conciliators appointed from outside the Panel of Conciliators shall possess the qualities stated in paragraph (1) of Article 14.

SECTION 3
Conciliation Proceedings

Article 32

(1) The Commission shall be the judge of its own competence.

(2) Any objection by a party to the dispute that that dispute is not within the jurisdiction of the Centre, or for other reasons is not within the competence of the Commission, shall be considered by the Commission which shall determine whether to deal with it as a preliminary question or to join it to the merits of the dispute.

Article 33

Any conciliation proceeding shall be conducted in accordance with the provisions of this Section and, except as the parties otherwise agree, in accordance with the Conciliation Rules in effect on the date on which the parties consented to conciliation. If any question of procedure arises which is not covered by this Section or the Conciliation Rules or any rules agreed by the parties, the Commission shall decide the question.

Article 34

(1) It shall be the duty of the Commission to clarify the issues in dispute between the parties and to endeavour to bring about agreement between them upon mutually acceptable terms. To that end, the Commission may at any stage of the proceedings and from time to time recommend terms of settlement to the parties. The parties shall cooperate in good faith with the

Commission in order to enable the Commission to carry out its functions, and shall give their most serious consideration to its recommendations.

(2) If the parties reach agreement, the Commission shall draw up a report noting the issues in dispute and recording that the parties have reached agreement. If, at any stage of the proceedings, it appears to the Commission that there is no likelihood of agreement between the parties, it shall close the proceedings and shall draw up a report noting the submission of the dispute and recording the failure of the parties to reach agreement. If one party fails to appear or participate in the proceedings, the Commission shall close the proceedings and shall draw up a report noting that party's failure to appear or participate.

Article 35

Except as the parties to the dispute shall otherwise agree, neither party to a conciliation proceeding shall be entitled in any other proceeding, whether before arbitrators or in a court of law or otherwise, to invoke or rely on any views expressed or statements or admissions or offers of settlement made by the other party in the conciliation proceedings, or the report or any recommendations made by the Commission.

CHAPTER IV
Arbitration

SECTION 1
Request for Arbitration

Article 36

(1) Any Contracting State or any national of a Contracting State wishing to institute arbitration proceedings shall address a request to that effect in writing to the Secretary-General who shall send a copy of the request to the other party.

(2) The request shall contain information concerning the issues in dispute, the identity of the parties and their consent to arbitration in accordance with the rules of procedure for the institution of conciliation and arbitration proceedings.

(3) The Secretary-General shall register the request unless he finds, on the basis of the information contained in the request, that the dispute is manifestly outside the jurisdiction of the Centre. He shall forthwith notify the parties of registration or refusal to register.

SECTION 2
Constitution of the Tribunal

Article 37

(1) The Arbitral Tribunal (hereinafter called the Tribunal) shall be constituted as soon

as possible after registration of a request pursuant to Article 36.

(2) (a) The Tribunal shall consist of a sole arbitrator or any uneven number of arbitrators appointed as the parties shall agree.

(b) Where the parties do not agree upon the number of arbitrators and the method of their appointment, the Tribunal shall consist of three arbitrators, one arbitrator appointed by each party and the third, who shall be the president of the Tribunal, appointed by agreement of the parties.

Article 38

If the Tribunal shall not have been constituted within 90 days after notice of registration of the request has been dispatched by the Secretary-General in accordance with paragraph (3) of Article 36, or such other period as the parties may agree, the Chairman shall, at the request of either party and after consulting both parties as far as possible, appoint the arbitrator or arbitrators not yet appointed. Arbitrators appointed by the Chairman pursuant to this Article shall not be nationals of the Contracting State party to the dispute or of the Contracting State whose national is a party to the dispute.

Article 39

The majority of the arbitrators shall be nationals of States other than the Contracting State party to the dispute and the Contracting State whose national is a party to the dispute; provided, however, that the foregoing provisions of this Article shall not apply if the sole arbitrator or each individual member of the Tribunal has been appointed by agreement of the parties.

Article 40

(1) Arbitrators may be appointed from outside the Panel of Arbitrators, except in the case of appointments by the Chairman pursuant to Article 38.

(2) Arbitrators appointed from outside the Panel of Arbitrators shall possess the qualities stated in paragraph (1) of Article 14.

SECTION 3
Powers and Functions of the Tribunal

Article 41

(1) The Tribunal shall be the judge of its own competence.

(2) Any objection by a party to the dispute that that dispute is not within the jurisdiction of the Centre, or for other reasons is not within the competence of the Tribunal, shall be considered by the Tribunal which shall determine whether to deal with it as a preliminary

question or to join it to the merits of the dispute.

Article 42

(1) The Tribunal shall decide a dispute in accordance with such rules of law as may be agreed by the parties. In the absence of such agreement, the Tribunal shall apply the law of the Contracting State party to the dispute (including its rules on the conflict of laws) and such rules of international law as may be applicable.

(2) The Tribunal may not bring in a finding of non liquet on the ground of silence or obscurity of the law.

(3) The provisions of paragraphs (1) and (2) shall not prejudice the power of the Tribunal to decide a dispute ex aequo et bono if the parties so agree.

Article 43

Except as the parties otherwise agree, the Tribunal may, if it deems it necessary at any stage of the proceedings,

(a) call upon the parties to produce documents or other evidence, and

(b) visit the scene connected with the dispute, and conduct such inquiries there as it may deem appropriate.

Article 44

Any arbitration proceeding shall be conducted in accordance with the provisions of this Section and, except as the parties otherwise agree, in accordance with the Arbitration Rules in effect on the date on which the parties consented to arbitration. If any question of procedure arises which is not covered by this Section or the Arbitration Rules or any rules agreed by the parties, the Tribunal shall decide the question.

Article 45

(1) Failure of a party to appear or to present his case shall not be deemed an admission of the other party's assertions.

(2) If a party fails to appear or to present his case at any stage of the proceedings the other party may request the Tribunal to deal with the questions submitted to it and to render an award. Before rendering an award, the Tribunal shall notify, and grant a period of grace to, the party failing to appear or to present its case, unless it is satisfied that that party does not intend to do so.

Article 46

Except as the parties otherwise agree, the Tribunal shall, if requested by a party, determine any incidental or additional claims or counter-claims arising directly out of the subject-matter of the dispute provided that they are within the scope of the consent of the parties and are otherwise within the jurisdiction of the Centre.

Article 47

Except as the parties otherwise agree, the Tribunal may, if it considers that the circumstances so require, recommend any provisional measures which should be taken to preserve the respective rights of either party.

SECTION 4
The Award

Article 48

(1) The Tribunal shall decide questions by a majority of the votes of all its members.

(2) The award of the Tribunal shall be in writing and shall be signed by the members of the Tribunal who voted for it.

(3) The award shall deal with every question submitted to the Tribunal, and shall state the reasons upon which it is based.

(4) Any member of the Tribunal may attach his individual opinion to the award, whether he dissents from the majority or not, or a statement of his dissent.

(5) The Centre shall not publish the award without the consent of the parties.

Article 49

(1) The Secretary-General shall promptly dispatch certified copies of the award to the parties. The award shall be deemed to have been rendered on the date on which the certified copies were dispatched.

(2) The Tribunal upon the request of a party made within 45 days after the date on which the award was rendered may after notice to the other party decide any question which it had omitted to decide in the award, and shall rectify any clerical, arithmetical or similar error in the award. Its decision shall become part of the award and shall be notified to the parties in the same manner as the award. The periods of time provided for under paragraph (2) of Article 51 and paragraph (2) of Article 52 shall run from the date on which the decision was rendered.

SECTION 5
Interpretation, Revision and Annulment of the Award

Article 50

(1) If any dispute shall arise between the parties as to the meaning or scope of an award, either party may request interpretation of the award by an application in writing addressed to the Secretary-General.

(2) The request shall, if possible, be submitted to the Tribunal which rendered the award. If this shall not be possible, a new Tribunal shall be constituted in accordance with Section 2 of this Chapter. The Tribunal may, if it considers that the circumstances so require, stay enforcement of the award pending its decision.

Article 51

(1) Either party may request revision of the award by an application in writing addressed to the Secretary-General on the ground of discovery of some fact of such a nature as decisively to affect the award, provided that when the award was rendered the fact was unknown to the Tribunal and to the applicant and that the applicant's ignorance of that fact was not due to negligence.

(2) The application shall be made within 90 days after the discovery of such fact and in any event within three years after the date on which the award was rendered.

(3) The request shall, if possible, be submitted to the Tribunal which rendered the award. If this shall not be possible, a new Tribunal shall be constituted in accordance with Section 2 of this Chapter.

(4) The Tribunal may, if it considers that the circumstances so require, stay enforcement of the award pending its decision. If the applicant requests a stay of enforcement of the award in his application, enforcement shall be stayed provisionally until the Tribunal rules on such request.

Article 52

(1) Either party may request annulment of the award by an application in writing addressed to the Secretary-General on one or more of the following grounds:

(a) that the Tribunal was not properly constituted;
(b) that the Tribunal has manifestly exceeded its powers;
(c) that there was corruption on the part of a member of the Tribunal;
(d) that there has been a serious departure from a fundamental rule of procedure; or
(e) that the award has failed to state the reasons on which it is based.

(2) The application shall be made within 120 days after the date on which the award was rendered except that when annulment is requested on the ground of corruption such application shall be made within 120 days after discovery of the corruption and in any event within three years after the date on which the award was rendered.

(3) On receipt of the request the Chairman shall forthwith appoint from the Panel of Arbitrators an ad hoc Committee of three persons. None of the members of the Committee shall have been a member of the Tribunal which rendered the award, shall be of the same nationality as any such member, shall be a national of the State party to the dispute or of the State whose national is a party to the dispute, shall have been designated to the Panel of Arbitrators by either of those States, or shall have acted as a conciliator in the same dispute. The Committee shall have the authority to annul the award or any part thereof on any of the grounds set forth in paragraph (1).

(4) The provisions of Articles 41-45, 48, 49, 53 and 54, and of Chapters VI and VII shall apply mutatis mutandis to proceedings before the Committee.

(5) The Committee may, if it considers that the circumstances so require, stay enforcement of the award pending its decision. If the applicant requests a stay of enforcement of the award in his application, enforcement shall be stayed provisionally until the Committee rules on such request.

(6) If the award is annulled the dispute shall, at the request of either party, be submitted to a new Tribunal constituted in accordance with Section 2 of this Chapter.

SECTION 6
Recognition and Enforcement of the Award

Article 53

(1) The award shall be binding on the parties and shall not be subject to any appeal or to any other remedy except those provided for in this Convention. Each party shall abide by and comply with the terms of the award except to the extent that enforcement shall have been stayed pursuant to the relevant provisions of this Convention.

(2) For the purposes of this Section, "award" shall include any decision interpreting, revising or annulling such award pursuant to Articles 50, 51, or 52.

Article 54

(1) Each Contracting State shall recognize an award rendered pursuant to this Convention as binding and enforce the pecuniary obligations imposed by that award within its territories as if it were a final judgment of a court in that State. A Contracting State with a federal constitution may enforce such an award in or through its federal courts and may provide

that such courts shall treat the award as if it were a final judgment of the courts of a constituent state.

(2) A party seeking recognition or enforcement in the territories of a Contracting State shall furnish to a competent court or other authority which such State shall have designated for this purpose a copy of the award certified by the Secretary-General. Each Contracting State shall notify the Secretary-General of the designation of the competent court or other authority for this purpose and of any subsequent change in such designation.

(3) Execution of the award shall be governed by the laws concerning the execution of judgments in force in the State in whose territories such execution is sought.

Article 55

Nothing in Article 54 shall be construed as derogating from the law in force in any Contracting State relating to immunity of that State or of any foreign State from execution.

CHAPTER V
Replacement and Disqualification of Conciliators and Arbitrators

Article 56

(1) After a Commission or a Tribunal has been constituted and proceedings have begun, its composition shall remain unchanged; provided, however, that if a conciliator or an arbitrator should die, become incapacitated, or resign, the resulting vacancy shall be filled in accordance with the provisions of Section 2 of Chapter III or Section 2 of Chapter IV.

(2) A member of a Commission or Tribunal shall continue to serve in that capacity notwithstanding that he shall have ceased to be a member of the Panel.

(3) If a conciliator or arbitrator appointed by a party shall have resigned without the consent of the Commission or Tribunal of which he was a member, the Chairman shall appoint a person from the appropriate Panel to fill the resulting vacancy.

Article 57

A party may propose to a Commission or Tribunal the disqualification of any of its members on account of any fact indicating a manifest lack of the qualities required by paragraph (1) of Article 14. A party to arbitration proceedings may, in addition, propose the disqualification of an arbitrator on the ground that he was ineligible for appointment to the Tribunal under Section 2 of Chapter IV.

Article 58

The decision on any proposal to disqualify a conciliator or arbitrator shall be taken by the other members of the Commission or Tribunal as the case may be, provided that where those members are equally divided, or in the case of a proposal to disqualify a sole conciliator or arbitrator, or a majority of the conciliators or arbitrators, the Chairman shall take that decision. If it is decided that the proposal is well-founded the conciliator or arbitrator to whom the decision relates shall be replaced in accordance with the provisions of Section 2 of Chapter III or Section 2 of Chapter IV.

CHAPTER VI
Cost of Proceedings

Article 59

The charges payable by the parties for the use of the facilities of the Centre shall be determined by the Secretary-General in accordance with the regulations adopted by the Administrative Council.

Article 60

(1) Each Commission and each Tribunal shall determine the fees and expenses of its members within limits established from time to time by the Administrative Council and after consultation with the Secretary-General.

(2) Nothing in paragraph (1) of this Article shall preclude the parties from agreeing in advance with the Commission or Tribunal concerned upon the fees and expenses of its members.

Article 61

(1) In the case of conciliation proceedings the fees and expenses of members of the Commission as well as the charges for the use of the facilities of the Centre, shall be borne equally by the parties. Each party shall bear any other expenses it incurs in connection with the proceedings.

(2) In the case of arbitration proceedings the Tribunal shall, except as the parties otherwise agree, assess the expenses incurred by the parties in connection with the proceedings, and shall decide how and by whom those expenses, the fees and expenses of the members of the Tribunal and the charges for the use of the facilities of the Centre shall be paid. Such decision shall form part of the award.

CHAPTER VII
Place of Proceedings

Article 62

Conciliation and arbitration proceedings shall be held at the seat of the Centre except as hereinafter provided.

Article 63

Conciliation and arbitration proceedings may be held, if the parties so agree,

(a) at the seat of the Permanent Court of Arbitration or of any other appropriate institution, whether private or public, with which the Centre may make arrangements for that purpose; or

(b) at any other place approved by the Commission or Tribunal after consultation with the Secretary-General.

CHAPTER VIII
Disputes between Contracting States

Article 64

Any dispute arising between Contracting States concerning the interpretation or application of this Convention which is not settled by negotiation shall be referred to the International Court of Justice by the application of any party to such dispute, unless the States concerned agree to another method of settlement.

CHAPTER IX
Amendment

Article 65

Any Contracting State may propose amendment of this Convention. The text of a proposed amendment shall be communicated to the Secretary-General not less than 90 days prior to the meeting of the Administrative Council at which such amendment is to be considered and shall forthwith be transmitted by him to all the members of the Administrative Council.

Article 66

(1) If the Administrative Council shall so decide by a majority of two-thirds of its members, the proposed amendment shall be circulated to all Contracting States for ratification, acceptance or approval. Each amendment shall enter into force 30 days after dispatch by the

depositary of this Convention of a notification to Contracting States that all Contracting States have ratified, accepted or approved the amendment.

(2) No amendment shall affect the rights and obligations under this Convention of any Contracting State or of any of its constituent subdivisions or agencies, or of any national of such State arising out of consent to the jurisdiction of the Centre given before the date of entry into force of the amendment.

CHAPTER X
Final Provisions

Article 67

This Convention shall be open for signature on behalf of States members of the Bank. It shall also be open for signature on behalf of any other State which is a party to the Statute of the International Court of Justice and which the Administrative Council, by a vote of two-thirds of its members, shall have invited to sign the Convention.

Article 68

(1) This Convention shall be subject to ratification, acceptance or approval by the signatory States in accordance with their respective constitutional procedures.

(2) This Convention shall enter into force 30 days after the date of deposit of the twentieth instrument of ratification, acceptance or approval. It shall enter into force for each State which subsequently deposits its instrument of ratification, acceptance or approval 30 days after the date of such deposit.

Article 69

Each Contracting State shall take such legislative or other measures as may be necessary for making the provisions of this Convention effective in its territories.

Article 70

This Convention shall apply to all territories for whose international relations a Contracting State is responsible, except those which are excluded by such State by written notice to the depositary of this Convention either at the time of ratification, acceptance or approval or subsequently.

Article 71

Any Contracting State may denounce this Convention by written notice to the depositary of this Convention. The denunciation shall take effect six months after receipt of such notice.

Article 72

Notice by a Contracting State pursuant to Articles 70 or 71 shall not affect the rights or obligations under this Convention of that State or of any of its constituent sub-divisions or agencies or of any national of that State arising out of consent to the jurisdiction of the Centre given by one of them before such notice was received by the depositary.

Article 73

Instruments of ratification, acceptance or approval of this Convention and of amendments thereto shall be deposited with the Bank which shall act as the depositary of this Convention. The depositary shall transmit certified copies of this Convention to States members of the Bank and to any other State invited to sign the Convention.

Article 74

The depositary shall register this Convention with the Secretariat of the United Nations in accordance with Article 102 of the Charter of the United Nations and the Regulations thereunder adopted by the General Assembly.

Article 75

The depositary shall notify all signatory States of the following:

(a) signatures in accordance with Article 67;
(b) deposits of instruments of ratification, acceptance and approval in accordance with Article 73;
(c) the date on which this Convention enters into force in accordance with Article 68;
(d) exclusions from territorial application pursuant to Article 70;
(e) the date on which any amendment of this Convention enters into force in accordance with Article 66; and
(f) denunciations in accordance with Article 71.

DONE at Washington, in the English, French and Spanish languages, all three texts being equally authentic, in a single copy which shall remain deposited in the archives of the International Bank for Reconstruction and Development, which has indicated by its signature below its agreement to fulfil the functions with which it is charged under this Convention.

* * *

UNITED NATIONS GENERAL ASSEMBLY RESOLUTION 3201 (S-VI): DECLARATION ON THE ESTABLISHMENT OF A NEW INTERNATIONAL ECONOMIC ORDER AND UNITED NATIONS GENERAL ASSEMBLY RESOLUTION 3202 (S-VI): PROGRAMME OF ACTION ON THE ESTABLISHMENT OF A NEW INTERNATIONAL ECONOMIC ORDER*

[excerpts]

The Declaration on the Establishment of a New International Economic Order (United Nations General Assembly resolution 3201 (S-VI)) and the Programme of Action on the Establishment of a New International Economic Order (United Nations General Assembly resolution 3202 (S-VI)) were adopted by the General Assembly at its sixth special session on 1 May 1974.

UNITED NATIONS GENERAL ASSEMBLY RESOLUTION 3201 (S-VI). DECLARATION ON THE ESTABLISHMENT OF A NEW INTERNATIONAL ECONOMIC ORDER

The General Assembly Adopts the following Declaration:

DECLARATION ON THE ESTABLISHMENT OF A NEW INTERNATIONAL ECONOMIC ORDER

We, the Members of the United Nations,

Having convened a special session of the General Assembly to study for the first time the problems of raw materials and development, devoted to the consideration of the most important economic problems facing the world community,

Bearing in mind the spirit, purposes and principles of the Charter of the United Nations to promote the economic advancement and social progress of all peoples,

* Source: United Nations (1974). "General Assembly Resolution 3201 (S-VI): Declaration on the Establishment of a New International Economic Order", and "General Assembly Resolution 3202 (S-VI): Programme of Action on the Establishment of a New International Economic Order", *Official Records of the General Assembly: Sixth Special Session*, Supplement No. 1 (A/9559) (New York: United Nations), pp. 3-12 [Note added by the editor].

Solemnly proclaim our united determination to work urgently for THE ESTABLISHMENT OF A NEW INTERNATIONAL ECONOMIC ORDER based on equity, sovereign equality, interdependence, common interest and cooperation among all States, irrespective of their economic and social systems which shall correct inequalities and redress existing injustices, make it possible to eliminate the widening gap between the developed and the developing countries and ensure steadily accelerating economic and social development and peace and justice for present and future generations, and, to that end, declare:

1. The greatest and most significant achievement during the last decades has been the independence from colonial and alien domination of a large number of peoples and nations which has enabled them to become members of the community of free peoples. Technological progress has also been made in all spheres of economic activities in the last three decades, thus providing a solid potential for improving the well-being of all peoples. However, the remaining vestiges of alien and colonial domination, foreign occupation, racial discrimination, *apartheid* and neo-colonialism in all its forms continue to be among the greatest obstacles to the full emancipation and progress of the developing countries and all the peoples involved. The benefits of technological progress are not shared equitably by all members of the international community. The developing countries, which constitute 70 per cent of the world's population, account for only 30 per cent of the world's income. It has proved impossible to achieve an even and balanced development of the international community under the existing international economic order. The gap between the developed and the developing countries continues to widen in a system which was established at a time when most of the developing countries did not even exist as independent States and which perpetuates inequality.

2. The present international economic order is in direct conflict with current developments in international political and economic relations. Since 1970, the world economy has experienced a series of grave crises which have had severe repercussions, especially on the developing countries because of their generally greater vulnerability to external economic impulses. The developing world has become a powerful factor that makes its influence felt in all fields of international activity. These irreversible changes in the relationship of forces in the world necessitate the active, full and equal participation of the developing countries in the formulation and application of all decisions that concern the international community.

3. All these changes have thrust into prominence the reality of interdependence of all the members of the world community. Current events have brought into sharp focus the realization that the interests of the developed countries and those of the developing countries can no longer be isolated from each other, that there is a close interrelationship between the prosperity of the developed countries and the growth and development of the developing countries, and that the prosperity of the international community as a whole depends upon the prosperity of its constituent parts. International co-operation for development is the shared goal and common duty of all countries. Thus the political, economic and social well-being of present and future generations depends more than ever on co-operation between all the members of the international community on the basis of sovereign equality and the removal of the disequilibrium that exists between them.

4. The new international economic order should be founded on full respect for the following principles:

(a) Sovereign equality of States, self-determination of all peoples, inadmissibility of the acquisition of territories by force, territorial integrity and noninterference in the internal affairs of other States;

(b) The broadest co-operation of all the States members of the international community, based on equity, whereby the prevailing disparities in the world may be banished and prosperity secured for all;

(c) Full and effective participation on the basis of equality of all countries in the solving of world economic problems in the common interest of all countries, bearing in mind the necessity to ensure the accelerated development of all the developing countries, while devoting particular attention to the adoption of special measures in favour of the least developed, land-locked and island developing countries as well as those developing countries most seriously affected by economic crises and natural calamities, without losing sight of the interests of other developing countries;

(d) The right of every country to adopt the economic and social system that it deems the most appropriate for its own development and not to be subjected to discrimination of any kind as a result;

(e) Full permanent sovereignty of every State over its natural resources and all economic activities. In order to safeguard these resources, each State is entitled to exercise effective control over them and their exploitation with means suitable to its own situation, including the right to nationalization or transfer of ownership to its nationals, this right being an expression of the full permanent sovereignty of the State. No State may be subjected to economic, political or any other type of coercion to prevent the free and full exercise of this inalienable right;

(f) The right of all States, territories and peoples under foreign occupation, alien and colonial domination or *apartheid* to restitution and full compensation for the exploitation and depletion of, and damages to, the natural resources and all other resources of those States, territories and peoples;

(g) Regulation and supervision of the activities of transnational corporations by taking measures in the interest of the national economies of the countries where such transnational corporations operate on the basis of the full sovereignty of those countries;

(h) The right of the developing countries and the peoples of territories under colonial and racial domination and foreign occupation to achieve their liberation and to regain effective control over their natural resources and economic activities;

(i) The extending of assistance to developing countries, peoples and territories which are under colonial and alien domination, foreign occupation, racial discrimination or *apartheid*

or are subjected to economic, political or any other type of coercive measures to obtain from them the subordination of the exercise of their sovereign rights and to secure from them advantages of any kind, and to neo-colonialism in all its forms, and which have established or are endeavouring to establish effective control over their natural resources and economic activities that have been or are still under foreign control;

(j) Just and equitable relationship between the prices of raw materials, primary commodities, manufactured and semi-manufactured goods exported by developing countries and the prices of raw materials, primary commodities, manufactures, capital goods and equipment imported by them with the aim of bringing about sustained improvement in their unsatisfactory terms of trade and the expansion of the world economy;

(k) Extension of active assistance to developing countries by the whole international community, free of any political or military conditions;

(l) Ensuring that one of the main aims of the reformed international monetary system shall be the promotion of the development of the developing countries and the adequate flow of real resources to them;

(m) Improving the competitiveness of natural materials facing competition from synthetic substitutes;

(n) Preferential and non-reciprocal treatment for developing countries, wherever feasible, in all fields of international economic co-operation whenever possible;

(o) Securing favourable conditions for the transfer of financial resources to developing countries;

(p) Giving to the developing countries access to the achievements of modern science and technology, and promoting the transfer of technology and the creation of indigenous technology for the benefit of the developing countries in forms and in accordance with procedures which are suited to their economies;

(q) The need for all States to put an end to the waste of natural resources, including food products;

(r) The need for developing countries to concentrate all their resources for the cause of development;

(s) The strengthening, through individual and collective actions, of mutual economic, trade, financial and technical co-operation among the developing countries, mainly on a preferential basis;

(t) Facilitating the role which producers' associations may play within the framework of international co-operation and, in pursuance of their aims, *inter alia* assisting in the promotion

of sustained growth of the world economy and accelerating the development of developing countries.

5. The unanimous adoption of the International Development Strategy for the Second United Nations Development Decade[1] was an important step in the promotion of international economic co-operation on a just and equitable basis. The accelerated implementation of obligations and commitments assumed by the international community within the framework of the Strategy, particularly those concerning imperative development needs of developing countries, would contribute significantly to the fulfilment of the aims and objectives of the present Declaration.

6. The United Nations as a universal organization should be capable of dealing with problems of international economic co-operation in a comprehensive manner and ensuring equally the interests of all countries. It must have an even greater role in the establishment of a new international economic order. The Charter of Economic Rights and Duties of States, for the preparation of which the present Declaration will provide an additional source of inspiration, will constitute a significant contribution in this respect. All the States Members of the United Nations are therefore called upon to exert maximum efforts with a view to securing the implementation of the present Declaration, which is one of the principal guarantees for the creation of better conditions for all peoples to reach a life worthy of human dignity.

7. The present Declaration on the Establishment of a New International Economic Order shall be one of the most important bases of economic relations between all peoples and all nations.

2229th plenary meeting
1 May 1974

* * *

[1]Resolution 2626 (XXV).

UNITED NATIONS GENERAL ASSEMBLY RESOLUTION 3202 (S-VI). PROGRAMME OF ACTION ON THE ESTABLISHMENT OF A NEW INTERNATIONAL ECONOMIC ORDER [excerpts]

The General Assembly Adopts the following Programme of Action:

PROGRAMME OF ACTION ON THE ESTABLISHMENT OF A NEW INTERNATIONAL ECONOMIC ORDER

CONTENTS

Section

Introduction

I. Fundamental problems of raw materials and primary commodities as related to trade and development

II. International monetary system and financing of the development of developing countries

III. Industrialization

IV. Transfer of technology

V. Regulation and control over the activities of transnational corporations

VI. Charter of Economic Rights and Duties of States

VII. Promotion of co-operation among developing countries

VIII. Assistance in the exercise of permanent sovereignty of States over natural resources

IX. Strengthening the role of the United Nations system in the field of international economic cooperation

X. Special Programme

INTRODUCTION

1. In view of the continuing severe economic imbalance in the relations between developed and developing countries, and in the context of the constant and continuing aggravation of the imbalance of the economies of the developing countries and the consequent need for the mitigation of their current economic difficulties, urgent and effective measures need

to be taken by the international community to assist the developing countries, while devoting particular attention to the least developed, land-locked and island developing countries and those developing countries most seriously affected by economic crises and natural calamities leading to serious retardation of development processes.

2. With a view to ensuring the application of the Declaration on the Establishment of a New International Economic Order,[2] it will be necessary to adopt and implement within a specified period a programme of action of unprecedented scope and to bring about maximum economic co-operation and understanding among all States, particularly between developed and developing countries, based on the principles of dignity and sovereign equality.

III. INDUSTRIALIZATION

All efforts should be made by the international community to take measures to encourage the industrialization of the developing countries, and to this end:

(a) The developed countries should respond favourably, within the framework of their official aid as well as international financial institutions, to the requests of developing countries for the financing of industrial projects;

(b) The developed countries should encourage investors to finance industrial production projects, particularly export-oriented production, in developing countries, in agreement with the latter and within the context of their laws and regulations;

(c) With a view to bringing about a new international economic structure which should increase the share of the developing countries in world industrial production, the developed countries and the agencies of the United Nations system, in co-operation with the developing countries, should contribute to setting up new industrial capacities including raw materials and commodity-transforming facilities as a matter of priority in the developing countries that produce those raw materials and commodities;

(d) The international community should continue and expand, with the aid of the developed countries and the international institutions, the operational and instruction-oriented technical assistance programmes, including vocational training and management development of national personnel of the developing countries, in the light of their special development requirements.

IV. TRANSFER OF TECHNOLOGY

All efforts should be made:

[2]Resolution 3201 (S-VI).

(a) To formulate an international code of conduct for the transfer of technology corresponding to needs and conditions prevalent in developing countries;

(b) To give access on improved terms to modern technology and to adapt that technology, as appropriate, to specific economic, social and ecological conditions and varying stages of development in developing countries;

(c) To expand significantly the assistance from developed to developing countries in research and development programmes and in the creation of suitable indigenous technology;

(d) To adapt commercial practices governing transfer of technology to the requirements of the developing countries and to prevent abuse of the rights of sellers;

(e) To promote international co-operation in research and development in exploration and exploitation, conservation and the legitimate utilization of natural resources and all sources of energy.

In taking the above measures, the special needs of the least developed and land-locked countries should be borne in mind.

V. REGULATION AND CONTROL OVER THE ACTIVITIES OF TRANSNATIONAL CORPORATIONS

All efforts should be made to formulate, adopt and implement an international code of conduct for transnational corporations:

(a) To prevent interference in the internal affairs of the countries where they operate and their collaboration with racist regimes and colonial administrations;

(b) To regulate their activities in host countries, to eliminate restrictive business practices and to conform to the national development plans and objectives of developing countries, and in this context facilitate, as necessary, the review and revision of previously concluded arrangements;

(c) To bring about assistance, transfer of technology and management skills to developing countries on equitable and favourable terms;

(d) To regulate the repatriation of the profits accruing from their operations, taking into account the legitimate interests of all parties concerned;

(e) To promote reinvestment of their profits in developing countries.

VI. CHARTER OF ECONOMIC RIGHTS AND DUTIES OF STATES

The Charter of Economic Rights and Duties of States, the draft of which is being prepared by a working group of the United Nations and which the General Assembly has already expressed the intention of adopting at its twenty-ninth regular session, shall constitute an effective instrument towards the establishment of a new system of international economic relations based on equity, sovereign equality, and interdependence of the interests of developed and developing countries. It is therefore of vital importance that the aforementioned Charter be adopted by the General Assembly at its twenty-ninth session.

VIII. ASSISTANCE IN THE EXERCISE OF PERMANENT SOVEREIGNTY OF STATES OVER NATURAL RESOURCES

All efforts should be made:

(a) To defeat attempts to prevent the free and effective exercise of the rights of every State to full and permanent sovereignty over its natural resources;

(b) To ensure that competent agencies of the United Nations system meet requests for assistance from developing countries in connexion with the operation of nationalized means of production.

2229th plenary meeting
May 1974

* * *

UNITED NATIONS GENERAL ASSEMBLY RESOLUTION 3281 (XXIX): CHARTER OF ECONOMIC RIGHTS AND DUTIES OF STATES*

The Charter of Economic Rights and Duties of States (United Nations General Assembly resolution 3281(XXIX)) was adopted by the General Assembly at its twenty-ninth session on 12 December 1974.

The General Assembly,

Recalling that the United Nations Conference on Trade and Development, in its resolution 45 (III) of 18 May 1972,[1] stressed the urgency to establish generally accepted norms to govern international economic relations systematically and recognized that it is not feasible to establish a just order and a stable world as long as a charter to protect the rights of all countries, and in particular the developing States, is not formulated,

Recalling further that in the same resolution it was decided to establish a Working Group of governmental representatives to draw up a draft Charter of Economic Rights and Duties of States, which the General Assembly, in its resolution 3037 (XXVII) of 19 December 1972, decided should be composed of forty Member States,

Noting that, in its resolution 3082 (XXVIII) of 6 December 1973, it reaffirmed its conviction of the urgent need to establish or improve norms of universal application for the development of international economic relations on a just and equitable basis and urged the Working Group on the Charter of Economic Rights and Duties of States to complete, as the first step in the codification and development of the matter, the elaboration of a final draft Charter of Economic Rights and Duties of States, to be considered and approved by the General Assembly at its twenty-ninth session,

Bearing in mind the spirit and terms of its resolutions 3201 (S-VI) and 3202 (S-VI) of 1 May 1974, containing, respectively, the Declaration and the Programme of Action on the Establishment of a New International Economic Order, which underlined the vital importance of the Charter to be adopted by the General Assembly at its twenty-ninth session and stressed the fact that the Charter shall constitute an effective instrument towards the establishment of a new

*Source: United Nations (1975). "General Assembly Resolution 3281 (XXIX): Charter of Economic Rights and Duties of States", *Official Records of the General Assembly: Twenty-Ninth Session*, Supplement No. 31 (A/9631) (New York: United Nations), pp.50-55 [Note added by the editor].

[1]See Proceedings of the United Nations Conference on Trade and Development, Third Session, vol. I, Report and Annexes (United Nations publication, Sales No.:E.73.II.D.4), annex I.A.

system of international economic relations based on equity, sovereign equality and interdependence of the interests of developed and developing countries,

Having examined the report of the Working Group on the Charter of Economic Rights and Duties of States on its fourth session,[2] transmitted to the General Assembly by the Trade and Development Board at its fourteenth session,

Expressing its appreciation to the Working Group on the Charter of Economic Rights and Duties of States which, as a result of the task performed in its four sessions held between February 1973 and June 1974, assembled the elements required for the completion and adoption of the Charter of Economic Rights and Duties of States at the twenty-ninth session of the General Assembly, as previously recommended,

Adopts and solemnly proclaims the following Charter:

CHARTER OF ECONOMIC RIGHTS AND DUTIES OF STATES

PREAMBLE

The General Assembly,

Reaffirming the fundamental purposes of the United Nations, in particular the maintenance of international peace and security, the development of friendly relations among nations and the achievement of international co-operation in solving international problems in the economic and social fields,

Affirming the need for strengthening international co-operation in these fields,

Reaffirming further the need for strengthening international co-operation for development,

Declaring that it is a fundamental purpose of the present Charter to promote the establishment of the new international economic order, based on equity, sovereign equality, interdependence, common interest and co-operation among all States, irrespective of their economic and social systems,

Desirous of contributing to the creation of conditions for:

(a) The attainment of wider prosperity among all countries and of higher standards of living for all peoples,

[2] *TD/B/AC.12/4 and Corr.1.*

(b) The promotion by the entire international community of the economic and social progress of all countries, especially developing countries,

(c) The encouragement of co-operation, on the basis of mutual advantage and equitable benefits for all peace-loving States which are willing to carry out the provisions of the present Charter, in the economic, trade, scientific and technical fields, regardless of political, economic or social systems,

(d) The overcoming of main obstacles in the way of the economic development of the developing countries,

(e) The acceleration of the economic growth of developing countries with a view to bridging the economic gap between developing and developed countries,

(f) The protection, preservation and enhancement of the environment,

Mindful of the need to establish and maintain a just and equitable economic and social order through:

(a) The achievement of more rational and equitable international economic relations and the encouragement of structural changes in the world economy,

(b) The creation of conditions which permit the further expansion of trade and intensification of economic co-operation among all nations,

(c) The strengthening of the economic independence of developing countries,

(d) The establishment and promotion of international economic relations, taking into account the agreed differences in development of the developing countries and their specific needs,

Determined to promote collective economic security for development, in particular of the developing countries, with strict respect for the sovereign equality of each State and through the co-operation of the entire international community,

Considering that genuine co-operation among States, based on joint consideration of and concerted action regarding international economic problems, is essential for fulfilling the international community's common desire to achieve a just and rational development of all parts of the world,

Stressing the importance of ensuring appropriate conditions for the conduct of normal economic relations among all States, irrespective of differences in social and economic systems, and for the full respect of the rights of all peoples, as well as strengthening instruments of international economic co-operation as a means for the consolidation of peace for the benefit of all,

Convinced of the need to develop a system of international economic relations on the basis of sovereign equality, mutual and equitable benefit and the close interrelationship of the interests of all States,

Reiterating that the responsibility for the development of every country rests primarily upon itself but that concomitant and effective international cooperation is an essential factor for the full achievement of its own development goals,

Firmly convinced of the urgent need to evolve a substantially improved system of international economic relations,

Solemnly adopts the present Charter of Economic Rights and Duties of States.

CHAPTER I
FUNDAMENTALS OF INTERNATIONAL ECONOMIC RELATIONS

Economic as well as political and other relations among States shall be governed, *inter alia,* by the following principles:

(a) Sovereignty, territorial integrity and political independence of States;

(b) Sovereign equality of all States;

(c) Non-aggression;

(d) Non-intervention;

(e) Mutual and equitable benefit;

(f) Peaceful coexistence;

(g) Equal rights and self-determination of peoples;

(h) Peaceful settlement of disputes;

(i) Remedying of injustices which have been brought about by force and which deprive a nation of the natural means necessary for its normal development;

(j) Fulfilment in good faith of international obligations;

(k) Respect for human rights and fundamental freedoms;

(l) No attempt to seek hegemony and spheres of influence;

(m) Promotion of international social justice;

(n) International co-operation for development;

(o) Free access to and from the sea by landlocked countries within the framework of the above principles.

CHAPTER II
ECONOMIC RIGHTS AND DUTIES OF STATES

Article 1

Every State has the sovereign and inalienable right to choose its economic system as well as its political, social and cultural systems in accordance with the will of its people, without outside interference, coercion or threat in any form whatsoever.

Article 2

1. Every State has and shall freely exercise full permanent sovereignty, including possession, use and disposal, over all its wealth, natural resources and economic activities.

2. Each State has the right:

(a) To regulate and exercise authority over foreign investment within its national jurisdiction in accordance with its laws and regulations and in conformity with its national objectives and priorities. No State shall be compelled to grant preferential treatment to foreign investment;

(b) To regulate and supervise the activities of transnational corporations within its national jurisdiction and take measures to ensure that such activities comply with its laws, rules and regulations and conform with its economic and social policies. Transnational corporations shall not intervene in the internal affairs of a host State. Every State should, with full regard for its sovereign rights, co-operate with other States in the exercise of the right set forth in this subparagraph;

(c) To nationalize, expropriate or transfer ownership of foreign property, in which case appropriate compensation should be paid by the State adopting such measures, taking into account its relevant laws and regulations and all circumstances that the State considers pertinent. In any case where the question of compensation gives rise to a controversy, it shall be settled under the domestic law of the nationalizing State and by its tribunals, unless it is freely and mutually agreed by all States concerned that other peaceful means be sought on the basis of the sovereign equality of States and in accordance with the principle of free choice of means.

Article 3

In the exploitation of natural resources shared by two or more countries, each State must co-operate on the basis of a system of information and prior consultations in order to achieve optimum use of such resources without causing damage to the legitimate interest of others.

Article 4

Every State has the right to engage in international trade and other forms of economic co-operation irrespective of any differences in political, economic and social systems. No State shall be subjected to discrimination of any kind based solely on such differences. In the pursuit of international trade and other forms of economic co-operation, every State is free to choose the forms of organization of its foreign economic relations and to enter into bilateral and multilateral arrangements consistent with its international obligations and with the needs of international economic co-operation.

Article 5

All States have the right to associate in organizations of primary commodity producers in order to develop their national economies, to achieve stable financing for their development and, in pursuance of their aims, to assist in the promotion of sustained growth of the world economy, in particular accelerating the development of developing countries. Correspondingly, all States have the duty to respect that right by refraining from applying economic and political measures that would limit it.

Article 6

It is the duty of States to contribute to the development of international trade of goods, particularly by means of arrangements and by the conclusion of long-term multilateral commodity agreements, where appropriate, and taking into account the interests of producers and consumers. All States share the responsibility to promote the regular flow and access of all commercial goods traded at stable, remunerative and equitable prices, thus contributing to the equitable development of the world economy, taking into account, in particular, the interests of developing countries.

Article 7

Every State has the primary responsibility to promote the economic, social and cultural development of its people. To this end, each State has the right and the responsibility to choose its means and goals of development, fully to mobilize and use its resources, to implement progressive economic and social reforms and to ensure the full participation of its people in the process and benefits of development. All States have the duty, individually and collectively, to co-operate in eliminating obstacles that hinder such mobilization and use.

Article 8

States should co-operate in facilitating more rational and equitable international economic relations and in encouraging structural changes in the context of a balanced world economy in harmony with the needs and interests of all countries, especially developing countries, and should take appropriate measures to this end.

Article 9

All States have the responsibility to co-operate in the economic, social, cultural, scientific and technological fields for the promotion of economic and social progress throughout the world, especially that of the developing countries.

Article 10

All States are juridically equal and, as equal members of the international community, have the right to participate fully and effectively in the international decision-making process in the solution of world economic, financial and monetary problems, *inter alia,* through the appropriate international organizations in accordance with their existing and evolving rules, and to share equitably in the benefits resulting therefrom.

Article 11

All States should co-operate to strengthen and continuously improve the efficiency of international organizations in implementing measures to stimulate the general economic progress of all countries, particularly of developing countries, and therefore should co-operate to adapt them, when appropriate, to the changing needs of international economic cooperation.

Article 12

1. States have the right, in agreement with the parties concerned, to participate in subregional, regional and interregional co-operation in the pursuit of their economic and social development. All States engaged in such co-operation have the duty to ensure that the policies of those groupings to which they belong correspond to the provisions of the present Charter and are outward-looking, consistent with their international obligations and with the needs of international economic co-operation, and have full regard for the legitimate interests of third countries, especially developing countries.

2. In the case of groupings to which the States concerned have transferred or may transfer certain competences as regards matters that come within the scope of the present Charter, its provisions shall also apply to those groupings in regard to such matters, consistent with the responsibilities of such States as members of such groupings. Those States shall co-operate in the observance by the groupings of the provisions of this Charter.

Article 13

1. Every State has the right to benefit from the advances and developments in science and technology for the acceleration of its economic and social development.

2. All States should promote international scientific and technological co-operation and the transfer of technology, with proper regard for all legitimate interests including, *inter alia,* the rights and duties of holders, suppliers and recipients of technology. In particular, all States should facilitate the access of developing countries to the achievements of modern science and technology, the transfer of technology and the creation of indigenous technology for the benefit of the developing countries in forms and in accordance with procedures which are suited to their economies and their needs.

3. Accordingly, developed countries should cooperate with the developing countries in the establishment, strengthening and development of their scientific and technological infrastructures and their scientific research and technological activities so as to help to expand and transform the economies of developing countries.

4. All States should co-operate in research with a view to evolving further internationally accepted guidelines or regulations for the transfer of technology, taking fully into account the interests of developing countries.

Article 14

Every State has the duty to co-operate in promoting a steady and increasing expansion and liberalization of world trade and an improvement in the welfare and living standards of all peoples, in particular those of developing countries. Accordingly, all States should co-operate, *inter alia,* towards the progressive dismantling of obstacles to trade and the improvement of the international framework for the conduct of world trade and, to these ends, co-ordinated efforts shall be made to solve in an equitable way the trade problems of all countries, taking into account the specific trade problems of the developing countries. In this connexion, States shall take measures aimed at securing additional benefits for the international trade of developing countries so as to achieve a substantial increase in their foreign exchange earnings, the diversification of their exports, the acceleration of the rate of growth of their trade, taking into account their development needs, an improvement in the possibilities for these countries to participate in the expansion of world trade and a balance more favourable to developing countries in the sharing of the advantages resulting from this expansion, through, in the largest possible measure, a substantial improvement in the conditions of access for the products of interest to the developing countries and, wherever appropriate, measures designed to attain stable, equitable and remunerative prices for primary products.

Article 15

All States have the duty to promote the achievement of general and complete disarmament under effective international control and to utilize the resources released by effective disarmament measures for the economic and social development of countries, allocating a substantial portion of such resources as additional means for the development needs of developing countries.

Article 16

1. It is the right and duty of all States, individually and collectively, to eliminate colonialism, *apartheid*, racial discrimination, neo-colonialism and all forms of foreign aggression, occupation and domination, and the economic and social consequences thereof, as a prerequisite for development. States which practise such coercive policies are economically responsible to the countries, territories and peoples affected for the restitution and full compensation for the exploitation and depletion of, and damages to, the natural and all other resources of those countries, territories and peoples. It is the duty of all States to extend assistance to them.

2. No State has the right to promote or encourage investments that may constitute an obstacle to the liberation of a territory occupied by force.

Article 17

International co-operation for development is the shared goal and common duty of all States. Every State should co-operate with the efforts of developing countries to accelerate their economic and social development by providing favourable external conditions and by extending active assistance to them, consistent with their development needs and objectives, with strict respect for the sovereign equality of States and free of any conditions derogating from their sovereignty.

Article 18

Developed countries should extend, improve and enlarge the system of generalized non-reciprocal and non-discriminatory tariff preferences to the developing countries consistent with the relevant agreed conclusions and relevant decisions as adopted on this subject, in the framework of the competent international organizations. Developed countries should also give serious consideration to the adoption of other differential measures, in areas where this is feasible and appropriate and in ways which will provide special and more favourable treatment, in order to meet the trade and development needs of the developing countries. In the conduct of international economic relations the developed countries should endeavour to avoid measures having a negative effect on the development of the national economies of the developing countries, as promoted by generalized tariff preferences and other generally agreed differential measures in their favour.

Article 19

With a view to accelerating the economic growth of developing countries and bridging the economic gap between developed and developing countries, developed countries should grant generalized preferential, non-reciprocal and non-discriminatory treatment to developing countries in those fields of international economic co-operation where it may be feasible.

Article 20

Developing countries should, in their efforts to increase their over-all trade, give due attention to the possibility of expanding their trade with socialist countries, by granting to these countries conditions for trade not inferior to those granted normally to the developed market economy countries.

Article 21

Developing countries should endeavour to promote the expansion of their mutual trade and to this end may, in accordance with the existing and evolving provisions and procedures of international agreements where applicable, grant trade preferences to other developing countries without being obliged to extend such preferences to developed countries, provided these arrangements do not constitute an impediment to general trade liberalization and expansion.

Article 22

1. All States should respond to the generally recognized or mutually agreed development needs and objectives of developing countries by promoting increased net flows of real resources to the developing countries from all sources, taking into account any obligations and commitments undertaken by the States concerned, in order to reinforce the efforts of developing countries to accelerate their economic and social development.

2. In this context, consistent with the aims and objectives mentioned above and taking into account any obligations and commitments undertaken in this regard, it should be their endeavour to increase the net amount of financial flows from official sources to developing countries and to improve the terms and conditions thereof.

3. The flow of development assistance resources should include economic and technical assistance.

Article 23

To enhance the effective mobilization of their own resources, the developing countries should strengthen their economic co-operation and expand their mutual trade so as to accelerate their economic and social development. All countries, especially developed countries, individually as well as through the competent international organizations of which they are members, should provide appropriate and effective support and co-operation.

Article 24

All States have the duty to conduct their mutual economic relations in a manner which takes into account the interests of other countries. In particular, all States should avoid prejudicing the interests of developing countries.

Article 25

In furtherance of world economic development, the international community, especially its developed members, shall pay special attention to the particular needs and problems of the least developed among the developing countries, of land-locked developing countries and also island developing countries, with a view to helping them to overcome their particular difficulties and thus contribute to their economic and social development.

Article 26

All States have the duty to coexist in tolerance and live together in peace, irrespective of differences in political, economic, social and cultural systems, and to facilitate trade between States having different economic and social systems. International trade should be conducted without prejudice to generalized non-discriminatory and non-reciprocal preferences in favour of developing countries, on the basis of mutual advantage, equitable benefits and the exchange of most-favoured-nation treatment.

Article 27

1. Every State has the right to enjoy fully the benefits of world invisible trade and to engage in the expansion of such trade.

2. World invisible trade, based on efficiency and mutual and equitable benefit, furthering the expansion of the world economy, is the common goal of all States. The role of developing countries in world invisible trade should be enhanced and strengthened consistent with the above objectives, particular attention being paid to the special needs of developing countries.

3. All States should co-operate with developing countries in their endeavours to increase their capacity to earn foreign exchange from invisible transactions, in accordance with the potential and needs of each developing country and consistent with the objectives mentioned above.

Article 28

All States have the duty to co-operate in achieving adjustments in the prices of exports of developing countries in relation to prices of their imports so as to promote just and equitable terms of trade for them, in a manner which is remunerative for producers and equitable for producers and consumers.

CHAPTER III
COMMON RESPONSIBILITIES TOWARDS THE INTERNATIONAL COMMUNITY

Article 29

The sea-bed and ocean floor and the subsoil thereof, beyond the limits of national jurisdiction, as well as the resources of the area, are the common heritage of mankind. On the basis of the principles adopted by the General Assembly in resolution 2749 (XXV) of 17 December 1970, all States shall ensure that the exploration of the area and exploitation of its resources are carried out exclusively for peaceful purposes and that the benefits derived therefrom are shared equitably by all States, taking into account the particular interests and needs of developing countries; an international regime applying to the area and its resources and including appropriate international machinery to give effect to its provisions shall be established by an international treaty of a universal character, generally agreed upon.

Article 30

The protection, preservation and enhancement of the environment for the present and future generations is the responsibility of all States. All States shall endeavour to establish their own environmental and developmental policies in conformity with such responsibility. The environmental policies of all States should enhance and not adversely affect the present and future development potential of developing countries. All States have the responsibility to ensure that activities within their jurisdiction or control do not cause damage to the environment of other States or of areas beyond the limits of national jurisdiction. All States should co-operate in evolving international norms and regulations in the field of the environment.

CHAPTER IV
FINAL PROVISIONS

Article 31

All States have the duty to contribute to the balanced expansion of the world economy, taking duly into account the close interrelationship between the well-being of the developed countries and the growth and development of the developing countries, and the fact that the prosperity of the international community as a whole depends upon the prosperity of its constituent parts.

Article 32

No State may use or encourage the use of economic, political or any other type of measures to coerce another State in order to obtain from it the subordination of the exercise of its sovereign rights.

Article 33

1. Nothing in the present Charter shall be construed as impairing or derogating from the provisions of the Charter of the United Nations or actions taken in pursuance thereof.

2. In their interpretation and application, the provisions of the present Charter are interrelated and each provision should be construed in the context of the other provisions.

Article 34

An item on the Charter of Economic Rights and Duties of States shall be included in the agenda of the General Assembly at its thirtieth session, and thereafter on the agenda of every fifth session. In this way a systematic and comprehensive consideration of the implementation of the Charter, covering both progress achieved and any improvements and additions which might become necessary, would be carried out and appropriate measures recommended. Such consideration should take into account the evolution of all the economic, social, legal and other factors related to the principles upon which the present Charter is based and on its purpose.

2315th plenary meeting
12 December 1974

* * *

ARBITRATION RULES OF THE UNITED NATIONS COMMISSION ON INTERNATIONAL TRADE LAW*

The Arbitration Rules of the United Nations Commission on International Trade Law (UNCITRAL Arbitration Rules) were adopted by the United Nations Commission on International Trade Law in 1976. In the same year, the United Nations General Assembly, by its resolution 31/98, recommended the use of the Rules in the settlement of international commercial disputes.

Section I. Introductory rules

SCOPE OF APPLICATION

Article 1

1. Where the parties to a contract have agreed in writing[1] that disputes in relation to that contract shall be referred to arbitration under the UNCITRAL Arbitration Rules, then such disputes shall be settled in accordance with these Rules subject to such modification as the parties may agree in writing.

2. These Rules shall govern the arbitration except that where any of these Rules is in conflict with a provision of the law applicable to the arbitration from which the parties cannot derogate, that provision shall prevail.

---

* Source: United Nations (1977). *UNCITRAL Arbitration Rules*, United Nations publication, Sales No. E.77.V.6 [Note added by the editor].

[1] MODEL ARBITRATION CLAUSE

Any dispute, controversy or claim arising out of or relating to this contract, or the breach, termination or invalidity thereof, shall be settled by arbitration in accordance with the UNCITRAL Arbitration Rules as at present in force.

Note - Parties may wish to consider adding

(a) The appointing authority shall be ... (name of institution or person)
(b) The number of arbitrators shall be ... (one or three)
(c) The place of arbitration shall be ... (town or country)
(d) The language(s) to be used in the arbitral proceedings shall be...

NOTICE, CALCULATION OF PERIODS OF TIME

Article 2

1. For the purposes of these Rules, any notice, including a notification, communication or proposal, is deemed to have been received if it is physically delivered to the addressee or if it is delivered at his habitual residence, place of business or mailing address, or, if none of these can be found after making reasonable inquiry, then at the addressees last-known residence or place of business. Notice shall be deemed to have been received on the day it is so delivered.

2. For the purposes of calculating a period of time under these Rules, such period shall begin to run on the day following the day when a notice, notification, communication or proposal is received. If the last day of such period is an official holiday or a non-business day at the residence or place of business of the addressee, the period is extended until the first business day which follows. Official holidays or non-business days occurring during the running of the period of time are included in calculating the period.

NOTICE OF ARBITRATION

Article 3

1. The party initiating recourse to arbitration (hereinafter called the "claimant") shall give to the other party (hereinafter called the "respondent") a notice of arbitration.

2. Arbitral proceedings shall be deemed to commence on the date on which the notice of arbitration is received by the respondent.

3. The notice of arbitration shall include the following:

(a) A demand that the dispute be referred to arbitration;
(b) The names and addresses of the parties;
(c) A reference to the arbitration clause or the separate arbitration agreement that is invoked;
(d) A reference to the contract out of or in relation to which the dispute arises;
(e) The general nature of the claim and an indication of the amount involved, if any;
(f) The relief or remedy sought;
(g) A proposal as to the number of arbitrators (i.e., one or three), if the parties have not previously agreed thereon.

4. The notice of arbitration may also include:

(a) The proposals for the appointments of a sole arbitrator and an appointing authority referred to in article 6, paragraph 1;
(b) The notification of the appointment of an arbitrator referred to in article 7;

(c) The statement of claim referred to in article l9.

REPRESENTATION AND ASSISTANCE

Article 4

The parties may be represented or assisted by persons of their choice. The names and addresses of such persons must be communicated in writing to the other party; such communication must specify whether the appointment is being made for purposes of representation or assistance.

Section II. Composition of the arbitral tribunal

NUMBER OF ARBITRATORS

Article 5

If the parties have not previously on the number of arbitrators (i.e. one or three), and if within fifteen days after the receipt by the respondent of the notice of arbitration the parties have not agreed that there shall be only one arbitrator, three arbitrators shall be appointed.

APPOINTMENT OF ARBITRATORS (ARTICLES 6 TO 8)

Article 6

l. If a sole arbitrator is to be appointed, either party may propose to the other:

(a) The names of one or more persons, one of whom would serve as the sole arbitrator; and

(b) If no appointing authority has been agreed upon by the parties, the name or names of one or more institutions or persons, one of whom would serve as appointing authority.

2. If within thirty days after receipt by a party of a proposal made in accordance with paragraph l the parties have not reached agreement on the choice of a sole arbitrator, the sole arbitrator shall be appointed by the appointing authority agreed upon by the parties. If no appointing authority has been agreed upon by the parties, or if the appointing authority agreed upon refused to act or fails to appoint the arbitrator within sixty days of the receipt of a party's request therefor, either party may request the Secretary-General of the Permanent Court of Arbitration at The Hague to designate an appointing authority.

3. The appointing authority shall, at the request of one of the parties, appoint the sole arbitrator as promptly as possible. In making the appointment the appointing authority shall use the following list-procedure, unless both parties agree that the list-procedure should not be used

or unless the appointing authority determines in its discretion that the use of the list-procedure is not appropriate for the case:

(a) At the request of one of the parties the appointing authority shall communicate to both parties an identical list containing at least three names;

(b) Within fifteen days after the receipt of this list, each party may return the list to the appointing authority after having deleted the name or names to which he objects and numbered the remaining names on the list in the order of his preference;

(c) After the expiration of the above period of time the appointing authority shall appoint the sole arbitrator from among the names approved on the lists returned to it and in accordance with the order of preference indicated by the parties;

(d) If for any reason the appointment cannot be made according to this procedure, the appointing authority may exercise its discretion in appointing the sole arbitrator.

4. In making the appointment, the appointing authority shall have regard to such considerations as are likely to secure the appointment of an independent and impartial arbitrator and shall take into account as well the advisability of appointing an arbitrator of a nationality other than the nationalities of the parties.

Article 7

1. If three arbitrators are to be appointed, each party shall appoint one arbitrator. The two arbitrators thus appointed shall choose the third arbitrator who will act as the presiding arbitrator of the tribunal.

2. If within thirty days after receipt of a party's notification of the appointment of an arbitrator the other party has not notified the first party of the arbitrator he has appointed:

(a) The first party may request the appointing authority previously designated by the parties to appoint the second arbitrator; or

(b) If no such authority has been previously designated by the parties, or if the appointing authority previously designated refuses to act or fails to appoint the arbitrator within thirty days after receipt of a party's request therefor, the first party may request the Secretary-General of the Permanent Court of Arbitration at The Hague to designate the appointing authority. The first party may then request the appointing authority so designated to appoint the second arbitrator. In either case, the appointing authority may exercise its discretion in appointing the arbitrator.

3. If within thirty days after the appointment of the second arbitrator the two arbitrators have not agreed on the choice of the presiding arbitrator, the presiding arbitrator shall be appointed

by an appointing authority in the same way as a sole arbitrator would be appointed under article 6.

Article 8

1. When an appointing authority is requested to appoint an arbitrator pursuant to article 6 or article 7, the party which makes the request shall send to the appointing authority a copy of the notice of arbitration, a copy of the contract out of or in relation to which the dispute has arisen and a copy of the arbitration agreement if it is not contained in the contract. The appointing authority may require from either party such information as it deems necessary to fulfil its function.

2. Where the names of one or more persons are proposed for appointment as arbitrators, their full names, addresses and nationalities shall be indicated, together with a description of their qualifications.

CHALLENGE OF ARBITRATORS (ARTICLES 9 TO 12)

Article 9

A prospective arbitrator shall disclose to those who approach him in connexion with his possible appointment any circumstances likely to give rise to justifiable doubts as to his impartiality or independence. An arbitrator, once appointed or chosen, shall disclose such circumstances to the parties unless they have already been informed by him of these circumstances.

Article 10

1. Any arbitrator may be challenged if circumstances exist that give rise to justifiable doubts as to the arbitrator's impartiality or independence.

2. A party may challenge the arbitrator appointed by him only for reasons of which he becomes aware after the appointment has been made.

Article 11

1. A party who intends to challenge an arbitrator shall send notice of his challenge within fifteen days after the appointment of the challenged arbitrator has been notified to the challenging party or within fifteen days after the circumstances mentioned in articles 9 and 10 became known to that party.

2. The challenge shall be notified to the other party, to the arbitrator who is challenged and to the other members of the arbitral tribunal. The notification shall be in writing and shall state the reasons for the challenge.

3. When an arbitrator has been challenged by one party, the other party may agree to the challenge. The arbitrator may also, after the challenge, withdraw from his office. In neither case does this imply acceptance of the validity of the grounds for the challenge. In both cases the procedure provided in article 6 or 7 shall be used in full for the appointment of the substitute arbitrator, even if during the process of appointing the challenged arbitrator a party had failed to exercise his right to appoint or to participate in the appointment.

Article 12

1. If the other party does not agree to the challenge and the challenged arbitrator does not withdraw, the decision on the challenge will be made:

(a) When the initial appointment was made by an appointing authority, by that authority;

(b) When the initial appointment was not made by an appointing authority, but an appointing authority has been previously designated, by that authority;

(c) In all other cases, by the appointing authority to be designated in accordance with the procedure for designating an appointing authority as provided for in article 6.

2. If the appointing authority sustains the challenge, a substitute arbitrator shall be appointed or chosen pursuant to the procedure applicable to the appointment or choice of an arbitrator as provided in articles 6 to 9 except that, when this procedure would call for the designation of an appointing authority, the appointment of the arbitrator shall be made by the appointing authority which decided on the challenge.

REPLACEMENT OF AN ARBITRATOR

Article 13

1. In the event of the death or resignation of an arbitrator during the course of the arbitral proceedings, a substitute arbitrator shall be appointed or chosen pursuant to the procedure provided for in articles 6 to 9 that was applicable to the appointment or choice of the arbitrator being replaced.

2. In the event that an arbitrator fails to act or in the event of the *de jure* or *de facto* impossibility of his performing his functions, the procedure in respect of the challenge and replacement of an arbitrator as provided in the preceding articles shall apply.

REPETITION OF HEARINGS IN THE EVENT OF THE REPLACEMENT OF AN ARBITRATOR

Article 14

If under articles 11 to 13 the sole or presiding arbitrator is replaced, any hearings held previously shall be repeated; if any other arbitrator is replaced, such prior hearings may be repeated at the discretion of the arbitral tribunal.

Section III. Arbitral proceedings

GENERAL PROVISIONS

Article 15

1. Subject to these Rules, the arbitral tribunal may conduct the arbitration in such manner as it considers appropriate, provided that the parties are treated with equality and that at any stage of the proceedings each party is given a full opportunity of presenting his case.

2. If either party so requests at any stage of the proceedings, the arbitral tribunal shall hold hearings for the presentation of evidence by witnesses, including expert witnesses, or for oral argument. In the absence of such a request, the arbitral tribunal shall decide whether to hold such hearings or whether the proceedings shall be conducted on the basis of documents and other materials.

3. All documents or information supplied to the arbitral tribunal by one party shall at the same time be communicated by that party to the other party.

PLACE OF ARBITRATION

Article 16

1. Unless the parties have agreed upon the place where the arbitration is to be held, such place shall be determined by the arbitral tribunal, having regard to the circumstances of the arbitration.

2. The arbitral tribunal may determine the locale of the arbitration within the country agreed upon by the parties. It may hear witnesses and hold meetings for consultation among its members at any place it deems appropriate, having regard to the circumstances of the arbitration.

3. The arbitral tribunal may meet any place it deems appropriate for the inspection of goods, other property or documents. The parties shall be given sufficient notice to enable them to be present at such inspection.

4. The award shall be made at the place of arbitration.

LANGUAGE

Article 17

1. Subject to an agreement by the parties, the arbitral tribunal shall, promptly after its appointment, determine the language or languages to be used in the proceedings. This determination shall apply to the statement of claim, the statement of defence, and any further written statements and, if oral hearings take place, to the language or languages to be used in such hearings.

2. The arbitral tribunal may order that any documents annexed to the statement of claim or statement of defence, and any supplementary documents or exhibits submitted in the course of the proceedings, delivered in their original language, shall be accompanied by a translation into the language or languages agreed upon by the parties or determined by the arbitral tribunal.

STATEMENT OF CLAIM

Article 18

1. Unless the statement of claim was contained in the notice of arbitration, within a period of time to be determined by the arbitral tribunal, the claimant shall communicate his statement of claim in writing to the respondent and to each of the arbitrators. A copy of the contract, and of the arbitration agreement if not contained in the contract, shall be annexed thereto.

2. The statement of claim shall include the following particulars:

(a) The names and addresses of the parties;
(b) A statement of the facts supporting the claim;
(c) The points at issue;
(d) The relief or remedy sought.

The claimant may annex to his statement of claim all documents he deems relevant or may add a reference to the documents or other evidence he will submit.

STATEMENT OF DEFENCE

Article 19

1. Within a period of time to be determined by the arbitral tribunal, the respondent shall communicate his statement of defence in writing to the claimant and to each of the arbitrators.

2. The statement of defence shall reply to the particulars (b), (c) and (d) of the statement

of claim (article 18, para. 2). The respondent may annex to his statement the documents on which he relies for his defence or may add a reference to the documents or other evidence he will submit.

3. In his statement of defence, or at a later stage in the arbitral proceedings if the arbitral tribunal decides that the delay was justified under the circumstances, the respondent may make a counter-claim arising out of the same contract or rely on a claim arising out of the same contract for the purpose of set-off.

4. The provisions of article 18, paragraph 2, shall apply to a counter-claim and a claim relied on for the purpose of a set-off.

AMENDMENTS TO THE CLAIM OR DEFENCE

Article 20

During the course of the arbitral proceedings either party may amend or supplement his claim or defence unless the arbitral tribunal considers it inappropriate to allow such amendment having regard to the delay in making it or prejudice to the other party or any other circumstances. However, a claim may not be amended in such a manner that the amended claim falls outside the scope of the arbitration clause or separate arbitration agreement.

PLEAS AS TO THE JURISDICTION OF THE ARBITRAL TRIBUNAL

Article 21

1. The arbitral tribunal shall have the power to rule on objections that it has no jurisdiction, including any objections with respect to the existence or validity of the arbitration clause or of the separate arbitration agreement.

2. The arbitral tribunal shall have the power to determine the existence or the validity of the contract of which an arbitration clause forms a part. For the purposes of article 2, an arbitration clause which forms part of a contract and which provides for arbitration under these Rules shall be treated as an agreement independent of the other terms of the contract. A decision by the arbitral tribunal that the contract is null and void shall not entail *ipso jure* the invalidity of the arbitration clause.

3. A plea that the arbitral tribunal does not have jurisdiction shall be raised not later than in the statement of defence or, with respect to a counter-claim, in the reply to the counter-claim.

4. In general, the arbitral tribunal should rule on a plea concerning its jurisdiction as a preliminary question. However, the arbitral tribunal may proceed with the arbitration and rule on such a plea in their final award.

FURTHER WRITTEN STATEMENTS

Article 22

The arbitral tribunal shall decide which further written statements, in addition to the statement of claim and the statement of defence, shall be required from the parties or may be presented by them and shall fix the periods of time for communicating such statements.

PERIODS OF TIME

Article 23

The periods of time fixed by the arbitral tribunal for the communication of written statements (including the statement of claim and statement of defence) should not exceed forty-five days. However, the arbitral tribunal may extend the time-limits if it concludes that an extension is justified.

EVIDENCE AND HEARINGS (ARTICLES 24 AND 25)

Article 24

1. Each party shall have the burden of proving the facts relied on to support his claim or defence.

2. The arbitral tribunal may, if it considers it appropriate, require a party to deliver to the tribunal and to the other party, within such a period of time as the arbitral tribunal shall decide, a summary of the documents and other evidence which that party intends to present in support of the facts in issue set out in his statement of claim or statement of defence.

3. At any time during the arbitral proceedings the arbitral tribunal may require the parties to produce documents, exhibits or other evidence within such a period of time as the tribunal shall determine.

Article 25

1. In the event of an oral hearing, the arbitral tribunal shall give the parties adequate advance notice of the date, time and place thereof.

2. If witnesses are to be heard, at least fifteen days before the hearing each party shall communicate to the arbitral tribunal and to the other party the names and addresses of the witnesses he intends to present, the subject upon and the languages in which such witnesses will give their testimony.

3. The arbitral tribunal shall make arrangements for the translation of oral statements made

at a hearing and for a record of the hearing if either is deemed necessary by the tribunal under the circumstances of the case or if the parties have agreed thereto and have communicated such agreement to the tribunal at least fifteen days before the hearing.

4. Hearings shall be held *in camera* unless the parties agree otherwise. The arbitral tribunal may require the retirement of any witness or witnesses during the testimony of other witnesses. The arbitral tribunal is free to determine the manner in which witnesses are examined.

5. Evidence of witnesses may also be presented in the form of written statements signed by them.

6. The arbitral tribunal shall determine the admissibility, relevance, materiality and weight of the evidence offered.

INTERIM MEASURES OF PROTECTION

Article 26

1. At the request of either party, the arbitral tribunal may take any interim measures it deems necessary in respect of the subject-matter of the dispute, including measures for the conservation of the goods forming the subject-matter in dispute, such as ordering their deposit with a third person or the sale of perishable goods.

2. Such interim measures may be established in the form of an interim award. The arbitral tribunal shall be entitled to require security for the costs of such measures.

3. A request for interim measures addressed by any party to a judicial authority shall not be deemed incompatible with the agreement to arbitrate, or as a waiver of that agreement.

EXPERTS

Article 27

1. The arbitral tribunal may appoint one or more experts to report to it, in writing, on specific issues to be determined by the tribunal. A copy of the expert's terms of reference, established by the arbitral tribunal, shall be communicated to the parties.

2. The parties shall give the expert any relevant information or produce for his inspection any relevant documents or goods that he may require of them. Any dispute between a party and such expert as to the relevance of the required information or production shall be referred to the arbitral tribunal for decision.

3. Upon receipt of the expert's report, the arbitral tribunal shall communicate a copy of the report to the parties who shall be given the opportunity to express, in writing, their opinion on

the report. A party shall be entitled to examine any document on which the expert has relied in his report.

4. At the request of either party the expert, after delivery of the report, may be heard at a hearing where the parties shall have the opportunity to be present and to interrogate the expert. At this hearing either party may present expert witnesses in order to testify on the points at issue. The provisions of article 25 shall be applicable to such proceedings.

DEFAULT

Article 28

1. If, within the period of time fixed by the arbitral tribunal, the claimant has failed to communicate his claim without showing sufficient cause for such failure, the arbitral tribunal shall issue an order for the termination of the arbitral proceedings. If, within the period of time fixed by the arbitral tribunal, the respondent has failed to communicate his statement of defence without showing sufficient cause for such failure, the arbitral tribunal shall order that the proceedings continue.

2. If one of the parties, duly notified under these Rules, fails to appear at a hearing, without showing sufficient cause for such failure, the arbitral tribunal may proceed with the arbitration.

3. If one of the parties, duly invited to produce documentary evidence, fails to do so within the established period of time, without showing sufficient cause for such failure, the arbitral tribunal may make the award on the evidence before it.

CLOSURE OF HEARINGS

Article 29

1. The arbitral tribunal may inquire of the parties if they have any further proof to offer or witnesses to be heard or submissions to make and, if there are none, it may declare the hearings closed.

2. The arbitral tribunal may, if it considers it necessary owing to exceptional circumstances, decide, on its own motion or upon application of a party, to reopen the hearings at any time before the award is made.

WAIVER OF RULES

Article 30

A party who knows that any provision of, or requirement under, these Rules has not been complied with and yet proceeds with the arbitration without promptly stating his objection to such non-compliance, shall be deemed to have waived his right to object.

Section IV. The award

DECISIONS

Article 31

1. When there are three arbitrators, any award or other decision of the arbitral tribunal shall be made by a majority of the arbitrators.

2. In the case of questions of procedure, when there is no majority or when the arbitral tribunal so authorizes, the presiding arbitrator may decide on his own, subject to revision, if any, by the arbitral tribunal.

FORM AND EFFECT OF THE AWARD

Article 32

1. In addition to making a final award, the arbitral tribunal shall be entitled to make interim, interlocutory, or partial awards.

2. The award shall be made in writing and shall be final and binding on the parties. The parties undertake to carry out the award without delay.

3. The arbitral tribunal shall state the reasons upon which the award is based, unless the parties have agreed that no reasons are to be given.

4. An award shall be signed by the arbitrators and it shall contain the date on which and the place where the award was made. Where there are three arbitrators and one of them fails to sign, the award shall state the reason for the absence of the signature.

5. The award may be made public only with the consent of both parties.

6. Copies of the award signed by the arbitrators shall be communicated to the parties by the arbitral tribunal.

7. If the arbitration law of the country where the award is made requires that the award be filed or registered by the arbitral tribunal, the tribunal shall comply with this requirement within the period of time required by law.

APPLICABLE LAW, AMIABLE COMPOSITEUR

Article 33

1. The arbitral tribunal shall apply the law designated by the parties as applicable to the substance of the dispute. Failing such designation by the parties, the arbitral tribunal shall apply the law determined by the conflict of laws rules which it considers applicable.

2. The arbitral tribunal shall decide as *amiable compositeur* or *ex aequo et bono* only if the parties have expressly authorized the arbitral tribunal to do so and if the law applicable to the arbitral procedure permits such arbitration.

3. In all cases, the arbitral tribunal shall decide in accordance with the terms of the contract and shall take into account the usages of the trade applicable to the transaction.

SETTLEMENT OR OTHER GROUNDS FOR TERMINATION

Article 34

1. If, before the award is made, the parties agree on a settlement of the dispute, the arbitral tribunal shall either issue an order for the termination of the arbitral proceedings or, if requested by both parties and accepted by the tribunal, record the settlement in the form of an arbitral award on agreed terms. The arbitral tribunal is not obliged to give reasons for such an award.

2. If, before the award is made, the continuation of the arbitral proceedings becomes unnecessary or impossible for any reason not mentioned in paragraph l, the arbitral tribunal shall inform the parties of its intention to issue an order for the termination of the proceedings. The arbitral tribunal shall have the power to issue such an order unless a party raises justifiable grounds for objection.

3. Copies of the order for the termination of the arbitral proceedings or of the arbitral award on agreed terms, signed by the arbitrators, shall be communicated by the arbitral tribunal to the parties. Where an arbitral award on agreed terms is made, the provisions of article 32, paragraphs 2 and 4 to 7, shall apply.

INTERPRETATION OF THE AWARD

Article 35

1. Within thirty days after the receipt of the award, either party, with notice to the other party, may request that the arbitral tribunal give an interpretation of the award.

2. The interpretation shall be given in writing within forty-five days after the receipt of the request. The interpretation shall form part of the award and the provisions of article 32,

paragraphs 2 to 7, shall apply.

CORRECTION OF THE AWARD

Article 36

1. Within thirty days after the receipt of the award, either party, with notice to the other party, may request the arbitral tribunal to correct in the award any errors in computation, any clerical or typographical errors, or any errors of similar nature. The arbitral tribunal may within thirty days after the communication of the award make such corrections on its own initiative.

2. Such corrections shall be in writing, and the provisions of article 32, paragraphs 2 to 7, shall apply.

ADDITIONAL AWARD

Article 37

1. Within thirty days after the receipt of the award, either party, with notice to the other party, may request the arbitral tribunal to make an additional award as to claims presented in the arbitral proceedings but omitted from the award.

2. If the arbitral tribunal considers the request for an additional award to be justified and considers that the omission can be rectified without any further hearings or evidence, it shall complete its award within sixty days after the receipt of the request.

3. When an additional award is made, the provisions of article 32, paragraphs 2 to 7, shall apply.

COSTS (ARTICLES 38 TO 40)

Article 38

The arbitral tribunal shall fix the costs of arbitration in its award. The term "costs" includes only:

(a) The fees of the arbitral tribunal to be stated separately as to each arbitrator and to be fixed by the tribunal itself in accordance with article 39;
(b) The travel and other expenses incurred by the arbitrators;
(c) The costs of expert advice and of other assistance required by the arbitral tribunal;
(d) The travel and other expenses of witnesses to the extent such expenses are approved by the arbitral tribunal;
(e) The costs of legal representation and assistance of the successful party if such costs were claimed during the arbitral proceedings, and only to the extent that the

arbitral tribunal determines that the amount of such costs is reasonable;

(f) Any fees and expenses of the appointing authority as well as the expenses of the Secretary-General of the Permanent Court of Arbitration at The Hague.

Article 39

1. The fees of the arbitral tribunal shall be reasonable in amount, taking into account the amount in dispute, the complexity of the subject-matter, the time spent by the arbitrators and any other relevant circumstances of the case.

2. If an appointing authority has been agreed upon by the parties or designated by the Secretary-General of the Permanent Court of Arbitration at The Hague, and if that authority has issued a schedule of fees for arbitrators in international cases which it administers, the arbitral tribunal in fixing its fees shall take that schedule of fees into account to the extent that it considers appropriate in the circumstances of the case.

3. If such appointing authority has not issued a schedule of fees for arbitrators in international cases, any party may at any time request the appointing authority to furnish a statement setting forth the basis for establishing fees which is customarily followed in international cases in which the authority appoints arbitrators. If the appointing authority consents to provide such a statement, the arbitral tribunal in fixing its fees shall take such information into account to the extent that it considers appropriate in the circumstances of the case.

4. In cases referred to in paragraphs 2 and 3, when a party so requests and the appointing authority consents to perform the function, the arbitral tribunal shall fix its fees only after consultation with the appointing authority which may make any comment it deems appropriate to the arbitral tribunal concerning the fees.

Article 40

1. Except as provided in paragraph 2, the costs of arbitration shall in principle be borne by the unsuccessful party. However, the arbitral tribunal may apportion each of such costs between the parties if it determines that apportionment is reasonable, taking into account the circumstances of the case.

2. With respect to the costs of legal representation and assistance referred to in article 38, paragraph (e), the arbitral tribunal, taking into account the circumstances of the case, shall be free to determine which party shall bear such costs or may apportion such costs between the parties if it determines that apportionment is reasonable.

3. When the arbitral tribunal issues an order for the termination of the arbitral proceedings or makes an award on agreed terms, it shall fix the costs of arbitration referred to in article 38 and article 39, paragraph 1, in the text of that order or award.

4. No additional fees may be charged by an arbitral tribunal for interpretation or correction or completion of its award under articles 35 to 37.

DEPOSIT OF COSTS

Article 41

1. The arbitral tribunal, on its establishment, may request each party to deposit an equal amount as an advance for the costs referred to in article 38, paragraphs (a), (b) and (c).

2. During the course of the arbitral proceedings the arbitral tribunal may request supplementary deposits from the parties.

3. If an appointing authority has been agreed upon by the parties or designated by the Secretary-General of the Permanent Court of Arbitration at The Hague, and when a party so requests and the appointing authority consents to perform the function, the arbitral tribunal shall fix the amounts of any deposits or supplementary deposits only after consultation with the appointing authority which may make any comments to the arbitral tribunal which it deems appropriate concerning the amount of such deposits and supplementary deposits.

4. If the required deposits are not paid in full within thirty days after the receipt of that request, the arbitral tribunal shall so inform the parties in order that one or another of them may make the required payment. If such payment is not made, the arbitral tribunal may order the suspension or termination of the arbitral proceedings.

5. After the award has been made, the arbitral tribunal shall render an accounting to the parties of the deposits received and return any unexpended balance to the parties.

* * *

ILO Tripartite Declaration of Principles concerning Multinational Enterprises and Social Policy

and

Procedurefor the examination of disputes concerning the application of the Tripartite Declaration of Principles concerning Multinational Enterprises and Social Policy by means of interpretation of its provisions

The ILO Tripartite Declaration of Principles concerning Multinational Enterprises and Social Policy was adopted by the Governing Body of the International Labour Office at its 204th session in Geneva on 16 November 1977 and took effect upon its publication in the ILO's Official Bulletin in 1978. The Procedure for the examination of disputes concerning the application of the Tripartite Declaration of Principles concerning Multinational Enterprises and Social Policy by means of interpretation of its provisions was adopted by the Governing Body of the International Labour Office at its 232nd session in Geneva in March 1986 to replace Part IV of the Procedures adopted by the Governing Body at its 214th session (November 1980). The "Addendum to the Tripartite Declaration of Principles concerning Multinational Enterprises and Social Policy: References to Conventions and Recommendations in the Tripartite Declaration of Principles concerning Multinational Enterprises and Social Policy" was adopted by the Governing Body of the International Labour Office at its 238th session in Geneva in November 1987. An update of the Addendum was approved by the Governing Body at its 264th (November 1995) Session (this Addendum has not been reproduced in this volume).

ILO Tripartite Declaration of Principles concerning Multinational Enterprises and Social Policy

(adopted by the Governing Body of the International Labour Office at its 204th Session (Geneva, November 1977)*)

The Governing Body of the International Labour Office;

Recalling that the International Labour Organisation for many years has been involved with certain social issues related to the activities of multinational enterprises;

*Official Bulletin (Geneva: ILO), 1978, Vol. LXI, Series A, No. 1, pp. 49-56.

Noting in particular that various Industrial Committees, Regional Conferences, and the International Labour Conference since the mid-1960s have requested appropriate action by the Governing Body in the field of multinational enterprises and social policy;

Having been informed of the activities of other international bodies, in particular the UN Commission on Transnational Corporations and the Organisation for Economic Co-operation and Development (OECD);

Considering that the ILO, with its unique tripartite structure, its competence, and its long-standing experience in the social field, has an essential role to play in evolving principles for the guidance of governments, workers' and employers' organisations, and multinational enterprises themselves;

Recalling that it convened a Tripartite Meeting of Experts on the Relationship between Multinational Enterprises and Social Policy in 1972, which recommended an ILO programme of research and study, and a Tripartite Advisory Meeting on the Relationship of Multinational Enterprises and Social Policy in 1976 for the purpose of reviewing the ILO programme of research and suggesting appropriate ILO action in the social and labour field;

Bearing in mind the deliberations of the World Employment Conference;

Having thereafter decided to establish a tripartite group to prepare a Draft Tripartite Declaration of Principles covering all of the areas of ILO concern which relate to the social aspects of the activities of multinational enterprises, including employment creation in the developing countries, all the while bearing in mind the recommendations made by the Tripartite Advisory Meeting held in 1976;

Having also decided to reconvene the Tripartite Advisory Meeting to consider the Draft Declaration of Principles as prepared by the tripartite group;

Having considered the Report and the Draft Declaration of Principles submitted to it by the reconvened Tripartite Advisory Meeting;

Hereby approves the following Declaration which may be cited as the Tripartite Declaration of Principles concerning Multinational Enterprises and Social Policy, adopted by the Governing Body of the International Labour Office, and invites governments of States Members of the ILO, the employers' and workers' organisations concerned and the multinational enterprises operating in their territories to observe the principles embodied therein.

1. Multinational enterprises play an important part in the economies of most countries and in international economic relations. This is of increasing interest to governments as well as to employers and workers and their respective organisations. Through international direct investment and other means such enterprises can bring substantial benefits to home and host countries by contributing to the more efficient utilisation of capital, technology and labour. Within the framework of development policies established by governments, they can also make an important

contribution to the promotion of economic and social welfare; to the improvement of living standards and the satisfaction of basic needs; to the creation of employment opportunities, both directly and indirectly; and to the enjoyment of basic human rights, including freedom of association, throughout the world. On the other hand, the advances made by multinational enterprises in organising their operations beyond the national framework may lead to abuse of concentrations of economic power and to conflicts with national policy objectives and with the interest of the workers. In addition, the complexity of multinational enterprises and the difficulty of clearly perceiving their diverse structures, operations and policies sometimes give rise to concern either in the home or in the host countries, or in both.

2. The aim of this Tripartite Declaration of Principles is to encourage the positive contribution which multinational enterprises can make to economic and social progress and to minimise and resolve the difficulties to which their various operations may give rise, taking into account the United Nations resolutions advocating the Establishment of a New International Economic Order.

3. This aim will be furthered by appropriate laws and policies, measures and actions adopted by the governments and by co-operation among the governments and the employers' and workers' organisations of all countries.

4. The principles set out in this Declaration are commended to the governments, the employers' and workers' organisations of home and host countries and to the multinational enterprises themselves.

5. These principles are intended to guide the governments, the employers' and workers' organisations and the multinational enterprises in taking such measures and actions and adopting such social policies, including those based on the principles laid down in the Constitution and the relevant Conventions and Recommendations of the ILO, as would further social progress.

6. To serve its purpose this Declaration does not require a precise legal definition of multinational enterprises; this paragraph is designed to facilitate the understanding of the Declaration and not to provide such a definition. Multinational enterprises include enterprises, whether they are of public, mixed or private ownership, which own or control production, distribution, services or other facilities outside the country in which they are based. The degree of autonomy of entities within multinational enterprises in relation to each other varies widely from one such enterprise to another, depending on the nature of the links between such entities and their fields of activity and having regard to the great diversity in the form of ownership, in the size, in the nature and location of the operations of the enterprises concerned. Unless otherwise specified, the term "multinational enterprise" is used in this Declaration to designate the various entities (parent companies or local entities or both or the organisation as a whole) according to the distribution of responsibilities among them, in the expectation that they will co-operate and provide assistance to one another as necessary to facilitate observance of the principles laid down in the Declaration.

7. This Declaration sets out principles in the fields of employment, training, conditions of work and life and industrial relations which governments, employers' and workers' organisations and multinational enterprises are recommended to observe on a voluntary basis; its provisions shall not limit or otherwise affect obligations arising out of ratification of any ILO Convention.

General policies

8. All the parties concerned by this Declaration should respect the sovereign rights of States, obey the national laws and regulations, give due consideration to local practices and respect relevant international standards. They should respect the Universal Declaration of Human Rights and the corresponding International Covenants adopted by the General Assembly of the United Nations as well as the Constitution of the International Labour Organisation and its principles according to which freedom of expression and association are essential to sustained progress. They should also honour commitments which they have freely entered into, in conformity with the national law and accepted international obligations.

9. Governments which have not yet ratified Conventions Nos. 87, 98, 111 and 122 are urged to do so and in any event to apply, to the greatest extent possible, through their national policies, the principles embodied therein and in Recommendations Nos. 111, 119 and 122.[1] Without prejudice to the obligation of governments to ensure compliance with Conventions they have ratified, in countries in which the Conventions and Recommendations cited in this paragraph are not complied with, all parties should refer to them for guidance in their social policy.

10. Multinational enterprises should take fully into account established general policy objectives of the countries in which they operate. Their activities should be in harmony with the development priorities and social aims and structure of the country in which they operate. To this effect, consultations should be held between multinational enterprises, the government and, wherever appropriate, the national employers' and workers' organisations concerned.

11. The principles laid down in this Declaration do not aim at introducing or maintaining inequalities of treatment between multinational and national enterprises. They reflect good practice for all. Multinational and national enterprises, wherever the principles of this Declaration are relevant to both, should be subject to the same expectations in respect of their conduct in general and their social practices in particular.

[1] Convention (No. 87) concerning Freedom of Association and Protection of the Right to Organise; Convention (No. 98) concerning the Application of the Principles of the Right to Organise and to Bargain Collectively; Convention (No. 111) concerning Discrimination in Respect of Employment and Occupation; Convention (No. 122) concerning Employment Policy; Recommendation (No. 111) concerning Discrimination in Respect of Employment and Occupation; Recommendation (No. 119) concerning Termination of Employment at the Initiative of the Employer; Recommendation (No. 122) concerning Employment Policy.

12. Governments of home countries should promote good social practice in accordance with this Declaration of Principles, having regard to the social and labour law, regulations and practices in host countries as well as to relevant international standards. Both host and home country governments should be prepared to have consultations with each other, whenever the need arises, on the initiative of either.

Employment

Employment promotion

13. With a view to stimulating economic growth and development, raising living standards, meeting manpower requirements and overcoming unemployment and underemployment, governments should declare and pursue, as a major goal, an active policy designed to promote full, productive and freely chosen employment.[2]

14. This is particularly important in the case of host country governments in developing areas of the world where the problems of unemployment and underemployment are at their most serious. In this connection, the general conclusions adopted by the Tripartite World Conference on Employment, Income Distribution and Social Progress and the International Division of Labour (Geneva, June 1976) should be kept in mind.[3]

15. Paragraphs 13 and 14 above establish the framework within which due attention should be paid, in both home and host countries, to the employment impact of multinational enterprises.

16. Multinational enterprises, particularly when operating in developing countries, should endeavour to increase employment opportunities and standards, taking into account the employment policies and objectives of the governments, as well as security of employment and the long-term development of the enterprise.

17. Before starting operations, multinational enterprises should wherever appropriate consult the competent authorities and the national employers' and workers' organisations in order to keep their manpower plans, as far as practicable, in harmony with national social development policies. Such consultation, as in the case of national enterprises, should continue between the multinational enterprises and all parties concerned, including the workers' organisations.

18. Multinational enterprises should give priority to the employment, occupational development, promotion and advancement of nationals of the host country at all levels in co-operation, as appropriate, with representatives of the workers employed by them or of the organisations of these workers and governmental authorities.

---

[2]Convention (No. 122) and Recommendation (No. 122) concerning Employment Policy.

[3] ILO, World Employment Conference, Geneva, 4-17 June 1976.

19. Multinational enterprises, when investing in developing countries, should have regard to the importance of using technologies which generate employment, both directly and indirectly. To the extent permitted by the nature of the process and the conditions prevailing in the economic sector concerned, they should adapt technologies to the needs and characteristics of the host countries. They should also, where possible, take part in the development of appropriate technology in host countries.

20. To promote employment in developing countries, in the context of an expanding world economy, multinational enterprises, wherever practicable, should give consideration to the conclusion of contracts with national enterprises for the manufacture of parts and equipment, to the use of local raw materials and to the progressive promotion of the local processing of raw materials. Such arrangements should not be used by multinational enterprises to avoid the responsibilities embodied in the principles of this Declaration.

Equality of opportunity and treatment

21. All governments should pursue policies designed to promote equality of opportunity and treatment in employment, with a view to eliminating any discrimination based on race, colour, sex, religion, political opinion, national extraction or social origin.[4]

22. Multinational enterprises should be guided by this general principle throughout their operations without prejudice to the measures envisaged in paragraph 18 or to government policies designed to correct historical patterns of discrimination and thereby to extend equality of opportunity and treatment in employment. Multinational enterprises should accordingly make qualifications, skill and experience the basis for the recruitment, placement, training and advancement of their staff at all levels.

23. Governments should never require or encourage multinational enterprises to discriminate on any of the grounds mentioned in paragraph 21, and continuing guidance from governments, where appropriate, on the avoidance of such discrimination in employment is encouraged.

Security of employment

24. Governments should carefully study the impact of multinational enterprises on employment in different industrial sectors. Governments, as well as multinational enterprises themselves, in all countries should take suitable measures to deal with the employment and labour market impacts of the operations of multinational enterprises.

---

[4] Convention (No. 111) and Recommendation (No. 111) concerning Discrimination in Respect of Employment and Occupation; Convention (No. 100) and Recommendation (No. 90) concerning Equal Remuneration for Men and Women Workers for Work of Equal Value.

25. Multinational enterprises equally with national enterprises, through active manpower planning, should endeavour to provide stable employment for their employees and should observe freely-negotiated obligations concerning employment stability and social security. In view of the flexibility which multinational enterprises may have, they should strive to assume a leading role in promoting security of employment, particularly in countries where the discontinuation of operations is likely to accentuate long-term unemployment.

26. In considering changes in operations (including those resulting from mergers, take-overs or transfers of production) which would have major employment effects, multinational enterprises should provide reasonable notice of such changes to the appropriate government authorities and representatives of the workers in their employment and their organisations so that the implications may be examined jointly in order to mitigate adverse effects to the greatest possible extent. This is particularly important in the case of the closure of an entity involving collective lay-offs or dismissals.

27. Arbitrary dismissal procedures should be avoided.[5]

28. Governments, in co-operation with multinational as well as national enterprises, should provide some form of income protection for workers whose employment has been terminated.[6]

Training

29. Governments, in co-operation with all the parties concerned, should develop national policies for vocational training and guidance, closely linked with employment.[7] This is the framework within which multinational enterprises should pursue their training policies.

30. In their operations, multinational enterprises should ensure that relevant training is provided for all levels of their employees in the host country, as appropriate, to meet the needs of the enterprise as well as the development policies of the country. Such training should, to the extent possible, develop generally useful skills and promote career opportunities. This responsibility should be carried out, where appropriate, in co-operation with the authorities of the country, employers' and workers' organisations and the competent local, national or international institutions.

31. Multinational enterprises operating in developing countries should participate, along with national enterprises, in programmes, including special funds, encouraged by host governments and supported by employers' and workers' organisations. These programmes should

---

[5]Recommendation (No. 119) concerning Termination of Employment at the Initiative of the Employer.

[6]ibid.

[7]Convention (No. 142) and Recommendation (No. 150) concerning Vocational Guidance and Vocational Training in the Development of Human Resources.

have the aim of encouraging skill formation and development as well as providing vocational guidance, and should be jointly administered by the parties which support them. Wherever practicable, multinational enterprises should make the services of skilled resource personnel available to help in training programmes organised by governments as part of a contribution to national development.

32. Multinational enterprises, with the co-operation of governments and to the extent consistent with the efficient operation of the enterprise, should afford opportunities within the enterprise as a whole to broaden the experience of local management in suitable fields such as industrial relations.

Conditions of work and life

Wages, benefits and conditions of work

33. Wages, benefits and conditions of work offered by multinational enterprises should be not less favourable to the workers than those offered by comparable employers in the country concerned.

34. When multinational enterprises operate in developing countries, where comparable employers may not exist, they should provide the best possible wages, benefits and conditions of work, within the framework of government policies.[8] These should be related to the economic position of the enterprise, but should be at least adequate to satisfy basic needs of the workers and their families. Where they provide workers with basic amenities such as housing, medical care or food, these amenities should be of a good standard.[9]

35. Governments, especially in developing countries, should endeavour to adopt suitable measures to ensure that lower income groups and less developed areas benefit as much as possible from the activities of multinational enterprises.

Safety and health

36. Governments should ensure that both multinational and national enterprises provide adequate safety and health standards for their employees. Those governments which have not yet ratified the ILO Conventions on Guarding of Machinery (No. 119), Ionising Radiation (No. 115), Benzene (No. 136) and Occupational Cancer (No. 139) are urged nevertheless to apply to the greatest extent possible the principles embodied in these Conventions and in their related Recommendations (Nos. 118, 114, 144 and 147). The Codes of Practice and Guides in the

---

[8] Recommendation (No. 116) concerning Reduction of Hours of Work.

[9] Convention (No. 110) and Recommendation (No. 110) concerning Conditions of Employment of Plantation Workers; Recommendation (No. 115) concerning Workers' Housing; Recommendation (No. 69) concerning Medical Care; Convention (No. 130) and Recommendation (No. 134) concerning Medical Care and Sickness.

current list of ILO publications on occupational safety and health should also be taken into account.[10]

37. Multinational enterprises should maintain the highest standards of safety and health, in conformity with national requirements, bearing in mind their relevant experience within the enterprise as a whole, including any knowledge of special hazards. They should also make available to the representatives of the workers in the enterprise, and upon request, to the competent authorities and the workers' and employers' organisations in all countries in which they operate, information on the safety and health standards relevant to their local operations, which they observe in other countries. In particular, they should make known to those concerned any special hazards and related protective measures associated with new products and processes. They, like comparable domestic enterprises, should be expected to play a leading role in the examination of causes of industrial safety and health hazards and in the application of resulting improvements within the enterprise as a whole.

38. Multinational enterprises should co-operate in the work of international organisations concerned with the preparation and adoption of international safety and health standards.

39. In accordance with national practice, multinational enterprises should co-operate fully with the competent safety and health authorities, the representatives of the workers and their organisations, and established safety and health organisations. Where appropriate, matters relating to safety and health should be incorporated in agreements with the representatives of the workers and their organisations.

Industrial relations

40. Multinational enterprises should observe standards of industrial relations not less favourable than those observed by comparable employers in the country concerned.

Freedom of association and the right to organise

41. Workers employed by multinational enterprises as well as those employed by national enterprises should, without distinction whatsoever, have the right to establish and, subject only to the rules of the organisation concerned, to join organisations of their own choosing without previous authorisation.[11] They should also enjoy adequate protection against acts of anti-union discrimination in respect of their employment.[12]

---

[10]The ILO Conventions and Recommendations referred to are listed in Publications on occupational safety and health, Geneva, ILO, 1976, pp. 1-3. An up-to-date list of codes of practice and guides can be found in the latest edition.

[11]Convention No. 87, Article 2.

[12]Convention No. 98, Article 1(1).

42. Organisations representing multinational enterprises or the workers in their employment should enjoy adequate protection against any acts of interference by each other or each other's agents or members in their establishment, functioning or administration.[13]

43. Where appropriate, in the local circumstances, multinational enterprises should support representative employers' organisations.

44. Governments, where they do not already do so, are urged to apply the principles of Convention No. 87, Article 5, in view of the importance, in relation to multinational enterprises, of permitting organisations representing such enterprises or the workers in their employment to affiliate with international organisations of employers and workers of their own choosing.

45. Where governments of host countries offer special incentives to attract foreign investment, these incentives should not include any limitation of the workers' freedom of association or the right to organise and bargain collectively.

46. Representatives of the workers in multinational enterprises should not be hindered from meeting for consultation and exchange of view among themselves, provided that the functioning of the operations of the enterprise and the normal procedures which govern relationships with representatives of the workers and their organisations are not thereby prejudiced.

47. Governments should not restrict the entry of representatives of employers' and workers' organisations who come from other countries at the invitation of the local or national organisations concerned for the purpose of consultation on matters of mutual concern, solely on the grounds that they seek entry in that capacity.

Collective bargaining

48. Workers employed by multinational enterprises should have the right, in accordance with national law and practice, to have representative organisations of their own choosing recognised for the purpose of collective bargaining.

49. Measures appropriate to national conditions should be taken, where necessary, to encourage and promote the full development and utilisation of machinery for voluntary negotiation between employers or employers' organisations and workers' organisations, with a view to the regulation of terms and conditions of employment by means of collective agreements.[14]

[13]Convention No. 98, Article 2(1).

[14] Convention No. 98, Article 4.

50. Multinational enterprises, as well as national enterprises, should provide workers' representatives with such facilities as may be necessary to assist in the development of effective collective agreements.[15]

51. Multinational enterprises should enable duly authorised representatives of the workers in their employment in each of the countries in which they operate to conduct negotiations with representatives of management who are authorised to take decisions on the matters under negotiation.

52. Multinational enterprises, in the context of bona fide negotiations with the workers' representatives on conditions of employment, or while workers are exercising the right to organise, should not threaten to utilise a capacity to transfer the whole or part of an operating unit from the country concerned in order to influence unfairly those negotiations or to hinder the exercise of the right to organise; nor should they transfer workers from affiliates in foreign countries with a view to undermining bona fide negotiations with the workers' representatives or the workers' exercise of their right to organise.

53. Collective agreements should include provisions for the settlement of disputes arising over their interpretation and application and for ensuring mutually respected rights and responsibilities.

54. Multinational enterprises should provide workers' representatives with information required for meaningful negotiations with the entity involved and, where this accords with local law and practices, should also provide information to enable them to obtain a true and fair view of the performance of the entity or, where appropriate, of the enterprise as a whole.[16]

55. Governments should supply to the representatives of workers' organisations on request, where law and practice so permit, information on the industries in which the enterprise operates, which would help in laying down objective criteria in the collective bargaining process. In this context, multinational as well as national enterprises should respond constructively to requests by governments for relevant information on their operations.

Consultation

56. In multinational as well as in national enterprises, systems devised by mutual agreement between employers and workers and their representatives should provide, in

[15] Convention (No. 135) concerning Protection and Facilities to be Afforded to Workers' Representatives in the Undertaking.

[16] Recommendation (No. 129) concerning Communications between Management and Workers within Undertakings.

accordance with national law and practice, for regular consultation on matters of mutual concern. Such consultation should not be a substitute for collective bargaining.[17]

Examination of grievances

57. Multinational as well as national enterprises should respect the right of the workers whom they employ to have all their grievances processed in a manner consistent with the following provision: any worker who, acting individually or jointly with other workers, considers that he has grounds for a grievance should have the right to submit such grievance without suffering any prejudice whatsoever as a result, and to have such grievance examined pursuant to an appropriate procedure.[18] This is particularly important whenever the multinational enterprises operate in countries which do not abide by the principles of ILO Conventions pertaining to freedom of association, to the right to organise and bargain collectively and to forced labour.[19]

Settlement of industrial disputes

58. Multinational as well as national enterprises jointly with the representatives and organisations of the workers whom they employ should seek to establish voluntary conciliation machinery, appropriate to national conditions, which may include provisions for voluntary arbitration, to assist in the prevention and settlement of industrial disputes between employers and workers. The voluntary conciliation machinery should include equal representation of employers and workers.[20]

Geneva, 16 November 1977.

* * *

[17]Recommendation (No. 94) concerning Consultation and Co-operation between Employers and Workers at the Level of the Undertaking; Recommendation (No. 129) concerning Communications within the Undertaking.

[18]Recommendation (No. 130) concerning the Examination of Grievances within the Undertaking with a View to their Settlement.

[19]Convention (No. 29) concerning Forced or Compulsory Labour; Convention (No. 105) concerning the Abolition of Forced Labour; Recommendation (No. 35) concerning Indirect Compulsion to Labour.

[20]Recommendation (No. 92) concerning Voluntary Conciliation and Arbitration.

Procedure for the examination of disputes concerning the application of the Tripartite Declaration of Principles concerning Multinational Enterprises and Social Policy by means of interpretation of its provisions

(adopted by the Governing Body of the International Labour Office at its 232nd Session (Geneva. March 1986)*)

1. The purpose of the procedure is to interpret the provisions of the Declaration when needed to resolve a disagreement on their meaning, arising from an actual situation, between parties to whom the Declaration is commended.

2. The procedure should in no way duplicate or conflict with existing national or ILO procedures. Thus, it cannot be invoked:

(a) in respect of national law and practice;

(b) in respect of international labour Conventions and Recommendations;

(c) in respect of matters failing under the freedom of association procedure.

The above means that questions regarding national law and practice should be considered through appropriate national machinery; that questions regarding international labour Conventions and Recommendations should be examined through the various procedures provided for in articles 19, 22. 24 and 26 of the Constitution of the ILO, or through government requests to the Office for informal interpretation; and that questions concerning freedom of association should be considered through the special ILO procedures applicable to that area.

3. When a request for interpretation of the Declaration is received by the International Labour Office, the Office shall acknowledge receipt and bring it before the Officers of the Committee on Multinational Enterprises. The Office will inform the government and the central organisations of employers and workers concerned of any request for interpretation received directly from an organisation under paragraph *5(b)* and (c).

4. The Officers of the Committee on Multinational Enterprises shall decide unanimously after consultations in the groups whether the request is receivable under the procedure. If they cannot reach agreement the request shall be referred to the full Committee for decision.

5. Requests for interpretation may be addressed to the Office:

***Official Bulletin* (Geneva, ILO), 1986, Vol. LXIX, Series A, No. 3. pp. 196-197 (to replace Part IV of the Procedures adopted by the Governing Body at its 214th Session (November 1980)). See *Official Bulletin*, 1981, Vol. LXIV, Series A, No. 1, pp. 89-90.

(a) as a rule by the government of a member State acting either on its own initiative or at the request of a national organisation of employers or workers;

(b) by a national organisation of employers or workers. which is representative at the national and/or sectoral level, subject to the conditions set out in paragraph 6. Such requests should normally be channelled through the central organisations in the country concerned;

(c) by an international organisation of employers or workers on behalf of a representative national affiliate.

6. In the case of *5(b)* and (c), requests may be submitted if it can be demonstrated:

(a) that the government concerned has declined to submit the request to the Office; or

(b) that three months have elapsed since the organisation addressed the government without a statement of the government's intention.

7. In the case of receivable requests the Office shall prepare a draft reply in consultation with the Officers of the Committee on Multinational Enterprises. All appropriate sources of information shall be used, including government. employers' and workers' sources in the country concerned. The Officers may ask the Office to indicate a period within which the information should be provided.

8. The draft reply to a receivable request shall be considered and approved by the Committee on Multinational Enterprises prior to submission to the Governing Body for approval.

9. The reply when approved by the Governing Body shall be forwarded to the parties concerned and published in the *Official Bulletin* of the International Labour Office.

* * *

DRAFT INTERNATIONAL AGREEMENT ON ILLICIT PAYMENTS*

The Draft International Agreement on Illicit Payments was elaborated by an Ad Hoc Intergovernmental Working Group and by the Committee on an International Agreement on Illicit Payments of the United Nations Economic and Social Council between 1976 and 1979. In May 1979, an almost complete text of the Draft International Agreement on Illicit Payments was transmitted through the Council to the General Assembly, together with a number of proposals for consideration by the conference of plenipotentiaries. These proposals have not been reproduced in this volume. The General Assembly took no action on the Council's recommendation to convene a conference to conclude and formalize the instrument.

Article 1

1. Each Contracting State undertakes to make the following acts punishable by appropriate criminal penalties under its national law:

(a) The offering, promising or giving of any payment, gift or other advantage by any natural person, on his own behalf or on behalf of any enterprise or any other person whether juridical or natural, to or for the benefit of a public official as undue consideration for performing or refraining from the performance of his duties in connection with an international commercial transaction.

(b) The soliciting, demanding, accepting or receiving, directly or indirectly, by a public official of any payment, gift or other advantage, as undue consideration for performing or refraining from the performance of his duties in connection with an international commercial transaction.

2. Each Contracting State likewise undertakes to make the acts referred to in paragraph 1 (a) of this article punishable by appropriate criminal penalties under its national law when committed by a juridical person, or, in the case of a State which does not recognize criminal responsibility of juridical persons, to take appropriate measures, according to its national law, with the objective of comparable deterrent effects.

---

*Source: United Nations Commission on Transnational Corporations (1991). "Efforts by the United Nations to address the issue of corrupt practices", Report of the Commission on Transnational Corporations at its seventeenth session to the Economic and Social Council: Addendum. United Nations document E/1991/31/Add.1 and E/C.10/1991/17/Add.1 (4 July 1991) Annex, pp.18-22 (reproducing document E/1979/104, Section III). The "Notes on the draft international agreement on illicit payments" can be found in E/1979/104, Sect. IV [Note added by the editor].

Article 2

For the purpose of this Agreement:

(a) "Public official" means any person, whether appointed or elected, whether permanently or temporarily, who, at the national, regional or local level holds a legislative, administrative, judicial or military office, or who, performing a public function, is an employee of a Government or of a public or governmental authority or agency or who otherwise performs a public function;

(b) International commercial transaction means, [inter alia] any sale, contract or any other business transaction, actual or proposed, with a national, regional or local Government or any authority or agency referred to in paragraph (a) of this article or any business transaction involving an application for governmental approval of a sale, contract or any other business transaction actual or proposed, relating to the supply or purchase of goods, services, capital or technology emanating from a State or States other than that in which those goods, services, capital or technology are to be delivered or rendered. It also means any application for or acquisition of proprietary interests or production rights from a Government by a foreign national or enterprise;

(c) "Intermediary" means any enterprise or any other person, whether juridical or natural, who negotiates with or otherwise deals with a public official on behalf of any other enterprise or any other person, whether juridical or natural, in connection with an international commercial transaction.

Article 3

Each Contracting State shall take all practicable measures for the purpose of preventing the offences mentioned in article 1.

Article 4

1. Each Contracting State shall take such measures as may be necessary to establish its jurisdiction:

(a) Over the offences referred to in article 1 when they are committed in the territory of that State;

(b) Over the offence referred to in article 1 (b) when it is committed by a public official of that State;

(c) Over the offence referred to in article 1, paragraph 1 (a) relating to any payment, gift or other advantage in connection with [the negotiation, conclusion, retention, revision or termination of] an international commercial transaction when the offence is committed by a national of that State, provided that any element of that offence, or any act aiding or abetting that offence, is connected with the territory of that State.

[(d) Over the offences referred to in article 1 when these have effects within the territory of that State.]

2. This Agreement does not exclude any criminal jurisdiction exercised in accordance with the national law of a Contracting State.

[3. Each Contracting State shall also take such measures as may be necessary to establish its jurisdiction over any other offence that may come within the scope of this Agreement when such offence is committed in the territory of that State, by a public official of that State, by a national of that State or by a juridical person established in the territory of that State.]

Article 5

1. A Contracting State in whose territory the alleged offender is found, shall, if it has jurisdiction under article 4, paragraph 1, be obliged without exception whatsoever to submit the case to its competent authorities for the purpose of prosecution, through proceedings in accordance with the laws of that State.

2. The obligation provided for in paragraph 1 of this article shall not apply if the Contracting State extradites the alleged offender.

Article 6

Each Contracting State shall ensure that enterprises or other juridical persons established in its territory maintain, under penalty of law, accurate records of payments made by them to an intermediary, or received by them as an intermediary, in connexion with an international commercial transaction. These records shall include the amount and date of any such payments and the name and address of the intermediary or intermediaries receiving such payments.

Article 7

1. Each Contracting State shall prohibit its nationals and enterprises of its nationality from making any royalty or tax payments to, or from knowingly transferring any assets or other financial resources in contravention of United Nations resolutions to facilitate trade with, or investment in a territory occupied by, an illegal minority regime in southern Africa.

2. Each Contracting State shall require, by law or regulation, its nationals and enterprises of its nationality to report to the competent authority of that State any royalties or taxes paid to an illegal minority regime in southern Africa in contravention of United Nations resolutions.

[3. Each Contracting State shall submit annually, to the Secretary-General of the United Nations, reports on the activities of transnational corporations of its nationality which collaborate directly or indirectly with illegal minority regimes in southern Africa in contravention of United Nations resolutions.]

Article 8

[Each Contracting State recognizes that if any of the offences that come within the scope of this Agreement is decisive in procuring the consent of a party to an international commercial transaction as defined in article 2, paragraph (b), such international commercial transaction should be voidable and agrees to ensure that its national law provide that such party may at its option institute judicial proceedings in order to have the international commercial transaction declared null and void or to obtain damages or both.]

Article 9

1. Contracting States shall inform each other upon request of measures taken in the implementation of this Agreement.

2. Each Contracting State shall furnish once every second year, in accordance with its national laws, to the Secretary-General of the United Nations, information concerning its implementation of this Agreement. Such information shall include legislative measures and administrative regulations as well as general information on judicial proceedings and other measures taken pursuant to such laws and regulations . Where final convictions have been obtained under laws within the scope of this Agreement, information shall also be furnished concerning the case, the decision and sanctions imposed in so far as they are not confidential under the national law of the State which provides the information.

3. The Secretary-General shall circulate a summary of the information referred to in paragraph 2 of this article to the Contracting States.

Article 10

1. Contracting States shall afford one another the greatest possible measure of assistance in connection with criminal investigations and proceedings brought in respect of any of the offences [referred to in article 1/within the scope of this Agreement]. The law of the State requested shall apply in all cases.

2. Contracting States shall also afford one another the greatest possible measure of assistance in connection with investigations and proceedings relating to the measures contemplated by article 1, paragraph 2, as far as permitted under their national laws.

3. Mutual assistance shall include, as far as permitted under the law of the State requested and taking into account the need for preserving the confidential nature of documents and other information transmitted to appropriate law enforcement authorities [and subject to the essential national interests of the requested State]:

(a) Production of documents or other information, taking of evidence and service of documents, relevant to investigations or court proceedings;

(b) Notice of the initiation and outcome of any public criminal proceedings concerning an offence referred to in article 1, to other Contracting States which may have jurisdiction over the same offence according to article 4;

(c) Production of the records maintained pursuant to article 6.

4. Contracting States shall upon mutual agreement enter into negotiations towards the conclusion of bilateral agreements with each other to facilitate the provision of mutual assistance in accordance with this article.

5. Any evidence or information obtained pursuant to the provisions of this article shall be used in the requesting State solely for the purposes for which it has been obtained, for the enforcement of this Agreement, and shall be kept confidential except to the extent that disclosure is required in proceedings for such enforcement. The approval of the requested State shall be obtained prior to any other use, including disclosure of such evidence or information.

6. The provisions of this article shall not affect obligations under any other treaty, bilateral or multilateral, which governs or will govern in whole or in part mutual assistance in criminal matters.

Article 11

1. The offences [referred to in article 1/ within the scope of this Agreement] shall be deemed to be included as extraditable offences in any extradition treaty existing between Contracting States. Contracting States undertake to include the said offences as extraditable offences in every extradition treaty to be concluded between them.

2. If a Contracting State which makes extradition conditional on the existence of a treaty receives a request for extradition from another Contracting State with which it has no extradition treaty, it [may at its option/shall] consider this Agreement as the legal basis for extradition in respect of the offence. Extradition shall be subject to the other conditions provided by the law of the requested State.

3. Contracting States which do not make extradition conditional on the existence of a treaty [shall/may at their option] recognize the offence as an extraditable offence between themselves subject to the conditions provided by the law of the requested State.

4. The offence shall be treated, for the purpose of extradition between Contracting States, as if it had been committed not only in the place in which it occurred but also in the territories of the States required to establish the jurisdiction in accordance with article 4, paragraph 1.

* * *

UNITED NATIONS MODEL DOUBLE TAXATIONCONVENTION BETWEEN DEVELOPED AND DEVELOPING COUNTRIES*

The United Nations Model Double Taxation Convention between Developed and Developing Countries and the associated commentaries was adopted by the Ad Hoc Group of Experts on Tax Treaties between Developed and Developing Countries at its eighth meeting in Geneva on 21 December 1979. The Ad Hoc Group was set up by the Secretary-General of the United Nations pursuant to resolution 1273 (XLII) adopted by the United Nations Economic and Social Council on 4 August 1967. The commentaries to the model Convention have not been reproduced in this volume.

SUMMARY OF THE CONVENTION

Title and Preamble

CHAPTER I
Scope of the Convention

Article 1 Personal Scope
Article 2 Taxes covered

CHAPTER II
Definitions

Article 3 General definitions
Article 4 Resident
Article 5 Permanent establishment

CHAPTER III
Taxation of income

Article 6 Income from immovable property
Article 7 Business profits
Article 8 A Shipping, inland waterways transport and air transport (alternative A)
Article 8 B Shipping, inland waterways transport and air transport (alternative B)
Article 9 Associated enterprises
Article 10 Dividends

---

*Source: United Nations (1980). *Articles of the United Nations Model Double Taxation Convention Between Developed and Developing Countries*, United Nations document ST/ESA/102, Sales No. E.80.XVI.3 (New York: United Nations). The commentaries on the Articles of the United Nations Model Double Taxation Convention can be found in the same source [Note added by the editor].

Article 11 Interest
Article 12 Royalties
Article 13 Capital gains
Article 14 Independent personal services
Article 15 Dependent personal services
Article 16 Directors' fees and remuneration of top-level managerial officials
Article 17 Income earned by entertainers and athletes
Article 18 A Pensions and social security payments (alternative A)
Article 18 B Pensions and social security payments (alternative B)
Article 19 Remuneration and pensions in respect of government service
Article 20 Payments received by students and apprentices
Article 21 Other income

CHAPTER IV
Taxation of capital

Article 22 Capital

CHAPTER V
Methods for elimination of double taxation

Article 23 A Exemption method
Article 23 B Credit method

CHAPTER VI
Special provisions

Article 24 Non-discrimination
Article 25 Mutual agreement procedure
Article 26 Exchange of information
Article 27 Diplomatic agents and consular officers

CHAPTER VII
Final provisions

Article 28 Entry into force
Article 29 Termination

TITLE OF THE CONVENTION

Convention between (State A) and (State B) for avoidance of double taxation with respect to taxes on income [and on capital].[1]

PREAMBLE OF THE CONVENTION

Chapter I
SCOPE OF THE CONVENTION

Article 1
PERSONAL SCOPE

This Convention shall apply to persons who are residents of one or both of the Contracting States.

Article 2
TAXES COVERED

1. This Convention shall apply to taxes on income [and on capital] imposed on behalf of a Contracting State or of its political subdivisions or local authorities, irrespective of the manner in which they are levied.

2. There shall be regarded as taxes on income [and on capital] all taxes imposed on total income, [on total capital,] or on elements of income [or of capital,] including taxes on gains from the alienation of movable or immovable property, taxes on the total amounts of wages or salaries paid by enterprises, as well as taxes on capital appreciation.

3. The existing taxes to which the Convention shall apply are in particular:
   (a) (in State A): ....
   (b) (in State B): ....

4. The Convention shall apply also to any identical or substantially similar taxes which are imposed after the date of signature of the Convention in addition to, or in place of, the existing taxes. At the end of each year, the competent authorities of the Contracting States shall notify each other of changes which have been made in their respective taxation laws.

---

[1]Throughout the Convention, the words in square brackets are to be deleted if it is not intended to include in the Convention an article on the taxation of capital (see also article 22). The Preamble of the Convention shall be drafted in accordance with the constitutional procedures of both Contracting States.

Chapter II
DEFINITIONS

Article 3
GENERAL DEFINITIONS

1. For the purposes of this Convention, unless the context otherwise requires:

(a) The term "person" includes an individual, a Company and any other body of persons;

(b) The term "company" means any body corporate or any entity which is treated as a body corporate for tax purposes;

(c) The terms "enterprise of a Contracting State" and "enterprise of the other Contracting State" mean respectively an enterprise carried on by a resident of a Contracting State and an enterprise carried on by a resident of the other Contracting State;

(d) The term "international traffic" means any transport by a ship or aircraft operated by an enterprise which has its place of effective management in a Contracting State, except when the ship or aircraft is operated solely between places in the other Contracting State;

(e) The term "competent authority" means:

(i) (In State A): ....

(ii) (In State B): ....

2. As regards the application of the Convention by a Contracting State, any term not defined therein shall, unless the context otherwise requires, have the meaning which it has under the law of that State concerning the taxes to which the Convention applies.

Article 4
RESIDENT

1. For the purposes of this Convention,the term "resident of a Contracting State" means any person who, under the laws of that State, is liable to tax therein by reason of his domicile, residence, place of management or any other criterion of a similar nature.

2. Where by reason of the provisions of paragraph 1 an individual is a resident of both Contracting States, then his status shall be determined as follows:

(a) He shall be deemed to be a resident of the State in which he has a permanent home available to him; if he has a permanent home available to him in both States, he shall be deemed to be a resident of the State with which his personal and economic relations are closer (centre of vital interests);

(b) If the State in which he has his centre of vital interests cannot be determined, or if he has not a permanent home available to him in either State, he shall be deemed to be a resident of the State in which he has an habitual abode;

(c) If he has an habitual abode in both States or in neither of them, he shall be deemed to be a resident of the State of which he is a national;

(d) If he is a national of both States or of neither of them, the competent authorities of the Contracting States shall settle the question by mutual agreement.

3. Where by reason of the provisions of paragraph a person other than an individual is a resident of both Contracting States, then it shall be deemed to be a resident of the State in which its place of effective management is situated.

Article 5

PERMANENT ESTABLISHMENT

1. For the purposes of this Convention, the term "permanent establishment" means a fixed place of business through which the business of an enterprise is wholly or partly carried on.

2. The term "permanent establishment" includes especially:

(a) A place of management;
(b) A branch;
(c) An office;
(d) A factory;
(e) A workshop;
(f) A mine, an oil or gas well, a quarry or any other place of extraction of natural resources.

3. The term "permanent establishment" likewise encompasses:

(a) A building site, a construction, assembly or installation project or supervisory activities in connection therewith, but only where such site, project or activities continue for a period of more than six months;

(b) The furnishing of services, including consultancy services, by an enterprise through employees or other personnel engaged by the enterprise for such purpose, but only where activities of that nature continue (for the same or a connected project) within the country for a period or periods aggregating more than six months within any 12-month period.

4. Notwithstanding the preceding provisions of this article, the term "permanent establishment" shall be deemed not to include:

(a) The use of facilities solely for the purpose of storage or display of goods or merchandise belonging to the enterprise;

(b) The maintenance of a stock of goods or merchandise belonging to the enterprise solely for the purpose of storage or display;

(c) The maintenance of a stock of goods or merchandise belonging to the enterprise solely for the purpose of processing by another enterprise;

(d) The maintenance of a fixed place of business solely for the purpose of purchasing goods or merchandise or of collecting information for the enterprise;

(e) The maintenance of a fixed place of business solely for the purpose of carrying on, for the enterprise, any other activity of a preparatory or auxiliary character.

5. Notwithstanding the provisions of paragraphs 1 and 2, where a person -- other than an agent of an independent status to whom paragraph 7 applies -- is acting in a Contracting state on behalf of an enterprise of the other Contracting State, that enterprise shall be deemed to have a permanent establishment in the first-mentioned Contracting State in respect of any activities which that person undertakes for the enterprise, if such a person:

(a) Has and habitually exercises in that State an authority to conclude contracts in the name of the enterprise, unless the activities of such person are limited to those mentioned in paragraph 4 which, if exercised through a fixed place of business, would not make this fixed place of business a permanent establishment under the provisions of that paragraph; or

(b) Has no such authority, but habitually maintains in the first-mentioned State a stock of goods or merchandise from which he regularly delivers goods or merchandise on behalf of the enterprise.

6. Notwithstanding the preceding provisions of this article, an insurance enterprise of a Contracting State shall, except in regard to re-insurance, be deemed to have a permanent establishment in the other Contracting State if it collects premiums in the territory of that other State or insures risks situated therein through a person other than an agent of an independent status to whom paragraph 7 applies.

7. An enterprise of a Contracting State shall not be deemed to have a permanent establishment in the other Contracting State merely because it carries on business in that other

State through a broker, general commission agent or any other agent of an independent status, provided that such persons are acting in the ordinary course of their business. However, when the activities of such an agent are devoted wholly or almost wholly on behalf of that enterprise, he will not be considered an agent of an independent status within the meaning of this paragraph.

8. The fact that a company which is a resident of a Contracting State controls or is controlled by a company which is a resident of the other Contracting State, or which carries on business in that other State (whether through a permanent establishment or otherwise) shall not of itself constitute either company a permanent establishment of the other.

Chapter III
TAXATION OF INCOME

Article 6
INCOME FROM IMMOVABLE PROPERTY

1. Income derived by a resident of a Contracting State from immovable property (including income from agriculture or forestry) situated in the other Contracting State may be taxed in that other State.

2. The term "immovable property" shall have the meaning which it has under the law of the Contracting State in which the property in question is situated. The term shall in any case include property accessory to immovable property, livestock and equipment used in agriculture and forestry, rights to which the provisions of general law respecting landed property apply, usufruct of immovable property and rights to variable or fixed payments as consideration for the working of, or the right to work, mineral deposits, sources and other natural resources; ships, boats and aircraft shall not be regarded as immovable property.

3. The provisions of paragraph 1 shall also apply to income derived from the direct use, letting or use in any other form of immovable property.

4. The provisions of paragraphs 1 and 3 shall also apply to time income from immovable property of an enterprise and to income of immovable property used for the performance of independent personal services.

Article 7
BUSINESS PROFITS

1. The profits of an enterprise of a Contracting State shall be taxable only in that State unless the enterprise carries on business in the other Contracting State through a permanent establishment situated therein. If the enterprise carries on business as aforesaid, the profits of the enterprise may be taxed in the other State but only so much of them as is attributable to (a) that permanent establishment; (b) sales in that other State of goods or merchandise of the same or similar kind as those sold through that permanent establishment; or (c) other business activities

carried on in that other State of the same or similar kind as those effected through that permanent establishment.

2. Subject to the provisions of paragraph 3, where an enterprise of a Contracting State carries on business in the other Contracting State through a permanent establishment situated therein, there shall in each Contracting State be attributed to that permanent establishment time profits which it might be expected to make if it were a distinct and separate enterprise engaged in the same or similar activities under the same or similar conditions and dealing wholly independently with the enterprise of which it is a permanent establishment.

3. In the determination of the profits of a permanent establishment, there shall be allowed as deductions expenses which are incurred for the purposes of the business of the permanent establishment including executive and general administrative expenses so incurred, whether in the State in which the permanent establishment is situated or elsewhere. However, no such deduction shall be allowed in respect of amounts, if any, paid (otherwise than towards reimbursement of actual expenses) by the permanent establishment to the head office of the enterprise or any of its other offices, by way of royalties, fees or other similar payments in return for the use of patents or other rights, or by way of commission, for specific services performed or for management, or, except in the case of a banking enterprise, by way of interest on moneys lent to the permanent establishment. Likewise, no account shall be taken, in the determination of the profits of a permanent establishment, for amounts charged (otherwise than towards reimbursement of actual expenses), by the permanent establishment to the head office of the enterprise or any of its other offices, by way of royalties, fees or other similar payments in return for the use of patents or other rights, or by way of commission for specific services performed or for management, or, except in the case of a banking enterprise by way of interest on moneys lent to the head office of the enterprise or any of its other offices.

4. In so far as it has been customary in a Contracting State to determine the profits to be attributed to a permanent establishment on the basis of an apportionment of the total profits of the enterprise to its various parts, nothing in paragraph 2 shall preclude that Contracting State from determining the profits to be taxed by such an apportionment as may be customary; the method of apportionment adopted shall, however, be such that the result shall be in accordance with the principles contained in this article.

5. For the purposes of the preceding paragraphs, the profits to be attributed to the permanent establishment shall be determined by the same method year by year unless there is good and sufficient reason to the contrary.

6. Where profits include items of income which are dealt with separately in other articles of this Convention, then the provisions of those articles shall not be affected by the provisions of this article.

(NOTE: the question of whether profits should be attributed to a permanent establishment by reason of the mere purchase by that permanent establishment of goods and merchandise for the enterprise was not resolved. It should therefore be settled in bilateral negotiations.)

Article 8
SHIPPING, INLAND WATERWAYS TRANSPORT AND AIR TRANSPORT

Article 8 A (alternative A)

1. Profits from the operation of ships or aircraft in international traffic shall be taxable only in the Contracting State in which the place of effective management of the enterprise is situated.

2. Profits from the operation of boats engaged in inland waterways transport shall be taxable only in the Contracting State in which the place of effective management of the enterprise is situated.

3. If the place of effective management of a shipping enterprise or of an inland waterways transport enterprise is aboard a ship or a boat, then it shall be deemed to be situated in the Contracting State in which the home harbour of the ship or boat situated, or, if there is no such home harbour, in the Contracting State of which the operator of the ship or boat is a resident.

4. The provisions of paragraph 1 shall also apply to profits from the participation in a pool, a joint business or an international operating agency.

Article 8 B (alternative B)

1. Profits from the operation of aircraft in international traffic shall be taxable only in the Contracting State in which the place of effective management of the enterprise is situated.

2. Profits from the operation of ships in international traffic shall be taxable only in the Contracting State in which the place of effective management of the enterprise is situated unless the shipping activities arising from such operation in the other Contracting State are more than casual. If such activities are more than casual, such profits may be taxed in that other State. The profits to be taxed in that other State shall be determined on the basis of an appropriate allocation of the over-all net profits derived by the enterprise from its shipping operations. The tax computed in accordance with such allocation shall then be reduced by ... per cent. (The percentage is to be established through bilateral negotiations.)

3. Profits from the operation of boats engaged in inland waterways transport shall be taxable only in the Contracting State in which the place of effective management of the enterprise is situated.

4. If the place of effective management of a shipping enterprise or of an inland waterways transport enterprise is aboard a ship or boat, then it shall be deemed to be situated in the Contracting State in which the home harbour of the ship or boat is situated, or if there is no such home harbour, in the Contracting State of which the operator of the ship or boat is a resident.

5. The provisions of paragraphs 1 and 2 shall also apply to profits from the participation in a pool, a joint business or an international operating agency.

Article 9
ASSOCIATED ENTERPRISES

1. Where:

(a) An enterprise of a Contracting State participates directly or indirectly in the management, control or capital of an enterprise of the other Contracting State, or

(b) The same persons participate directly or indirectly in management, control or capital of an enterprise of a Contracting State and an enterprise of the other Contracting State,

and in either case conditions are made or imposed between the two enterprises in their commercial or financial relations which differ from those which would be made between independent enterprises, then any profits which would, but for those conditions, have not so accrued, may be included in the profits of that enterprise and taxed accordingly.

2. Where a Contracting State includes in the profits of an enterprise of that State -- and taxes accordingly -- profits on which an enterprise of the other Contracting State has been charged to tax in that other State and the profits so included are profits which would have accrued to the enterprise of the first-mentioned State if the conditions made between the two enterprises had been those which would have been made between independent enterprises, then that other State shall make an appropriate adjustment to the amount of the tax charged therein on those profits. In determining such adjustment, due regard shall be had to the other provisions of the Convention and the competent authorities of the Contracting States shall, if necessary, consult each other.

Article 10
DIVIDENDS

1. Dividends paid by a company which is a resident of a Contracting State to a resident of the other Contracting State may be taxed in that other State.

2. However, such dividends may also be taxed in the Contracting State of which the company paying the dividends is a resident and according to the laws of that State, but if the recipient is the beneficial owner of the dividends the tax so charged shall not exceed:

(a) ... per cent (the percentage is to be established through bilateral negotiations) of the gross amount of the dividends if the beneficial owner is a company (other than a partnership) which holds directly at least 10 per cent of the capital of the company paying the dividends;

(b) ... per cent (the percentage is to be established through bilateral negotiations) of the gross amount of the dividends in all other cases.

The competent authorities of the Contracting States shall by mutual agreement settle the mode of application of these limitations.

This paragraph shall not affect the taxation of the company in respect of the profits out of which the dividends are paid.

3. The term "dividends" as used in this article means income from shares, "jouissance" shares or "jouissance" rights, mining shares, founders' shares or other rights, not being debt-claims, participating in profits, as well as income from other corporate rights which is subjected to the same taxation treatment as income from shares by the laws of the State of which the company making the distribution is a resident.

4. The provisions of paragraphs 1 and 2 shall not apply if the beneficial owner of the dividends, being a resident of a Contracting State, carries on business in the other Contracting State of which the company paying the dividends is a resident, through a permanent establishment situated therein, or performs in that other State independent personal services from a fixed base situated therein, and the holding in respect of which the dividends are paid is effectively connected with such permanent establishment or fixed base. In such case the provisions of article 7 or article 14, as the case may be, shall apply.

5. Where a company which is a resident of a Contracting State derives profits or income from the other Contracting State, that other State may not impose any tax on the dividends paid by the company, except in so far as such dividends are paid to a resident of that other State or in so far as the holding in respect of which the dividends are paid is effectively connected with a permanent establishment or a fixed base situated in that other State, nor subject the company's undistributed profits to a tax on the company's undistributed profits, even if the dividends paid or the undistributed profits consist wholly or partly of profits or income arising in such other State.

Article 11
INTEREST

1. Interest arising in a Contracting State and paid to a resident of the other Contracting State may be taxed in that other State.

2. However, such interest may also be taxed in the Contracting State in which it arises and according to the laws of that State, but if the recipient is the beneficial owner of the interest the tax so charged shall not exceed ... per cent (the percentage is to be established through bilateral negotiations) of the gross amount of the interest. The competent authorities of the Contracting States shall by mutual agreement settle the mode of application of this limitation.

3. The term "interest" as used in this article means income from debt-claims of every kind, whether or not secured by mortgage and whether or not carrying a right to participate in the debtor's profits, and in particular, income from government securities and income from bonds or

debentures, including premiums and prizes attaching to such securities, bonds or debentures. Penalty charges for late payment shall not be regarded as interest for the purpose of this article.

4. The provisions of paragraphs 1 and 2 shall not apply if the beneficial owner of the interest, being a resident of a Contracting State, carries on business in the other Contracting State in which the interest arises, through a permanent establishment situated therein, or performs in that other State independent personal services from a fixed base situated therein, and the debt-claim in respect of which the interest is paid is effectively connected with (a) such permanent establishment or fixed base, or with (b) business activities referred to under (c) of paragraph 1 of article 7. In such cases the provisions of article 7 or article 14, as the case may be, shall apply.

5. Interest shall be deemed to arise in a Contracting State when the payer is that State itself, a political subdivision, a local authority or a resident of that State. Where, however, the person paying the interest, whether he is a resident of a Contracting State or not, has in a Contracting State a permanent establishment or a fixed base in connexion with which the indebtedness on which the interest is paid was incurred, and such interest is borne by such permanent establishment or fixed base, then such interest shall be deemed to arise in the State in which the permanent establishment or fixed base is situated.

6. Where by reason of a special relationship between the payer and the beneficial owner or between both of them and some other person, the amount of the interest, having regard to the debt-claim for which it is paid, exceeds the amount which would have been agreed upon by the payer and the beneficial owner in the absence of such relationship, the provisions of this article shall apply only to the last-mentioned amount. In such case, the excess part of the payments shall remain taxable according to the laws of each Contracting State, due regard being had to the other provisions of this Convention.

Article 12
ROYALTIES

1. Royalties arising in a Contracting State and paid to a resident of the other Contracting State may be taxed in that other State.

2. However, such royalties may also be taxed in the Contracting State in which they arise and according to the laws of that State, but if the recipient is the beneficial owner of the royalties, the tax so charged shall not exceed ... per cent (the percentage is to be established through bilateral negotiations) of the gross amount of the royalties. The competent authorities of the Contracting States shall by mutual agreement settle the mode of application of this limitation.

3. The term "royalties" as used in this article means payments of any kind received as a consideration for the use of, or the right to use, any copyright of literary, artistic or scientific work including cinematograph films, or films or tapes used for radio or television broadcasting, any patent, trade mark, design or model, plan, secret formula or process, or for the use of, or the

right to use, industrial, commercial, or scientific equipment, or for information concerning industrial, commercial or scientific experience.

4. The provisions of paragraphs 1 and 2 shall not apply if the beneficial owner of the royalties, being a resident of a Contracting State, carries on business in the other Contracting State in which the royalties arise, through a permanent establishment situated therein, or performs in that other State independent personal services from a fixed base situated therein, and the right or property in respect of which the royalties are paid is effectively connected with (a) such permanent establishment or fixed base, or with (b) business activities referred to under (c) of paragraph 1 of article 7. In such cases the provisions of article 7 or article 14, as the case may be, shall apply.

5. Royalties shall be deemed to arise in a Contracting State when the payer is that State itself, a political subdivision, a local authority or a resident of that State. Where, however, the person paying the royalties, whether he is a resident of a Contracting State or not, has in a Contracting State a permanent establishment or a fixed base in connexion with which the liability to pay the royalties was incurred, and such royalties are borne by such permanent establishment or fixed base, then such royalties shall be deemed to arise in the State in which the permanent establishment or fixed base is situated.

6. Where by reason of a special relationship between the payer and the beneficial owner or between both of them and some other person, the amount of the royalties, having regard to the use, right or information for which they are paid, exceeds the amount which would have been agreed upon by the payer and the beneficial owner in the absence of such relationship, the provisions of this article shall apply only to the last-mentioned amount. In such case, the excess part of the payments shall remain taxable according to the laws of each Contracting State, due regard being had to the other provisions of this Convention.

Article 13
CAPITAL GAINS

1. Gains derived by a resident of a Contracting State from the alienation of immovable property referred to in article 6 and situated in the other Contracting State may be taxed in that other State.

2. Gains from the alienation of immovable property forming part of the business property of a permanent establishment which an enterprise of a Contracting State has in the other Contracting State or of movable property pertaining to a fixed base available to a resident of a Contracting State in the other Contracting State for the purpose of performing independent personal services, including such gains from the alienation of such a permanent establishment (alone or with the whole enterprise) or of such fixed base, may be taxed in that other State.

3. Gains from the alienation of ships or aircraft operated in international traffic, boats engaged in inland waterways transport or movable property pertaining to the operation of such

ships, aircraft or boats, shall be taxable only in the Contracting State in which the place of effective management of the enterprise is situated.

4. Gains from the alienation of shares of the capital stock of a company the property of which consists directly or indirectly principally of immovable property situated in a Contracting State may be taxed in that State.

5. Gains from the alienation of shares other than those mentioned in paragraph 4 representing a participation of ... per cent (the percentage is to be established through bilateral negotiations) in a company which is a resident of a Contracting State may be taxed in that State.

6. Gains from the alienation of any property other than that referred to in paragraphs 1, 2, 3, 4 and 5 shall be taxable only in the Contracting State of which the alienator is a resident.

Article 14

INDEPENDENT PERSONAL SERVICES

1. Income derived by a resident of a Contracting State in respect of professional services or other activities of an independent character shall be taxable only in that State except in the following circumstances, when such income may also be taxed in the other Contracting State:

(a) If he has a fixed base regularly available to him in the other Contracting State for the purpose of performing his activities; in that case, only so much of the income as is attributable to that fixed base may be taxed in that other Contracting State; or

(b) If his stay in the other Contracting State is for a period or periods amounting to or exceeding in the aggregate 183 days in the fiscal year concerned; in that case, only so much of the income as is derived from his activities performed in that other State may be taxed in that other State; or

(c) If the remuneration for his activities in the other Contracting State is paid by a resident of that Contracting State or is borne by a permanent establishment or a fixed base situated in that Contracting State and exceeds in the fiscal year ... (the amount is to be established through bilateral negotiations).

2. The term "professional services" includes especially independent scientific, literary, artistic, educational or teaching activities as well as the independent activities of physicians, lawyers, engineers, architects, dentists and accountants.

Article 15

DEPENDENT PERSONAL SERVICES

1. Subject to the provisions of articles 16, 18 and 19, salaries, wages and other similar remuneration derived by a resident of a Contracting State in respect of an employment shall be

taxable only in that State unless the employment is exercised in the other Contracting State. If the employment is so exercised, such remuneration as is derived therefrom may be taxed in that other State.

2. Notwithstanding the provisions of paragraph 1, remuneration derived by a resident of a Contracting State in respect of an employment exercised in the other Contracting State shall be taxable only in the first-mentioned State if:

(a) The recipient is present in the other State for a period or periods not exceeding in the aggregate 183 days in the fiscal year concerned; and

(b) The remuneration is paid by, or on behalf of, an employer who is not a resident of the other State; and

(c) The remuneration is not borne by a permanent establishment or a fixed base which the employer has in the other State.

3. Notwithstanding the preceding provisions of this article, remuneration derived in respect of an employment exercised aboard a ship or aircraft operated in international traffic, or aboard a boat engaged in inland waterways transport, may be taxed in the Contracting State in which the place of effective management of the enterprise is situated.

Article 16
DIRECTORS' FEES AND REMUNERATION OF TOP-LEVEL MANAGERIAL OFFICIALS

1. Directors' fees and other similar payments derived by a resident of a Contracting State in his capacity as a member of the Board of Directors of a company which is a resident of the other Contracting State may be taxed in that other State.

2. Salaries, wages and other similar remuneration derived by a resident of a Contracting State in his capacity as an official in a top-level managerial position of a company which is a resident of the other Contracting State may be taxed in that other State.

Article 17
INCOME EARNED BY ENTERTAINERS AND ATHLETES

1. Notwithstanding the provisions of articles 14 and 15, income derived by a resident of a Contracting State as an entertainer, such as a theatre, motion picture, radio or television artiste, or a musician, or as an athlete, from his personal activities as such exercised in the other Contracting State, may be taxed in that other State.

2. Where income in respect of personal activities exercised by an entertainer or an athlete in his capacity as such accrues not to the entertainer or athlete himself but to another person, that

income may, notwithstanding the provisions of articles 7, 14 and 15, be taxed in the Contracting State in which the activities of the entertainer or athlete are exercised.

Article 18
PENSIONS AND SOCIAL SECURITY PAYMENTS

Article 18 A (alterative A)

1. Subject to the provisions of paragraph 2 of Article 19, pensions and other similar remuneration paid to a resident of a Contracting State in consideration of past employment shall be taxable only in that State.

2. Notwithstanding the provisions of paragraph 1, pensions paid and other payments made under a public scheme which is part of the social security system of a Contracting State or a political subdivision or a local authority thereof shall be taxable only in that State.

Article 18 B (alternative B)

1. Subject to the provisions of paragraph 2 of article 19, pensions and other similar remuneration paid to a resident of a Contracting State in consideration of past employment may be taxed in that State.

2. However, such pensions and other similar remuneration may also be taxed in the other Contracting State if the payment is made by a resident of that other State or a permanent establishment situated therein.

3. Notwithstanding the provisions of paragraphs 1 and 2, pensions paid and other payments made under a public scheme which is part of the social security system of a Contracting State or a political subdivision or a local authority thereof shall be taxable only in that State.

Article 19
REMUNERATION AND PENSIONS IN RESPECT OF GOVERNMENT SERVICE

1. (a) Remuneration, other than a pension, paid by a Contracting State or a political subdivision or a local authority thereof to an individual in respect of services rendered to that State or subdivision or authority shall be taxable in that State.

(b) However, such remuneration shall be taxable only in the other Contracting State if the services are rendered in that other State and the individual is a resident of that State who:

(i) Is a national of that State; or

(ii) Did not become a resident of that State solely for the purpose of rendering the services.

2. (a) Any pension paid by, or out of funds created by, a Contracting State or a political subdivision or a local authority thereof to an individual in respect of services rendered to that State or subdivision or authority shall be taxable only in that State.

(b) However, such pension shall be taxable only in the other Contracting State if the individual is a resident of, and a national of, that other State.

3. The provisions of articles 15, 16 and 18 shall apply to remuneration and pensions in respect of services rendered in connexion with a business carried on by a Contracting State or a political subdivision or a local authority thereof.

Article 20
PAYMENTS RECEIVED BY STUDENTS AND APPRENTICES

1. Payments which a student or business apprentice who is or was immediately before visiting a Contracting State a resident of the other Contracting State and who is present in the first-mentioned State solely for the purpose of his education or training receives for the purpose of his maintenance, education or training shall not be taxed in that State, provided that such payments arise from sources outside that State.

2. In respect of grants, scholarships and remuneration from employment not covered by paragraph 1, a student or business apprentice described in paragraph 1 shall, in addition, be entitled during such education or training to the same exemptions, reliefs or reductions in respect of taxes available to residents of the State which he is visiting.

Article 21
OTHER INCOME

1. Items of income of a resident of a Contracting State, wherever arising, not dealt with in the foregoing articles of this Convention shall be taxable only in that State.

2. The provisions of paragraph 1 shall not apply to income, other than income from immovable property as defined in paragraph 2 of article 6, if the recipient of such income, being a resident of a Contracting State, carries on business in the other Contracting State through a permanent establishment situated therein, or performs in that other State independent personal services from a fixed base situated therein, and the right or property in respect of which the income is paid is effectively connected with such permanent establishment or fixed base. In such case the provisions of article 7 or article 14, as the case may be, shall apply.

3. Notwithstanding the provisions of paragraphs 1 and 2, items of income of a resident of a Contracting State not dealt with in the foregoing articles of this Convention and arising in the other Contracting State may also be taxed in that other State.

Chapter IV
TAXATION OF CAPITAL

Article 22
CAPITAL

1. [Capital represented by immovable property referred to in article 6, owned by a resident of a Contracting State and situated in the other Contracting State, may be taxed in that other State.]

2. [Capital represented by movable property forming part of the business property of a permanent establishment which an enterprise of a Contracting State has in the other Contracting State or by movable property pertaining to a fixed base available to a resident of a Contracting State in the other Contracting State for the purpose of performing independent personal services, may be taxed in that other State.]

3. [Capital represented by ships and aircraft operated in international traffic and by boats engaged in inland waterways transport, and by movable property pertaining to the operation of such ships, aircraft and boats, shall be taxable only in the Contracting State in which the place of effective management of the enterprise is situated.]

4. [All other elements of capital of a resident of a Contracting State shall be taxable only in that State.]

(The Group decided to leave to bilateral negotiations the question of the taxation of the capital represented by immovable property and movable property and of all other elements of capital of a resident of a Contracting State. Should the negotiating parties decide to include in the Convention an article on the taxation of capital, they will have to determine whether to use the wording of paragraph 4 as shown or wording that leaves taxation to the State in which the capital is located.)

Chapter V
METHODS FOR THE ELIMINATION OF DOUBLE TAXATION

Article 23 A
EXEMPTION METHOD

1. Where a resident of a Contracting State derives income [or owns capital] which, in accordance with the provisions of this Convention, may be taxed in the other Contracting State, the first-mentioned State shall, subject to the provisions of paragraphs 2 and 3, exempt such income [or capital] from tax.

2. Where a resident of a Contracting State derives items of income which, in accordance with the provisions of articles 10, 11 and 12, may be taxed in the other Contracting State, the

first-mentioned State shall allow as a deduction from the tax on the income of that resident an amount equal to the tax paid in that other State. Such deduction shall not, however, exceed that part of the tax, as computed before the deduction is given, which is attributable to such items of income derived from that other State.

3. Where in accordance with any provision of this Convention income derived [or capital owned] by a resident of a Contracting State is exempt from tax in that State, such State may nevertheless, in calculating the amount of tax on the remaining income [or capital] of such resident, take into account the exempted income [or capital].

Article 23 B

CREDIT METHOD

1. Where a resident of a Contracting State derives income [or owns capital] which, in accordance with the provisions of this Convention, may be taxed in the other Contracting State, the first-mentioned State shall allow as a deduction from the tax on the income of that resident an amount equal to the income tax paid in that other State]; and as a deduction from the tax on the capital of that resident, an amount equal to the capital tax paid in that other State]. Such deduction [in either case] shall not, however, exceed that part of the income tax [or capital tax,] as computed before the deduction is given, which is attributable, as the case may be, to the income [or the capital] which may be taxed in that other State.

2. Where, in accordance with any provision of this Convention, income derived [or capital owned] by a resident of a Contracting State is exempt form tax in that State, such State may nevertheless, in calculating the amount of tax on the remaining income [or capital] of such resident, take into account the exempted income [or capital].

Chapter VI
SPECIAL PROVISIONS

Article 24

NON-DISCRIMINATION

1. Nationals of a Contracting State shall not be subjected in the other Contracting State to any taxation or any requirement connected therewith which is other or more burdensome than the taxation and connected requirements to which nationals of that other State in the same circumstances are or may be subjected. This provision shall, notwithstanding the provisions of article 1, also apply to persons who are not residents of one or both of the Contracting States.

2. The term "nationals" means:

(a) All individuals possessing the nationality of a Contracting State;

(b) All legal persons, partnerships and associations deriving their status as such from the laws in force in a Contracting State.

3. Stateless persons who are residents of a Contracting State shall not be subjected in either Contracting State to any taxation or any requirement connected therewith which is other or more burdensome than the taxation and connected requirements to which nationals of the State concerned in the same circumstances are or may be subjected.

4. The taxation on a permanent establishment which an enterprise of a Contracting State has in the other Contracting State shall not be less favourably levied in that other State than the taxation levied on enterprises of that other State carrying on the same activities. This provision shall not be construed as obliging a Contracting State to grant to residents of the other Contracting State any personal allowances, reliefs and reductions for taxation purposes on account of civil status or family responsibilities which it grants to its own residents.

5. Except where the provisions of paragraph 1 of article 9, paragraph 6 of article 11, or paragraph 6 of article 12 apply, interest, royalties and other disbursements paid by an enterprise of a Contracting State to a resident of the other Contracting State shall, for the purpose of determining the taxable profits of such enterprise, be deductible under the same conditions as if they had been paid to a resident of the first-mentioned State. [Similarly, any debts of an enterprise of a Contracting State to a resident of the other Contracting State shall, for the purpose of determining the taxable capital of such enterprise, be deductible under the same conditions as if they had been contracted to a resident of the first-mentioned State.]

6. Enterprises of a Contracting State, the capital of which is wholly or partly owned or controlled, directly or indirectly, by one or more residents of the other Contracting State, shall not be subjected in the first-mentioned State to any taxation or any requirement connected therewith which is other or more burdensome than the taxation and connected requirements to which other similar enterprises of the first-mentioned State are or may be subjected.

7. The provisions of this article shall, notwithstanding the provisions of article 2, apply to taxes of every kind and description.

Article 25
MUTUAL AGREEMENT PROCEDURE

1. Where a person considers that the actions of one or both of the Contracting States result or will result for him in taxation not in accordance with the provisions of this Convention, he may, irrespective of the remedies provided by the domestic law of those States, present his case to the competent authority of the Contracting State of which he is a resident or, if his case comes under paragraph 1 of article 24, to that of the Contracting State of which he is a national. The case must be presented within three years from the first notification of the action resulting in taxation not in accordance with the provisions of the Convention.

2. The competent authority shall endeavour, if the objection appears to it to be justified and if it is not itself able to arrive at a satisfactory solution, to resolve the case by mutual agreement with the competent authority of the other Contracting State, with a view to the avoidance of taxation which is not in accordance with this Convention. Any agreement reached shall be implemented notwithstanding any time-limits in the domestic law of the Contracting States.

3. The competent authorities of the Contracting States shall endeavour to resolve by mutual agreement any difficulties or doubts arising as to the interpretation or application of the Convention. They may also consult together for the elimination of double taxation in cases not provided for in the Convention.

4. The competent authorities of the Contracting States may communicate with each other directly for the purpose of reaching an agreement in the sense of the preceding paragraphs. The competent authorities, through consultations, shall develop appropriate bilateral procedures, conditions, methods and techniques for the implementation of the mutual agreement procedure provided for in this article. In addition, a competent authority may devise appropriate unilateral procedures, conditions, methods and techniques to facilitate the above-mentioned bilateral actions and the implementation of the mutual agreement procedure.

Article 26
EXCHANGE OF INFORMATION

1. The competent authorities of the Contracting States shall exchange such information as is necessary for carrying out the provisions of this Convention or of the domestic laws of the Contracting States concerning taxes covered by the Convention, in so far as the taxation thereunder is not contrary to the Convention, in particular for the prevention of fraud or evasion of such taxes. The exchange of information is not restricted by article 1. Any information received by a Contracting State shall be treated as secret in the same manner as information obtained under the domestic laws of that State. However, if the information is originally regarded as secret in the transmitting State it shall be disclosed only to persons or authorities (including courts and administrative bodies) involved in the assessment or collection of, the enforcement or prosecution in respect of, or the determination of appeals in relation to, the taxes which are the subject of the Convention. Such persons or authorities shall use the information only for such purposes but may disclose the information in public court proceedings or in judicial decisions. The competent authorities shall, through consultation, develop appropriate conditions, methods and techniques concerning the matters in respect of which such exchanges of information shall be made, including, where appropriate, exchanges of information regarding tax avoidance.

2. In no case shall the provisions of paragraph 1 be construed so as to impose on a Contracting State the obligation:

(a) To carry out administrative measures at variance with the laws and administrative practice of that or of the other Contracting State;

(b) To supply information which is not obtainable under the laws or of the normal course of the administration of that or of the other Contracting State;

(c) To supply information which would disclose any trade, business, industrial, commercial or professional secret or trade process, or information, the disclosure of which would be contrary to public policy (ordre public).

Article 27
DIPLOMATIC AGENTS AND CONSULAR OFFICERS

Nothing in this Convention shall affect the fiscal privileges of diplomatic agents or consular officers under the general rules of international law or under the provisions of special agreements.

Chapter VII
FINAL PROVISIONS

Article 28
ENTRY INTO FORCE

1. This Convention shall be ratified and the instruments of ratification shall be exchanged at .... as soon as possible.

2. The Convention shall enter into force upon the exchange of instruments of ratification and its provisions shall have effect:

(a) (In State A): ....

(b) (In State B): ....

Article 29
TERMINATION

This Convention shall remain in force until terminated by a Contracting State. Either Contracting State may terminate the Convention, through diplomatic channels, by giving notice of termination at least six months before the end of any calendar year after the year .... In such event, the Convention shall cease to have effect:

(a) (In State A): ....

(b) (In State B): ....

TERMINAL CLAUSE

NOTE: The provisions relating to the entry into force and termination and the terminal clause concerning the signing of the Convention shall be drafted in accordance with the constitutional procedure of both Contracting States.

* * *

THE SET OF MULTILATERALLY AGREED EQUITABLE PRINCIPLES AND RULES FOR THE CONTROL OF RESTRICTIVE BUSINESS PRACTICES*[1] AND RESOLUTION ADOPTED BY THE CONFERENCE STRENGTHENING THE IMPLEMENTATION OF THE SET**

The Set of Multilaterally Agreed Equitable Principles and Rules for the Control of Restrictive Business Practices was adopted by the United Nations General Assembly at its thirty-fifth session on 5 December 1980 by its resolution 35/63. The Second United Nations Conference to Review all Aspects of the Multilaterally Agreed Equitable Principles and Rules for the Control of Restrictive Business Practices was held in Geneva from 26 November to 7 December 1990. That Conference adopted a resolution on "Strengthening the implementation of the Set" at its sixth meeting on 7 December 1990. A Third Review Conference took place on 13-21 November 1995. This Conference adopted a resolution calling for a number of concrete actions to give effect to the implementation of the Set.

THE SET OF MULTILATERALLY AGREED EQUITABLE PRINCIPLES AND RULES FOR THE CONTROL OF RESTRICTIVE BUSINESS PRACTICES

The United Nations Conference on Restrictive Business Practices,

Recognizing that restrictive business practices can adversely affect international trade, particularly that of developing countries, and the economic development of these countries,

Affirming that a set of multilaterally agreed equitable principles and rules for the control of restrictive business practices can contribute to attaining the objective in the establishment of a new international economic order to eliminate restrictive business practices adversely affecting

---

*<u>Source</u>: United Nations Conference on Trade and Development (1981). *The Set of Multilaterally Agreed Equitable Principles and Rules for the Control of Restrictive Business Practices*, United Nations document TD/RBP/CONF/10/Rev.1 (New York: United Nations) [Note added by the editor].

[1] The Set of Principles and Rules was adopted by the United Nations Conference on Restrictive Business Practices as an annex to its resolution of 22 April 1980.

**<u>Source</u>: United Nations Conference on Trade and Development (1991). "Resolution Adopted by the Conference Strengthening the Implementation of the Set", *Report of the Second United Nations Conference to Review all Aspects of the Multilaterally Agreed Equitable Principles and Rules for the Control of Restrictive Business Practices*, United Nations document TD/RBP/CONF.3/9 (Geneva: United Nations), Annex, pp.48-51 [Note added by the editor].

international trade and thereby contribute to development and improvement of international economic relations on a just and equitable basis,

Recognizing also the need to ensure that restrictive business practices do not impede or negate the realization of benefits that should arise from the liberalization of tariff and non-tariff barriers affecting international trade, particularly those affecting the trade and development of developing countries,

Considering the possible adverse impact of restrictive business practices, including among others those resulting from the increased activities of transnational corporations, on the trade and development of developing countries,

Convinced of the need for action to be taken by countries in a mutually reinforcing manner at the national, regional and international levels to eliminate or effectively deal with restrictive business practices, including those of transnational corporations, adversely affecting international trade, particularly that of developing countries, and the economic development of these countries,

Convinced also of the benefits to be derived from a universally applicable set of multilaterally agreed equitable principles and rules for the control of restrictive business practices and that all countries should encourage their enterprises to follow in all respects the provisions of such a set of multilaterally agreed equitable principles and rules,

Convinced further that the adoption of such a set of multilaterally agreed equitable principles and rules for the control of restrictive business practices will thereby facilitate the adoption and strengthening of laws and policies in the area of restrictive business practices at the national and regional levels and thus lead to improved conditions and attain greater efficiency and participation in international trade and development, particularly that of developing countries, and to protect and promote social welfare in general, and in particular the interests of consumers in both developed and developing countries,

Affirming also the need to eliminate the disadvantages to trade and development which may result from the restrictive business practices of transnational corporations or other enterprises, and thus help to maximize benefits to international trade and particularly the trade and development of developing countries,

Affirming further the need that measures adopted by the States for the control of restrictive business practices should be applied fairly, equitably, on the same basis to all enterprises and in accordance with established procedures of law; and for States to take into account the principles and objectives of the Set of Multilaterally Agreed Equitable Principles and Rules,

Hereby agrees on the following Set of Principles and Rules for the control of restrictive business practices, which take the form of recommendations:

A. Objectives

Taking into account the interests of all countries, particularly those of developing countries, the Set of Multilaterally Agreed Equitable Principles and Rules are framed in order to achieve the following objectives:

1. To ensure that restrictive business practices do not impede or negate the realization of benefits that should arise from the liberalization of tariff and non-tariff barriers affecting world trade, particularly those affecting the trade and development of developing countries;

2. To attain greater efficiency in international trade and development, particularly that of developing countries, in accordance with national aims of economic and social development and existing economic structures, such as through:

(a) The creation, encouragement and protection of competition;

(b) Control of the concentration of capital and/or economic power;

(c) Encouragement of innovation;

3. To protect and promote social welfare in general and, in particular, the interests of consumers in both developed and developing countries;

4. To eliminate the disadvantages to trade and development which may result from the restrictive business practices of transnational corporations or other enterprises, and thus help to maximize benefits to international trade and particularly the trade and development of developing countries;

5. To provide a Set of Multilaterally Agreed Equitable Principles and Rules for the control of restrictive business practices for adoption at the international level and thereby to facilitate the adoption and strengthening of laws and policies in this area at the national and regional levels.

B. Definitions and scope of application

For the purpose of this Set of Multilaterally Agreed Equitable Principles and Rules:

(i) Definitions

1. Restrictive business practices means acts or behaviour of enterprises which, through an abuse or acquisition and abuse of a dominant position of market power, limit access to markets or otherwise unduly restrain competition, having or being likely to have adverse effects on international trade, particularly that of developing countries, and on the economic development of these countries, or which through formal, informal, written or unwritten agreements or arrangements among enterprises, have the same impact.

2. Dominant position of market power refers to a situation where an enterprise, either by itself or acting together with a few other enterprises, is in a position to control the relevant market for a particular good or service or group of goods or services.

3. Enterprises means firms, partnerships, corporations, companies, other associations, natural or juridical persons, or any combination thereof, irrespective of the mode of creation or control or ownership, private or State, which are engaged in commercial activities, and includes their branches, subsidiaries, affiliates, or other entities directly or indirectly controlled by them.

(ii) Scope of application

4. The Set of Principles and Rules applies to restrictive business practices, including those of transnational corporations, adversely affecting international trade, particularly that of developing countries and the economic development of these countries. It applies irrespective of whether such practices involve enterprises in one or more countries.

5. The "principles and rules for enterprises, including transnational corporations" apply to all transactions in goods and services.

6. The "principles and rules for enterprises, including transnational corporations" are addressed to all enterprises.

7. The provisions of the Set of Principles and Rules shall be universally applicable to all countries and enterprises regardless of the parties involved in the transactions, acts or behaviour.

8. Any reference to "States" or "Governments" shall be construed as including any regional groupings of States, to the extent that they have competence in the area of restrictive business practices.

9. The Set of Principles and Rules shall not apply to intergovernmental agreements, nor to restrictive business practices directly caused by such agreements.

C. Multilaterally agreed equitable principles for the control of restrictive business practices

In line with the objectives set forth, the following principles are to apply:

(i) General principles

1. Appropriate action should be taken in a mutually reinforcing manner at national, regional and international levels to eliminate, or effectively deal with, restrictive business practices, including those of transnational corporations, adversely affecting international trade, particularly that of developing countries and the economic development of these countries.

2. Collaboration between Governments at bilateral and multilateral levels should be established and, where such collaboration has been established, it should be improved to facilitate the control of restrictive business practices.

3. Appropriate mechanisms should be devised at the international level and/or the use of existing international machinery improved to facilitate exchange and dissemination of information among Governments with respect to restrictive business practices.

4. Appropriate means should be devised to facilitate the holding of multilateral consultations with regard to policy issues relating to the control of restrictive business practices.

5. The provisions of the Set of Principles and Rules should not be construed as justifying conduct by enterprises which is unlawful under applicable national or regional legislation.

(ii) Relevant factors in the application of the Set of Principles and Rules

6. In order to ensure the fair and equitable application of the Set of Principles and Rules, States, while bearing in mind the need to ensure the comprehensive application of the Set of Principles and Rules, should take due account of the extent to which the conduct of enterprises, whether or not created or controlled by States, is accepted under applicable legislation or regulations, bearing in mind that such laws and regulations should be clearly defined and publicly and readily available, or is required by States.

(iii) Preferential or differential treatment for developing countries

7. In order to ensure the equitable application of the Set of Principles and Rules, States, particularly developed countries, should take into account in their control of restrictive business practices the development, financial and trade needs of developing countries, in particular of the least developed countries, for the purposes especially of developing countries in:

(a) Promoting the establishment or development of domestic industries and the economic development of other sectors of the economy, and

(b) Encouraging their economic development through regional or global arrangements among developing countries.

D. Principles and rules for enterprises, including transnational corporations

1. Enterprises should conform to the restrictive business practices laws, and the provisions concerning restrictive business practices in other laws, of the countries in which they operate, and, in the event of proceedings under these laws, should be subject to the competence of the courts and relevant administrative bodies therein.

2. Enterprises should consult and co-operate with competent authorities of countries directly affected in controlling restrictive business practices adversely affecting the interests of those countries. In this regard, enterprises should also provide information, in particular details of restrictive arrangements, required for this purpose, including that which may be located in foreign countries, to the extent that in the latter event such production or disclosure is not prevented by applicable law or established public policy. Whenever the provision of information is on a voluntary basis, its provision should be in accordance with safeguards normally applicable in this field.

3. Enterprises, except when dealing with each other in the context of an economic entity wherein they are under common control, including through ownership, or otherwise not able to act independently of each other, engaged on the market in rival or potentially rival activities, should refrain from practices such as the following when, through formal, informal, written or unwritten agreements or arrangements, they limit access to markets or otherwise unduly restrain competition, having or being likely to have adverse effects on international trade, particularly that of developing countries, and on the economic development of these countries:

(a) Agreements fixing prices, including as to exports and imports;

(b) Collusive tendering;

(c) Market or customer allocation arrangements;

(d) Allocation by quota to sales and production;

(e) Collective action to enforce arrangements, e.g. by concerted refusals to deal;

(f) Concerted refusal of supplies to potential importers;

(g) Collective denial of access to an arrangement, or association, which is crucial to competition.

4. Enterprises should refrain from the following acts or behaviour in a relevant market when, through an abuse* or acquisition and abuse of a dominant position of market

*Whether acts or behaviour are abusive or not should be examined in terms of their purpose and effects in the actual situation, in particular with reference to whether they limit access to markets or otherwise unduly restrain competition, having or being likely to have adverse effects on international trade, particularly that of developing countries, and on the economic development of these countries, and to whether they are:

(a) Appropriate in the light of the organizational, managerial and legal relationship among the enterprises concerned, such as in the context of relations within an economic entity and not having restrictive effects outside the related enterprises;

power, they limit access to markets or otherwise unduly restrain competition, having or being likely to have adverse effects on international trade, particularly that of developing countries, and on the economic development of these countries:

(a) Predatory behaviour towards competitors, such as using below-cost pricing to eliminate competitors;

(b) Discriminatory (i.e. unjustifiably differentiated) pricing or terms or conditions in the supply or purchase of goods or services, including by means of the use of pricing policies in transactions between affiliated enterprises which overcharge or undercharge for goods or services purchased or supplied as compared with prices for similar or comparable transactions outside the affiliated enterprises;

(c) Mergers, takeovers, joint ventures or other acquisitions of control, whether of a horizontal, vertical or a conglomerate nature;

(d) Fixing the prices at which goods exported can be resold in importing countries;

(e) Restrictions on the importation of goods which have been legitimately marked abroad with a trademark identical with or similar to the trademark protected as to identical or similar goods in the importing country where the trademarks in question are of the same origin, i.e. belong to the same owner or are used by enterprises between which there is economic, organizational, managerial or legal interdependence and where the purpose of such restrictions is to maintain artificially high prices;

(f) When not for ensuring the achievement of legitimate business purposes, such as quality, safety, adequate distribution or service:

(i) Partial or complete refusals to deal on the enterprise's customary commercial terms;

(ii) Making the supply of particular goods or services dependent upon the acceptance of restrictions on the distribution or manufacture of competing or other goods;

(b) Appropriate in light of special conditions or economic circumstances in the relevant market such as exceptional conditions of supply and demand or the size of the market;

(c) Of types which are usually treated as acceptable under pertinent national or regional laws and regulations for the control of restrictive business practices;

(d) Consistent with the purposes and objectives of these principles and rules.

(iii) Imposing restrictions concerning where, or to whom, or in what form or quantities, goods supplied or other goods may be resold or exported;

(iv) Making the supply of particular goods or services dependent upon the purchase of other goods or services from the supplier or his designee.

E. Principles and rules for States at national, regionaland subregional levels

1. States should, at the national level or through regional groupings, adopt, improve and effectively enforce appropriate legislation and implementing judicial and administrative procedures for the control of restrictive business practices, including those of transnational corporations.

2. States should base their legislation primarily on the principle of eliminating or effectively dealing with acts or behaviour of enterprises which, through an abuse or acquisition and abuse of a dominant position of market power, limit access to markets or otherwise unduly restrain competition, having or being likely to have adverse effects on their trade or economic development, or which through formal, informal, written or unwritten agreements or arrangements among enterprises have the same impact.

3. States, in their control of restrictive business practices, should ensure treatment of enterprises which is fair, equitable, on the same basis to all enterprises, and in accordance with established procedures of law. The laws and regulations should be publicly and readily available.

4. States should seek appropriate remedial or preventive measures to prevent and/or control the use of restrictive business practices within their competence when it comes to the attention of States that such practices adversely affect international trade, and particularly the trade and development of the developing countries.

5. Where, for the purposes of the control of restrictive business practices, a State obtains information from enterprises containing legitimate business secrets, it should accord such information reasonable safeguards normally applicable in this field, particularly to protect its confidentiality.

6. States should institute or improve procedures for obtaining information from enterprises, including transnational corporations, necessary for their effective control of restrictive business practices, including in this respect details of restrictive agreements, undertakings and other arrangements.

7. States should establish appropriate mechanisms at the regional and subregional levels to promote exchange of information on restrictive business practices and on the application of national laws and policies in this area, and to assist each other to their mutual advantage regarding control of restrictive business practices at the regional and subregional levels.

8. States with greater expertise in the operation of systems for the control of restrictive business practices should, on request, share their experience with, or otherwise provide technical assistance to, other States wishing to develop or improve such systems.

9. States should, on request, or at their own initiative when the need comes to their attention, supply to other States, particularly developing countries, publicly available information and, to the extent consistent with their laws and established public policy, other information necessary to the receiving interested State for its effective control of restrictive business practices.

F. International measures

Collaboration at the international level should aim at eliminating or effectively dealing with restrictive business practices, including those of transnational corporations, through strengthening and improving controls over restrictive business practices adversely affecting international trade, particularly that of developing countries, and the economic development of these countries. In this regard, action should include:

1. Work aimed at achieving common approaches in national policies relating to restrictive business practices compatible with the Set of Principles and Rules.

2. Communication annually to the Secretary-General of UNCTAD of appropriate information on steps taken by States and regional groupings to meet their commitment to the Set of Principles and Rules, and information on the adoption, development and application of legislation, regulations and policies concerning restrictive business practices.

3. Continued publication annually by UNCTAD of a report on developments in restrictive business practices legislation and on restrictive business practices adversely affecting international trade, particularly the trade and development of developing countries, based upon publicly available information and as far as possible other information, particularly on the basis of requests addressed to all member States or provided at their own initiative and, where appropriate, to the United Nations Centre on Transnational Corporations and other competent international organizations.

4. Consultations:

(a) Where a State, particularly of a developing country, believes that a consultation with another State or States is appropriate in regard to an issue concerning control of restrictive business practices, it may request a consultation with those States with a view to finding a mutually acceptable solution. When a consultation is held, the States involved may request the Secretary-General of UNCTAD to provide mutually agreed conference facilities for such a consultation;

(b) States should accord full consideration to requests for consultations and, upon agreement as to the subject of and the procedures for such a consultation, the consultation should take place at an appropriate time;

(c) If the States involved so agree, a joint report on the consultations and their results should be prepared by the States involved and, if they so wish, with the assistance of the UNCTAD secretariat, and be made available to the Secretary-General of UNCTAD for inclusion in the annual report on restrictive business practices.

5. Continued work within UNCTAD on the elaboration of a model law or laws on restrictive business practices in order to assist developing countries in devising appropriate legislation. States should provide necessary information and experience to UNCTAD in this connection.

6. Implementation within or facilitation by UNCTAD, and other relevant organizations of the United Nations system in conjunction with UNCTAD, of technical assistance, advisory and training programmes on restrictive business practices, particularly for developing countries:

(a) Experts should be provided to assist developing countries, at their request, in formulating or improving restrictive business practices legislation and procedures;

(b) Seminars, training programmes or courses should be held, primarily in developing countries, to train officials involved or likely to be involved in administering restrictive business practices legislation and, in this connection, advantage should be taken, *inter alia*, of the experience and knowledge of administrative authorities, especially in developed countries, in detecting the use of restrictive business practices;

(c) A handbook on restrictive business practices should be compiled;

(d) Relevant books, documents, manuals and any other information on matters related to restrictive business practices should be collected and made available, particularly to developing countries;

(e) Exchange of personnel between restrictive business practices authorities should be arranged and facilitated;

(f) International conferences on restrictive business practices legislation and policy should be arranged;

(g) Seminars for an exchange of views on restrictive business practices among persons in public and private sectors should be arranged.

7. International organizations and financing programmes, in particular the United Nations Development Programme, should be called upon to provide resources through appropriate channels and modalities for the financing of activities set out in paragraph 6 above. Furthermore, all countries are invited, in particular the developing countries, to make voluntary financial and other contributions for the above-mentioned activities.

G. International institutional machinery

(i) Institutional arrangements

1. An Intergovernmental Group of Experts on Restrictive Business Practices operating within the framework of a Committee of UNCTAD will provide the institutional machinery.

2. States which have accepted the Set of Principles and Rules should take appropriate steps at the national or regional levels to meet their commitment to the Set of Principles and Rules.

(ii) Functions of the Intergovernmental Group

3. The Intergovernmental Group shall have the following functions:

(a) To provide a forum and modalities for the multilateral consultations, discussion and exchange of views between States on matters related to the Set of Principles and Rules, in particular its operation and the experience arising therefrom;

(b) To undertake and disseminate periodically studies and research on restrictive business practices related to the provisions of the Set of Principles and Rules, with a view to increasing exchange of experience and giving greater effect to the Set of Principles and Rules;

(c) To invite and consider relevant studies, documentation and reports from relevant organizations of the United Nations system;

(d) To study matters relating to the Set of Principles and Rules and which might be characterized by data covering business transactions and other relevant information obtained upon request addressed to all States;

(e) To collect and disseminate information on matters relating to the Set of Principles and Rules to the over-all attainment of its goals and to the appropriate steps States have taken at the national or regional levels to promote an effective Set of Principles and Rules, including its objectives and principles;

(f) To make appropriate reports and recommendations to States on matters within its competence, including the application and implementation of the Set of Multilaterally Agreed Equitable Principles and Rules;

(g) To submit reports at least once a year on its work.

4. In the performance of its functions, neither the Intergovernmental Group nor its subsidiary organs shall act like a tribunal or otherwise pass judgement on the activities or conduct of individual Governments or of individual enterprises in connection with a specific business transaction. The Intergovernmental Group or its subsidiary organs should avoid becoming involved when enterprises to a specific business transaction are in dispute.

5. The Intergovernmental Group shall establish such procedures as may be necessary to deal with issues related to confidentiality.

(iii) Review procedure

6. Subject to the approval of the General Assembly, five years after the adoption of the Set of Principles and Rules, a United Nations Conference shall be convened by the Secretary-General of the United Nations under the auspices of UNCTAD for the purpose of reviewing all aspects of the Set of Principles and Rules. Towards this end, the Intergovernmental Group shall make proposals to the Conference for the improvement and further development of the Set of Principles and Rules.

* * *

RESOLUTION ADOPTED BY THE CONFERENCE STRENGTHENING THE IMPLEMENTATION OF THE SET

The Second United Nations Conference to Review all Aspects of the Set of Multilaterally Agreed Equitable Principles and Rules for the Control of Restrictive Business Practices,

Having reviewed all aspects of the Set, 10 years after its adoption,

Reaffirming the importance of the Set of Multilaterally Agreed Equitable Principles and Rules for the Control of Restrictive Business Practices ("the Set") adopted by the General Assembly in its resolution 35/63 of 5 December 1980,

Further reaffirming the need to ensure that restrictive business practices do not impede or negate the realization of benefits that should arise from the liberalization of tariff and non-tariff barriers affecting world trade, particularly those affecting the trade and development of developing countries,

Recalling the agreement in the Final Act of the seventh session of the United Nations conference on Trade and Development, paragraph 105 (18), to continue and strengthen the ongoing work in UNCTAD in respect of restrictive business practices, particularly with a view to ensuring transparency and to defining consultation procedures, and to continue the UNCTAD technical assistance programme in the field of restrictive business practices,

Decides that the implementation of the Set should be strengthened and to this end:

1. Expresses concern at the continued existence of restrictive business practices adversely affecting international trade, particularly the trade and development of developing countries, and calls upon States to implement fully all provisions of the Set in order to ensure its effective application;

2. Considers that one of the important means of achieving this goal is the adoption and effective enforcement of national restrictive business practices legislation and that the increasing number of countries which have taken such action since the First Review Conference is an encouraging development, and therefore calls upon all States to adopt, improve and effectively enforce appropriate legislation and to implement judicial and administrative procedures;

3. Suggests to this end that:

(a) States without any legislation to control restrictive business practices may wish to request information on restrictive business practices legislation and seek consultations with developed and developing countries which have experience of introducing such laws, as well as appropriate technical assistance. The latter may consist of introductory seminars directed at an audience which would include government officials and academics, as well as business and consumer-oriented circles;

(b) States which are in the process of drafting restrictive business practice legislation or have recently done so may wish to request information on restrictive business practice legislation and consultations with countries having experience of such laws, as well as technical assistance. This may consist of advisory services and assistance, training workshops and seminars for national officials for implementing restrictive business practice control legislation and on-the-job training with restrictive business practice control authorities in countries having experience in restrictive business practice control;

(c) States which have already adopted such legislation and seek to enforce those laws more effectively, as well as all other States, may wish to seek information or consultations with other countries on general matters of restrictive business practice legislation, issues of importance to restrictive business practice authorities in actual enforcement and specific restrictive business practices cases. Such States may also seek appropriate technical assistance;

(d) Any State so addressed should give full and sympathetic consideration to such requests and supply such publicly available information, and, to the extent consistent with their laws and established public policy, other information;

<u>Information</u>

4. <u>Considers</u> that, in the light of States' needs for information, a list of RBP authorities through which requests for information should be channelled is a useful device for increasing the flow of information, and requests the Secretary-General of UNCTAD to issue a directory of restrictive business practices authorities and to update it regularly;

5. <u>Considers</u> further that it would be helpful for States requesting information to have guidance and <u>requests</u> the Secretary-General of UNCTAD to prepare an indicative checklist of items which may include <u>inter alia</u>:

(a) A description of the restrictive business practice case in question;

(b) The enterprises involved;

(c) The legal basis for instituting proceedings;

(d) The reasons for requesting the information;

(e) The specific information sought;

(f) The intended use of the information.

6. <u>Requests</u>, on the basis of paragraphs 2 and 3 of section F of the Set, that:

(a) States supply to the UNCTAD secretariat annually or as the information becomes available if appropriate, preferably in one of the official languages of the United Nations:

(i) Information concerning new restrictive business practice legislation or amendments to existing laws, with a copy of the legislation or amendments;

(ii) A report on their activities concerning the control of RBPs including details of the more important cases dealt with, as provided for in section F, paragraph 3 of the Set;

(iii) Any relevant studies, guidelines or reports on restrictive business practices matters or details thereof which they may have published;

(b) The UNCTAD secretariat, on the basis of the information received and of other available information:

(i) Maintain its data base and make it available to States upon request;

(ii) Disseminate this information through appropriate publications;

(iii) Complete and update the Handbook on restrictive business practices legislation.

<u>Consultations</u>

7. Considering that the existing provisions of the Set provide a good basis for consultations, <u>emphasizes</u> the importance of section F, paragraph 4 of the Set and, in order to improve implementation of the Set in this respect, requests the UNCTAD secretariat to prepare a checklist of possible steps which countries may wish to follow in the preparation of a case, and in their request for consultation. Such a checklist could include, <u>inter alia</u>, explaining the reasons for the request for consultations, and indicating the specific details of the behaviour or activity about which the consultation is

8. <u>Recommends</u> that, following a request for consultation, the state addressed should take whatever action it considers appropriate, including action under its legislation on restrictive business practices or administrative measures, on a voluntary basis and considering its legitimate interests;

9. <u>Considers</u> that the multilateral consultations, discussions and exchanges of views that have taken place under section G, paragraph 3 (a) of the Set among restrictive business practices experts at sessions of the Intergovernmental Group of Experts on Restrictive Business Practices have provided a useful forum for consideration of particular restrictive business practices issues and have served to establish important contacts between experts from interested countries, and <u>requests</u> the Intergovernmental Group of Experts to serve as a forum for exchanges

of information and consultations at each of its sessions. Topics should be selected in advance of each session and time made available for the discussions;

Technical assistance

10. Recognizes the importance of both bilateral and multilateral technical assistance as an important way to secure the implementation of the Set. Both types of technical assistance are especially effective in introducing large groups of officials from several countries to basic restrictive business practices control principles and have been very effective in providing in-depth technical co-operation between restrictive business practice control authorities, particularly where it can be tailored to specific needs;

11. Notes the commitment of States members of Group B to continue to provide technical assistance on both a bilateral and multilateral basis, subject to the availability of resources and tailored to the requirements of individual countries or groups of countries;

12. Concludes that the UNCTAD secretariat's proposals for a framework for technical assistance in its report TD/RBP/CONF.3/4 contain useful elements. In order to facilitate a meaningful evaluation of the secretariat's proposed framework, the secretariat should suggest priorities from among the different types of technical assistance set out in paragraph 71 of its report and taking into account the three categories of countries requesting assistance identified in paragraph 3 above;

13. Requests the UNCTAD secretariat to take into account the costs of the various types of technical assistance and the most effective use of resources and to undertake a regular evaluation of its technical assistance activities in order to determine their effectiveness;

14. Invites the UNCTAD secretariat to continue organizing national, regional and subregional seminars, workshops and symposia, as appropriate, including with respect to regional grouping of States willing to adopt restrictive business practices control systems;

15. Urges intergovernmental organizations and financing programmes, in particular the United Nations Development Programme (UNDP), to provide the necessary resources for the activities mentioned above;

16. Appeals to States, in particular developed countries, to increase voluntary financial contributions and to provide necessary expertise for the implementation of the activities mentioned above;

Review procedure

17. Recommends to the General Assembly that a Third Review Conference be convened in 1995.

6th (closing) meeting
7 December 1990

* * *

INTERNATIONAL CODE OF MARKETING OF BREAST-MILK SUBSTITUTES*

The International Code of Marketing of Breast-milk Substitutes was adopted by the Thirty-fourth World Health Assembly (resolution WHA34.22) of the World Health Organization on 21 May 1981.

The Member States of the World Health Organization:

Affirming the right of every child and every pregnant and lactating woman to be adequately nourished as a means of attaining and maintaining health;

Recognizing that infant malnutrition is part of the wider problems of lack of education, poverty and social injustice;

Recognizing that the health of infants and young children cannot be isolated from the health and nutrition of women, their socio-economic status and their role as mothers;

Conscious that breast-feeding is an unequalled way of providing ideal food for the healthy growth and development of infants; that it forms a unique biological and emotional basis for the health of both mother and child; that the anti-infective properties of breast milk help to protect infants against disease; and that there is an important relationship between breast-feeding and child-spacing;

Recognizing that the encouragement and protection of breast-feeding is an important part of the health, nutrition and other social measures required to promote healthy growth, nutrition and other social measures required to promote healthy growth and development of infants and young children; and that breast-feeding is an important aspect of primary health care;

Considering that when mothers do not breast-feed, or only do so partially, there is a legitimate market for infant formula and for suitable ingredients from which to prepare it; that all these products should accordingly be made accessible to those who need them through commercial or non-commercial distribution systems; and that they should not be marketed or distributed in ways that may interfere with the protection and promotion of breast-feeding;

Recognizing further that inappropriate feeding practices lead to infant malnutrition, morbidity and mortality in all countries, and that improper practices in the marketing of breast-milk substitutes and related products can contribute to these major public health problems;

---

*Source: World Health Organization (1981). "International Code of Marketing of Breast-milk Substitutes", *International Code of Marketing of Breast-milk Substitutes* (Geneva: World Health Organization), pp. 9-22 [Note added by the editor].

Convinced that it is important for infants to receive appropriate complementary foods, usually when the infant reaches four to six months of age, and that every effort should be made to use locally available foods; and convinced, nevertheless, that such complementary foods should not be used as breast-milk substitutes;

Appreciating that there are a number of social and economic factors affecting breast-feeding, and that, accordingly, governments should develop social support systems to protect, facilitate and encourage it, and that they should create an environment that fosters breast-feeding, provides appropriate family and community support, and protects mothers from factors that inhibit breast-feeding;

Affirming that health care systems, and the health professional and other health workers serving in them, have an essential role to play in guiding infant feeding practices, encouraging and facilitating breast-feeding, and providing objective and consistent advice to mothers and families about the superior value of breast-feeding, or, where needed, on the proper use of infant formula, whether manufactured industrially or home-prepared;

Affirming further that educational systems and other social services should be involved in the protection and promotion of breast-feeding, and in the appropriate use of complementary foods;

Aware that families, communities, women's organizations and other nongovernmental organizations have a special role to play in the protection and promotion of breast-feeding and in ensuring the support needed by pregnant women and mothers of infants and young children, whether breast-feeding or not;

Affirming the need for governments, organizations of the United Nations system, nongovernmental organizations, experts in various related disciplines, consumer groups and industry to co-operate in activities aimed at the improvement of maternal, infant and young child health and nutrition;

Recognizing that governments should undertake a variety of health, nutrition and other social measures to promote healthy growth and development of infants and young children, and that this Code concerns only one aspect of these measures;

Considering that manufacturers and distributors of breast-milk substitutes have an important and constructive role to play in relation to infant feeding, and in the promotion of the aim of this Code and its proper implementation;

Affirming that governments are called upon to take action appropriate to their social and legislative framework and their overall development objectives to give effect to the principles and aim of this Code, including the enactment of legislation, regulations or other suitable measures;

Believing that, in the light of the foregoing considerations, and in view of the vulnerability of infants in the early months of life and the risks involved in inappropriate feeding practices, including the unnecessary and improper use of breast-milk substitutes, the marketing of breast-milk substitutes requires special treatment, which makes usual marketing practices unsuitable for these products;

THEREFORE:

The Member States hereby agree the following articles which are recommended as a basis for action

Article 1
Aim of the Code

The aim of this Code is to contribute to the provisions of safe and adequate nutrition for infants, by the protection and promotion of breast-feeding, and by ensuring the proper use of breast-milk substitutes, when these are necessary, on the basis of adequate information and through appropriate marketing and distribution.

Article 2
Scope of the Code

The Code applies to the marketing, and practices related thereto, of the following products: breast-milk substitutes, including infant formula; other milk products, foods and beverages, including bottle-fed complementary foods, when marketed or otherwise represented to be suitable, with or without modification, for use as a partial or total replacement of breast-milk; feeding bottles and teats. It also applies to their quality and availability, and to information concerning their use.

Article 3
Definitions

For the purposes of this Code;

"Breast-milk substitute" means — any food being marketed or otherwise represented as a partial or total replacement for breast-milk, whether or not suitable for that purpose.

"Complementary food" means — any food, whether manufactured or locally prepared, suitable as a complement to breast-milk or to infant formula, when either becomes insufficient to satisfy the nutritional requirements of the infant. Such food is also commonly called "weaning food" or "breast-milk supplement".

"Container" means	any form of packaging of products for sale as a normal retail unit, including wrappers.
"Distribute" means	a person, corporation or any other entity in the public or private sector engaged in the business (whether directly or indirectly) of marketing at the wholesale or retail level a product within the scope of this Code. A "primary distributor" is a manufacturer's sales agent, representative, national distributor or broker.
"Health care system" means	governmental, nongovernmental or private institutions or organizations engaged, directly or indirectly, in health care for mothers, infants and pregnant women; and nurseries or child-care institutions. It also include health workers in private practice. For the purposes of this Code, the health care system does not include pharmacies or other established sales outlets.
"Health worker" means	a person working in a component of such a health care system, whether professional or non-professional, including voluntary, unpaid workers.
"Infant formula" means	a breast-milk substitute formulated industrially in accordance with applicable Codex Alimentarius standards, to satisfy the normal nutritional requirements of infants up to between four and six months of age, and adapted to their physiological characteristics. Infant formula may also be prepared at home, in which case it is described as "home-prepared".
"Label" means	any tag, brand, mark, pictorial or other descriptive matter, written, printed, stencilled, marked, embossed or impressed on, or attached to, a container (see above) of any products within the scope of this Code.
"Manufacturer" means	a corporation or other entity in the public or private sector engaged in the business or function (whether directly or through an agent or through an entity controlled by or under contract with it) of manufacturing a product within the scope of this Code.
"Marketing" means	product promotion, distribution, selling, advertising, product public relations, and information services.

"Marketing personnel" means any persons whose functions involve the marketing of a product or products coming within the scope of this Code.

"Samples" means single or small quantities of a product provided without cost.

"Supplies" means quantities of a product provided for use over an extended period, free or at a low price, for social purposes, including those provided to families in need.

Article 4
Information and education

4.1 Governments should have the responsibility to ensure that objective and consistent information is provided on infant and young child feeding for use by families and those involved in the field of infant and young child nutrition. This responsibility should cover either the planning, provision, design and disseminations of information, or their control.

4.2 Informational and educational materials, whether written, audio, or visual, dealing with the feeding of infants and intended to reach pregnant women and mothers of infants and young children, should include clear information on all the following points: (a) the benefits and superiority of breast-feeding; (b) maternal nutrition, and the preparation for and maintenance of breast-feeding; (c) the negative effect on breast-feeding of introducing partial bottle feeding; (d) the difficulty of reversing the decision not to breast-feed; and (e) where needed, the proper use of infant formula, whether manufactured industrially or home-prepared. When such materials contain information about the use of infant formula, they should include the social and financial implications of its use; the health hazards of inappropriate foods or feeding methods; and, in particular, the health hazards of unnecessary or improper use of infant formula and other breast-milk substitutes. Such materials should not use any pictures or text which may idealize the use of breast-milk substitutes.

4.3 Donations of informational or educational equipment or materials by manufacturers or distributors should be made only at the request and with the written approval of the appropriate government authority or within guidelines given by governments for this purpose. Such equipment or materials may bear the donating company's name or logo, but should not refer to a proprietary product that is within the scope of this Code, and should be distributed only through the health care system.

Article 5
The general public and mothers

5.1 There should be no advertising or other form of promotion to the general public of products within the scope of this Code.

5.2 Manufacturers and distributors should not provide, directly or indirectly, to pregnant women, mothers or members of their families, samples of products within the scope of this Code.

5.3 In conformity with paragraphs 1 and 2 of this Article, there should be no point of sale advertising, giving of samples, or any other promotion device to induce sales directly to the consumer at the retail level, such as special displays, discount coupons, premiums, special sales, loss-leaders and tie-in sales, for products within the scope of this Code. This provision should not restrict the establishment of pricing policies and practices intended to provide products at lower prices on a long-term basis.

5.4 Manufacturers and distributors should not distribute to pregnant women or mothers of infants and young children any gifts of articles or utensils which may promote the use of breast-milk substitutes or bottle-feeding.

5.5 Marketing personnel, in their business capacity, should not seek direct or indirect contact of any kind with pregnant women or with mothers of infants and young children.

Article 6
Health care systems

6.1 The health authorities in Member States should take appropriate measures to encourage and protect breast-feeding and promote the principles of this Code, and should give appropriate information and advice to health workers in regard to their responsibilities, including the information specified in Article 4.2.

6.2 No facility of a health care system should be used for the purpose of promoting infant formula or other products within the scope of this Code. This Code does not, however, preclude the dissemination of information to health professionals as provided in Article 7.2.

6.3 Facilities of health care systems should not be used for the display of products within the scope of this Code, for placards or posters concerning such products, or for the distribution of material provided by a manufacturer or distributor other than that specified in Article 4.3.

6.4 The use by the health care system of "professional service representatives", "mothercraft nurses" or similar personnel, provided or paid for by manufacturers or distributors, should not be permitted.

6.5 Feeding with infant formula, whether manufactured or home-prepared, should be demonstrated only by health workers, or other community workers if necessary; and only to the mothers or family members who need to use it, and the information given should include a clear explanation of the hazards of improper use.

6.6. Donations or low-price sales to institutions or organizations of supplies of infant formula or other products within the scope of this Code, whether for use in the institutions or for distribution outside them, may be made. Such supplies should only be used or distributed for infants who have to be fed on breast-milk substitutes. If these supplies are distributed for use outside the institutions, this should be done only by the institutions or organizations concerned. Such donations or low-price sales should not be used by manufacturers or distributors as a sales inducement.

6.7 Where donated supplies of infant formula or other products within the scope of this Code are distributed outside an institution, the institution or organization should take steps to ensure that supplies can be continued as long as the infants concerned need them. Donors, as well as institutions or organizations concerned, should bear in mind this responsibility.

6.8 Equipment and materials, in addition to those referred to in Article 4.3, donated to a health care system may bear a company's name or logo, but should not refer to any proprietary product within the scope of this Code.

Article 7
Health workers

7.1 Health workers should encourage and protect breast-feeding; and those who are concerned in particular with maternal and infant nutrition should make themselves familiar with their responsibilities under this Code, including the information specified in Article 4.2.

7.2 Information provided by manufacturers and distributors to health professionals regarding products within the scope of this Code should be restricted to scientific and factual matters, and such information should not imply or create a belief that bottle-feeding is equivalent or superior to breast-feeding. It should also include the information specified in Article 4.2.

7.3 No financial or material inducements to promote products within the scope of this Code should be offered by manufacturers or distributors to health workers or members of their families, nor should these be accepted by health workers or members of their families.

7.4 Samples of infant formula or other products within the scope of this Code, or of equipment or utensils for their preparations or use, should not be provided to health workers except when necessary for the purpose of professional evaluation or research at the institutional level. Health workers should not give samples of infant formula to pregnant women, mothers of infants and young children, or members of their families.

7.5 Manufacturers and distributors of products within the scope of this Code should disclose to the institutions to which a recipient health worker is affiliated any contribution made to him or on his behalf for fellowships, study tours, research grants, attendance at professional conferences, or the like. Similar disclosures should be made by the recipient.

Article 8
Persons employed by manufacturers and distributors

8.1 In systems of sales incentives for marketing personnel, the volume of sales of products within the scope of this Code should not be included in the calculation of bonuses, nor should quotas be set specifically for sales of these products. This should not be understood to prevent the payment of bonuses based on the overall sales by a company of other products marketed by it.

8.2 Personnel employed in marketing products within the scope of this Code should not, as part of their job responsibilities, perform educational functions in relation to pregnant women or mothers of infants and young children. This should not be understood as preventing such personnel from being used for other functions by the health care system at the request and with the written approval of the appropriate authority of the government concerned.

Article 9
Labelling

9.1 Labels should be designed to provide the necessary information about the appropriate use of the product, and so as not to discourage breast-feeding.

9.2 Manufacturers and distributors of infant formula should ensure that each container has a clear, conspicuous, and easily readable and understandable message printed on it, or on a label which cannot readily become separated from it, in an appropriate language, which includes all the following points: (a) the words "Important Notice" or their equivalent; (b) a statement of the superiority of breast-feeding; (c) a statement that the product should be used only on the advice of a health worker as to the need for its use and the proper method of use; (d) instructions for appropriate preparation, and a warning against the health hazards of inappropriate preparation. Neither the container not the label should have pictures of infants, nor should they have other pictures or texts which may idealize the use of infant formula. They may, however, have graphics for easy identification of the product as a breast-milk substitute and for illustrating methods of preparation. The terms "humanized", "maternalized" or similar terms should not be used. Inserts giving additional information about the product and its proper use, subject to the above conditions, may be included in the package or retail unit. When labels give instructions for modifying a product into infant formula, the above should apply.

9.3 Food products within the scope of this Code, marketed for infant formula, which do not meet all the requirements of an infant formula, but which can be modified to do so, should carry on the label a warning that the unmodified product should not be the sole source of nourishment of an infant. Since sweetened condensed milk is not suitable for infant feeding, nor for use as a main ingredient of infant feeding, its label should not contain purported instructions on how to modify it for that purpose.

9.4 The label of food products within the scope of this Code should also state all the following points: (a) the ingredients used; (b) the composition/analysis of the product; (c) the storage conditions required; and (d) the batch number and the date before which the product is to be consumed, taking into account the climatic and storage conditions of the country concerned.

Article 10
Quality

10.1 The quality of products is an essential element for the protection of the health of infants and therefore should be of a high recognized standard.

10.2 Food products within the scope of this Code should, when sold or otherwise distributed, meet applicable standards recommended by the Codex Alimentarius Commission and also the Codex Code of Hygienic Practice for Foods for Infants and Children.

Article 11
Implementation and monitoring

11.1 Governments should take action to give effect to the principles and aim of this Code, as appropriate to their social and legislative framework, including the adoption of national legislation, regulations or other suitable measures. For this purpose, government should seek, when necessary, the cooperation of WHO, UNICEF and other agencies of the United Nations system. National policies and measures, including laws and regulations, which are adopted to give effect to the principles and aim of this Code should be publicly stated, and should apply on the same basis to all those involved in the manufacture and marketing of products within the scope of this Code.

11.2 Monitoring the application of this Code lies with governments acting individually, and collectively through the World Health Organization as provided in paragraphs 6 and 7 of this Article. The manufacturers and distributors of products within the scope of this Code, and appropriate nongovernmental organizations, professional groups, and consumer organizations should collaborate with governments to this end.

11.3 Independently of any other measures taken for implementation of this Code, manufacturers and distributors of products within the scope of this Code should regard themselves as responsible for monitoring their marketing practices according to the principles and aim of this Code, and for taking steps to ensure that their conduct at every level conforms to them.

11.4 Nongovernmental organizations, professional groups, institutions, and individuals concerned should have the responsibility of drawing the attention of manufacturers or distributors to activities which are incompatible with the principles and aim of this Code, so that appropriate action can be taken. The appropriate governmental authority should also be informed.

11.5 Manufacturers and primary distributors of products within the scope of this Code should apprise each member of their marketing personnel of the Code and their responsibilities under it.

11.6 In accordance with Article 62 of the Constitutions of the World Health Organization, Member States shall communicate annually to the Director-General information on action taken to give effect to the principles and aim of this Code.

11.7 The Director-General shall report in even years to the World Health Assembly on the status of implementation of the Code, and shall, on request, provide technical support to Member States preparing national legislation or regulations, or taking other appropriate measures in implementation and furtherance of the principles and aim of this Code.

* * *

DRAFT UNITED NATIONS CODE OF CONDUCT ON TRANSNATIONAL CORPORATIONS*
[1983 version]

The elaboration of the United Nations Code of Conduct on Transnational Corporations was one of the main tasks of the Commission on Transnational Corporations (established by the Economic and Social Council under resolution 1913 (LVII) of 5 December 1974). The preparation of the text of the Draft Code was entrusted first to an Ad Hoc Inter-Governmental Working Group. The Group submitted its report to the Commission at its eighth session in 1982 (United Nations document E/C.10/1982/6). The next stage of the negotiations was entrusted to a special session of the Commission on Transnational Corporations which began deliberations in 1983 and was open to the participation of all States. The special session was reconvened a number of times between 1983 and 1990.

In 1988, the Chairman of the reconvened special session and the Secretary-General of the United Nations prepared a text of a draft code (E/1988/39/Add.1), drawing upon discussions and proposals presented over the years. In an effort to facilitate compromise while preserving the already agreed texts, the Chairman, at the meeting on 24 May 1990, transmitted to the Economic and Social Council a revised text of the draft code of conduct, based on the 1988 draft. The text of the Draft Code of Conduct on Transnational Corporations reproduced in this volume reflects the status of negotiations as at 1986.

PREAMBLE AND OBJECTIVES** a/

DEFINITIONS AND SCOPE OF APPLICATION

1. (a) [The term "transnational corporations" as used in this Code means an enterprise, comprising entities in two or more countries, regardless of the legal form and fields of activity of these entities, which operates under a system of decision-making, permitting coherent policies and a common strategy through one or more decision-making centres, in which the entities are so linked, by ownership or otherwise, that one or more of them may be able to exercise a significant influence over the activities of others, and, in particular, to share knowledge, resources and responsibilities with the others.]

---

*Source: Commission on Transnational Corporations, Report on the Special Session (7-18 March and 9-21 May 1983) *Official Records of the Economic and Social Council*, 1983, Supplement No. 7 (E/1983/17/Rev. 1), Annex II. This text of the Code was also reproduced in United Nations Centre on Transnational Corporations (1986). *The United Nations Code of Conduct on Transnational Corporations*, Current Studies, Series A (New York: United Nations) United Nations publication sales No. E.86.II.A.15, (ST/CTC/SER.A/4), Annex I, pp.28-45 [Note added by the editor].

**No final decision regarding the use and contents of headings and subheadings appearing in the text has yet been taken.

[The term "transnational corporation" as used in this Code means an enterprise whether of public, private or mixed ownership, comprising entities in two or more countries, regardless of the legal form and fields of activity of these entities, which operates under a system of decision-making, permitting coherent policies and a common strategy through one or more decision-making centres, in which the entities are so linked, by ownership or otherwise, that one or more of them [may be able to] exercise a significant influence over the activities of others, and, in particular, to share knowledge, resources and responsibilities with the others.]

(b) The term "entities" in the Code refers to both parent entities - that is, entities which are the main source of influence over others - and other entities, unless otherwise specified in the Code.

(c) The term "transnational corporation" in the Code refers to the enterprise as a whole or its various entities.

(d) The term "home country" means the country in which the parent entity is located. The term "host country" means a country in which an entity other than the parent entity is located.

(e) The term "country in which a transnational corporation operates" refers to a home or host country in which an entity of a transnational corporation conducts operations.

2. [The Code is universally applicable in, and to this end is open to adoption by, all States.]

[The Code is universally applicable in [home and host countries of transnational corporations] [as defined in paragraph 1 (a)], and to this end is open to adoption by, all States [regardless of their political and economic systems and their level of development] .]

[The Code is open to adoption by all States and is applicable in all States where an entity of a transnational corporation conducts operations.]

[The Code is universally applicable to all States regardless of their political and economic systems and their level of development.]

3. [This Code applies to all enterprises as defined in paragraph 1 (a) above.]

[To be placed in paragraph 1 (a).]

[4. The provisions of the Code addressed to transnational corporations reflect good practice for all enterprises. They are not intended to introduce differences of conduct between transnational corporations and domestic enterprises. Wherever the provisions are relevant to both, transnational corporations and domestic enterprises should be subject to the same expectations in regard to their conduct.]

[to be deleted][*]

[5. Any reference in this Code to States, countries or Governments also includes regional groupings of States, to the extent that the provisions of this Code relate to matters within these groupings' own competence, with respect to such competence.]

[To be deleted]

ACTIVITIES OF TRANSNATIONAL CORPORATIONS

A. General and political

Respect for national sovereignty and observance of domestic laws, regulations and administrative practices

6. Transnational corporations should/shall respect the national sovereignty of the countries in which they operate and the right of each State to exercise its [full permanent sovereignty] [in accordance with international law] [in accordance with agreements reached by the countries concerned on a bilateral and multilateral basis] over its natural resources [wealth and economic activities] within its territory.

7. [Transnational corporations] [Entities of transnational corporations] [shall/should observe] [are subject to] the laws, regulations [jurisdiction] and [administrative practices] [explicitly declared administrative practices] of the countries in which they operate. [Entities of transnational corporations are subject to the jurisdiction of the countries in which they operate to the extent required by the national law of these countries.]

8. Transnational corporations should/shall respect the right of each State to regulate and monitor accordingly the activities of their entities operating within its territory.

Adherence to economic goals and development objectives, policies and priorities

9. Transnational corporations shall/should carry on their activities in conformity with the development policies, objectives and priorities set out by the Governments of the countries in which they operate and work seriously towards making a positive contribution to the achievement of such goals at the national and, as appropriate, the regional level, within the framework of regional integration programmes. Transnational corporations shall/should co-operate with the Governments of the countries in which they operate with a view to contributing to the development process and shall/should be responsive to requests for consultation in this respect, thereby establishing mutually beneficial relations with these countries.

---

[*] On the grounds, inter alia, that the text within the first pair of brackets goes beyond the mandate of the Intergovernmental Working Group on a Code of Conduct.

10. Transnational corporations shall/should carry out their operations in conformity with relevant intergovernmental co-operative arrangements concluded by countries in which they operate.

Review and renegotiation of contracts

11. Contracts between Governments and transnational corporations should be negotiated and implemented in good faith. In such contracts, especially long-term ones, review or renegotiation clauses should normally be included.

In the absence of such clauses and where there has been a fundamental change of the circumstances on which the contract or agreement was based, transnational corporations, acting in good faith, shall/should co-operate with Governments for the review or renegotiation of such contract or agreement.

Review or renegotiation of such contracts or agreements shall/should be subject to [the laws of the host country] [relevant national laws and international legal principles].

Adherence to socio-cultural objectives and values

12. Transnational corporations should/shall respect the social and cultural objectives, values and traditions of the countries in which they operate. While economic and technological development is normally accompanied by social change, transnational corporations should/shall avoid practices, products or services which cause detrimental effects on cultural patterns and socio-cultural objectives as determined by Governments. For this purpose,transnational corporations should/shall respond positively to requests for consultations from Governments concerned.

Respect for human rights and fundamental freedoms

13. Transnational corporations should/shall respect human rights and fundamental freedoms in the countries in which they operate. In their social and industrial relations, transnational corporations should/shall not discriminate on the basis of race, colour, sex, religion, language, social, national and ethnic origin or political or other opinion. Transnational corporations should/shall conform to government policies designed to extend equality of opportunity and treatment.

Non-collaboration by transnational corporations with racist minority regimes in southern Africa

14. In accordance with the efforts of the international community towards the elimination of apartheid in South Africa and its continued illegal occupation of Namibia,

[(a) Transnational corporations shall progressively reduce their business activities and make no further investment in South Africa and immediately cease all business activities in Namibia;

(b) Transnational corporations shall refrain from collaborating directly or indirectly with that regime especially with regard to its racist practices in South Africa and illegal occupation of Namibia to ensure the successful implementation of United Nations resolutions in relation to these two countries.]

[Transnational corporations operating in southern Africa

(a) Should respect the national laws and regulations adopted in pursuance of Security Council decisions concerning southern Africa;

(b) Should within the framework of their business activities engage in appropriate activities with a view to contributing to the elimination of racial discrimination practices under the system of apartheid.]

Non-interference in internal political affairs

15. Transnational corporations should/shall not interfere [illegally] in the internal [political] affairs of the countries in which they operate [by resorting to] [They should refrain from any] [subversive and other [illicit]] activities [aimed at] undermining the political and social systems in these countries.

16. Transnational corporations should/shall not engage in activities of a political nature which are not permitted by the laws and established policies and administrative practices of the countries in which they operate.

Non-interference in intergovernmental relations

17. Transnational corporations should/shall not interfere in [any affairs concerning] intergovernmental relations [, which are the sole concern of Governments].

18. Transnational corporations shall/should not request Governments acting on their behalf to take the measures referred to in the second sentence of paragraph 65.

19. With respect to the exhaustion of local remedies, transnational corporations should/shall not request Governments to act on their behalf in any manner inconsistent with paragraph 65.

Abstention from corrupt practices

20. [Transnational corporations shall refrain, in their transactions, from the offering, promising or giving of any payment, gift or other advantage to or for the benefit of a public official as

consideration for performing or refraining from the performance of his duties in connection with those transactions.

Transnational corporations shall maintain accurate records of payments made by them, in connection with their transactions, to any public official or intermediary. They shall make available these records to the competent authorities of the countries in which they operate, upon request, for investigations and proceedings concerning those payments.]

[For the purposes of this Code, the principles set out in the International Agreement on Illicit Payments adopted by the United Nations should apply in the area of abstention from corrupt practices.]*

B. Economic, financial and social

Ownership and control

21. Transnational corporations should/shall make every effort so to allocate their decision-making powers among their entities as to enable them to contribute to the economic and social development of the countries in which they operate.

22. To the extent permitted by national laws, policies and regulations of the country in which it operates, each entity of a transnational corporation should/shall co-operate with the other entities, in accordance with the actual distribution of responsibilities among them and consistent with paragraph 21, so as to enable each entity to meet effectively the requirements established by the laws, policies and regulations of the country in which it operates.

23. Transnational corporations shall/should co-operate with Governments and nationals of the countries in which they operate in the implementation of national objectives for local equity participation and for the effective exercise of control by local partners as determined by equity, contractual terms in non-equity arrangements or the laws of such countries.

24. Transnational corporations should/shall carry out their personnel policies in accordance with the national policies of each of the countries in which they operate which give priority to the employment and promotion of its [adequately qualified] nationals at all levels of management and direction of the affairs of each entity so as to enhance the effective participation of its nationals in the decision-making process.

25. Transnational corporations should/shall contribute to the managerial and technical training of nationals of the countries in which they operate and facilitate their employment at all levels of management of the entities and enterprises as a whole.

---

*To be included in one of the substantive introductory parts of the Code.

Balance of payments and financing b/

26. Transnational corporations should/shall carry on their operations in conformity with laws and regulations and with full regard to the policy objectives set out by the countries in which they operate, particularly developing countries, relating to balance of payments, financial transactions and other issues dealt with in the subsequent paragraphs of this section.

27. Transnational corporations should/shall respond positively to requests for consultation on their activities from the Governments of the countries in which they operate, with a view to contributing to the alleviation of pressing problems of balance of payments and finance of such countries.

28. [As required by government regulations and in furtherance of government policies] [Consistent with the purpose, nature and extent of their operations] transnational corporations should/shall contribute to the promotion of exports and the diversification of exports [and imports] in the countries in which they operate and to an increased utilization of goods, services and other resources which are available in these countries.

29. Transnational corporations should/shall be responsive to requests by Governments of the countries in which they operate, particularly developing countries, concerning the phasing over a limited period of time of the repatriation of capital in case of disinvestment or remittances of accumulated profits, when the size and timing of such transfers would cause serious balance-of-payments difficulties for such countries.

30. Transnational corporations should/shall not, contrary to generally accepted financial practices prevailing in the countries in which they operate, engage in short-term financial operations or transfers or defer or advance foreign exchange payments, including intra-corporate payments, in a manner which would increase currency instability and thereby cause serious balance-of-payments difficulties for the countries concerned.

31. Transnational corporations should/shall not impose restrictions on their entities, beyond generally accepted commercial practices prevailing in the countries in which they operate, regarding the transfer of goods, services and funds which would cause serious balance-of-payments difficulties for the countries in which they operate.

32. When having recourse to the money and capital markets of the countries in which they operate, transnational corporations should/shall not, beyond generally accepted financial practices prevailing in such countries, engage in activities which would have a significant adverse impact on the working of local markets, particularly by restricting the availability of funds to other enterprises. When issuing shares with the objective of increasing local equity participation in an entity operating in such a country, or engaging in long-term borrowing in the local market, transnational corporations shall/should consult with the Government of the country concerned upon its request on the effects of such transactions on the local money and capital markets.

Transfer pricing

33. In respect of their intra-corporate transactions, transnational corporations, should/shall not use pricing policies that are not based on relevant market prices, or, in the absence of such prices, the arm's length principle, which have the effect of modifying the tax base on which their entities are assessed or of evading exchange control measures [or customs valuation regulations] [or which [contrary to national laws and regulations] adversely affect economic and social conditions] of the countries in which they operate.

Taxation

34. Transnational corporations should/shall not, contrary to the laws and regulations of the countries in which they operate, use their corporate structure and modes of operation, such as the use of intra-corporate pricing which is not based on the arm's length principle, or other means, to modify the tax base on which their entities are assessed.

Competition and restrictive business practices

35. For the purpose of this Code, the relevant provisions of the Set of Multilaterally Agreed Equitable Principles and Rules for the Control of Restrictive Business Practices adopted by the General Assembly in its resolution 35/63 of 5 December 1980 shall/should also apply in the field of restrictive business practices. c/

Transfer of technology

36. [Transnational corporations shall conform to the transfer of technology laws and regulations of the countries in which they operate. They shall co-operate with the competent authorities of those countries in assessing the impact of international transfers of technology in their economies and consult with them regarding the various technological options which might help those countries, particularly developing countries, to attain their economic and social development.

Transnational corporations in their transfer of technology transactions, including intra-corporate transactions, shall avoid practices which adversely affect the international flow of technology, or otherwise hinder the economic and technological development of countries, particularly developing countries.

Transnational corporations shall contribute to the strengthening of the scientific and technological capacities of developing countries, in accordance with the science and technology policies and priorities of those countries. Transnational corporations shall undertake substantial research and development activities in developing countries and make full use of local resources and personnel in this process.]

[For the purposes of this Code the relevant provisions of the International Code of Conduct on the Transfer of Technology adopted by the General Assembly in its resolution ________ of ________ shall/should apply in the field of transfer of technology.]*

Consumer protection

37. Transnational corporations shall/should carry out their operations, in particular production and marketing, in accordance with national laws, regulations, administrative practices and policies concerning consumer protection of the countries in which they operate. Transnational corporations shall/should also perform their activities with due regard to relevant international standards, so that they do not cause injury to the health or endanger the safety of consumers or bring about variations in the quality of products in each market which would have detrimental effects on consumers.

38. Transnational corporations shall/should, in respect of the products and services which they produce or market or propose to produce or market in any country, supply to the competent authorities of that country on request or on a regular basis, as specified by these authorities, all relevant information concerning:

Characteristics of these products or services which may be injurious to the health and safety of consumers including experimental uses and related aspects;

Prohibitions, restrictions, warnings and other public regulatory measures imposed in other countries on grounds of health and safety protection on these products or services.

39. Transnational corporations shall/should disclose to the public in the countries in which they operate all appropriate information on the contents and, to the extent known, on possible hazardous effects of the products they produce or market in the countries concerned by means of proper labelling, informative and accurate advertising or other appropriate methods. Packaging of their products should be safe and the contents of the product should not be misrepresented.

40. Transnational corporations shall/should be responsive to requests from Governments of the countries in which they operate and be prepared to co-operate with international organizations in their efforts to develop and promote national and international standards for the protection of the health and safety of consumers and to meet the basic needs of consumers.

Environmental protection

41. Transnational corporations shall/should carry out their activities in accordance with national laws, regulations, administrative practices and policies relating to the preservation of the environment of the countries in which they operate and with due regard to relevant international

*To be included in one of the substantive introductory parts of the Code.

standards. Transnational corporations shall/should, in performing their activities, take steps to protect the environment and where damaged to [restore it to the extent appropriate and feasible] [rehabilitate it] and should make efforts to develop and apply adequate technologies for this purpose.

42. Transnational corporations shall/should, in respect of the products, processes and services they have introduced or propose to introduce in any country, supply to the competent authorities of that country on request or on a regular basis, as specified by these authorities, all relevant information concerning:

Characteristics of these products, processes and other activities including experimental uses and related aspects which may harm the environment and the measures and costs necessary to avoid or at least to mitigate their harmful effects;

Prohibitions, restrictions, warnings and other public regulatory measures imposed in other countries on grounds of protection of the environment on these products, processes and services.

43. Transnational corporations shall/should be responsive to requests from Governments of the countries in which they operate and be prepared where appropriate to co-operate with international organizations in their efforts to develop and promote national and international standards for the protection of the environment.

C. Disclosure of information

44. Transnational corporations should disclose to the public in the countries in which they operate, by appropriate means of communication, clear, full and comprehensible information on the structure, policies, activities and operations of the transnational corporation as a whole. The information should include financial as well as non-financial items and should be made available on a regular annual basis, normally within six months and in any case not later than 12 months from the end of the financial year of the corporation. In addition, during the financial year, transnational corporations should wherever appropriate make available a semi-annual summary of financial information.

The financial information to be disclosed annually should be provided where appropriate on a consolidated basis, together with suitable explanatory notes and should include, inter alia, the following:

(a) A balance sheet;

(b) An income statement, including operating results and sales;

(c) A statement of allocation of net profits or net income;

(d) A statement of the sources and uses of funds;

(e) Significant new long-term capital investment;

(f) Research and development expenditure.

The non-financial information referred to in the first subparagraph should include, inter alia:

(a) The structure of the transnational corporation, showing the name and location of the parent company, its main entities, its percentage ownership, direct and indirect, in these entities, including shareholdings between them;

(b) The main activity of its entities;

(c) Employment information including average number of employees;

(d) Accounting policies used in compiling and consolidating the information published;

(e) Policies applied in respect of transfer pricing.

The information provided for the transnational corporation as a whole should as far as practicable be broken down:

By geographical area or country, as appropriate, with regard to the activities of its main entities, sales, operating results, significant new investments and number of employees;

By major line of business as regards sales and significant new investment.

The method of breakdown as well as details of information provided should/shall be determined by the nature, scale and interrelationships of the transnational corporation's operations, with due regard to their significance for the areas or countries concerned.

The extent, detail and frequency of the information provided should take into account the nature and size of the transnational corporation as a whole, the requirements of confidentiality and effects on the transnational corporation's competitive position as well as the cost involved in producing the information.

The information herein required should, as necessary, be in addition to information required by national laws, regulations and administrative practices of the countries in which transnational corporations operate.

45. Transnational corporations should/shall supply to the competent authorities in each of the countries in which they operate, upon request or on a regular basis as specified by those authorities, and in accordance with national legislation, all information required for legislative

and administrative purposes relevant to the activities and policies of their entities in the country concerned.

Transnational corporations should/shall, to the extent permitted by the provisions of the relevant national laws, regulations, administrative practices and policies of the countries concerned, supply to competent authorities in the countries in which they operate information held in other countries needed to enable them to obtain a true and fair view of the operations of the transnational corporation concerned as a whole in so far as the information requested relates to the activities of the entities in the countries seeking such information.

The provisions of paragraph 51 concerning confidentiality shall apply to information supplied under the provisions of this paragraph.

46. With due regard to the relevant provisions of the ILO Tripartite Declaration of Principles concerning Multinational Enterprises and Social Policy and in accordance with national laws, regulations and practices in the field of labour relations, transnational corporations should/shall provide to trade unions or other representatives of employees in their entities in each of the countries in which they operate, by appropriate means of communication, the necessary information on the activities dealt with in this code to enable them to obtain a true and fair view of the performance of the local entity and, where appropriate, the corporation as a whole. Such information should/shall include, where provided for by national law and practices, inter alia, prospects or plans for future development having major economic and social effects on the employees concerned.

Procedures for consultation on matters of mutual concern should/shall be worked out by mutual agreement between entities of transnational corporations and trade unions or other representatives of employees in accordance with national law and practice.

Information made available pursuant to the provisions of this paragraph should be subject to appropriate safeguards for confidentiality so that no damage is caused to the parties concerned.

TREATMENT OF TRANSNATIONAL CORPORATIONS

A. General treatment of transnational corporations by the countries in which they operate

47. States have the right to regulate the entry and establishment of transnational corporations including determining the role that such corporations may play in economic and social development and prohibiting or limiting the extent of their presence in specific sectors.

48. Transnational corporations should receive [fair and] equitable [and non-discriminatory] treatment [under] [in accordance with] the laws, regulations and administrative practices of the countries in which they operate [as well as intergovernmental

obligations to which the Governments of these countries have freely subscribed] [consistent with their international obligations] [consistent with international law].

49. Consistent with [national constitutional systems and] national needs to [protect essential/national economic interests,] maintain public order and to protect national security, [and with due regard to provisions of agreements among countries, particularly developing countries,] entities of transnational corporations should be given by the countries in which they operate [the treatment] [treatment no less favourable than that] [appropriate treatment].* accorded to domestic enterprises under their laws, regulations and administrative practices [when the circumstances in which they operate are similar/identical] [in like situations]. [Transnational corporations should not claim preferential treatment or the incentives and concessions granted to domestic enterprises of the countries in which they operate.] [Such treatment should not necessarily include extension to entities of transnational corporations of incentives and concessions granted to domestic enterprises in order to promote self-reliant development or protect essential economic interests.]**

[50. Endeavouring to assure the clarity and stability of national policies, laws, regulations and administrative practices is of acknowledged importance. Laws, regulations and other measures affecting transnational corporations should be publicly and readily available. Changes in them should be made with proper regard to the legitimate rights and interests of all concerned parties, including transnational corporations.]

[To be deleted]

51. Information furnished by transnational corporations to the authorities in each of the countries in which they operate containing [legitimate business secrets] [confidential business information] should be accorded reasonable safeguards normally applicable in the area in which the information is provided, particularly to protect its confidentiality.

[52. In order to achieve the purposes of paragraph 25 relating to managerial and technical training and employment of nationals of the countries in which transnational corporations operate, the transfer of those nationals between the entities of a transnational corporation should, where consistent with the laws and regulations of the countries concerned, be facilitated.]

[To be deleted]

53. Transnational corporations should be able to transfer freely and without restriction all payments relating to their investments such as income from invested capital and the repatriation of this capital when this investment is terminated, and licensing and technical assistance fees and

---

*In this alternative, the sentence will end here.

**Some delegations preferred not to have a second sentence.

other royalties, without prejudice to the relevant provisions of the "Balance of payments and financing" section of this Code and, in particular, its paragraph 29.]

[To be deleted]

B. Nationalization and compensation

54. [In the exercise of its right to nationalize or expropriate totally or partially the assets of transnational corporations operating in its territory, the State adopting those measures should pay adequate compensation taking into account its own laws and regulations and all the circumstances which the State may deem relevant. When the question of compensation gives rise to controversy or should there be a dispute as to whether a nationalization or expropriation has taken place, it shall be settled under the domestic law of the nationalizing or expropriating State and by its tribunals.]

[In the exercise of their sovereignty, States have the right to nationalize or expropriate foreign-owned property in their territory. Any such taking of property whether direct or indirect, consistent with international law, must be non-discriminatory, for a public purpose, in accordance with due process of law, and not be in violation of specific undertakings to the contrary by contract or other agreement; and be accompanied by the payment of prompt, adequate and effective compensation. Such compensation should correspond to the full value of the property interests taken, on the basis of their fair market value, including going concern value, or where appropriate other internationally accepted methods of valuation, determined apart from any effects on value caused by the expropriatory measure or measures, or the expectation of them. Such compensation payments should be freely convertible and transferable, and should not be subject to any restrictive measures applicable to transfers of payments, income or capital.]

[In the exercise of its sovereignty, a State has the right to nationalize or expropriate totally or partially the assets of transnational corporations in its territory, and appropriate compensation should be paid by the State adopting such measures, in accordance with its own laws and regulations and all the circumstances which the State deems relevant. Relevant international obligations freely undertaken by the States concerned apply.]

[A State has the right to nationalize or expropriate the assets of transnational corporations in its territory against compensation, in accordance with its own laws and regulations and its international obligations.]

C. Jurisdiction

[55.] [Entities of transnational corporations are subject to the jurisdiction of the countries in which they operate.]

[An entity of a transnational corporation operating in a given country is subject to the jurisdiction of such a country] [in respect of its operations in that country.]

[To be deleted]

56. [Disputes between a State and an entity of a transnational corporation operating in its territory are subject to the jurisdiction of the courts and other competent authorities of that State unless amicably settled between the parties.]

[Disputes between a State and an entity of a transnational corporation which are not amicably settled between the parties or resolved in accordance with previously agreed dispute settlement procedures, should be submitted to competent courts or other authorities, or to other agreed means of settlement, such as arbitration.]

[Disputes between States and entities of transnational corporations, which are not amicably settled between the parties, shall/should be submitted to competent national courts or authorities in conformity with the principle of paragraph 7. Where the parties so agree, such disputes may be referred to other mutually acceptable dispute settlement procedures.]

[57. In contracts in which at least one party is an entity of a transnational corporation the parties should be free to choose the applicable law and the form for settlement of disputes, including arbitration, it being understood that such a choice may be limited in its effects by the law of the countries concerned.]

[To be deleted]

58. [States should [use moderation and restraint in order to] [seek to] avoid [undue] encroachment on a Jurisdiction more [properly appertaining to, or more] appropriately exercisable, by another State.] Where the exercise of jurisdiction over transnational corporations and their entities by more than one State may lead to conflicts of jurisdiction, States concerned should endeavour to adopt mutually acceptable [principles and procedures, bilaterally or multilaterally, for the avoidance or settlement of such conflicts,] [arrangements] on the basis of respect for [their mutual interests] [the principle of sovereign equality and mutual interests.]

[To be placed in the section on intergovernmental co-operation.]

INTERGOVERNMENTAL CO-OPERATION

59. [It is acknowledged] [States agree] that intergovernmental co-operation is essential in accomplishing the objectives of the Code.

60. [States agree that] intergovernmental co-operation should be established or strengthened at the international level and, where appropriate, at the bilateral, regional and interregional levels [with a view to promoting the contribution of transnational corporations to their developmental

goals, particularly those of developing countries, while controlling and eliminating their negative effects].*

61. States [agree to] [should] exchange information on the measures they have taken to give effect to the Code and on their experience with the Code.

62. States [agree to] [should] consult on a bilateral or multilateral basis, as appropriate, on matters relating to the Code and its application [in particular on conflicting requirements imposed on transnational corporations by the countries in which they operate and issues of conflicting national jurisdictions] [in particular in relation to conflicting requirements imposed by parent companies on their entities operating in different countries] and with respect to the development of international agreements and arrangements on issues related to the Code.

63. States [agree to] [should] take into consideration the objectives of the Code as reflected in its provisions when negotiating bilateral or multilateral agreements concerning transnational corporations.

64. States [agree not to use] [should not use] transnational corporations as instruments to intervene in the internal or external affairs of other States [and agree to take appropriate action within their jurisdiction to prevent transnational corporations from engaging in activities referred to in paragraph 15 to 17 of this Code].

65. Government action on behalf of a transnational corporation operating in another country should/shall be subject to the principle of exhaustion of local remedies provided in such a country and, when agreed among the Governments concerned, to procedures for dealing with international legal claims. Such action should not in any event amount to the use of any type of coercive measures not consistent with the Charter of the United Nations and the Declaration on Principles of International Law concerning Friendly Relations and Co-operation among States in accordance with the Charter of the United Nations.

IMPLEMENTATION OF THE CODE OF CONDUCT

A. Action at the national level

66. In order to ensure and promote implementation of the Code at the national level, States shall/should, inter alia:

(a) Publicize and disseminate the Code;

(b) Follow the implementation of the Code within their territories;

* It is agreed that the last bracketed text will be deleted provided that the concept embodied therein is referred to in the section on objectives.

(c) Report to the United Nations Commission on Transnational Corporations on the action taken at the national level to promote the code and on the experience gained from its implementation;

(d) Take actions to reflect their support for the Code and take into account the objectives of the Code as reflected in its provisions when introducing implementing and reviewing laws, regulations and administrative practices on matters dealt with in the Code.

B. International institutional machinery

67. The United Nations Commission on Transnational Corporations shall assume the functions of the international institutional machinery for the implementation of the Code. In this capacity, the Commission shall be open to the participation of all States having accepted the Code. [It may establish the subsidiary bodies and specific procedures it deems necessary for the effective discharge of its functions.] The United Nations Centre of Transnational Corporations shall act as the secretariat to the Commission.

68. The Commission shall act as the focal international body within the United Nations system for all matters related to the Code. It shall establish and maintain close contacts with other United Nations organizations and specialized agencies dealing with matters related to the Code and its implementation with a view to co-ordinating work related to the Code. When matters covered by international agreements or arrangements, specifically referred to in the Code, which have been worked out in other United Nations forums, arise, the Commission shall forward such matters to the competent bodies concerned with such agreements or arrangements.

69. The Commission shall have the following functions:

(a) To discuss at its annual sessions matters related to the Code. If agreed by the Governments engaged in consultations on specific issues related to the Code, the Commission shall facilitate such intergovernmental consultations to the extent possible. [Representatives of trade unions, business, consumer and other relevant groups may express their views on matters related to the Code through the non-governmental organizations represented in the Commission.]

(b) Periodically to assess the implementation of the Code, such assessments being based on reports submitted by Governments and, as appropriate, on documentation from United Nations organizations and specialized agencies performing work relevant to the Code and non-governmental organizations represented in the Commission. The first assessment shall take place not earlier than two years and not later than three years after the adoption of the Code. The second assessment shall take place two years after the first one. The Commission shall determine whether a periodicity of two years is to be maintained or modified for subsequent assessments. The format of assessments shall be determined by the Commission.

[(c) To provide [, upon the request of a Government,] clarification of the provisions of the Code in the light of actual situations in which the applicability and implications of the Code have been the subject of intergovernmental consultations. In clarifying the provisions of the Code, the Commission shall not draw conclusions concerning the conduct of the parties involved in the situation which led to the request for clarification. The clarification is to be restricted to issues illustrated by such a situation. The detailed procedures regarding clarification are to be determined by the Commission.]

[To be deleted.]

(d) To report annually to the General Assembly [through the Economic and Social Council] on its activities regarding the implementation of the Code.

(e) To facilitate intergovernmental arrangements or agreements on specific aspects relating to transnational corporations upon request of the Governments concerned.

70. The United Nations Centre on Transnational Corporations shall provide assistance relating to the implementation of the Code, inter alia, by collecting, analysing and disseminating information and conducting research and surveys, as required and specified by the Commission.

C. Review procedure

71. The Commission shall make recommendations to the General Assembly [through the Economic and Social Council] for the purpose of reviewing the Code. The first review shall take place not later than six years after the adoption of the Code. The General Assembly shall establish, as appropriate, the modalities for reviewing the Code.*

Notes

a/ No drafting was done on the Preamble and Objectives of the Code. However, the following text was drafted during the discussion on other parts of the Code and the decision was taken to place it in one of the substantive introductory parts of the Code:

"For the purposes of this Code, the principles set out in the Tripartite Declaration of Principles concerning Multinational Enterprises and Social Policy, adopted by the Governing Body of the International Labour Office, should apply in the field of employment, training, conditions of work and life and industrial relations."
(No decision has yet been taken on the exact location of this paragraph.)

---

*Further discussion of this provision will take place after related issues, such as the mode of adoption and the legal nature of the code, have been settled.

b/ Some delegations accepted paragraphs 26, 30, 31 and 32 on balance of payments and financing on an ad referendum basis.

c/ The placement of this paragraph has not yet been decided.

Appendix

NON-COLLABORATION BY TRANSNATIONAL CORPORATIONS WITH RACIST MINORITY REGIMES IN SOUTHERN AFRICA a/

14. In accordance with the efforts of the international community towards the elimination of apartheid in South Africa and its illegal occupation of Namibia,

(a) Transnational corporations shall/should refrain from operations and activities supporting and sustaining the racist minority regime of South Africa in maintaining the system of apartheid and the illegal occupation of Namibia;

(b) Transnational corporations shall/should engage in appropriate activities within their competence with a view to eliminating racial discrimination and all other aspects of the system of apartheid;

(c) Transnational corporations shall/should comply strictly with obligations resulting from Security Council decisions and shall/should fully respect those resulting from all relevant United Nations resolutions;

(d) With regard to investment in Namibia, transnational corporations shall/should comply strictly with obligations resulting from Security Council resolution 283 (1970) and other relevant Security Council decisions and shall/should fully respect those resulting from all relevant United Nations resolutions.

Notes

a/ The text of paragraph 14 was agreed ad referendum in the working group on paragraph 14, but no final decision thereon was taken by the Commission.

* * *

DRAFT INTERNATIONAL CODE OF CONDUCT ON THE TRANSFER OF TECHNOLOGY*
[1985 VERSION]

The Draft International Code of Conduct on the Transfer of Technology was negotiated under the auspices of the United Nations Conference on Trade and Development between 1976 and 1985. The text reproduced in this volume is that of the Draft Code as it stood at the close of the sixth session of the Conference on an International Code of Conduct on the Transfer of Technology on 5 June 1985. The Draft Code includes a number of appendices that reflect outstanding issues and alternative wording proposed for portions of the Draft Code. The appendices have not been reproduced in this volume. The draft Code has not been adopted by the United Nations General Assembly.

Preamble

The United Nations Conference on an International Code of Conduct on the Transfer of Technology,

1. Recognizing the fundamental role of science and technology in the socio-economic development of all countries, and in particular, in the acceleration of the development of the developing countries;

2. Believing that technology is key to the progress of mankind and that all peoples have the right to benefit from the advances and developments in science and technology in order to improve their standards of living;

3. Bearing in mind relevant decisions of the General Assembly and other bodies of the United Nations, in particular UNCTAD, on the transfer and development of technology;

4. Recognizing the need to facilitate an adequate transfer and development of technology so as to strengthen the scientific and technological capabilities of all countries, particularly the developing countries, and to co-operate with the developing countries in their own efforts in this field as a decisive step in the progress towards the establishment of a new international economic order;

---

* Source: United Nations Conference on Trade and Development (1985). "Draft International Code of Conduct on the Transfer of Technology", Note by the UNCTAD Secretariat to the United Nations Conference on an International Code of Conduct on the Transfer of Technology, Document TD/CODE TOT/47 (New York: UNCTAD). The Appendices A, B, C, D, E and F referred to in the text and the endnotes can be found in the source document. In the present text, the following key is used to identify the sponsorship of a text, where the text is not an agreed one: Group of 77 text: *; Group B: **; Group D and Mongolia: ***. [Note added by the editor].

5. Desirous of promoting international scientific and technological co-operation in the interest of peace, security and national independence and for the benefit of all nations;

6. Striving to promote an increase of the international transfer of technology with an equal opportunity for all countries to participate irrespective of their social and economic system and of their level of economic development;

7. Recognizing the need for developed countries to grant special treatment to the developing countries in the field of the transfer of technology;

8. Drawing attention to the need to improve the flow of technological information, and in particular to promote the widest and fullest flow of information on the availability of alternative technologies, and on the selection of appropriate technologies suited to the specific needs of developing countries;

9. Believing that a Code of Conduct will effectively assist the developing countries in their selection, acquisition and effective use of technologies appropriate to their needs in order to develop improved economic standards and living conditions;

10. Believing that a Code of Conduct will help to create conditions conducive to the promotion of the international transfer of technology, under mutually agreed and advantageous terms to all parties;

11. 1/

12. 1/

Chapter 1

Definitions and scope of application

1.1. For the purposes of the present Code of Conduct:

(a) "Party" means any person, either natural or juridical, of public or private law, either individual or collective, such as corporations, companies, firms, partnerships and other associations, or any combination thereof, whether created, owned or controlled by States, Government agencies, juridical persons, or individuals, wherever they operate, as well as States, Government agencies and international, regional and subregional organizations, when they engage in an international transfer of technology transaction which is usually considered to be of a commercial nature. The term "party" includes, among the entities enumerated above, incorporated branches, subsidiaries and affiliates, joint ventures or other legal entities regardless of the economic and other relationships between and among them. 2/

(b) "Acquiring party" means the party which obtains a licence to use or to exploit, purchases or otherwise acquires technology of a proprietary or non-proprietary nature and/or rights related thereto in a transfer of technology.

(c) "Supplying party" means the party which licenses, sells, assigns or otherwise provides technology of a proprietary or non-proprietary nature and/or rights related thereto in a transfer of technology.

1.2. Transfer of technology under this Code is the transfer of systematic knowledge for the manufacture of a product, for the application of a process or for the rendering of a service and does not extend to the transactions involving the mere sale or mere lease of goods.

1.3. Transfer of technology transactions are arrangements between parties involving transfer of technology, as defined in paragraph 1.2 above, particularly in each of the following cases:

(a) The assignment, sale and licensing of all forms of industrial property, except for trade marks, service marks and trade names when they are not part of transfer of technology transactions;

(b) The provision of know-how and technical expertise in the form of feasibility studies, plans, diagrams, models, instructions, guides, formulae, basic or detailed engineering designs, specifications and equipment for training, services involving technical advisory and managerial personnel, and personnel training;

(c) The provision of technological knowledge necessary for the installation, operation and functioning of plant and equipment, and turnkey projects;

(d) The provision of technological knowledge necessary to acquire, install and use machinery, equipment, intermediate goods and/or raw materials which have been acquired by purchase, lease or other means;

(e) The provision of technological contents of industrial and technical co-operation arrangements.

1.4. International transfer of technology transactions. 3/

1.5. The Code of Conduct is universally applicable in scope and is addressed to all parties to transfer of technology transactions and to all countries and groups of countries, irrespective of their economic and political systems and their levels of development.

1.6. Regional groupings of States. 4/

Chapter 2

Objectives and principles

2. The Code of Conduct is based on the following objectives and principles:

2.1. Objectives

(i) To establish general and equitable standards on which to base the relationships among parties to transfer of technology transactions and governments concerned, taking into consideration their legitimate interests, and giving due recognition to special needs of developing countries for the fulfilment of their economic and social development objectives.

(ii) To promote mutual confidence between parties as well as their governments.

(iii) To encourage transfer of technology transactions, particularly those involving developing countries, under conditions where bargaining positions of the parties to the transactions are balanced in such a way as to avoid abuses of a stronger position and thereby to achieve mutually satisfactory agreements.

(iv) To facilitate and increase the international flow of technological information, particularly on the availability of alternative technologies, as a prerequisite for the assessment, selection, adaptation, development and use of technologies in all countries, particularly in developing countries.

(v) To facilitate and increase the international flow of proprietary and non-proprietary technology for strengthening the growth of the scientific and technological capabilities of all countries, in particular developing countries, so as to increase their participation in world production and trade.

(vi) To increase the contributions of technology to the identification and solution of social and economic problems of all countries, particularly the developing countries, including the development of basic sectors of their national economies.

(vii) To facilitate the formulation, adoption and implementation of national policies, laws and regulations on the subject of transfer of technology by setting forth international norms.

(viii) To promote adequate arrangements as regards unpackaging in terms of information concerning the various elements of the technology to be transferred, such as that required for technical, institutional and financial evaluation of the transaction, thus avoiding undue or unnecessary packaging.

(ix) To specify restrictive [business] practices from which parties to technology transfer transactions [shall] [should] refrain. 5/

(x) To set forth an appropriate set of responsibilities and obligations of parties to transfer of technology transactions, taking into consideration their legitimate interests as well as differences in their bargaining positions.

2.2. Principles

(i) The Code of Conduct is universally applicable in scope.

(ii) States have the right to adopt all appropriate measures for facilitating and regulating the transfer of technology, in a manner consistent with their international obligations, taking into consideration the legitimate interests of all parties concerned, and encouraging transfers of technology under mutually agreed, fair and reasonable terms and conditions.

(iii) The principles of sovereignty and political independence of States (covering, inter alia, the requirements of foreign policy and national security) and sovereign equality of States, should be recognized in facilitating and regulating transfer of technology transactions.

(iv) States should co-operate in the international transfer of technology in order to promote economic growth throughout the world, especially that of the developing countries. Co-operation in such transfer should be irrespective of any differences in political, economic and social systems; this is one of the important elements in maintaining international peace and security and promoting international economic stability and progress, the general welfare of nations and international co-operation free from discrimination based on such differences. Nothing in this Code may be construed as impairing or derogating from the provisions of the Charter of the United Nations or actions taken in pursuance thereof. It is understood that special treatment in transfer of technology should be accorded to developing countries in accordance with the provisions in this Code on the subject.

(v) The separate responsibilities of parties to transfer of technology transactions, on the one hand, and those of governments when not acting as parties, on the other, should be clearly distinguished.

(vi) Mutual benefits should accrue to technology supplying and recipient parties in order to maintain and increase the international flow of technology.

(vii) Facilitating and increasing the access to technology, particularly for developing countries, under mutually agreed fair and reasonable terms and conditions, are fundamental elements in the process of technology transfer and development.

(viii) Recognition of the protection of industrial property rights granted under national law.

(ix) Technology supplying parties when operating in an acquiring country should respect the sovereignty and the laws of that country, act with proper regard for that country's declared development policies and priorities and endeavour to contribute substantially to the development of the acquiring country. The freedom of parties to negotiate, conclude and perform agreements for the transfer of technology on mutually acceptable terms and conditions should be based on respect for the foregoing and other principles set forth in this Code.

Chapter 3

National regulation of transfer of technology transactions

3.1. In adopting, and in the light of evolving circumstances making necessary changes in laws, regulations and rules, and policies with respect to transfer of technology transactions, States have the right to adopt measures such as those listed in paragraph 3.4 of this chapter and should act on the basis that these measures should:

(i) Recognize that a close relationship exists between technology flows [and] the conditions under which such flows are admitted and treated;

(ii) Promote a favourable and beneficial climate for the international transfer of technology;

(iii) Take into consideration in an equitable manner the legitimate interests of all parties;

(iv) Encourage and facilitate transfers of technology to take place under mutually agreed, fair and reasonable terms and conditions having regard to the principles and objectives of the Code;

(v) Take into account the differing factors characterizing the transactions such as local conditions, the nature of the technology and the scope of the undertaking;

(vi) Be consistent with their international obligations.

3.2. Measures adopted by States including decisions of competent administrative bodies should be applied fairly, equitably, and on the same basis to all parties in accordance with established procedures of law and the principles and objectives of the Code. Laws and regulations should be clearly defined and publicly and readily available. To the extent appropriate, relevant information regarding decisions of competent administrative bodies should be disseminated.

3.3. Each country adopting legislation on the protection of industrial property should have regard to its national needs of economic and social development, and should ensure an effective protection of industrial property rights granted under its national law and other related rights recognized by its national law.

3.4. Measures on regulation of the flow and effects of transfer of technology, finance and technical aspects of technology transactions and on organizational forms and mechanisms may deal with:

Finance

(a) Currency regulations of foreign exchange payments and remittances;

(b) Conditions of domestic credit and financing facilities;

(c) Transferability of payments;

(d) Tax treatment;

(e) Pricing policies;

Renegotiation

(f) Terms, conditions and objective criteria for the renegotiation of transfer of technology transactions;

Technical aspects

(g) Technology specifications and standards for the various components of the transfer of technology transactions and their payments;

(h) Analysis and evaluation of transfer of technology transactions to assist parties in their negotiations;

(i) Use of local and imported components;

Organizational forms and mechanisms

(j) Evaluation, negotiation, and registration of transfer of technology transactions;

(k) Terms, conditions, duration, of transfer of technology transactions;

(l) Loss of ownership and/or control of domestic acquiring enterprises;

(m) Regulation of foreign collaboration arrangements and agreements that could displace national enterprises from the domestic market;

(n) The definition of fields of activity of foreign enterprises and the choice of channels, mechanisms, organizational forms for the transfer of technology and the prior or subsequent approval of transfer of technology transactions and their registration in these fields;

(o) The determination of the legal effect of transactions which are not in conformity with national laws, regulations and administrative decisions on the transfer of technology;

(p) The establishment or strengthening of national administrative mechanisms for the implementation and application of the Code of Conduct and of national laws, regulations and policies on the transfer of technology;

(q) Promotion of appropriate channels for the international exchange of information and experience in the field of the transfer of technology.

Chapter 4 6/

[The regulation of practices and arrangements involving the transfer of technology] [Restrictive business practices] [Exclusion of political discrimination and restrictive business practices] 7/

Section A: (Chapeau) 8/

Section B: (List of practices) 9/

1. [Exclusive] ** Grant-back provisions 10/

Requiring the acquiring party to transfer or grant back to the supplying party, or to any other enterprise designated by the supplying party, improvements arising from the acquired technology, on an exclusive basis [or]* without offsetting consideration or reciprocal obligations from the supplying party, or when the practice will constitute an abuse of a dominant market position of the supplying party.

2. Challenges to validity 10/

[Unreasonably] ** requiring the acquiring party to refrain from challenging the validity of patents and other types of protection for inventions involved in the transfer or the validity of other such grants claimed or obtained by the supplying party, recognizing that any issues concerning the mutual rights and obligations of the parties following such a challenge will be determined by the appropriate applicable law and the terms of the agreement to the extent consistent with that law. 11/

3. Exclusive dealing

Restrictions on the freedom of the acquiring party to enter into sales, representation or manufacturing agreements relating to similar or competing technologies or products or to obtain competing technology, when such restrictions are not needed for ensuring the achievement of legitimate interests, particularly including securing the confidentiality of the technology transferred or best effort distribution or promotional obligations.

4. Restrictions on research 10/

[Unreasonably]**/*** restricting the acquiring party either in undertaking research and development directed to absorb and adapt the transferred technology to local conditions or in initiating research and development programmes in connection with new products, processes or equipment.

5. Restrictions on use of personnel 10/

[Unreasonably] ** requiring the acquiring party to use personnel designated by the supplying party, except to the extent necessary to ensure the efficient transmission phase for the transfer of technology and putting it to use or thereafter continuing such requirement beyond the time when adequately trained local personnel are available or have been trained; or prejudicing the use of personnel of the technology acquiring country.

6. Price fixing 10/

[Unjustifiably]** imposing regulation of prices to be charged by acquiring parties in the relevant market to which the technology was transferred for products manufactured or services produced using the technology supplied.

7. Restrictions on adaptations 10/

Restrictions which [unreasonably]** prevent the acquiring party from adapting the imported technology to local conditions or introducing innovations in it, or which oblige the acquiring party to introduce unwanted or unnecessary design or specification changes, if the acquiring party makes adaptations on his own responsibility and without using the technology supplying party's name, trade or service marks or trade names, and except to the extent that this adaptation unsuitably affects those products, or the process for their manufacture, to be supplied to the supplying party, his designates, or his other licensees, or to be used as a component or spare part in a product to be supplied to his customers.

8. Exclusive sales or representation agreements

Requiring the acquiring party to grant exclusive sales or representation rights to the supplying party or any person designated by the supplying party, except as to subcontracting or manufacturing arrangements wherein the parties have agreed that all or part of the production under the technology transfer arrangement will be distributed by the supplying party or any person designated by him.

9. Tying arrangements 10/

[Unduly]** imposing acceptance of additional technology, future inventions and improvements, goods or services not wanted by the acquiring party or [unduly]** restricting sources of technology, goods or services, as a condition for obtaining the technology required when not required to maintain the quality of the product or service when the supplier's trade or service mark or other identifying item is used by the acquiring party, or to fulfil a specific performance obligation which has been guaranteed, provided further that adequate specification of the ingredients is not feasible or would involve the disclosure of additional technology not covered by the arrangement.

10. Export restrictions 8/

11. Patent pool or cross-licensing agreements and other arrangements

Restrictions on territories, quantities, prices, customers or markets arising out of patent pool or cross-licensing agreements or other international transfer of technology interchange arrangements among technology suppliers which unduly limit access to new technological developments or which would result in an abusive domination of an industry or market with adverse effects on the transfer of technology, except for those restrictions appropriate and ancillary to co-operative arrangements such as co-operative research arrangements.

12. Restrictions on publicity 10/

Restrictions [unreasonably]** regulating the advertising or publicity by the acquiring party except where restrictions of such publicity may be required to prevent injury to the supplying party's goodwill or reputation where the advertising or publicity makes reference to the supplying party's name, trade or service marks, trade names or other identifying items, or for legitimate reasons of avoiding product liability when the supplying party may be subject to such liability, or where appropriate for safety purposes or to protect consumers, or when needed to secure the confidentiality of the technology transferred.

13. Payments and other obligations after expiration of industrial property rights

Requiring payments or imposing other obligations for continuing the use of industrial property rights which have been invalidated, cancelled or have expired recognizing that any other issue, including other payment obligations for technology, shall be dealt with by the appropriate applicable law and the terms of the agreement to the extent consistent with that law. 11/

14. Restrictions after expiration of arrangement. 8/

Chapter 5

Responsibilities and Obligations of Parties

Common provision on negotiating as well as contractual phase

5.1. When negotiating and concluding a technology transfer agreement, the parties should, in accordance with this chapter, be responsive to the economic and social development objectives of the respective countries of the parties and particularly of the technology acquiring country, and when negotiating, concluding and performing a technology transfer agreement, the parties should observe fair and honest business practices and take into account the specific circumstances of the individual case and recognition should be given to certain circumstances, mainly the stage of development of technology, the economic and technical capabilities of the parties, the nature and type of the transaction such as any ongoing or continuous flow of technology between the parties.

Negotiating phase

5.2. In being responsive to the economic and social development objectives mentioned in this chapter each party should take into account the other's request to include in the agreements, to the extent technically and commercially practicable and for adequate consideration, when appropriate, such as the case in which the supplying party incurs additional costs or efforts, items clearly related to the official economic and social development objectives of the country of the requesting party as enunciated by its government. Such items include, inter alia, where applicable:

(a) Use of locally available resources

(i) specific provisions for the use for the tasks concerned of adequately trained or otherwise suitable local personnel to be designated and subsequently made available by the potential technology recipient including managerial personnel, as well as for the training of suitably skilled local personnel to be designated and subsequently made available by the potential technology recipient;

(ii) specific provisions for the use of locally available materials, technologies, technical skills, consultancy and engineering services and other resources to be indicated and subsequently made available by the potential technology recipient;

(b) Rendering of technical services

Specific provisions for the rendering of technical services in the introduction and operation of the technology to be transferred;

(c) Unpackaging

Upon request of the potential acquiring party, the potential supplying party should, to the extent practicable, make adequate arrangements as regards unpackaging in terms of information concerning the various elements of the technology to be transferred, such as that required for technical, institutional and financial evaluation of the potential supplying party's offer.

5.3. Business negotiating practices

When negotiating a technology transfer agreement, the parties should observe fair and honest business practices and therefore:

(a) Both potential parties

(i) Fair and reasonable terms and conditions

(i) Should negotiate in good faith with the aim of reaching, in a timely manner, an agreement containing fair and reasonable commercial terms and conditions, including agreement on payments such as licence fees, royalties and other considerations;

(ii) The price or consideration to be charged should be fair and reasonable, it should be clearly indicated and, to the extent practicable, specified in such a manner that the acquiring party would be able to appreciate its reasonableness and fairness by comparing it to the price or consideration for other comparable technologies transferred under similar conditions, which may be known to him;

(ii) Relevant information

Should consider requests to inform each other, to the extent appropriate, about their prior arrangements which may affect the contemplated technology transfer;

(iii) Confidential information

Should keep secret, in accordance with any obligation, either legal or contractual, all confidential information received from the other party and make use of the confidential information received from a potential party only for the purpose of evaluating this party's offer or request for other purposes agreed upon by the parties;

(iv) Termination of negotiations

May cease negotiations if, during the negotiations, either party determines that a satisfactory agreement cannot be reached;

(b) The potential acquiring party

Relevant information

Should provide the potential technology supplier in a timely manner with the available specific information concerning the technical conditions and official economic and social development objectives as well as legislation of the acquiring country relevant to the particular transfer and use of the technology under negotiation as far as such information is needed for the supplying party's responsiveness under this chapter;

(c) The potential supplying party

Relevant information

(i) Should disclose, in a timely manner, to the potential technology acquiring party any reason actually known to him, on account of which the technology to be supplied, when used in accordance with the terms and conditions of the proposed agreement, would not meet particular health, safety and environmental requirements in the technology acquiring country, already known to him as being relevant in the specific case or which have been specifically drawn to his attention, as well as any serious health, safety and environmental risks known by the supplier associated with the use of the technology and of products to be produced by it;

(ii) Should disclose to the potential technology acquiring party, to the actual extent known to him, any limitation, including any pending official procedures or litigation which adversely concerns, in a direct manner, the existence or validity of the rights to be transferred, on his entitlement to grant the rights or render the assistance and services specified in the proposed agreement;

Provision of accessories, spare parts and components

(iii) Should to the extent feasible, take into account the request of the acquiring party to provide it for a period to be specified with accessories, spare parts and components produced by the supplying party and necessary for using the technology to be transferred, particularly where alternative sources are unavailable.

Contractual phase - Chapeau

5.4. The technology transfer agreement should, in accordance with 5.1., provide for mutually acceptable contractual obligations, including those relating to payments and, where appropriate, inter alia, the following:

(i) Access to improvements

Access for a specified period or for the lifetime of the agreement to improvements to the technology transferred under the agreement;

(ii) Confidentiality 12/

(iii) Dispute settlement and applicable law 12/

(iv) Description of the technology

The technology supplier's guarantee that the technology meets the description contained in the technology transfer agreement;

(v) Suitability for use

The technology supplier's guarantee that the technology, if used in accordance with the supplier's specific instructions given pursuant to the agreement, is suitable for manufacturing of goods or production of services as agreed upon by the parties and stipulated in the agreement;

(vi) Rights to the technology transferred

The technology supplier's representation that on the date of the signing of the agreement, it is, to the best of its knowledge, not aware of third parties' valid patent rights or similar protection for inventions which would be infringed by the use of the technology when used as specified in the agreement;

(vii) Quality levels and goodwill

The technology recipient's commitment to observe quality levels agreed upon in cases where the agreement includes the use of the supplier's trade marks, trade names or similar identification of goodwill, and both parties' commitment to avoid taking actions primarily or deliberately intended to injure the other's goodwill or reputation;

(viii) Performance guarantees

Specification to technical performance parameters which the supplying party has agreed to guarantee, including specification of requirements for the achievement of such parameters, details of the manner of determining whether the performance has been met and the consequences of failure to meet that performance;

(ix) Transmission of documentation

The supplying party's commitment that relevant technical documentation and other data required from him for a particular purpose defined in terms directly specified in the agreement will be transferred in a timely manner and as correctly and completely for such purpose as agreed upon;

(x) Training of personnel and provision of accessories, spare parts and components

Where negotiations under paragraphs 5.2 (a) (i) and 5.5 (c) (iii) have taken place, suitable provisions for training of personnel and supply of accessories, spare parts and components would be made, consistent with the results of the negotiations;

(xi) Liability

Disposition concerning liability for the non-fulfilment by either party of its responsibilities under the technology transfer agreement including questions of loss, damage or injury.

Chapter 6

Special treatment for developing countries

6.1. Taking into consideration the needs and problems of developing countries, particularly of the least developed countries, governments of developed countries, directly or through appropriate international organizations, in order to facilitate and encourage the initiation and strengthening of the scientific and technological capabilities of developing countries so as to assist and co-operate with them in their efforts to fulfil their economic and social objectives, should take adequate specific measures, inter alia, to:

(i) facilitate access by developing countries to available information regarding the availabilities, description, location and, as far as possible, approximate cost of technologies which might help those countries to attain their economic and social development objectives;

(ii) give developing countries the freest and fullest possible access to technologies whose transfer is not subject to private decisions; 13/

(iii) facilitate access by developing countries, to the extent practicable, to technologies whose transfer is subject to private decisions; 13/

(iv) assist and co-operate with developing countries in the assessment and adaptation of existing technologies and in the development of national technologies by facilitating access, as far as possible, to available scientific and industrial research data;

(v) co-operate in the development of scientific and technological resources in developing countries, including the creation and growth of innovative capacities;

(vi) assist developing countries in strengthening their technological capacity, especially in the basic sectors of their national economy, through creation of and support for laboratories, experimental facilities and institutes for training and research;

(vii) co-operate in the establishment or strengthening of national, regional and/or international institutions, including technology transfer centres, to help developing countries to develop and obtain the technology and skills required for the establishment, development and enhancement of their technological capabilities including the design, construction and operation of plants;

(viii) encourage the adaptation of research and development, engineering and design to conditions and factor endowments prevailing in developing countries;

(ix) co-operate in measures leading to greater utilization of the managerial, engineering, design and technical experience of the personnel and the institutions of developing countries in specific economic and other development projects undertaken at the bilateral and multilateral levels;

(x) encourage the training of personnel from developing countries.

6.2. Governments of developed countries, directly or through appropriate international organizations, in assisting in the promotion of transfer of technology to developing countries - particularly to the least developed countries - should, as a part of programmes for development assistance and co-operation, take into account requests from developing countries to:

(i) contribute to the development of national technologies in developing countries by providing experts under development assistance and research exchange programmes;

(ii) provide training for research, engineering, design and other personnel from developing countries engaged in the development of national technologies or in the adaptation and use of technologies transferred;

(iii) provide assistance and co-operation in the development and administration of laws and regulations with a view to facilitating the transfer of technology;

(iv) provide support for projects in developing countries for the development and adaptation of new and existing technologies suitable to the particular needs of developing countries;

(v) grant credits on terms more favourable than the usual commercial terms for financing the acquisition of capital and intermediate goods in the context of approved development projects involving transfer of technology transactions so as to reduce the cost of projects and improve the quality of technology received by the developing countries;

(vi) provide assistance and co-operation in the development and administration of laws and regulations designed to avoid health, safety and environmental risks associated with technology or the products produced by it.

6.3. Governments of developed countries should take measures in accordance with national policies, laws and regulations to encourage and to endeavour to give incentive to enterprises and institutions in their countries, either individually or in collaboration with enterprises and institutions in developing countries, particularly those in the least developed countries, to make special efforts, inter alia, to:

(i) assist in the development of technological capabilities of the enterprises in developing countries, including special training as required by the recipients;

(ii) undertake the development of technology appropriate to the needs of developing countries;

(iii) undertake R and D activity in developing countries of interest to such countries, as well as to improve co-operation between enterprises and scientific and technological institutions of developed and developing countries;

(iv) assist in projects by enterprises and institutions in developing countries for the development and adaptation of new and existing technologies suitable to the particular needs and conditions of developing countries.

6.4. The special treatment accorded to developing countries should be responsive to their economic and social objectives vis-a-vis their relative stage of economic and social development and with particular attention to the special problems and conditions of the least developed countries.

Chapter 7

International collaboration

7.1. The States recognize the need for appropriate international collaboration among governments, intergovernmental bodies, and organs and agencies of the United Nations system, including the international institutional machinery provided for in this Code, with a view to facilitating an expanded international flow of technology for strengthening the technological capabilities of all countries, taking into account the objectives and principles of this Code, and to promoting the effective implementation of its provisions.

7.2. Such international collaboration between governments at the bilateral or multilateral, subregional, regional or interregional levels may include, inter alia, the following measures:

(i) Exchange of available information on the availability and description of technologies and technological alternatives;

(ii) Exchange of available information on experience in seeking solutions to problems relating to the transfer of technology, particularly restrictive [business]** practices in the transfer of technology; 14/

(iii) Exchange of information on development of national legislation with respect to the transfer of technology;

(iv) Promotion of the conclusion of international agreements which should provide equitable treatment for both technology supplying and recipient parties and governments;

(v) Consultations which may lead to greater harmonization, where appropriate, of national legislation and policies with respect to the transfer of technology;

(vi) Promotion, where appropriate, of common programmes for searching for, acquiring and disseminating technologies;

(vii) Promotion of programmes for the adaptation and development of technology in the context of development objectives;

(viii) Promotion of the development of scientific and technological resources and capabilities stimulating the development of indigenous technologies;

(ix) Action through international agreements to avoid, as far as possible, imposition of double taxation on earnings and payments arising out of transfer of technology transactions.

Chapter 8

International Institutional Machinery

8.1. Institutional arrangements

(a) 15/

(b) 15/

(c) States which have accepted the Code of Conduct on the Transfer of Technology should take appropriate steps at the national level to meet their commitment to the Code.

8.2. Functions of the International Institutional Machinery

8.2.1. The International Institutional Machinery shall have the following functions:

(a) To provide a forum and modalities for consultations, discussion, and exchange of views between States on matters related to the Code, in particular its application and its greater harmonization, and the experience gained in its operations;

(b) To undertake and disseminate periodically studies and research on transfer of technology related to the provisions of the code, with a view to increasing exchange of experience and giving greater effect to the application and implementation of the Code;

(c) To invite and consider relevant studies, documentation and reports from within the United Nations system, particularly from UNIDO and WIPO;

(d) To study matters relating to the Code and which might be characterized by data covering transfer of technology transactions and other relevant information obtained upon request addressed to all States;

(e) To collect and disseminate information on matters relating to the Code, to the over-all attainment of its goals and to the appropriate steps States have taken at the national level to promote an effective Code, including its objective and principles;

(f) To make appropriate reports and recommendations to States on matters within its competence including the application and implementation of the Code;

(g) To organize symposia, workshops and similar meetings concerning the application of the provisions of the Code, subject to the approval of the Trade and Development Board where financing from the regular budget is involved;

(h) To submit reports at least once a year on its work to the Trade and Development Board.

8.2.2. In the performance of its functions, the International Institutional Machinery may not act like a tribunal or otherwise pass judgement on the activities or conduct of individual Governments or of individual parties in connection with a specific transfer of technology transaction. The International Institutional Machinery should avoid becoming involved when parties in a specific transfer of technology transaction are in dispute.

8.2.3. The International Institutional Machinery shall establish such procedures as may be necessary to deal with issues related to confidentiality.

8.3. Review procedure 15/

8.4. Secretariat

The secretariat for the International Institutional Machinery shall be the UNCTAD secretariat. At the request of the International Institutional Machinery the secretariat shall submit relevant studies, documentation and other information to the International Institutional Machinery. It shall consult with and render assistance, by the relevant services, to States, particularly the developing countries, at their request, in the application of the Code at the national level, to the extent that resources are available.

8.5. General provisions 15/

Chapter 9

Applicable law and settlement of disputes 16/

ENDNOTES

1/ For texts under consideration, see appendices A and F.

2/ Group 2 accepts inclusion of this sentence subject to agreement to be reached on qualifications relating to the application of the Code to the relations of these entities in relevant parts of the Code.

3/ For texts under consideration, see appendices A and C.

4/ Text under consideration. See proposal in appendix C.

5/ Text under consideration. See also appendix A.

6/ In view of continuing negotiations on the chapter, no attempt has been made to number the provisions of this chapter consistently with the other chapters.

7/ Title of Chapter 4 under consideration.

8/ For texts under consideration, see appendices A and D.

9/ With regard to practices 15 to 20, see appendix A.l for text of agreed statement for inclusion in the report of the Conference, and for texts under consideration see appendix D.

10/ Text under consideration. See appendix A.

11/ The spokesman for the regional groups noted that their acceptance of agreed language which makes reference to the term "applicable law" is conditional upon acceptable resolution of differences in the group texts concerning applicable law and national regulation of this Code.

12/ For text under consideration, see appendix A.

13/ The term "private decision" in the particular context of this chapter should be officially interpreted in the light of the legal order of the respective country.

14/ Text under consideration; see also appendix A.

15/ For texts under consideration, see appendices A and E.

16/ For texts under consideration, see appendices A and F.

* * *

UNITED NATIONS GENERAL ASSEMBLY RESOLUTION 39/248: GUIDELINES FOR CONSUMER PROTECTION*

The Guidelines for Consumer Protection (United Nations General Assembly resolution 39/248) were adopted by the General Assembly at its 106th plenary meeting on 9 April 1985.

The General Assembly,

Recalling Economic and Social Council resolution 1981/62 of 23 July 1981, in which the Council requested the Secretary-General to continue consultations on consumer protection with a view to elaborating a set of general guidelines for consumer protection, taking particularly into account the needs of the developing countries,

Recalling further General Assembly resolution 38/147 of 19 December 1983,

Noting Economic and Social Council resolution 1984/63 of 26 July 1984,

1. *Decides* to adopt the guidelines for consumer protection annexed to the present resolution;

2. *Requests* the Secretary-General to disseminate the guidelines to Governments and other interested parties;

3. *Requests* all organizations of the United Nations system that elaborate guidelines and related documents on specific areas relevant to consumer protection to distribute them to the appropriate bodies of individual States.

Annex

GUIDELINES FOR CONSUMER PROTECTION

I. Objectives

1. Taking into account the interests and needs of consumers in all countries, particularly those in developing countries; recognizing that consumers often face imbalances in economic terms, educational levels, and bargaining power; and bearing in mind that consumers should have the right of access to non-hazardous products, as well as the right to promote just, equitable and

*Source: United Nations (1986). *Guidelines for Consumer Protection*, United Nations document ST/ESA/170, (New York, United Nations) Sales No. E.86.IV.2 [Note added by the editor].

sustainable economic and social development, these guidelines for consumer protection have the following objectives:

(a) To assist countries in achieving or maintaining adequate protection for their population as consumers;

(b) To facilitate production and distribution patterns responsive to the needs and desires of consumers;

(c) To encourage high levels of ethical conduct for those engaged in the production and distribution of goods and services to consumers;

(d) To assist countries in curbing abusive business practices by all enterprises at the national and international levels which adversely affect consumers;

(e) To facilitate the development of independent consumer groups;

(f) To further international co-operation in the field of consumer protection;

(g) To encourage the development of market conditions which provide consumers with greater choice at lower prices.

II. General principles

2. Governments should develop, strengthen or maintain a strong consumer protection policy, taking into account the guidelines set out below. In so doing, each Government must set its own priorities for the protection of consumers in accordance with the economic and social circumstances of the country, and the needs of its population, and bearing in mind the costs and benefits of proposed measures.

3. The legitimate needs which the guidelines are intended to meet are the following:

(a) The protection of consumers from hazards to their health and safety;

(b) The promotion and protection of the economic interests of consumers;

(c) Access of consumers to adequate information to enable them to make informed choices according to individual wishes and needs;

(d) Consumer education;

(e) Availability of effective consumer redress;

(f) Freedom to form consumer and other relevant groups or organizations and the opportunity of such organizations to present their views in decision-making processes affecting them.

4. Governments should provide or maintain adequate infrastructure to develop, implement and monitor consumer protection policies. Special care should be taken to ensure that measures for consumer protection are implemented for the benefit of all sectors of the population, particularly the rural population.

5. All enterprises should obey the relevant laws and regulations of the countries in which they do business. They should also conform to the appropriate provisions of international standards for consumer protection to which the competent authorities of the country in question have agreed. (Hereinafter references to international standards in the guidelines should be viewed in the context of this paragraph.)

6. The potential positive role of universities and public and private enterprises in research should be considered when developing consumer protection policies.

III. Guidelines

7. The following guidelines should apply both to home-produced goods and services and to imports.

8. In applying any procedures or regulations for consumer protection, due regard should be given to ensuring that they do not become barriers to international trade and that they are consistent with international trade obligations.

A. Physical safety

9. Governments should adopt or encourage the adoption of appropriate measures, including legal systems, safety regulations, national or international standards, voluntary standards and the maintenance of safety records to ensure that products are safe for either intended or normally foreseeable use.

10. Appropriate policies should ensure that goods produced by manufacturers are safe for either intended or normally foreseeable use. Those responsible for bringing goods to the market, in particular suppliers, exporters, importers, retailers and the like (hereinafter referred to as "distributors"), should ensure that while in their care these goods are not rendered unsafe through improper handling or storage and that while in their care they do not become hazardous through improper handling or storage. Consumers should be instructed in the proper use of goods and should be informed of the risks involved in intended or normally foreseeable use. Vital safety information should be conveyed to consumers by internationally understandable symbols wherever possible.

11. Appropriate policies should ensure that if manufacturers or distributors become aware of unforeseen hazards after products are placed on the market, they should notify the relevant authorities and, as appropriate, the public without delay. Governments should also consider ways of ensuring that consumers are properly informed of such hazards.

12. Governments should, where appropriate, adopt policies under which, if a product is found to be seriously defective and/or to constitute substantial and severe hazard even when properly used, manufacturers and/or distributors should recall it and replace or modify it, or substitute another product for it; if it is not possible to do this within a reasonable period of time, the consumer should be adequately compensated.

B. Promotion and protection of consumers' economic interests

13. Government policies should seek to enable consumers to obtain optimum benefit from their economic resources. They should also seek to achieve the goals of satisfactory production and performance standards, adequate distribution methods, fair business practices, informative marketing and effective protection against practices which could adversely affect the economic interests of consumers and the exercise of choice in the market-place.

14. Governments should intensify their efforts to prevent practices which are damaging to the economic interests of consumers through ensuring that manufacturers, distributors and others involved in the provision of goods and services adhere to established laws and mandatory standards. Consumer organizations should be encouraged to monitor adverse practices, such as the adulteration of foods, false or misleading claims in marketing and service frauds.

15. Governments should develop, strengthen or maintain, as the case may be, measures relating to the control of restrictive and other abusive business practices which may be harmful to consumers, including means for the enforcement of such measures. In this connection, Governments should be guided by their commitment to the Set of Multilaterally Agreed Equitable Principles and Rules for the Control of Restrictive Business Practices adopted by the General Assembly in resolution 35/63 of 5 December 1980.

16. Governments should adopt or maintain policies that make clear the responsibility of the producer to ensure that goods meet reasonable demands of durability, utility and reliability, and are suited to the purpose for which they are intended, and that the seller should see that these requirements are met. Similar policies should apply to the provision of services.

17. Governments should encourage fair and effective competition in order to provide consumers with the greatest range of choice among products and services at the lowest cost.

18. Governments should, where appropriate, see to it that manufacturers and/or retailers ensure adequate availability of reliable after-sales service and spare parts.

19. Consumers should be protected from such contractual abuses as one-sided standard contracts, exclusion of essential rights in contracts, and unconscionable conditions of credit by sellers.

20. Promotional marketing and sales practices should be guided by the principle of fair treatment of consumers and should meet legal requirements. This requires the provision of the information necessary to enable consumers to take informed and independent decisions, as well as measures to ensure that the information provided is accurate.

21. Governments should encourage all concerned to participate in the free flow of accurate information on all aspects of consumer products.

22. Governments should, within their own national context, encourage the formulation and implementation by business, in co-operation with consumer organizations, of codes of marketing and other business practices to ensure adequate consumer protection. Voluntary agreements may also be established jointly by business, consumer organizations and other interested parties. These codes should receive adequate publicity.

23. Governments should regularly review legislation pertaining to weights and measures and assess the adequacy of the machinery for its enforcement.

C. Standards for the safety and quality of consumer goods and services

24. Governments should, as appropriate, formulate or promote the elaboration and implementation of standards, voluntary and other, at the national and international levels for the safety and quality of goods and services and give them appropriate publicity. National standards and regulations for product safety and quality should be reviewed from time to time, in order to ensure that they conform, where possible, to generally accepted international standards.

25. Where a standard lower than the generally accepted international standard is being applied because of local economic conditions, every effort should be made to raise that standard as soon as possible.

26. Governments should encourage and ensure the availability of facilities to test and certify the safety, quality and performance of essential consumer goods and services.

D. Distribution facilities for essential consumer goods and services

27. Governments should, where appropriate, consider:

(a) Adopting or maintaining policies to ensure the efficient distribution of goods and services to consumers; where appropriate, specific policies should be considered to ensure the distribution of essential goods and services where this distribution

is endangered, as could be the case particularly in rural areas. Such policies could include assistance for the creation of adequate storage and retail facilities in rural centres, incentives for consumer self-help and better control of the conditions under which essential goods and services are provided in rural areas;

(b) Encouraging the establishment of consumer co-operatives and related trading activities, as well as information about them, especially in rural areas.

E. Measures enabling consumers to obtain redress

28. Governments should establish or maintain legal and/or administrative measures to enable consumers or, as appropriate, relevant organizations to obtain redress through formal or informal procedures that are expeditious, fair, inexpensive and accessible. Such procedures should take particular account of the needs of low-income consumers.

29. Governments should encourage all enterprises to resolve consumer disputes in a fair, expeditious and informal manner, and to establish voluntary mechanisms, including advisory services and informal complaints procedures, which can provide assistance to consumers.

30. Information on available redress and other dispute-resolving procedures should be made available to consumers.

F. Education and information programmes

31. Governments should develop or encourage the development of general consumer education and information programmes, bearing in mind the cultural traditions of the people concerned. The aim of such programmes should be to enable people to act as discriminating consumers, capable of making an informed choice of goods and services, and conscious of their rights and responsibilities. In developing such programmes, special attention should be given to the needs of disadvantaged consumers, in both rural and urban areas, including low-income consumers and those with low or non-existent literacy levels.

32. Consumer education should, where appropriate, become an integral part of the basic curriculum of the educational system, preferably as a component of existing subjects.

33. Consumer education and information programmes should cover such important aspects of consumer protection as the following:

(a) Health, nutrition, prevention of food-borne diseases and food adulteration;

(b) Product hazards;

(c) Product labelling;

(*d*) Relevant legislation, how to obtain redress, and agencies and organizations for consumer protection;

(*e*) Information on weights and measures, prices, quality, credit conditions and availability of basic necessities; and

(*f*) As appropriate, pollution and environment.

34. Governments should encourage consumer organizations and other interested groups, including the media, to undertake education and information programmes, particularly for the benefit of low-income consumer groups in rural and urban areas.

35. Business should, where appropriate, undertake or participate in factual and relevant consumer education and information programmes.

36. Bearing in mind the need to reach rural consumers and illiterate consumers, Governments should, as appropriate, develop or encourage the development of consumer information programmes in the mass media.

37. Governments should organize or encourage training programmes for educators, mass media professionals and consumer advisers, to enable them to participate in carrying out consumer information and education programmes.

G. Measures relating to specific areas

38. In advancing consumer interests, particularly in developing countries, Governments should, where appropriate, give priority to areas of essential concern for the health of the consumer, such as food, water and pharmaceuticals. Policies should be adopted or maintained for product quality control, adequate and secure distribution facilities, standardized international labelling and information, as well as education and research programmes in these areas. Government guidelines in regard to specific areas should be developed in the context of the provisions of this document.

39. Food. When formulating national policies and plans with regard to food, Governments should take into account the need of all consumers for food security and should support and, as far as possible, adopt standards from the Food and Agriculture Organization of the United Nations and the World Health Organization Codex Alimentarius or, in their absence, other generally accepted international food standards. Governments should maintain, develop or improve food safety measures, including, *inter alia*, safety criteria, food standards and dietary requirements and effective monitoring, inspection and evaluation mechanisms.

40. Water. Governments should, within the goals and targets set for the International Drinking Water Supply and Sanitation Decade, formulate, maintain or strengthen national policies to improve the supply, distribution and quality of water for drinking. Due regard should be paid

to the choice of appropriate levels of service, quality and technology, the need for education programmes and the importance of community participation.

41. Pharmaceuticals. Governments should develop or maintain adequate standards, provisions and appropriate regulatory systems for ensuring the quality and appropriate use of pharmaceuticals through integrated national drug policies which could address, inter alia, procurement, distribution , production, licensing arrangements, registration systems and the availability of reliable information on pharmaceuticals. In so doing, Governments should take special account of the work and recommendations of the World Health Organization on pharmaceuticals. For relevant products, the use of that organization's Certification Scheme on the Quality of Pharmaceutical Products Moving in Inter-national Commerce and other international information systems on pharmaceuticals should be encouraged. Measures should also be taken, as appropriate, to promote the use of international non-proprietary names (INNs) for drugs, drawing on the work done by the World Health Organization.

42. In addition to the priority areas indicated above, Governments should adopt appropriate measures in other areas, such as pesticides and chemicals in regard, where relevant, to their use, production and storage, taking into account such relevant health and environmental information as Governments may require producers to provide and include in the labelling of products.

IV. International co-operation

43. Governments should, especially in a regional or subregional context:

(a) Develop, review, maintain or strengthen, as appropriate, mechanisms for the exchange of information on national policies and measures in the field of consumer protection;

(b) Co-operate or encourage co-operation in the implementation of consumer protection policies to achieve greater results within existing resources. Examples of such co-operation could be collaboration in the setting up or joint use of testing facilities, common testing procedures, exchange of consumer information and education programmes, joint training programmes and joint elaboration of regulations;

(c) Co-operate to improve the conditions under which essential goods are offered to consumers, giving due regard to both price and quality. Such co-operation could include joint procurement of essential goods, exchange of information on different procurement possibilities and agreement on regional product specifications.

44. Governments should develop or strengthen information links regarding products which have been banned, withdrawn or severely restricted in order to enable other importing countries to protect themselves adequately against the harmful effects of such products.

45. Governments should work to ensure that the quality of products, and information relating to such products, does not vary from country to country in a way that would have detrimental effects on consumers.

46. Governments should work to ensure that policies and measures for consumer protection are implemented with due regard to their not becoming barriers to international trade, and that they are consistent with international trade obligations.

* * *

CONVENTION ESTABLISHING THE MULTILATERAL INVESTMENT GUARANTEE AGENCY*

The Convention Establishing the Multilateral Investment Guarantee Agency was submitted to Governments by the Board of Governors of the International Bank for Reconstruction and Development on 11 October 1985. The Convention entered into force on 12 April 1988. As of 31 May 1995, the MIGA Convention had been signed by 152 States. The Convention included two schedules: Schedule A on Membership and Subscriptions and Schedule B on Election of Directors. The schedules have not been reproduced in this volume.

PREAMBLE

The Contracting States

Considering the need to strengthen international co-operation for economic development and to foster the contribution to such development of foreign investment in general and private foreign investment in particular;

Recognizing that the flow of foreign investment to developing countries would be facilitated and further encouraged by alleviating concerns related to non-commercial risks;

Desiring to enhance the flow to developing countries of capital and technology for productive purposes under conditions consistent with their development needs, policies and objectives, on the basis of fair and stable standards for the treatment of foreign investment;

Convinced that the Multilateral Investment Guarantee Agency can play an important role in the encouragement of foreign investment complementing national and regional investment guarantee programs and private insurers of non-commercial risk; and

Realizing that such Agency should, to the extent possible, meet its obligations without resort to its callable capital and that such an objective would be served by continued improvement in investment conditions,

---

*Source: Multilateral Investment Guarantee Agency (1985). "Convention Establishing the Multilateral Investment Guarantee Agency", *Convention Establishing the Multilateral Investment Guarantee Agency and Commentary on the Convention* (Washington, D.C.: MIGA), pp. 1-34. The Schedules attached to the Convention can be found in the same source [Note added by the editor].

Have Agreed as follows:

CHAPTER I

Establishment, Status, Purposes and Definitions

Article 1. Establishment and Status of the Agency

(a) There is hereby established the Multilateral Investment Guarantee Agency (hereinafter called the Agency).

(b) The Agency shall possess full and juridical personality and, in particular, the capacity to:

(i) contract;
(ii) acquire and dispose of movable and immovable property; and
(iii) institute legal proceedings.

Article 2. Objectives and Purposes

The objectives of the Agency shall be to encourage the flow of investments for productive purposes among member countries, and in particular to developing member countries, thus supplementing the activities of the International Bank for Reconstruction and Development (hereinafter referred to as the Bank), the International Finance Corporation and other international development finance institutions.

To serve its objective, the Agency shall:

(a) issue guarantees, including coinsurance and reinsurance, against non-commercial risks in respect of investments in a member country which flow from other member countries;

(b) carry out appropriate complementary activities to promote the flow of investments to and among developing member countries; and

(c) exercise such other incidental powers as shall be necessary or desirable in the furtherance of its objective.

The Agency shall be guided in all its decisions by the provisions of this Article.

Article 3. Definitions

For the purposes of this Convention:

(a) "Member" means a State with respect to which this Convention has entered into force in accordance with Article 61.

(b) "Host country" or "host government" means a member, its government, or any public authority of a member in whose territories, as defined in Article 66, an investment which has been guaranteed or reinsured, or is considered for guarantee or reinsurance, by the Agency is to be located.

(c) A "developing member country" means a member which is listed as such in Schedule A hereto as this Schedule may be amended from time to time by the Council of Governors referred to in Article 30 (hereinafter called the Council).

(d) A "special majority" means an affirmative vote of not less than two-thirds of the total voting power representing not less than fifty-five per cent of the subscribed shares of the capital stock of the Agency.

(e) A "freely usable currency" means (i) any currency designated as such by the International Monetary Fund from time to time and (ii) any other freely available and effectively usable currency which the Board of Directors referred to in Article 30 (hereinafter called the Board) may designate for the purposes of this Convention after consultation with the International Monetary Fund and with the approval of the country of such currency.

CHAPTER II
Membership and Capital

Article 4. Membership

(a) Membership in the Agency shall be open to all members of the Bank and to Switzerland.

(b) Original members shall be the States which are listed in Schedule A hereto and become parties to this Convention on or before October 30, 1987.

Article 5. Capital

(a) The authorized capital stock of the Agency shall be one billion Special Drawing Rights (SDR 1,000,000,000). The capital stock shall be divided into 100,000 shares having a par value of SDR 10,000 each, which shall be available for subscription by members. All payment obligations of members with respect to capital stock shall be settled on the basis of the average value of the SDR in terms of United States dollars for the period January 1, 1981 to June 30, 1985, such value being 1.082 United States dollars per SDR.

(b) The capital stock shall increase on the admission of a new member to the extent that the then authorized shares are insufficient to provide the shares to be subscribed by such member pursuant to Article 6.

(c) The Council, by special majority, may at any time increase the capital stock of the Agency.

Article 6. Subscription of Shares

Each original member of the Agency shall subscribe at par to the number of shares of capital stock set forth opposite its name in Schedule A hereto. Each other member shall subscribe to such number of shares of capital stock on such terms and conditions as may be determined by the Council, but in no event at an issue price of less than par. No member shall subscribe to less than fifty shares. The Council may prescribe rules by which members may subscribe to less than fifty shares. The Council may prescribe rules by which members may subscribe to additional shares of the authorized capital stock.

Article 7. Division and Calls of Subscribed Capital

The initial subscription of each member shall be paid as follows:

(i) Within ninety days from the date on which this Convention enters into force with respect to such member, ten per cent of the price of each share shall be paid in cash as stipulated in Section (a) of Article 8 and an additional ten per cent in the form of non-negotiable, non-interest-bearing promissory notes or similar obligations to be encashed pursuant to a decision of the Board in order to meet the Agency's obligations.

(ii) The remainder shall be subject to call by the Agency when required to meet its obligations.

Article 8. Payment of Subscription of Shares

(a) Payments of subscriptions shall be made in freely usable currencies except that payments by developing member countries may be made in their own currencies up to twenty-five per cent of the paid-in cash portion of their subscriptions payable under Article 7 (i).

(b) Calls on any portion of unpaid subscriptions shall be uniform on all shares.

(c) If the amount received by the Agency on a call shall be insufficient to meet the obligations which have necessitated the call, the Agency may make further successive calls on unpaid subscriptions until the aggregate amount received by it shall be sufficient to meet such obligations.

(d) Liability on shares shall be limited to the unpaid portion of the issue price.

Article 9. Valuation of Currencies

Whenever it shall be necessary for the purposes of this Convention to determine the value of one currency in terms of another, such value shall be reasonably determined by the Agency, after consultation with the International Monetary Fund.

Article 10. Refunds

(a) The Agency shall, as soon as practicable, return to members amounts paid on calls on subscribed capital if and to the extent that:

(i) the call shall have been made to pay a claim resulting from a guarantee or reinsurance contract and thereafter the Agency shall have recovered its payment, in whole or in part, in a freely usable currency; or

(ii) the call shall have been made because of a default in payment by a member and thereafter such member shall have made good such default in whole or in part; or

(iii) the Council, by special majority, determines that the financial position of the Agency permits all or part of such amounts to be returned out of the Agency's revenue.

(b) Any refund effected under this Article to a member shall be made in freely usable currency in the proportion of the payments made by that member to the total amount paid pursuant to calls made prior to such refund.

(c) The equivalent of amounts refunded under this Article to a member shall become part of the callable capital obligations of the member under Article 7 (ii).

CHAPTER III
Operations

Article 11. Covered risks

(a) Subject to the provisions of Sections (b) and (c) below, the Agency may guarantee eligible investment against a loss resulting from one or more of the following types of risk:

(i) *Currency Transfer*

any introduction attributable to the host government of restrictions on the transfer outside the host country of its currency into a freely usable currency or another currency acceptable to the holder of the guarantee, including a failure of the host government to act within a reasonable period of time on an application by such holder for such transfer;

(ii) *Expropriation and Similar Measures*

any legislative action or administrative action or omission attributable to the host government which has the effect of depriving the holder of a guarantee of his ownership or control of, or a substantial benefit from, his investment, with the exception of non-discriminatory measures of general application which governments normally take for the purpose of regulating economic activity in their territories;

(iii) *Breach of Contract*

any repudiation or breach by the host government of a contract with the holder of a guarantee, when (a) the holder of a guarantee does not have recourse to a judicial or arbitral forum to determine the claim of repudiation or breach, or (b) a decision by such forum is not rendered within such reasonable period of time as shall be prescribed in the contracts of guarantee pursuant to the Agency's regulations, or (c) such a decision cannot be enforced; and

(iv) *War and Civil Disturbance*

any military action or civil disturbance in any territory of the host country to which this Convention shall be applicable as provided in Article 66.

(b) Upon the joint application of the investor and the host country, the Board, by special majority, may approve the extension of coverage under this Article to specific non-commercial risks other than those referred to in Section (a) above, but in no case to the risk of devaluation or depreciation of currency.

(c) Losses resulting from the following action shall not be covered:

(i) any host government action or omission to which the holder of the guarantee has agreed or for which he has been responsible; and

(ii) any host government action or omission or any other event occurring before the conclusion of the contract of guarantee.

Article 12. Eligible Investments

(a) Eligible investments shall include equity interests, including medium- or long-term loans made or guaranteed by holders of equity in the enterprise concerned, and such forms of direct investment as may be determined by the Board.

(b) The Board, by special majority, may extend eligibility to any other medium- or long-term form of investment, except that loans other than those mentioned in Section (a) above may be eligible only if they are related to a specific investment covered or to be covered by the Agency.

(c) Guarantees shall be restricted to investments the implementation of which begins subsequent to the registration of the application for the guarantee by the Agency. Such investments may include:

(i) any transfer of foreign exchange made to modernize, expand, or develop an existing investment; and

(ii) the use of earnings from existing investments which could otherwise be transferred outside the host country.

(d) In guaranteeing an investment, the Agency shall satisfy itself as to:

(i) the economic soundness of the investment and its contribution to the development of the host country;

(ii) compliance of the investment with the host country's laws and regulations;

(iii) consistency of the investment with the declared development objectives and priorities of the host country; and

(iv) the investment conditions in the host country, including the availability of fair and equitable treatment and legal protection for the investment.

Article 13. Eligible Investors

(a) Any natural person and any juridical person may be eligible to receive the Agency's guarantee provided that:

(i) such natural person is a national of a member other than the host country;

(ii) such juridical person is incorporated and has its principal place of business in a member or the majority of its capital is owned by a member or members or nationals thereof, provided that such member is not the host country in any of the above cases; and

(iii) such juridical person, whether or not it is privately owned, operates on a commercial basis.

(b) In case the investor has more than one nationality, for the purposes of Section (a) above the nationality of a member shall prevail over the nationality of a non-member, and the nationality of the host country shall prevail over the nationality of any other member.

(c) Upon the joint application of the investor and the host country, the Board, by special majority, may extend eligibility to a natural person who is a national of the host country or a juridical person which is incorporated in the host country or the majority of whose capital is owned by nationals, provided that the assets invested are transferred from outside the host country.

Article 14. Eligible Host Countries

Investments shall be guaranteed under this Chapter only if they are to be made in the territory of a developing member country.

Article 15. Host Country Approval

The Agency shall not conclude any contract of guarantee before the host government has approved the issuance of the guarantee by the Agency against the risks designated for cover.

Article 16. Terms and Conditions

The terms and conditions of each contract of guarantee shall be determined by the Agency subject to such rules and regulations as the Board shall issue, provided that the Agency shall not cover the total loss of the guaranteed investment. Contracts of guarantee shall be approved by the President under the direction of the Board.

Article 17. Payment of Claims

The President under the direction of the Board shall decide on the payment of claims to a holder of a guarantee in accordance with the contract of guarantee and such policies as the Board may adopt. Contracts of guarantee shall require holders of guarantees to seek, before a payment is made by the Agency, such administrative remedies as may be appropriate under the circumstances, provided that they are readily available to them under the laws of the host country. Such contracts may require the lapse of certain reasonable periods between the occurrence of events giving rise to claims and payments of claims.

Article 18. Subrogation

(a) Upon paying or agreeing to pay compensation to holder of a guarantee, the Agency shall be subrogated to such rights or claims related to the guaranteed investment as the holder of a guarantee may have had against the host country and other obligors. The contract of guarantee shall provide the terms and conditions of such subrogation.

(b) The rights of the Agency pursuant to Section (a) above shall be recognized by all members.

(c) Amounts in the currency of the host country acquired by the Agency as subrogee pursuant to Section (a) above shall be accorded, with respect to use and conversion, treatment by the host country as favorable as the treatment to which such funds would be entitled in the hands of the holder of the guarantee. In any case, such amounts may be used by the Agency for the payment of its administrative expenditures and other costs.

The Agency shall also seek to enter into arrangements with host countries on other uses of such currencies to the extent that they are not freely usable.

Article 19. Relationship to National and Regional Entities

The Agency shall co-operate with, and seek to complement the operations of, national entities of members and regional entities the majority of whose capital is owned by members, which carry out activities similar to those of the Agency, with a view to maximizing both the efficiency of their respective services and their contribution to increased flows of foreign investment. To this end, the Agency may enter into arrangements with such entities on the details of such co-operation, including in particular the modalities of reinsurance and coinsurance.

Article 20. Reinsurance of National and Regional Entities

(a) The Agency may issue reinsurance in respect of a specific investment against a loss resulting from one or more of the non-commercial risks underwritten by a member or agency thereof or by a regional investment guarantee agency the majority of whose capital is owned by members. The Board, by special majority, shall from time to time prescribe maximum amounts of contingent liability which may be assumed by the Agency with respect to reinsurance contracts. In respect of specific investments which have been completed more than twelve months prior to receipt of the application for reinsurance by the Agency, the maximum amount shall initially be set at ten per cent of the aggregate contingent liability of the Agency under this Chapter. The conditions of eligibility specified in Articles 11 to 14 shall apply to reinsurance operations, except that the reinsured investments need not be implemented subsequent to the application for reinsurance.

(b) The mutual rights and obligations of the Agency and a reinsured member or agency shall be stated in contracts of reinsurance subject to such rules and regulations as the Board shall issue. The Board shall approve each contract for reinsurance covering an investment which has been made prior to receipt of the application for reinsurance by the Agency, with a view to minimizing risks, assuring that the Agency receives premiums commensurate with its risk, and assuring that the reinsured entity is appropriately committed toward promoting new investment in developing member countries.

(c) The Agency shall, to the extent possible, assure that it or the reinsured entity shall have the rights of subrogation and arbitration equivalent to those the Agency would have if it were the primary guarantor. The terms and conditions of reinsurance shall require that administrative remedies are sought in accordance with Article 17 before a payment is made by the Agency. Subrogation shall be effective with respect to the host country concerned only after its approval of the reinsurance by the Agency. The Agency shall include in the contracts of reinsurance provisions requiring the reinsured to pursue with due diligence the rights or claims related to the reinsured investment.

Article 21. Co-operation with Private Insurers and with Reinsurers

(a) The Agency may enter into arrangements with private insurers in member countries to enhance its own operations and encourage such insurers to provide coverage of non-commercial risks in developing member countries on conditions similar to those applied by the Agency. Such arrangements may include the provision of reinsurance by the Agency under the conditions and procedures specified in Article 20.

(b) The Agency may reinsure with any appropriate reinsurance entity, in whole or in part, any guarantee or guarantees issued by it.

(c) The Agency will in particular seek to guarantee investments for which comparable coverage on reasonable terms is not available from private insurers and reinsurers.

Article 22. Limits of Guarantee

(a) Unless determined otherwise by the Council by special majority, the aggregate amount of contingent liabilities which may be assumed by the Agency under this Chapter shall not exceed one hundred and fifty per cent of the amount of the Agency's unimpaired subscribed capital and its reserves plus such portion of its reinsurance cover as the Board may determine. The Board shall from time to time review the risk profile of the Agency's portfolio in the light of its experience with claims, degree of risk diversification, reinsurance cover and other relevant factors with a view to ascertaining whether changes in the maximum aggregate amount of contingent liabilities should be recommended to the Council. The maximum amount determined by the Council shall not under any circumstances exceed five times the amount of the Agency's unimpaired subscribed capital, its reserves and such portion of its reinsurance cover as may be deemed appropriate.

(b) Without prejudice to the general limit of guarantee referred to in Section (a) above, the Board may prescribe:

(i) maximum aggregate amounts of contingent liability which may be assumed by the Agency under this Chapter for all guarantees issued to investors of each individual member. In determining such maximum amounts, the Board shall give due consideration to the share of the respective member in the capital of the Agency and the need to apply more liberal limitations in respect of investments originating in developing member countries; and

(ii) maximum aggregate amounts of contingent liability which may be assumed by the Agency with respect to such risk diversification factors as individual projects, individual host countries and types of investment or risk.

Article 23. Investment Promotion

(a) The Agency shall carry out research, undertake activities to promote investment flows and disseminate information on investment opportunities in developing member countries, with a view to improving the environment for foreign investment flows to such countries. The Agency may, upon the request of a member, provide technical advice and assistance to improve the investment conditions in the territories of that member. In performing these activities, the Agency shall:

(i) be guided by relevant investment agreements among member countries;

(ii) seek to remove impediments, in both developed and developing member countries, to the flow of investment to developing member countries; and

(iii) co-ordinate with other agencies concerned with the promotion of foreign investment, and in particular the International Finance Corporations.

(b) The Agency also shall:

(i) encourage the amicable settlement of disputes between investors and host countries;

(ii) endeavour to conclude agreements with developing member countries, and in particular with prospective host countries, which will assure that the Agency, with respect to investment guaranteed by it, has treatment at least as favorable as that agreed by the member concerned for the most favored investment guarantee agency or State in an agreement relating to investment, such agreements to be approved by special majority of the Board; and

(iii) promote and facilitate the conclusion of agreements, among its members, on the promotion and protection of investments.

(c) The Agency shall give particular attention in its promotional efforts to the importance of increasing the flow of investments among developing member countries.

Article 24. Guarantees of Sponsored Investments

In addition to the guarantee operations undertaken by the Agency under this Chapter, the Agency may guarantee investments under the sponsorship arrangements provided for in Annex I to this Convention.

CHAPTER IV
Financial Provisions

Article 25. Financial Management

The Agency shall carry out its activities in accordance with sound business and prudent financial management practices with a view to maintaining under all circumstances its ability to meet its financial obligations.

Article 26. Premiums and Fees

The Agency shall establish and periodically review the rates of premiums, fees and other charges, if any, applicable to each type of risk.

Article 27. Allocation of Net Income

(a) Without prejudice to the provisions of Section (a)(iii) of Article 10, the Agency shall allocate net income to reserves until such reserves reach five times the subscribed capital of the Agency.

(b) After the reserves of the Agency have reached the level prescribed in Section (a) above, the Council shall decide whether, and to what extent, the Agency's net income shall be allocated to reserves, be distributed to the Agency's members or be used otherwise. Any distribution of net income to the Agency's members shall be made in proportion to the share of each member in the capital of the Agency in accordance with a decision of the Council acting by special majority.

Article 28. Budget

The President shall prepare an annual budget of revenues and expenditures of the Agency for approval by the Board.

Article 29. Accounts

The Agency shall publish an Annual Report which shall include statements of its accounts and of the accounts of the Sponsorship Trust Fund referred to in Annex I to this Convention, as audited by independent auditors. The Agency shall circulate to members at appropriate intervals a summary statement of its financial position and a profit and loss statement showing the results of its operations.

CHAPTER V
Organization and Management

Article 30. Structure of the Agency

The Agency shall have a Council of Governors, a Board of Directors, a President and staff to perform such duties as the Agency may determine.

Article 31. The Council

(a) All the powers of the Agency shall be vested in the Council, except such powers as are, by the terms of this Convention, specifically conferred upon another organ of the Agency. The Council may delegate to the Board the exercise of any of its powers, except the power to:

(i) admit new members and determine the conditions of their admission;

(ii) suspend a member;

(iii) decide on any increase or decrease in the capital;

(iv) increase the limit of the aggregate amount of contingent liabilities pursuant to Section (a) of Article 22;

(v) designate a member as a developing country member pursuant to Section (c) of Article 3;

(vi) classify a new member as belonging to Category One or Category Two for voting purposes pursuant to Section (a) of Article 39 or reclassify an existing member for the same purposes;

(vii) determine the compensation of Directors and their Alternates;

(viii) cease operations and liquidate the Agency;

(ix) distribute assets to members upon liquidation; and

(x) amend this Convention, its Annexes and Schedules.

(b) The Council shall be composed of one Governor and on Alternate appointed by each member in such a manner as it may determine. No Alternate may vote except in the absence of his principal. The Council shall select one of the Governors as Chairman.

(c) The Council shall hold an annual meeting and such other meetings as may be determined by the Council or called by the Board. The Board shall call a meeting of the Council whenever requested by five members or by members having twenty-five per cent of the total voting power.

Article 32. The Board

(a) The Board shall be responsible for the general operations of the Agency and shall take, in the fulfillment of this responsibility, any action required or permitted under this Convention.

(b) The Board shall consist of not less then twelve Directors. The number of Directors may be adjusted by the Council to take into account changes in membership. Each Director may appoint an Alternate with full power to act for him in case of the Director's absence or inability to act. The President of the Bank shall be ex officio Chairman of the Board, but shall have no vote except a deciding vote in case of an equal division.

(c) The Council shall determine the term of office of the Directors. The first Board shall be constituted by the Council at its inaugural meeting.

(d) The Board shall meet at the call of its Chairman acting on his own initiative or upon request of three Directors.

(e) Until such time as the Council may decide that the Agency shall have a resident Board which functions in continuous session, the Directors and Alternates shall receive compensation only for the cost of attendance at the meetings of the Board and the discharge of other official functions on behalf of the Agency. Upon the establishment of a Board in continuous session, the Directors and Alternates shall receive such remuneration as may be determined by the Council.

Article 33. President and Staff

(a) The President shall, under the general control of the Board, conduct the ordinary business of the Agency. He shall be responsible for the organization, appointment and dismissal of the staff.

(b) The President shall be appointed by the Board on the nomination of its Chairman. The Council shall determine the salary and terms of the contract of service of the President.

(c) In the discharge of their offices, the President and the staff owe their duty entirely to the Agency and to no other authority. Each member of the Agency shall respect the international character of this duty and shall refrain from all attempts to influence the President or the staff in the discharge of their duties.

(d) In appointing the staff, the President shall, subject to the paramount importance of securing the highest standards of efficiency and of technical competence, pay due regard to the importance of recruiting personnel on as wide a geographic basis as possible.

(e) The President and staff shall maintain at all times the confidentiality of information obtained in carrying out the Agency's operations.

Article 34. Political Activity Prohibited

The Agency, its President and staff shall not interfere in the political affairs of any member. Without prejudice to the right of the Agency to take into account all the circumstances surrounding an investment, they shall not be influenced in their decisions by the political character of the member or members concerned. Considerations relevant to their decisions shall be weighed impartially in order to achieve the purposes stated in Article 2.

Article 35. Relations with International Organizations

The Agency shall, within the terms of the Convention, co-operate with the United Nations and with other inter-governmental organizations having specialized responsibilities in related fields, including in particular the Bank and the International Finance Corporation.

Article 36. Location of Principal Office

(a) The principal office of the Agency shall be located in Washington, D.C., unless the Council, by special majority, decides to establish it in another location.

(b) The Agency may establish other offices as may be necessary for its work.

Article 37. Depositories for Assets

Each member shall designate its central bank as a depository in which the Agency may keep holdings of such member's currency or other assets of the Agency or, if it has no central bank, it shall designate for such purpose such other institution as may be acceptable to the Agency.

Article 38. Channel of Communication

(a) Each member shall designate an appropriate authority with which the Agency may communicate in connection with any matter arising under this Convention. The Agency may rely on statements of such authority as being statements of the member. The Agency, upon the request of a member, shall consult with that member with respect to matters dealt with in Articles 19 to 21 and related to entities or insurers of that member.

(b) Whenever the approval of any member is required before any act may be done by the Agency, approval shall be deemed to have been given unless the member presents an objection within such reasonable period as the Agency may fix in notifying the member of the proposed act.

CHAPTER VI
Voting, Adjustments of Subscriptions and Representation

Article 39. Voting and Adjustments of Subscriptions

(a) In order to provide for voting arrangements that reflect the equal interest in the Agency of the two Categories of States listed in Schedule A of this Convention, as well as the importance of each member's financial participation, each member shall have 177 membership votes plus one subscription vote for each share of stock held by that member.

(b) If at any time within three years after the entry into force of this Convention the aggregate sum of membership and subscription votes of members which belong to either of the two Categories of States listed in Schedule A of this Convention is less than forty per cent of the total voting power, members from such a Category shall have such number of supplementary votes as shall be necessary for the aggregate voting power of the Category to equal such a percentage of the total voting power. Such supplementary votes shall be distributed among the members of such Category in the proportion that the subscription votes of each bears to the aggregate of subscription votes of the Category. Such supplementary votes shall be subject to automatic adjustment to ensure that such percentage is maintained and shall be cancelled at the end of the above-mentioned three-year period.

(c) During the third year following the entry into force of this Convention, the Council shall review the allocation of shares and shall be guided in its decision by the following principles:

(i) the votes of members shall reflect actual subscriptions to the Agency's capital and the membership votes as set out in Section (a) of this Article;

(ii) shares allocated to countries which shall not have signed the Convention and shall be made available for reallocation to such members and in such manner as to make possible voting parity between the above-mentioned Categories; and

(iii) the Council will take measures that will facilitate members' ability to subscribe to shares allocated to them.

(d) Within the three-year period provided for in Section (b) of this Article, all decisions of the Council and Board shall be taken by special majority, except that decisions requiring a higher majority under this Convention shall be taken by such higher majority.

(e) In case the capital stock of the Agency is increased pursuant to Section (c) of Article 5, each member which so requests shall be authorized to subscribe a proportion of the increase equivalent to the proportion which its stock theretofore subscribed bears to the total capital stock of the Agency, but no member shall be obligated to subscribe any part of the increased capital.

(f) The Council shall issue regulations regarding the making of additional subscriptions under Section (e) of this Article. Such regulations shall prescribe reasonable time limits for the submission by members of requests to make such subscriptions.

Article 40. Voting in the Council

(a) Each Governor shall be entitled to cast the votes of the member he represents. Except as otherwise specified in this Convention, decisions of the Council shall be taken by a majority of the votes cast.

(b) A quorum for any meeting of the Council shall be constituted by a majority of the Governors exercising not less than two-thirds of the total voting power.

(c) The Council may by regulation establish a procedure whereby the Board, when it deems such action to be in the best interests of the Agency, may request a decision of the Council on a specific question without calling a meeting of the Council.

Article 41. Election of Directors

(a) Directors shall be elected in accordance with Schedule B.

(b) Directors shall continue in office until their successors are elected. If the office of a Director become vacant more than ninety days before the end of his term, another Director shall be elected for the remainder of the term by the Governors who elected the former Director. A majority of the votes cast shall be required for election. While the office remains vacant, the Alternate of the former Director shall exercise his powers, except that of appointing an Alternate.

Article 42. Voting in the Board

(a) Each Director shall be entitled to cast the number of votes of the member whose vote counted towards his election. All the votes which a Director is entitled to cast shall be cast as a unit. Except as otherwise specified in this Convention, decisions of the Board shall be taken by a majority of the votes cast.

(b) A quorum for a meeting of the Board shall be constituted by a majority of the Directors exercising not less than one-half of the total voting power.

(c) The Board may by regulation establish a procedure whereby its Chairman, when he deems such action to be in the best interests of the Agency, may request a decision of the Board on a specific question without calling a meeting of the Board.

CHAPTER VII
Privileges and Immunities

Article 43. Purposes of Chapter

To enable the Agency to fulfill its functions, the immunities and privileges set forth in this Chapter shall be accorded to the Agency in the territories of each member.

Article 44. Legal Process

Actions other than those within the scope of Articles 57 and 58 may be brought against the Agency only in a court of competent jurisdiction in the territories of a member in which the Agency has an office or has appointed an agent for the purposes of accepting service or notice of process. No such action against the Agency shall be brought (i) by members or persons acting for or deriving claims from members or (ii) in respect of personnel matters. The property and assets of the Agency shall, wherever located and by whomsoever held, be immune from all forms of seizure, attachment or execution before the delivery of the final judgment or award against the Agency.

Article 45. Assets

(a) The property and assets of the Agency, wherever located and by whomsoever held, shall be immune from search, requisition, confiscation, expropriation or any other form of seizure by executive or legislative action.

(b) To the extent necessary to carry out its operations under this Convention, all property and assets of the Agency shall be free from restrictions, regulations, controls and moratoria of any nature; provided that property and assets acquired by the Agency as successor to or subrogee of a holder of a guarantee, a reinsured entity or an investor insured by a reinsured entity shall be free from applicable foreign exchange restrictions, regulations and controls in force in the territories of the member concerned to the extent that the holder, entity or investor to whom the Agency was subrogated was entitled to such treatment.

(c) For the purposes of this Chapter, the term "assets" shall include the assets of the Sponsorship Trust Fund referred to in Annex I of this Convention and other assets administered by the Agency in furtherance of its objective.

Article 46. Archives and Communications

(a) The archives of the Agency shall be inviolable, wherever they may be.

(b) The official communications of the Agency shall be accorded by each member the same treatment that is accorded to the official communications of the Bank.

Article 47. Taxes

(a) The Agency, its assets, property and income, and its operations and transactions authorized by this Convention, shall be immune from all taxes and customs duties. The Agency shall also be immune from liability for the collection or payment of any tax or duty.

(b) Except in the case of local nationals, no tax shall be levied on or in respect of expense allowances paid by the Agency or Governors and their Alternate or on or in respect of salaries, expense allowances or other emoluments paid by the Agency to the Chairman of the Board, Directors, their Alternates, the President or staff of the Agency.

(c) No taxation of any kind shall be levied on any investment guaranteed or reinsured by the Agency (including any earnings therefrom) or any insurance policies reinsured by the agency (including any premiums and other revenues therefrom) by whomsoever held; (i) which discriminates against such investment or insurance policy solely because it is guaranteed or reinsured by the Agency; or (ii) if the sole jurisdictional basis for such taxation is the location of any office or place of business maintained by the Agency.

Article 48. Officials of the Agency

All Governors, Directors, Alternates, the President and staff of the Agency:

(i) shall be immune from legal process with respect to acts performed by them in their official capacity;

(ii) not being local nationals, shall be accorded the same immunities from immigration restrictions, alien registration requirements and national service obligations, and the same facilities as regards exchange restrictions as are accorded by the members concerned to the representatives, officials and employees of comparable rank of other members; and

(iii) shall be granted the same treatment in respect of travelling facilities as is accorded by the members concerned to representatives, officials and employees of comparable rank of other members.

Article 49. Application of the Chapter

Each member shall take such action as is necessary in its own territories for the purpose of making effective in terms of its own law the principles set forth in this Chapter and shall inform the Agency of the detailed action which it has taken.

Article 50. Waiver

The immunities, exemptions and privileges provided in this Chapter are granted in the interests of the Agency and may be waived, to such extent and upon such conditions as the Agency may determine, in cases where such a waiver would not prejudice its interests. The Agency shall waive the immunity of any of its staff in cases where, in its opinion, the immunity would impede the course of justice and can be waived without prejudice to the interests of the Agency.

CHAPTER VIII

Withdrawal, Suspension of Membership and Cessation of Operations

Article 51. Withdrawal

Any member may, after the expiration of three years following the date upon which this Convention has entered into force with respect to such member, withdraw from the Agency at any time by giving notice in writing to the Agency at its principal office. The Agency shall notify the Bank, as depository of this Convention, of the receipt of such notice. Any withdrawal shall become effective ninety days following the date of the receipt of such notice by the Agency. A member may revoke such notice as long as it has not become effective.

Article 52. Suspension of Membership

(a) If a member fails to fulfill any of its obligations under the Convention, the Council may, by a majority of its members exercising a majority of the total voting power, suspend its membership.

(b) While under suspension a member shall have no rights under this Convention, except for the right of withdrawal and other rights provided in this Chapter and Chapter IX, but shall remain subject to all its obligations.

(c) For purposes of determining eligibility for a guarantee or reinsurance to be issued under Chapter III or Annex I to this Convention, a suspended member shall not be treated as a member of the Agency.

(d) The suspended member shall automatically cease to be a member one year from the date of its suspension unless the Council decides to extend the period of suspension or to restore the member to good standing.

Article 53. Rights and Duties of States Ceasing to be Members

(a) When a State ceases to be a member, it shall remain liable for all its obligations, including its contingent obligations, under this Convention which shall have been in effect before the cessation of its membership.

(b) Without prejudice to Section (a) above, the Agency shall enter into an arrangement with such State for the settlement of their respective claims and obligations. Any such arrangement shall be approved by the Board.

Article 54. Suspension of Operations

(a) The Board may, whenever it deems it justified, suspend the issuance of new guarantees for a specified period.

(b) In an emergency, the Board may suspend all activities of the Agency for a period not exceeding the duration of such emergency, provided that the necessary arrangements shall be made for the protection of the interests of the Agency and of third parties.

(c) The decision to suspend operations shall have no effect on the obligations of the members under this Convention or on the obligations of the Agency towards holders of a guarantee or reinsurance policy towards third parties.

Article 55. Liquidation

(a) The Council, by special majority, may decide to cease operations and to liquidate the Agency. Thereupon the Agency shall forthwith cease all activities, except those incident to the orderly realization, conservation and preservation of assets and settlement of obligations. Until final settlement and distribution of assets, the Agency shall remain in existence and all rights and obligations of members under this Convention shall continue unimpaired.

(b) No distribution of assets shall be made to members until all liabilities to holders of guarantees and other creditors shall have been discharged or provided for and until the Council shall have decided to make such distribution.

(c) Subject to the foregoing, the Agency shall distribute its remaining assets to members in proportion to each member's share in the subscribed capital. The Agency shall also distribute any remaining assets of the Sponsorship Trust Fund referred to in Annex I to this Convention to sponsoring members in the proportion which the investments sponsored by each bears to the total of sponsored investments. No member shall be entitled to share in the assets of the Agency or the Sponsorship Trust Fund unless that member has settled all outstanding claims by the Agency against it. Every distribution of assets shall be made at such times as the Council shall determine and in such manner as it shall deem fair and equitable.

CHAPTER IX
Settlement of Disputes

Article 56. Interpretation and Application of the Convention

(a) Any question of interpretation or application of the provisions of this Convention arising between any member of the Agency and the Agency or among members of the Agency shall be submitted to the Board for its decision. Any member which is particularly affected by the question and which is not otherwise represented by a national in the

Board may send a representative to attend any meeting of the Board at which such question is considered.

(b) In any case where the Board has given a decision under Section (a) above, any member may require that the question be referred to the Council, whose decision shall be final. Pending the result of the referral to the Council, the Agency may, so far as it deems necessary, act on the basis of the decision of the Board.

Article 57. Disputes between the Agency and Members

(a) Without prejudice to the provisions of Article 56 and of Section (b) of this Article, any dispute between the Agency and a member or an agency thereof and any dispute between the Agency and a country (or agency thereof) which has ceased to be a member, shall be settled in accordance with the procedure set out in Annex II to this Convention.

(b) Disputes concerning claims of the Agency acting as subrogee of an investor shall be settled in accordance with either (i) the procedure set out in Annex II to this Convention, or (ii) an agreement to be entered into between the Agency and the member concerned on an alternative method or methods for the settlement of such disputes. In the latter case, Annex II to this Convention shall serve as a basis for such an agreement which shall, in each case, be approved by the Board by special majority prior to the undertaking by the Agency of operations in the territories of the member concerned.

Article 58. Disputes Involving Holders of a Guarantee or Reinsurance

Any dispute arising under a contract of guarantee or reinsurance between the parties thereto shall be submitted to arbitration for final determination in accordance with such rules as shall be provided for or referred to in the contract of guarantee or reinsurance.

CHAPTER X
Amendments

Article 59. Amendment by Council

(a) This Convention and its Annexes may be amended by vote of three-fifths of the Governors exercising four-fifths of the total voting power, provided that:

(i) any amendments modifying the right to withdraw from the Agency provided in Article 51 or the limitation on liability provided in Section (d) of Article 8 shall require the affirmative vote of all Governors; and

(ii) any amendment modifying the loss-sharing arrangement provided in Articles 1 and 3 of Annex I to this Convention which will result in an increase in any member's liability thereunder shall require the affirmative vote of the Governor of each such member.

(b) Schedules A and B to this Convention may be amended by the Council by special majority.

(c) If an amendment affects any provision of Annex I to this Convention, total votes shall include the additional votes allotted under Article 7 of such Annex to sponsoring members and countries hosting sponsored investments.

Article 60. Procedure

Any proposal to amend this Convention, whether emanating from a member or a Governor or a Director, shall be communicated to the Chairman of the Board who shall bring the proposal before the Board. If the proposed amendment is recommended by the Board, it shall be submitted to the Council for approval in accordance with Article 59. When an amendment has been duly approved by the Council, the Agency shall so certify by formal communication addressed to all members. Amendments shall enter into force for all members ninety days after the date of the formal communication unless the Council shall specify a different date.

CHAPTER XI
Final Provisions

Article 61. Entry into Force

(a) This Convention shall be open for signature on behalf of all members of the Bank and Switzerland and shall be subject to ratification, acceptance or approval by the signatory States in accordance with their constitutional procedures.

(b) This Convention shall enter into force on the day when not less than five instruments of ratification, acceptance or approval have been deposited on behalf of signatory States in Category One, and not less than fifteen such instruments shall have been deposited on behalf of signatory States in Category Two; provided that the total subscriptions of these States amount to not less than one-third of the authorized capital of the Agency as prescribed in Article 5.

(c) For each State which deposits its instrument of ratification, acceptance or approval after this Convention shall have entered into force, this Convention shall enter into force on the date of such deposit.

(d) If this Convention shall not have entered into force within two years after its opening for signature, the President of the Bank shall convene a conference of interested countries to determine the future course of action.

Article 62. Inaugural Meeting

Upon entry into force of this Convention, the President of the Bank shall call the inaugural meeting of the Council. This meeting shall be held at the principal office of the Agency within sixty days from the date on which this Convention has entered into force or as soon as practicable thereafter.

Article 63. Depository

Instruments of ratification, acceptance or approval of this Convention and amendments thereto shall be deposited with the Bank which shall act as the depository of this Convention. The depository shall transmit certified copies of this Convention to States members of the Bank and to Switzerland.

Article 64. Registration

The depository shall register this Convention with the Secretariat of the United Nations in accordance with Article 102 of the Charter of the United Nations and the Regulations thereunder adopted by the General Assembly.

Article 65. Notification

The depository shall notify all signatory States and, upon the entry into force of this Convention, the Agency of the following:

(a) signatures of this Convention;

(b) deposits of instruments of ratification, acceptance and approval in accordance with Article 63;

(c) The date on which this Convention enters into force in accordance with Article 61;

(d) exclusions from territorial application pursuant to Article 66; and

(e) withdrawal of a member from the Agency pursuant to Article 51.

Article 66. Territorial Application

This Convention shall apply to all territories under the jurisdiction of a member including the territories for whose international relations a member is responsible, except those which are excluded by such member by written notice to the depository of this Convention either at the time of ratification, acceptance or approval or subsequently.

Article 67. Periodic Reviews

(a) The Council shall periodically undertake comprehensive reviews of the activities of the Agency as well as the results achieved with a view to introducing any changes required to enhance the Agency's ability to serve its objectives.

(b) The first such review shall take place five years after the entry into force of this Convention. The dates of subsequent reviews shall be determined by the Council.

DONE at Seoul, in a single copy which shall remain deposited in the archives of the International Bank for Reconstruction and Development, which has indicated by its signature below its agreement to fulfill the functions with which it is charged under this Convention.

ANNEX I
Guarantees of Sponsored Investments Under Article 24

Article 1. Sponsorship

(a) Any member may sponsor for guarantee an investment to be made by an investor of any nationality or by investors of any or several nationalities.

(b) Subject to the provisions of Sections (b) and (c) of Article 3 of this Annex, each sponsoring member shall share with the other sponsoring members in losses under guarantees of sponsored investments, when and to the extent that such losses cannot be covered out of the Sponsorship Trust Fund referred to in Article 2 of this Annex, in the proportion which the amount of maximum contingent liability under the guarantees of investments sponsored by it bears to the total amount of maximum contingent liability under the guarantees of investments sponsored by all members.

(c) In its decisions on the issuance of guarantees under this Annex, the Agency shall pay due regard to the prospects that the sponsoring member will be in a position to meet its obligations under this Annex and shall give priority to investments which are co-sponsored by the host countries concerned.

(d) The Agency shall periodically consult with sponsoring members with respect to its operations under this Annex.

Article 2. Sponsorship Trust Fund

(a) Premiums and other revenues attributable to guarantees of sponsored investments, including returns on the investment of such premiums and revenues, shall be held in a separate account which shall be called the Sponsorship Trust Fund.

(b) All administrative expenses and payments on claims attributable to guarantees issued under this Annex shall be paid out of the Sponsorship Trust Fund.

(c) The assets of the Sponsorship Trust Fund shall be held and administered for the joint account of sponsoring members and shall be kept separate and apart from the assets of the Agency.

Article 3. Calls on Sponsoring Members

(a) To the extent that any amount is payable by the Agency on account of a loss under a sponsored guarantee and such amount cannot be paid out of the assets of the Sponsorship Trust Fund, the Agency shall call on each sponsoring member to pay into such Fund its share of such amount as shall be determined in accordance with Section (b) of Article 1 of this Annex.

(b) No member shall be liable to pay any amount on a call pursuant to the provisions of this Article if as a result total payments made by that member will exceed the total amount of guarantees covering investments sponsored by it.

(c) Upon the expiry of any guarantee covering an investment sponsored by a member, the liability of that member shall be decreased by an amount equivalent to the amount of such guarantee; such liability shall also be decreased on a pro rata basis upon payment by the Agency of any claim related to a sponsored investment and shall otherwise continue in effect until the expiry of all guarantees of sponsored investments outstanding at the time of such payment.

(d) If any sponsoring member shall not be liable for an amount of a call pursuant to the provisions of this Article because of the limitation contained in Sections (b) and (c) above, or if any sponsoring member shall default in payment of an amount due in response to any such call, the liability for payment of such amount shall be shared *pro rata* by the other sponsoring members. Liability of members pursuant to this Section shall be subject to the limitation set forth in Sections (b) and (c) above.

(e) Any payment by a sponsoring member pursuant to a call in accordance with this Article shall be made promptly and in freely usable currency.

Article 4. Valuation of Currencies and Refunds

The provisions on valuation of currencies and refunds contained in this Convention with respect to capital subscriptions shall be applied *mutatis mutandis* to funds paid by members on account of sponsored investments.

Article 5. Reinsurance

(a) The Agency may, under the conditions set forth in Article 1 of this Annex, provide reinsurance to a member, an agency thereof, a regional agency as defined in Section (a) of Article 20 of this Convention or a private insurer in a member country. The provisions of this Annex concerning guarantees and of Articles 20 and 21 of this Convention shall be applied *mutatis mutandis* to reinsurance provided under this Section.

(b) The Agency may obtain reinsurance for investments guaranteed by it under this Annex and shall meet the cost of such reinsurance out of the Sponsorship Trust Fund. The

Board may decide whether and to what extent the loss-sharing obligation of sponsoring members referred to in Section (b) of Article 1 of this Annex may be reduced on account of the reinsurance cover obtained.

Article 6. Operational Principles

Without prejudice to the provisions of this Annex, the provisions with respect to guarantee operations under Chapter III of this Convention and to financial management under Chapter IV of this Convention shall be applied *mutatis mutandis* to guarantees of sponsored investments except that (i) such investments shall qualify for sponsorship if made in the territories of any member, and in particular of any developing member, by an investor or investors eligible under Section (a) of Article 1 of this Annex, and (ii) the Agency shall not be liable with respect to its own assets for any guarantee or reinsurance issued under this Annex and each contract of guarantee or reinsurance concluded pursuant to this Annex shall expressly so provide.

Article 7. Voting

For decisions relating to sponsored investments, each sponsoring member shall have one additional vote for each 10,000 Special Drawing Rights equivalent of the amount guaranteed or reinsured on the basis of its sponsorship, and each member hosting a sponsored investment shall have one additional vote for each 10,000 Special Drawing Rights equivalent of the amount guaranteed or reinsured with respect to any sponsored investment hosted by it. Such additional votes shall be cast only for decisions related to sponsored investments and shall otherwise be disregarded in determining the voting power of members.

ANNEX II
Settlement of Disputes Between a Member and the Agency Under Article 57

Article 1. Application of the Annex

All disputes within the scope of Article 57 of this Convention shall be settled in accordance with the procedure set out in this Annex, except in the cases where the Agency has entered into an agreement with a member pursuant to Section (b)(ii) of Article 57.

Article 2. Negotiation

The parties to a dispute within the scope of this Annex shall attempt to settle such dispute by negotiation before seeking conciliation or arbitration. Negotiations shall be deemed to have been exhausted if the parties fail to reach a settlement within a period of one hundred and twenty days from the date of the request to enter into negotiation.

Article 3. Conciliation

(a) If the dispute is not resolved through negotiation, either party may submit the dispute to arbitration in accordance with the provisions of Article 4 of this Annex, unless the parties, by mutual consent, have decided to resort first to the conciliation procedure provided for in this Article.

(b) The agreement for recourse to conciliation shall specify the matter in dispute, the claims of the parties in respect thereof and, if available, the name of the conciliator agreed upon by the parties. In the absence of agreement on the conciliator, the parties may jointly request either the Secretary-General of the International Centre for Settlement of Investment Disputes (hereinafter called ICSID) or the President of the International Court of Justice to appoint a conciliator. The conciliation procedure shall terminate if the conciliator has not been appointed within ninety days after the agreement for recourse to conciliation.

(c) Unless otherwise provided in this Annex or agreed upon by the parties, the conciliator shall determine the rules governing the conciliation procedure and shall be guided in this regard by the conciliation rules adopted pursuant to the Convention on the Settlement of Investment Disputes between States and Nationals of Other States.

(d) The parties shall cooperate in good faith with the conciliator and shall, in particular, provide him with all information and documentation which would assist him in the discharge of his functions; they shall give their most serious consideration to his recommendations.

(e) Unless otherwise agreed upon by the parties, the conciliator shall, within a period not exceeding one hundred and eighty days from the date of his appointment, submit to the parties a report recording the results of his efforts and setting out the issues controversial between the parties and his proposals for their settlement.

(f) Each party shall, within sixty days from the date of the receipt of the report, express in writing its views on the report to the other party.

(g) Neither party to a conciliation proceeding shall be entitled to have recourse to arbitration unless:

(i) the conciliator shall have failed to submit his report within the period established in Section (e) above; or

(ii) the parties shall have failed to accept all of the proposals contained in the report within sixty days after its receipt; or

(iii) the parties, after an exchange of views on the report, shall have failed to agree on a settlement of all controversial issues within sixty days after receipt of the conciliator's report; or

(iv) a party shall have failed to express its views on the report as prescribed in Section (f) above.

(h) Unless the parties agree otherwise, the fees of the conciliator shall be determined on the basis of the rates applicable to ICSID conciliation. These fees and the other costs of the conciliation proceedings shall be borne equally by the parties. Each party shall defray its own expenses.

Article 4. Arbitration

(a) Arbitration proceedings shall be instituted by means of a notice by the party seeking arbitration (the claimant) addressed to the other party or parties to the dispute (the respondent). The notice shall specify the nature of the dispute, the relief sought and the name of the arbitrator appointed by the claimant. The respondent shall, within thirty days after the date of receipt of the notice, notify the claimant of the name of the arbitrator appointed by it. The two parties shall, within a period of thirty days from the date of appointment of the second arbitrator, select a third arbitrator, who shall act as President of the Arbitral Tribunal (the Tribunal).

(b) If the Tribunal shall not have been constituted within sixty days from the date of the notice, the arbitrator not yet appointed or the President not yet selected shall be appointed, at the joint request of the parties, by the Secretary-General of ICSID. If there is no such joint request, or if the Secretary-General shall fail to make the appointment within thirty days of the request, either party may request the President of the International Court of Justice to make the appointment.

(c) No party shall have the right to change the arbitrator appointed by it once the hearing of the dispute has commenced. In case any arbitrator (including the President of the Tribunal) shall resign, die, or become incapacitated, a successor shall be appointed in the manner followed in the appointment of his predecessor and such successor shall have the same powers and duties of the arbitrator he succeeds.

(d) The Tribunal shall convene first at such time and place as shall be determined by the President. Thereafter, the Tribunal shall determine the place and dates of its meetings.

(e) Unless otherwise provided in this Annex or agreed upon by the parties, the Tribunal shall determine its procedure and shall be guided in this regard by the arbitration rules adopted pursuant to the Convention on the Settlement of Investment Disputes between States and Nationals of Other States.

(f) The Tribunal shall be the judge of its own competence except that, if an objection is raised before the Tribunal to the effect that the dispute falls within the jurisdiction of the

Board or the Council under Article 56 or within the jurisdiction of a judicial or arbitral body designated in an agreement under Article 1 of this Annex and the Tribunal is satisfied that the objection is genuine, the objection shall be referred by the Tribunal to the Board or the Council or the designated body, as the case may be, and the arbitration proceedings shall be stayed until a decision has been reached on the matter, which shall be binding upon the Tribunal.

(g) The Tribunal shall, in any dispute within the scope of this Annex, apply the provisions of this Convention, any relevant agreement between the parties to the dispute, the Agency's by-laws and regulations, the applicable rules of international law, the domestic law of the member concerned as well as the applicable provisions of the investment contract, if any. Without prejudice to the provisions of this Convention, the Tribunal may decide a dispute *ex aequo et bono* if the Agency and the member concerned so agree. The Tribunal may not bring a finding of *non liquet* on the ground of silence or obscurity of the law.

(h) The Tribunal shall afford a fair hearing to all the parties. All decisions of the Tribunal shall be taken by a majority vote and shall state the reasons on which they are based. The award of the Tribunal shall be in writing, and shall be signed by at least two arbitrators and a copy thereof shall be transmitted to each party. The award shall be final and binding upon the parties and shall not be subject to appeal, annulment or revision.

(i) If any dispute shall arise between the parties as to the meaning or scope of an award, either party may, within sixty days after the award was rendered, request interpretation of the award by an application in writing to the President of the Tribunal which rendered the award. The President shall, if possible, submit the request to the Tribunal which rendered the award and shall convene such Tribunal within sixty days after receipt of the application. If this shall not be possible, a new Tribunal shall be constituted in accordance with the provisions of Sections (a) to (d) above. The Tribunal may stay enforcement of the award pending its decision on the requested interpretation.

(j) Each member shall recognize an award rendered pursuant to this Article as binding and enforceable within its territories as if it were a final judgment of a court in that member. Execution of the award shall be governed by the laws concerning the execution of judgments in force in the State in whose territories such execution is sought and shall not derogate from the law in force relating to immunity from execution.

(k) Unless the parties shall agree otherwise, the fees and remuneration payable to the arbitrators shall be determined on the basis of the rates applicable to ICSID arbitration. Each party shall defray its own costs associated with the arbitration proceedings. The costs of the Tribunal shall be borne by the parties in equal proportion unless the Tribunal decides otherwise. Any question concerning the division of the costs of the Tribunal or the procedure for payment of such costs shall be decided by the Tribunal.

Article 5. Service of Process

Service of any notice or process in connection with any proceeding under this Annex shall be made in writing. It shall be made by the Agency upon the authority designated by the member concerned pursuant to Article 38 of this Convention and by that member at the principal office of the Agency.

* * *

CRITERIA FOR SUSTAINABLE DEVELOPMENT MANAGEMENT: TOWARDS ENVIRONMENTALLY SUSTAINABLE DEVELOPMENT*

The United Nations Centre on Transnational Corporations, at the request of the United Nations Economic and Social Council at its July 1989 session, elaborated a set of "Criteria for Sustainable Development Management". The Criteria were presented to the Economic and Social Council at its July 1990 session.

First corporate steps

1. Establish and publish a transnational corporate sustainable development policy statement emphasizing sustainable growth, environmental protection, resource use, worker safety and accident prevention. Translate the policy statement into all the working languages of affiliate enterprises.

2. Review strategic planning, resource acquisition plans, and operating procedures so as to align them with the sustainable development policy. Announce significant efforts to reduce the use of natural resources and minimize the generation of wastes.

3. Review and modify corporate structure, lines of responsibility and internal reporting mechanisms to reflect the sustainable development policy. Encourage overseas affiliates to modify procedures in order to reflect local ecological and social realities.

4. Educate staff on the ways in which sustainable development affects their firm and how they can utilize these criteria in their specific tasks. Reward employees who discover and report environmental problems or who recommend new, environmentally sound products and processes.

5. Prepare sustainable development assessments of all major upcoming investment and operating decisions. Distribute them to affilate offices as models for their own sustainable development assessments.

6. Perform an environmental audit of on-going activities, particularly those in developing countries, to verify that the criteria have been adequately considered. Establish a comparative scale for identifying affiliates with strong and weak environmental track records.

---

*Source: United Nations Centre on Transnational Corporations (1991). "Towards Environmentally Sustainable Development: First Corporate Steps", in *Criteria for Sustainable Development Management*, (New York: United Nations), p. 10 [Note added by the editor].

7. Report publicly on the enterprise's most hazardous products, processes and toxic emissions. Distribute widely information on the methods in place to reduce these potential hazards and to cope with unanticipated emergencies.

8. Institute research and development work on the reduction and/or elimination of industrial products and processes which generate greenhouse gases. Arrange for environmentally safer technologies to be available to affiliates in developing countries without extra internal charges.

9. Inform joint venture partners and subcontractors about the corporate sustainable development policy. Establish ground rules for discountinuing business relationships with associated firms which operate with a disregard for basic health and environmental concerns.

10. Disseminate these criteria to other firms in relevant trade associations, local areas, or affiliated companies. Share the experiences with these criteria with local governments, national authorities, and the United Nations.

* * *

GUIDELINES ON THE TREATMENT OF FOREIGN DIRECT INVESTMENT*

The Guidelines on the Treatment of Foreign Direct Investment were prepared by the Development Committee of the Board of Governors of the International Monetary Fund and the World Bank. In September 1992, the Development Committee brought them to the attention of member countries.

The Development Committee

Recognizing

that a greater flow of foreign direct investment brings substantial benefits to bear on the world economy and on the economies of developing countries in particular, in terms of improving the long term efficiency of the host country through greater competition, transfer of capital, technology and managerial skills and enhancement of market access and in terms of the expansion of international trade;

that the promotion of private foreign investment is a common purpose of the International Bank for Reconstruction and Development, the International Finance Corporation and the Multilateral Investment Guarantee Agency;

that these institutions have pursued this common objective through their operations, advisory services and research;

that at the request of the Development Committee, a working group established by the President of these institutions and consisting of their respective General Counsel has, after reviewing existing legal instruments and literature, as well as best available practice identified by these institutions, prepared a set of guidelines representing a desirable overall framework which embodies essential principles meant to promote foreign direct investment in the common interest of all members;

that these guidelines, which have benefitted from a process of broad consultation inside and outside these institutions, constitute a further step in the evolutionary process where several international efforts aim to establish a favorable investment environment free from non-commercial risks in all countries, and thereby foster the confidence of international investors; and

---

*Source: World Bank Group (1992). "Guidelines on the Treatment of Foreign Direct Investment", ***Legal Framework for the Treatment of Foreign Investment: Volume II: Guidelines*** (Washington, D.C.: The International Bank for Reconstruction and Development/THE WORLD BANK), pp. 35-44 [Note added by the editor].

that these guidelines are not ultimate standards but an important step in the evolution of generally acceptable international standards which complement, but do not substitute for, bilateral investment treaties,

therefore *calls the attention* of member countries to the following Guidelines as useful parameters in the admission and treatment of private foreign investment in their territories, without prejudice to the binding rules of international law at this stage of its development.

I
SCOPE OF APPLICATION

1. These Guidelines may be applied by members for the World Bank Group institutions to private foreign investment in their respective territories, as a complement to applicable bilateral and multilateral treaties and other international instruments, to the extent that these Guidelines do not conflict with such treaties and binding instruments, and as a possible source on which national legislation governing the treatment of private foreign investment may draw. Reference to the "State" in these Guidelines, unless the context otherwise indicates, includes the State or any constituent subdivision, agency or instrumentality of the State and reference to "nationals" includes natural and juridical persons who enjoy the nationality of the State.

2. The application of these Guidelines extends to existing and new investment established and operating at all times as *bona fide* private foreign investments, in full conformity with the laws and regulations of the host State.

3. These Guidelines are based on the general premise that equal treatment of investors in similar circumstances and free competition among them are prerequisites of a positive investment environment. Nothing in these Guidelines therefore suggests that foreign investors should receive a privileged treatment denied to national investors in similar circumstances.

II
ADMISSION

1. Each State will encourage nationals of other States to invest capital, technology and managerial skill in its territory and, to that end, is expected to admit such investments in accordance with the following provisions.

2. In furtherance of the foregoing principle, each State will:

   (a) facilitate the admission and establishment of investments by nationals of other States, and

   (b) avoid making unduly cumbersome or complicated procedural regulations for, or imposing unnecessary conditions on, the admission of such investments.

3. Each State maintains the right to make regulations to govern the admission of private foreign investments. In the formulation and application of such regulations, States will note that experience suggests that certain performance requirements introduced as conditions of admission are often counterproductive and that open admission, possibly subject to a restricted list of investments (which are either prohibited or require screening and licensing), is a more effective approach. Such performance requirements often discourage foreign investors from initiating investment in the State concerned or encourage evasion and corruption. Under the restricted list approach, investments in non-listed activities, which proceed without approval, remain subject to the laws and regulations applicable to investments in the State concerned.

4. Without prejudice to the general approach of free admission recommended in Section 3 above, a State may, as an exception, refuse admission to a proposed investment:

(i) which is, in the considered opinion of the State, inconsistent with clearly defined requirements of national security; or

(ii) which belongs to sectors reserved by the law of the State to its nationals on account of the State's economic development objectives or the strict exigencies of its national interest.

5. Restrictions applicable to national investment on account of public policy (*ordre public*), public health and the protection of the environment will equally apply to foreign investment.

6. Each State is encouraged to publish, in the form of a handbook or other medium easily accessible to other States and their investors, adequate and regularly updated information about its legislation, regulations and procedures relevant to foreign investment and other information relating to its investment policies including, *inter alia*, an indication of any classes of investment which it regards as falling under Sections 4 and 5 of this Guideline.

III
TREATMENT

1. For the promotion of international economic cooperation through the medium of private foreign investment, the establishment, operation, management, control, and exercise of rights in such an investment, as well as such other associated activities necessary therefor or incidental thereto, will be consistent with the following standards which are meant to apply simultaneously to all States without prejudice to the provisions of applicable international instruments, and to firmly established rules of customary international law.

2. Each State will extend to investments established in its territory by nationals of any other State fair and equitable treatment according to the standards recommended in these Guidelines.

3. (a) With respect to the protection and security of their person, property rights and interests, and to the granting of permits, import and export licenses and the authorization to

employ, and the issuance of the necessary entry and stay visas to their foreign personnel, and other legal matters relevant to the treatment of foreign investors as described in Section 1 above, such treatment will, subject to the requirement of fair and equitable treatment mentioned above, be as favorable as that accorded by the State to national investors in similar circumstances. In all cases, full protection and security will be accorded to the investor's rights regarding ownership, control and substantial benefits over his property, including intellectual property.

(b) As concerns such other matters as are not relevant to national investors, treatment under the State's legislation and regulations will not discriminate among foreign investors on grounds of nationality.

4. Nothing in this Guideline will automatically entitle nationals of other States to the more favorable standards of treatment accorded to the nationals of certain States under any customs union or free trade area agreement.

5. Without restricting the generality of the foregoing, each State will:

(a) promptly issue such licenses and permits and grant such concessions as as may be necessary for the uninterrupted operation of the admitted investment; and

(b) to the extent necessary for the efficient operation of the investment, authorize the employment of foreign personnel. While a State may require the foreign investor to reasonably establish his inability to recruit the required personnel locally, e.g. through local advertisement, before he resorts to the recruitment of foreign personnel, labor market flexibility in this and other areas is recognized as an important element in a positive investment environment. Of particular importance in this respect is the investor's freedom to employ top managers regardless of their nationality.

6. (1) Each State will, with respect to private investment in its territory by nationals of the other States:

(a) freely allow regular periodic transfer of a reasonable part of the salaries and wages of foreign personnel; and, on liquidation of the investment or earlier termination of the employment, allow immediate transfer of all savings from such salaries and wages;

(b) freely allow transfer of the net revenues realized from the investment;

(c) allow the transfer of such sums as may be necessary for the payment of debts contracted, or the discharge of other contractual obligations incurred in connection with the investment as they fall due;

(d) on liquidation or sale of the investment (whether covering the investment as a whole or a part thereof), allow the repatriation and transfer of the net proceeds of such liquidation or sale and all accretions thereto all at once; in the exceptional cases where the State faces foreign exchange stringencies, such transfer may as an exception be made in installments within a period which will be as short as possible and will not in any case exceed five years from the date of liquidation or sale, subject to interest as provided for in Section 6 (3) of this Guidelines; and

(e) allow the transfer of any other amounts to which the investor is entitled such as those which become due under the conditions provided for in Guidelines IV and V.

(2) Such transfer as provided for in Section 6 (1) of this Guidelines will be made (a) in the currency brought in by the investor where it remains convertible, in another currency designated as freely usable currency by the International Monetary Fund or in any other currency accepted by the investor, and (b) at the applicable market rate of exchange at the time of the transfer.

(3) In the case of transfers under Section 6(1) of this Guideline, and without prejudice to Sections 7 and 8 of Guideline IV where they apply, any delay in effecting the transfers to be made through the central bank (or another authorized public authority) of the host State will be subject to interest at the normal rate applicable to the local currency involved in respect of any period intervening between the date on which such local currency has been provided to the central bank (or the other authorized public authority) for transfer and the date on which the transfer is actually effected.

(4) The provisions set forth in this Guideline with regard to the transfer of capital will also apply to the transfer of any compensation for loss due to war, armed conflict, revolution or insurrection to the extent that such compensation may be due to the investor under applicable law.

7. Each State will permit and facilitate the reinvestment in its territory of the profits realized from existing investments and the proceeds of sale or liquidation of such investments.

8. Each State will take appropriate measures for the prevention and control of corrupt business practices and the promotion of accountability and transparency in its dealings with foreign investors, and will cooperate with other States in developing international procedures and mechanisms to ensure the same.

9. Nothing in this Guideline suggests that a State should provide foreign investors with tax exemptions or other fiscal incentives. Where such incentives are deemed to be justified by the State, they may to the extent possible be automatically granted, directly linked to the type of activity to be encouraged and equally extended to national investors in similar circumstances. Competition among States in providing such incentives, especially tax exemptions, is not

recommended. Reasonable and stable tax rates are deemed to provide a better incentive than exemptions followed by uncertain or excessive rates.

10. Developed and capital surplus States will not obstruct flows of investment from their territories to developing States and are encouraged to adopt appropriate measures to facilitate such flows, including taxation agreements, investment guarantees, technical assistance and the provision of information. Fiscal incentives provided by some investors' governments for the purpose of encouraging investment in developing States are recognized in particular as a possibly effective element in promoting such investment.

IV
EXPROPRIATION AND UNILATERAL ALTERATIONS OR TERMINATION OF CONTRACTS

1. A State may not expropriate or otherwise take in whole or in part a foreign private investment in its territory, or take measures which have similar effects, except where this is done in accordance with applicable legal procedures, in pursuance in good faith of a public purpose, without discrimination on the basis of nationality and against the payment of appropriate compensation.

2. Compensation for a specific investment taken by the State will, according to the details provided below, be deemed "appropriate" if it is adequate, effective and prompt.

3. Compensation will be deemed "adequate" if it is based on the fair market value of the taken asset as such value is determined immediately before the time at which the taking occurred or the decision to take the asset became publicly known.

4. Determination of the "fair market value" will be acceptable if conducted according to a method agreed by the State and the foreign investor (hereinafter referred to as the parties) or by a tribunal or another body designated by the parties.

5. In the absence of a determination agreed by, or based on the agreement of, the parties, the fair market value will be acceptable if determined by the State according to reasonable criteria related to the market value of the investment, i.e., in an amount that a willing buyer would normally pay to a willing seller after taking into account the nature of the investment, the circumstances in which it would operate in the future and its specific characteristics, including the period in which it has been in existence, the proportion of tangible assets in the total investment and other relevant factors pertinent to the specific circumstances of each case.

6. Without implying the exclusive validity of a single standard for the fairness by which compensation is to be determined and as an illustration of the reasonable determination by a State of the market value of the investment under Section 5 above, such determination will be deemed reasonable if conducted as follows:

(i) for a going concern with a proven record of profitability, on the basis of the discounted cash flow value;

(ii) for an enterprise which, not being a proven going concern, demonstrates lack of profitability, on the basis of the liquidation value;

(iii) for other assets, on the basis of (a) the replacement value or (b) the book value in case such value has been recently assessed or has been determined as of the date of the taking and can therefore be deemed to represent a reasonable replacement value.

For the purpose of this provision:

-- a "*going concern*" means an enterprise consisting of income-producing assets which has been in operation for a sufficient period of time to generate the data required for the calculation of future income and which could have been expected with reasonable certainty, if the taking had not occurred, to continue producing legitimate income over the course of its economic life in the general circumstances following the taking by the State;

-- "*discounted cash flow value*" means the cash receipts realistically expected from the enterprise in each future year of its economic life as reasonably projected minus that year's expected cash expenditure, after discounting this net cash flow for each year by a factor which reflects the time value of money, expected inflation, and the risk associated with such cash flow under realistic circumstances. Such discount rate may be measured by examining the rate of return available in the same market on alternative investments of comparable risk on the basis of their present value;

-- "*liquidation value*" means the amounts at which individual assets comprising the enterprise or the entire assets of the enterprise could be sold under conditions of liquidation to a willing buyer less any liabilities which the enterprise has to meet;

-- "*replacement value*" means the cash amount required to replace the individual assets of the enterprise in their actual state as of the date of the taking; and

-- "*book value*" means the difference between the enterprise's assets and liabilities as recorded on its financial statements or the amount at which the taken tangible assets appear on the balance sheet of the enterprise, representing their cost after deducting accumulated depreciation in accordance with generally accepted accounting principles.

7. Compensation will be deemed "effective" if it is paid in the currency brought in by the investor where it remains convertible, in another currency designated as freely usable by the International Monetary Fund or in any other currency accepted by the investor.

8. Compensation will be deemed to be "prompt" in normal circumstances if paid without delay. In cases where the State faces exceptional circumstances, as reflected in an arrangement for the use of the resources of the International Monetary Fund or under similar objective circumstances of established foreign exchange stringencies, compensation in the currency designated under Section 7 above may be paid in installments within a period which will be as short as possible and which will not in any case exceed five years from the time of the taking, provided that reasonable, market-related interest applies to the deferred payments in the same currency.

9. Compensation according to the above criteria will not be due, or will be reduced in case the investment is taken by the State as a sanction against an investor who has violated the State's law and regulations which have been in force prior to the taking, as such violation is determined by a court of law. Further disputes regarding claims for compensation in such a case will be settled in accordance with the provisions of Guideline V.

10. In case of comprehensive non-discriminatory nationalizations effected in the process of large scale social reforms under exceptional circumstances of revolution, war and similar exigencies, the compensation may be determined through negotiations between the host State and the investors' home State and failing this, through international arbitration.

11. The provisions of Section 1 of this Guideline will apply with respect to the conditions under which a State may unilaterally terminate, amend or otherwise disclaim liability under a contract with a foreign private investor for other than commercial reasons, i.e., where the State acts as a sovereign and not as a contracting party. Compensation due to the investor in such cases will be determined in the light of the provisions of Sections 2 to 9 of this Guideline. Liability for repudiation of contract for commercial reasons, i.e., where the State acts as a contracting party, will be determined under the applicable law of the contract.

V
SETTLEMENT OF DISPUTES

1. Disputes between private foreign investors and the host State will normally be settled through negotiations between them and failing this, through national courts or through other agreed mechanisms including conciliation and binding independent arbitration.

2. Independent arbitration for the purpose of this Guidelines will include any *ad hoc* or institutional arbitration agreed upon in writing by the State and the investor or between the State and the investor's home State where the majority of the arbitrators are not solely appointed by one party to the dispute.

3. In case of agreement on independent arbitration, each State is encouraged to accept the settlement of such disputes through arbitration under the Convention establishing the International Centre for Settlement of Investment Disputes (ICSID) if it is a party to the ICSID Convention or through the "ICSID Additional Facility" if it is not a party to the ICSID Convention.

* * *

PERMANENT COURT OF ARBITRATION OPTIONAL RULES FOR ARBITRATING DISPUTES BETWEEN TWO PARTIES OF WHICH ONLY ONE IS A STATE*

The Permanent Court of Arbitration Optional Rules for Arbitrating Disputes between Two Parties of which only One is a State were adopted by the Permanent Court of Arbitration and became effective on 6 July 1993. These Rules supersede the "1962 Rules of Arbitration and Conciliation for Settlement of International Disputes Between Two Parties of Which Only One is a State."

SECTION I. INTRODUCTORY RULES

Scope of Application

Article 1

1. Where the parties to a contract have agreed in writing that disputes in relation to that contract shall be referred to arbitration under the Permanent Court of Arbitration Optional Rules for Arbitrating Disputes Between two parties of which only one is a State, then such disputes shall be referred to arbitration in accordance with these Rules subject to such modification as the parties may agree in writing.

2. Agreement by a party to arbitration under these Rules constitutes a waiver of any right to sovereign immunity from jurisdiction, in respect of the dispute in question, to which such party might otherwise be entitled. A waiver of immunity relating to the execution of an arbitral award must be explicitly expressed.

3. These Rules shall govern the arbitration except that where any of these Rules is in conflict with a provision of the law applicable to the arbitration from which the parties cannot derogate, that provision shall prevail.

4. The International Bureau of the Permanent Court of Arbitration at The Hague (the "International Bureau") shall have charge of the archives of the arbitration proceedings. In addition, the International Bureau shall, upon written request of all the parties or of the arbitral tribunal, act as a channel of communications between the parties and the arbitral tribunal, and provide secretariat services including, *inter alia*, arranging for hearing rooms, interpretation, and stenographic or electronic records of hearings.

---

*Source: International Bureau of the Permanent Court of Arbitration (1993). ***Permanent Court of Arbitration Optional Rules for Arbitrating Disputes Between Two Parties of which only One is a State,*** (The Hague, The Netherlands: International Bureau of the Permanent Court of Arbitration) [Note added by the editor].

Notice, Calculation of Periods of Time

Article 2

1. For the purposes of these Rules, any notice, including a notification, communication or proposal, is deemed to have been received if it is physically delivered to the addressee or if it is delivered at the addressee's habitual residence, place of business or mailing address, or, if none of these can be found after making reasonable inquiry, then at the addressee's last-known residence or place of business or mailing address. Notice shall be deemed to have been received on the day it is so delivered.

2. For the purposes of calculating a period of time under these Rules, such period shall begin to run on the day following the day when a notice, notification, communication or proposal is received. If the last day of such period is an official holiday or a non-business day at the residence or place of business of the addressee, the period is extended until the first business day which follows. Official holidays or non-business days occurring during the running of the period of time are included in calculating the period.

Notice of Arbitration

Article 3

1. The party initiating recourse to arbitration (hereinafter called the "claimant") shall give to the other party (hereinafter called the "respondent") a notice of arbitration.

2. Arbitral proceedings shall be deemed to commence on the date on which the notice of arbitration is received by the respondent.

3. The notice of arbitration shall include the following:

(a) A demand that the dispute be referred to arbitration;

(b) The names and addresses of the parties;

(c) A reference to the arbitration clause or the separate arbitration agreement that is invoked;

(d) A reference to the contract out of or in relation to which the dispute arises;

(e) The general nature of the claim and an indication of the amount involved, if any;

(f) The relief or remedy sought;

(g) A proposal as to the number of arbitrators (i.e., one or three), if the parties have not previously agreed thereon.

4. The notice of arbitration may also include:

(a) The proposals for the appointments of a sole arbitrator and an appointing authority referred to in article 6, paragraph 1;

(b) The notification of the appointment of an arbitrator referred to in article 7;

(c) The statement of claim referred to in article 18.

Representation and Assistance

Article 4

The parties may be represented or assisted by persons of their choice. The names and addresses of such persons must be communicated in writing to the other party, to the International Bureau, and to the arbitral tribunal after it has been appointed; such communication must specify whether the appointment is being made for purposes of representation or assistance.

SECTION II. COMPOSITION OF THE ARBITRAL TRIBUNAL

Number of Arbitrators

Article 5

1. If the parties have not previously agreed on the number of arbitrators (i.e., one or three), and if within thirty days after the receipt by the respondent of the notice of arbitration the parties have not agreed that there shall be only one arbitrator, three arbitrators shall be appointed.

Appointment of Arbitrators (Articles 6 to 8)

Article 6

1. If a sole arbitrator is to be appointed, either party may propose to the other:

(a) The names of one or more persons, one of whom would serve as the sole arbitrator; and

(b) If no appointing authority has been agreed upon by the parties, the name or names of one or more institutions or persons, one of whom would serve as appointing authority.

2. If within thirty days after receipt by a party of a proposal made in accordance with paragraph 1 the parties have not reached agreement on the choice of a sole arbitrator, the sole arbitrator shall be appointed by the appointing authority agreed upon by the parties. If no

appointing authority has been agreed upon by the parties, or if the appointing authority agreed upon refuses to act or fails to appoint the arbitrator within sixty days of the receipt of a party's request therefor, either party may request the Secretary-General of the Permanent Court of Arbitration at The Hague ("the Secretary-General") to designate an appointing authority.

3. The appointing authority shall, at the request of one of the parties, appoint the sole arbitrator as promptly as possible. In making the appointment the appointing authority shall use the following list-procedure, unless both parties agree that the list-procedure should not be used or unless the appointing authority determines in its discretion that the use of the list-procedure is not appropriate for the case:

(a) At the request of one of the parties the appointing authority shall communicate to both parties an identical list containing at least three names;

(b) Within thirty days after the receipt of this list, each party may return the list to the appointing authority after having deleted the name or names to which he objects and numbered the remaining names on the list in the order of its preference;

(c) After the expiration of the above period of time the appointing authority shall appoint the sole arbitrator from among the names approved on the lists returned to it and in accordance with the order of preference indicated by the parties;

(d) If for any reason the appointment cannot be made according to this procedure, the appointing authority may exercise its discretion in appointing the sole arbitrator.

4. In making the appointment, the appointing authority shall have regard to such considerations as are likely to secure the appointment of an independent and impartial arbitrator and shall take into account as well the advisability of appointing an arbitrator of a nationality other than the nationalities of the parties.

Article 7

1. If three arbitrators are to be appointed, each party shall appoint one arbitrator. The two arbitrators thus appointed shall choose the third arbitrator who will act as the presiding arbitrator of the tribunal.

2. If within thirty days after the receipt of a party's notification of the appointment of an arbitrator the other party has not notified the first party of the arbitrator it has appointed:

(a) The first party may request the appointing authority previously designated by the parties to appoint the second arbitrator; or

(b) If no such authority has been previously designated by the parties, or if the appointing authority previously designated refuses to act or fails to appoint the arbitrator within thirty days after receipt of a party's request therefor, the first party may request the Secretary-General to designate the appointing authority. The first party may then request the appointing authority so designated to appoint the second arbitrator. In either case, the appointing authority may exercise its discretion in appointing the arbitrator.

3. If within thirty days after the appointment of the second arbitrator the two arbitrators have not agreed on the choice of the presiding arbitrator, the presiding arbitrator shall be appointed by an appointing authority in the same way as a sole arbitrator would be appointed under article 6.

Article 8

1. When an appointing authority is requested to appoint an arbitrator pursuant to article 6 or article 7, the party which makes the request shall send to the appointing authority a copy of the notice of arbitration, a copy of the contract out of or in relation to which the dispute has arisen and a copy of the arbitration agreement if it is not contained in the contract. The appointing authority may require from either party such information as it deems necessary to fulfil its function.

2. Where the names of one or more persons are proposed for appointment as arbitrators, their full names, addresses and nationalities shall be indicated, together with a description of their qualifications.

3. In appointing arbitrators pursuant to these Rules, the parties and the appointing authority are free to designate persons who are not members of the Permanent Court of Arbitration at The Hague.

Challenge of Arbitrators (Articles 9 to 12)

Article 9

A prospective arbitrator shall disclose to those who approach him/her in connection with his/her possible appointment any circumstances likely to give rise to justifiable doubts as to his/her impartially or independence. An arbitrator, once appointed or chosen, shall disclose such circumstances to the parties unless they have already been informed by him/her of these circumstances.

Article 10

1. Any arbitrator may be challenged if circumstances exist that give rise to justifiable doubts as to the arbitrator's impartiality or independence.

2. A party may challenge the arbitrator appointed by it only for reasons of which it becomes aware after the appointment has been made.

Article 11

1. A party which intends to challenge an arbitrator shall send notice of its challenge within thirty days after the appointment of the challenged arbitrator has been notified to the challenging party or within thirty days after the circumstances mentioned in articles 9 and 10 became known to that party.

2. The challenge shall be notified to the other party, to the arbitrator who is challenged and to the other members of the arbitral tribunal. The notification shall be in writing and shall state the reasons for the challenge.

3. When an arbitrator has been challenged by one party, the other party may agree to the challenge. The arbitrator may also, after the challenge, withdraw from his/her office. In neither case does this imply acceptance of the validity of the grounds for the challenge. In both cases the procedure provided in article 6 or 7 shall be used in full for the appointment of the substitute arbitrator, even if during the process of appointing the challenged arbitrator a party had failed to exercise its right to appoint or to participate in the appointment.

Article 12

1. If the other party does not agree to the challenge and the challenged arbitrator does not withdraw, the decision on the challenge will be made:

(a) When the initial appointment was made by an appointing authority, by that authority;

(b) When the initial appointment was not made by an appointing authority, but an appointing authority has been previously designated, by that authority;

(c) In all other cases, by the appointing authority to be designated in accordance with the procedure for designating an appointing authority as provided for in article 6.

2. If the appointing authority sustains the challenge, a substitute arbitrator shall ... appointed or chosen pursuant to the procedure applicable to the appointment or choice of an arbitrator as provided in articles 6 to 9 except that, when this procedure would call for the designation of an appointing authority, the appointment of the arbitrator shall be made by the appointing authority which decided on the challenge.

Replacement of an Arbitrator

Article 13

1. In the event of the death or resignation of an arbitrator during the course of the arbitral proceedings, a substitute arbitrator shall be appointed or chosen pursuant to the procedure provided for in articles 6 to 9 that was applicable to the appointment or choice of the arbitrator

being replaced. Any resignation by an arbitrator shall be addressed to the arbitral tribunal and shall not be effective unless the arbitral tribunal determines that there are sufficient reasons to accept the resignation, and if the arbitral tribunal so determines the resignation shall become effective on the date designated by the arbitral tribunal. In the event that an arbitrator whose resignation is not accepted by the tribunal nevertheless fails to participate in the arbitration, the provisions of paragraph 3 of this Article shall apply.

2. In the event that an arbitrator fails to act or in the event of the *de jure* or *de facto* impossibility of his/her performing his/her functions, the procedure in respect of the challenge and replacement of an arbitrator as provided in the preceding articles shall apply, subject to the provisions of paragraph 3 of this Article.

3. If an arbitrator on a three-person tribunal fails to participate in the arbitration, the other arbitrators shall, unless the parties agree otherwise, have the power in their sole discretion to continue the arbitration and to make any decision, ruling or award, notwithstanding the failure of one arbitrator to participate. In determining whether to continue the arbitration or to render any decision, ruling, or award without the participation of an arbitrator, the other arbitrators shall take into account the stage of the arbitration, the reason, if any, expressed by the arbitrator for such nonparticipation, and such other matters as they consider appropriate in the circumstances of the case. In the event that the other arbitrators determine not to continue the arbitration without the nonparticipating arbitrator, the arbitral tribunal shall declare the office vacant, and a substitute arbitrator shall be appointed pursuant to the provisions of Articles 6 to 9, unless the parties otherwise agree on a different method of appointment.

Repetition of Hearings in the Event of the Replacement of an Arbitrator

Article 14

If under articles 11 to 13 the sole or presiding arbitrator is replaced, any hearings held previously shall be repeated; if any other arbitrator is replaced, such prior hearings may be repeated at the discretion of the arbitral tribunal.

SECTION III. ARBITRAL PROCEEDINGS

General Provisions

Article 15

1. Subject to these Rules, the arbitral tribunal may conduct the arbitration in such manner as it considers appropriate, provided that the parties are treated with equality and that at any stage of the proceedings each party is given a full opportunity of presenting its case.

2. If either party so requests at any appropriate stage of the proceedings, the arbitral tribunal shall hold hearings for the presentation of evidence by witnesses, including expert witnesses, or

for oral argument. In the absence of such a request, the arbitral tribunal shall decide whether to hold such hearings or whether the proceedings shall be conducted on the basis of documents and other materials.

3. All documents or information supplied to the arbitral tribunal by one party shall at the same time be communicated by that party to the other party and a copy shall be filed with the International Bureau.

Place of Arbitration

Article 16

1. Unless the parties have agreed upon the place where the arbitration is to be held, such place shall be The Hague, The Netherlands. If the parties agree that the arbitration shall be held at a place other than The Hague, the International Bureau shall inform the parties and the arbitral tribunal whether it is willing to provide the secretariat and registrar services referred to in Article 1, paragraph 4, and the services referred to in Article 25, paragraph 3.

2. The arbitral tribunal may determine the locale of the arbitration within the country agreed upon by the parties. It may hear witnesses and hold meetings for consultation among its members at any place it deems appropriate, having regard to the circumstances of the arbitration.

3. After inviting the views of the parties, the arbitral tribunal may meet at any place it deems appropriate for the inspection of goods, other property or documents. The parties shall be given sufficient notice to enable them to be present at such inspection.

4. The award shall be made at the place of arbitration.

Language

Article 17

1. Subject to an agreement by the parties, the arbitral tribunal shall, promptly after its appointment, determine the language or languages to be used in the proceedings. This determination shall apply to the statement of claim, the statement of defence, and any further written statements and, if oral hearings take place, to the language or languages to be used in such hearings.

2. The arbitral tribunal may order that any documents annexed to the statement of claim or statement of defence, and any supplementary documents or exhibits submitted in the course of the proceedings, delivered in their original language, shall be accompanied by a translation into the language or languages agreed upon by the parties or determined by the arbitral tribunal.

Statement of Claim

Article 18

1. Unless the statement of claim was contained in the notice of arbitration, within a period of time to be determined by the arbitral tribunal, the claimant shall communicate its statement of claim in writing to the respondent and to each of the arbitrators. A copy of the contract, and of the arbitration agreement if not contained in the contract, shall be annexed thereto.

2. The statement of claim shall include the following particulars:

(a) The names and addresses of the parties;

(b) A statement of the facts supporting the claim;

(c) The points at issue;

(d) The relief or remedy sought.

The claimant may annex to its statement of claim all documents it deems relevant or may add a reference to the documents or other evidence it will submit.

Statement of Defence

Article 19

1. Within a period of time to be determined by the arbitral tribunal, the respondent shall communicate its statement of defence in writing to the claimant and to each of the arbitrators.

2. The statement of defence shall reply to the particulars (b), (c) and (d) of the statement of claim (article 18, para. 2). The respondent may annex to its statement the documents on which it relies for its defence or may add a reference to the documents or other evidence it will submit.

3. In its statement of defence, or at a later stage in the arbitral proceedings if the arbitral tribunal decides that the delay was justified under the circumstances, the respondent may make a counter-claim arising out of the same contract or rely on a claim arising out of the same contract for the purpose of a set-off.

4. The provisions of article 18, paragraph 2, shall apply to a counter-claim and a claim relied on for the purpose of a set-off.

Amendments to the Claim or Defence

Article 20

During the course of the arbitral proceedings either party may amend or supplement its claim or defence unless the arbitral tribunal considers it inappropriate to allow such amendment having regard to the delay in making it or prejudice to the other party or any other circumstances. However, a claim may not be amended in such a manner that the amended claim falls outside the scope of the arbitration clause or separate arbitration agreement.

Pleas as to the Jurisdiction of the Arbitral Tribunal

Article 21

1. The arbitral tribunal shall have the power to rule on objections that it has no jurisdiction, including any objections with respect to the existence or validity of the arbitration clause or of the separate arbitration agreement.

2. The arbitral tribunal shall have the power to determine the existence or the validity of the contract of which an arbitration clause forms a part. For the purposes of this article, an arbitration clause which forms part of a contract and which provides for arbitration under these Rules shall be treated as an agreement independent of the other terms of the contract. A decision by the arbitral tribunal that the contract is null and void shall not entail *ipso jure* the invalidity of the arbitration clause.

3. A plea that the arbitral tribunal does not have jurisdiction shall be raised not later than in the statement of defence or, with respect to a counter-claim, in the reply to the counter-claim.

4. In general, the arbitral tribunal should rule on a plea concerning its jurisdiction as a preliminary question. However, the arbitral tribunal may proceed with the arbitration and rule on such a plea in their final award.

Further Written Statements

Article 22

The arbitral tribunal shall decide which further written statements, in addition to the statement of claim and the statement of defence, shall be required from the parties or may be presented by them and shall fix the periods of time for communicating such statements.

Periods of Time

Article 23

The periods of time fixed by the arbitral tribunal for the communication of written statements (including the statement of claim and statement of defence) should not exceed forty-five days. However, the arbitral tribunal may set longer time limits, or extend the time limits, if it concludes that either is justified.

Evidence and Hearings (Articles 24 and 25)

Article 24

1. Each party shall have the burden of proving the facts relied on to support its claim or defence.

2. The arbitral tribunal may, if it considers it appropriate, require a party to deliver to the tribunal and to the other party, within such a period of time as the arbitral tribunal shall decide, a summary of the documents and other evidence which that party intends to present in support of the facts in issue set out in its statement of claim or statement of defence.

3. At any time during the arbitral proceedings the arbitral tribunal may call upon the parties to produce documents, exhibits or other evidence within such a period of time as the tribunal shall determine. The Tribunal shall take formal note of any refusal to do so, as well as any reasons given for such refusal.

Article 25

1. In the event of an oral hearing, the arbitral tribunal shall give the parties adequate advance notice of the date, time and place thereof.

2. If witnesses are to be heard, at least thirty days before the hearing each party shall communicate to the arbitral tribunal and to the other party the names and addresses of the witnesses it intends to present, the subject upon and the languages in which such witnesses will give their testimony.

3. The International Bureau shall make arrangements for the translation of oral statements made at a hearing and for a record of the hearing if either is deemed necessary by the tribunal under the circumstances of the case, or if the parties have agreed thereto and have communicated such agreement to the tribunal and the International Bureau at least thirty days before the hearing, or such longer period before the hearing as the arbitral tribunal may determine.

4. Hearings shall be held *in camera* unless the parties agree otherwise. The arbitral tribunal may require the retirement of any witness or witnesses during the testimony of other witnesses. The arbitral tribunal is free to determine the manner in which witnesses are examined.

5. Evidence of witnesses may also be presented in the form of written statements signed by them.

6. The arbitral tribunal shall determine the admissibility, relevance, materiality and weight of the evidence offered.

Interim Measures of Protection

Article 26

1. Unless the parties agree otherwise, the arbitral tribunal may, at the request of either party, take any interim measures it deems necessary to preserve the respective rights of either party or in respect of the subject-matter of the dispute, including measures for conservation of the goods forming the subject-matter in dispute, such as ordering their deposit with a third person or the sale of perishable goods.

2. Such interim measures may be established in the form of an interim award. The arbitral tribunal shall be entitled to require security for the costs of such measures.

3. A request for interim measures addressed by any party to a judicial authority shall not be deemed incompatible with the agreement to arbitrate, or as a waiver of that agreement.

Experts

Article 27

1. The arbitral tribunal may appoint one or more experts to report to it, in writing, on specific issues to be determined by the tribunal. A copy of the expert's terms of reference, established by the arbitral tribunal, shall be communicated to the parties.

2. The parties shall give the expert any relevant information or produce for his/her inspection any relevant documents or goods that he/she may require of them. Any dispute between a party and such expert as to the relevance of the required information or production shall be referred to the arbitral tribunal for decision.

3. Upon receipt of the expert's report, the arbitral tribunal shall communicate a copy of the report to the parties which shall be given the opportunity to express, in writing, their opinion on the report. A party shall be entitled to examine any document on which the expert has relied in his/her report.

4. At the request of either party the expert, after delivery of the report, may be heard at a hearing where the parties shall have the opportunity to be present and to interrogate the expert. At this hearing either party may present expert witnesses in order to testify on the points at issue. The provisions of article 25 shall be applicable to such proceedings.

Failure to Appear or to Make Submissions

Article 28

1. If, within the period of time fixed by the arbitral tribunal, the claimant has failed to communicate its claim without showing sufficient cause for such failure, the arbitral tribunal shall issue an order for the termination of the arbitral proceedings. If, within the period of time fixed by the arbitral tribunal, the respondent has failed to communicate its statement of defence without showing sufficient cause for such failure, the arbitral tribunal shall order that the proceedings continue.

2. If one of the parties, duly notified under these Rules, fails to appear at a hearing, without showing sufficient cause for such failure, the arbitral tribunal may proceed with the arbitration.

3. If one of the parties, duly invited to produce documentary evidence, fails to do so within the established period of time, without showing sufficient cause for such failure, the arbitral tribunal may make the award on the evidence before it.

Closure of Hearings

Article 29

1. The arbitral tribunal may inquire of the parties if they have any further proof to offer or witnesses to be heard or submissions to make and, if there are none, it may declare the hearings closed.

2. The arbitral tribunal may, if it considers it necessary owing to exceptional circumstances, decide, on its own motion or upon application of a party, to reopen the hearings at any time before the award is made.

Waiver of Rules

Article 30

A party which knows that any provision of, or requirement under, these Rules has not been complied with and yet proceeds with the arbitration without promptly stating its objection to such non-compliance, shall be deemed to have waived its right to object.

SECTION IV. THE AWARD

Decisions

Article 31

1. When there are three arbitrators, any award or other decision of the arbitral tribunal shall

be made by a majority of the arbitrators.

2. In the case of questions of procedure, when there is no majority or when the arbitral tribunal so authorizes, the presiding arbitrator may decide on his/her own, subject to revision, if any, by the arbitral tribunal.

Form and Effect of the Award

Article 32

1. In addition to making a final award, the arbitral tribunal shall be entitled to make interim, interlocutory, or partial awards.

2. The award shall be made in writing and shall be final and binding on the parties. The parties undertake to carry out the award without delay.

3. The arbitral tribunal shall state the reasons upon which the award is based, unless the parties have agreed that no reasons are to be given.

4. An award shall be signed by the arbitrators and it shall contain the date on which and the place where the award was made. Where there are three arbitrators and one of them fails to sign, the award shall state the reason for the absence of the signature.

5. The award may be made public only with the consent of both parties.

6. Copies of the award signed by the arbitrators shall be communicated to the parties by the International Bureau. The International Bureau may withhold communicating the award to the parties until all costs of the arbitration have been paid.

7. If the arbitration law of the country where the award is made requires that the award be filed or registered by the arbitral tribunal, the tribunal shall comply with this requirement within the period of time required by law.

Applicable Law, Amiable Compositeur

Article 33

1. The arbitral tribunal shall apply the law designated by the parties as applicable to the substance of the dispute. Failing such designation by the parties, the arbitral tribunal shall apply the law determined by the conflict of laws rules which it considers applicable.

2. The arbitral tribunal shall decide as *amiable compositeur* or *ex aequo et bono* only if the parties have expressly authorized the arbitral tribunal to do so and if the law applicable to the arbitral procedure permits such arbitration.

3. In all cases, the arbitral tribunal shall decide in accordance with the terms of the contract and shall take into account the usages of the trade applicable to the transaction.

Settlement or other Grounds for Termination

Article 34

1. If, before the award is made, the parties agree on a settlement of the dispute, the arbitral tribunal shall either issue an order for the termination of the arbitral proceedings or, if requested by both parties and accepted by the tribunal, record the settlement in the form of an arbitral award on agreed terms. The arbitral tribunal is not obliged to give reasons for such an award.

2. If, before the award is made, the continuation of the arbitral proceedings becomes unnecessary or impossible for any reason not mentioned in paragraph 1, the arbitral tribunal shall inform the parties of its intention to issue an order for the termination of the proceedings. The arbitral tribunal shall have the power to issue such an order unless a party raises justifiable grounds for objection.

3. Copies of the order for termination of the arbitral proceedings or of the arbitral award on agreed terms, signed by the arbitrators, shall be communicated to the parties by the International Bureau. Where an arbitral award on agreed terms is made, the provisions of article 32, paragraphs 2 and 4 to 7, shall apply.

Interpretation of the Award

Article 35

1. Within thirty days after the receipt of the award, either party, with notice to the other party, may request that the arbitral tribunal give an interpretation of the award.

2. The interpretation shall be given in writing within forty-five days after the receipt of the request. The interpretation shall form part of the award and the provisions of article 32, paragraphs 2 to 7, shall apply.

Correction of the Award

Article 36

1. Within thirty days after the receipt of the award, either party, with notice to the other party, may request the arbitral tribunal to correct in the award any errors in computation, any clerical or typographical errors, or any errors of similar nature. The arbitral tribunal may within thirty days after the communication of the award make such corrections on its own initiative.

2. Such corrections shall be in writing, and the provisions of article 32, paragraphs 2 to 7, shall apply.

Additional Award

Article 37

1. Within sixty days after the receipt of the award, either party, with notice to the other party, may request the arbitral tribunal to make an additional award as to claims presented in the arbitral proceedings but omitted from the award.

2. If the arbitral tribunal considers the request for an additional award to be justified and considers that the omission can be rectified without any further hearings or evidence, it shall complete its award within sixty days after the receipt of the request.

3. When an additional award is made, the provisions of article 32, paragraphs 2 to 7, shall apply.

Costs (Articles 38 to 40)

Article 38

The arbitral tribunal shall fix the costs of arbitration in its award. The term "costs" includes only:

(a) The fees of the arbitral tribunal to be stated separately as to each arbitrator and to be fixed by the tribunal itself in accordance with article 39;

(b) The travel and other expenses incurred by the arbitrators;

(c) The costs of expert advice and of other assistance required by the arbitral tribunal;

(d) The travel and other expenses of witnesses to the extent such expenses are approved by the arbitral tribunal;

(e) The costs for legal representation and assistance of the successful party if such costs were claimed during the arbitral proceedings, and only to the extent that the arbitral tribunal determines that the amount of such costs is reasonable;

(f) Any fees and expenses of the appointing authority as well as the expenses of the Secretary-General and the International Bureau.

Article 39

1. The fees of the arbitral tribunal shall be reasonable in amount, taking into account the amount in dispute, the complexity of the subject-matter, the time spent by the *arbitrators* and any other relevant circumstances of the case.

2. If an appointing authority has been agreed upon by the parties or designated by the Secretary-General of the Permanent Court of Arbitration at The Hague, and if that authority has issued a schedule of fees for arbitrators in international cases which it administers, the arbitral tribunal in fixing its fees shall take that schedule of fees into account to the extent that it considers appropriate in the circumstances of the case.

3. If such appointing authority has not issued a schedule of fees for arbitrators in international cases, any party may at any time request the appointing authority to furnish a statement setting forth the basis for establishing fees which is customarily followed in international cases in which the authority appoints arbitrators. If the appointing authority consents to provide such a statement, the arbitral tribunal in fixing its fees shall take such information into account to the extent that it considers appropriate in the circumstances of the case.

4. In cases referred to in paragraphs 2 and 3, when a party so requests and the appointing authority consents to perform the function, the arbitral tribunal shall fix its fees only after consultation with the appointing authority which may make any comment it deems appropriate to the arbitral tribunal concerning the fees.

Article 40

1. Except as provided in paragraph 2, the costs of arbitration shall in principle be borne by the unsuccessful party. However, the arbitral tribunal may apportion each of such costs between the parties if it determines that apportionment is reasonable, taking into account the circumstances of the case.

2. With respect to the costs of legal representation and assistance referred to in article 38, paragraph (e), the arbitral tribunal, taking into account the circumstances of the case shall be free to determine which party shall bear such costs or may apportion such costs between the parties if it determines that apportionment is reasonable.

3. When the arbitral tribunal issues an order for the termination of the arbitral proceedings or makes an award on agreed terms, it shall fix the costs of arbitration referred to in articles 38 and 39, paragraph 1, in the text of that order or award.

4. No additional fees may be charged by an arbitral tribunal for interpretation or correction or completion of its award under articles 35 to 37.

Deposit of Costs

Article 41

1. The arbitral tribunal, on its establishment, may request each party to deposit an equal amount as an advance for the costs referred to in article 38, paragraph (a), (b), (c) and (f). All amounts deposited by the parties pursuant to this paragraph and paragraph 2 of this Article shall

be paid to the International Bureau, and shall be disbursed by it for such costs, including, *inter alia*, fees to the arbitrators, the Secretary-General and the International Bureau.

2. During the course of the arbitral proceedings the arbitral tribunal may request supplementary deposits from the parties.

3. If an appointing authority has been agreed upon by the parties or designated by the Secretary-General of the Permanent Court of Arbitration at The Hague, and when a party so requests and the appointing authority consents to perform the function, the arbitral tribunal shall fix the amounts of any deposits or supplementary deposits only after consultation with the appointing authority which may make any comments to the arbitral tribunal which it deems appropriate concerning the amount of such deposits and supplementary deposits.

4. If the required deposits are not paid in full within thirty days after the receipt of the request, the arbitral tribunal shall so inform the parties in order that one or another of them may make the required payment. If such payment is not made, the arbitral tribunal may order the suspension or termination of the arbitral proceedings.

5. After the award has been made, the International Bureau shall render an accounting to the parties of the deposits received and return any unexpended balance to the parties.

MODEL ARBITRATION CLAUSES FOR USE IN CONNECTION WITH PERMANENT COURT OF ARBITRATION OPTIONAL RULES FOR ARBITRATING BILATERAL DISPUTES BETWEEN TWO PARTIES OF WHICH ONLY ONE IS A STATE

Future Disputes

Where a State and a private entity are parties to a contract and wish to have any dispute referred to arbitration under these Rules, they may insert in the contract an arbitration clause in the following form:

1. If any dispute arises between the parties as to the interpretation application or performance of this contract, including its existence, validity or termination, either party may submit the dispute to final and binding arbitration in accordance with the Permanent Court of Arbitration Optional Rules for Arbitrating Disputes Between Two Parties of which only one is a State, as in effect on the date of this contract.[1]

[1]Parties may agree to vary this model clause. If they consider doing so, they may consult with the Secretary-General of the Permanent Court of Arbitration to ensure that the clause to which they agree will be appropriate in the context of the Rules, and that the functions of the Secretary-General and the International Bureau can be carried out effectively.

Parties may wish to consider adding:

2. *The number of arbitrators shall be...* [insert "one" or "three"].[2]

3. *The language(s) to be used in the arbitral proceedings shall be* [insert choice of one or more languages].[3]

4. *The appointing authority shall be...* [insert choice].[4]

5. *This agreement to arbitrate constitutes a waiver of any right to sovereign immunity from execution to which a party might otherwise be entitled with respect to the enforcement of any award rendered by an arbitral tribunal constituted pursuant to this agreement.*[5]

Existing Disputes

If the parties have not already entered into an arbitration agreement, or if they mutually agree to change a previous agreement in order to provide for arbitration under these Rules, they may enter into an agreement in the following form:

1. The parties agree to submit the following dispute to final and binding arbitration in accordance with the Permanent Court of Arbitration Optional Rules for Arbitrating Bilateral Disputes Between Two Parties of which only one is a State, as in effect on the date of this agreement: . . . [insert brief description of dispute].

Parties may wish to consider adding paragraphs 2-5 of the arbitration clause for future disputes as set forth above.

---

[2]If the parties do not agree on the number of arbitrators, the number shall be three, in accordance with Article 5 of the Rules.

[3]If the parties do not agree on the language, or languages, to be used in the arbitral proceedings, this shall be determined by the arbitral tribunal in accordance with Article 17 of the Rules.

[4]Parties are free to agree upon any appointing authority, e.g., the President of the International Court of Justice, or the head of a specialized body expert in the relevant subject-matter, or an ad hoc panel chosen by the parties, or any other officer, institution or individual. The Secretary-General of the Permanent Court of Arbitration will consider accepting designation as appointing authority in appropriate cases. Before inserting the name of an appointing authority in an arbitration clause, it is advisable for the parties to inquire whether the proposed authority is willing to act. If the parties do not agree on the appointing authority, the Secretary-General of the Permanent Court of Arbitration at The Hague will designate the appointing authority in accordance with Article 6 or 7 of the Rules, as the case may be.

[5]Waiver of sovereign immunity from jurisdiction is provided in Article 1, paragraph 2 of the Rules.

GUIDELINES FOR ADAPTING THESE RULES FOR USE IN ARBITRATING DISPUTES ARISING UNDER MULTIPARTY CONTRACTS

The Permanent Court of Arbitration Optional Rules for Arbitrating Disputes Between Two Parties of which only one is a State can be adapted for use in resolving disputes arising under multiparty contracts. All of the provisions in these Rules are appropriate, except that modifications are needed in the mechanisms for naming arbitrators and sharing costs.

Particular care should be taken in drafting the provisions for appointing arbitrators where there may be so many parties in the arbitration that the tribunal would be of impractical size or structure if each party appointed an arbitrator. One solution sometimes considered in multiparty arbitrations is for the parties to agree that the appointing authority will designate all of the arbitrators if the parties do not do so within a specified period.

Modifications may also be needed in the provisions for sharing the costs of the arbitration.

It is recommended that parties that contemplate including an arbitration provision in a multiparty contract consult in advance with the Secretary-General of the Permanent Court of Arbitration concerning the drafting of that provision in order to ensure that the functions of the Secretary-General and the International Bureau of the Permanent Court of Arbitration can be carried out effectively.

NOTES TO THE TEXT

These Rules are based on the UNCITRAL Arbitration Rules, with the following modifications:

(i) Modifications to facilitate effective arbitration between a State or State entity, on the one hand, and a non-State party, on the other hand:

Article 1, para. 1; para. 2 (added); para. 3 (renumbered)
Article 2, para. 1
Article 8, para. 3 (added)
Article 13, paras. 1 and 2; para. 3 (added)
Article 15, para. 2
Article 16, para. 3
Article 23
Article 24, para. 3
Article 25, para. 3
Article 26, para. 1
Article 41, para. 1

Throughout the Rules, all fifteen-day time limits placed upon the parties have been made twice as long, i.e., "thirty days" substituted for "fifteen days."

Throughout the Rules, all references to "his" have been changed to "his/hers". The pronoun "it" ("its") is used when referring to parties and means any person, natural and juridical.

(ii) Modifications to indicate the functions of the Secretary-General and the International Bureau of the Permanent Court of Arbitration:

Article 1,	para. 4 (added)
Article 4	
Article 15,	para. 3
Article 16,	para. 1
Article 25,	para. 3
Article 32,	para. 6
Article 34,	para. 3
Article 38	
Article 41,	paras. 1 and 5

* * *

MARRAKESH AGREEMENT ESTABLISHING THE WORLD TRADE ORGANIZATION

ANNEX 1A: MULTILATERAL AGREEMENTS ON TRADE IN GOODS

AGREEMENT ON TRADE-RELATED INVESTMENT MEASURES*

The Agreement on Trade-Related Investment Measures is an integral part of the Marrakesh Agreement Establishing the World Trade Organization (as one of the Agreements in Annex 1A: Multilateral Agreements on Trade in Goods) which was signed on 15 April 1994 by the participants in the Uruguay Round of Multilateral Trade Negotiations held under the auspices of GATT. The Agreement came into force on 1 January 1995 and had been ratified by 105 States as of 5 July 1995.

Members,

Considering that Ministers agreed in the Punta del Este Declaration that "Following an examination of the operation of GATT Articles related to the trade-restrictive and distorting effects of investment measures, negotiations should elaborate, as appropriate, further provisions that may be necessary to avoid such adverse effects on trade";

Desiring to promote the expansion and progressive liberalisation of world trade and to facilitate investment across international frontiers so as to increase the economic growth of all trading partners, particularly developing country Members, while ensuring free competition;

Taking into account the particular trade, development and financial needs of developing country Members, particularly those of the least-developed country Members;

Recognizing that certain investment measures can cause trade-restrictive and distorting effects;

Hereby *agree* as follows:

Article 1
Coverage

This Agreement applies to investment measures related to trade in goods only (referred

* Source: World Trade Organization (1995). "Marrakesh Agreement Establishing the World Trade Organization. Annex 1A: Multilateral Agreements on Trade in Goods - Agreement on Trade-Related Investment Measures", *The Results of the Uruguay Round of Multilateral Trade Negotiations: The Legal Texts* (Geneva: World Trade Organization), pp. 163-167 [Note added by the editor].

to in this Agreement as "TRIMs").

Article 2
National Treatment and Quantitative Restrictions

1. Without prejudice to other rights and obligations under GATT 1994, no Member shall apply any TRIM that is inconsistent with the provisions of Article III or Article XI of GATT 1994.

2. An illustrative list of TRIMs that are inconsistent with the obligation of national treatment provided for in paragraph 4 of Article III of GATT 1994 and the obligation of general elimination of quantitative restrictions provided for in paragraph 1 of Article XI of GATT 1994 is contained in the Annex to this Agreement.

Article 3
Exceptions

All exceptions under GATT 1994 shall apply, as appropriate, to the provisions of this Agreement.

Article 4
Developing Country Members

A developing country Member shall be free to deviate temporarily from the provisions of Article 2 to the extent and in such a manner as Article XVIII of GATT 1994, the Understanding on the Balance-of-Payments Provisions of GATT 1994, and the Declaration on Trade Measures Taken for Balance-of-Payments Purposes adopted on 28 November 1979 (BISD 26S/205-209) permit the Member to deviate from the provisions of Articles III and XI of GATT 1994.

Article 5
Notification and Transitional Arrangements

1. Members, within 90 days of the date of entry into force of the WTO Agreement, shall notify the Council for Trade in Goods of all TRIMs they are applying that are not in conformity with the provisions of this Agreement. Such TRIMs of general or specific application shall be notified, along with their principal features.[1]

2. Each Member shall eliminate all TRIMs which are notified under paragraph 1 within two years of the date of entry into force of the WTO Agreement in the case of a developed country Member, within five years in the case of a developing country Member, and within

[1] In the case of TRIMs applied under discretionary authority, each specific application shall be notified. Information that would prejudice the legitimate commercial interests of particular enterprises need not be disclosed.

seven years in the case of a least-developed country Member.

3. On request, the Council for Trade in Goods may extend the transition period for the elimination of TRIMs notified under paragraph 1 for a developing country Member, including a least-developed country Member, which demonstrates particular difficulties in implementing the provisions of this Agreement. In considering such a request, the Council for Trade in Goods shall take into account the individual development, financial and trade needs of the Member in question.

4. During the transition period, a Member shall not modify the terms of any TRIM which it notifies under paragraph 1 from those prevailing at the date of entry into force of the WTO Agreement so as to increase the degree of inconsistency with the provisions of Article 2. TRIMs introduced less than 180 days before the date of entry into force of the WTO Agreement shall not benefit from the transitional arrangements provided in paragraph 2.

5. Notwithstanding the provisions of Article 2, a Member, in order not to disadvantage established enterprises which are subject to a TRIM notified under paragraph 1, may apply during the transition period the same TRIM to a new investment (*i*) where the products of such investment are like products to those of the established enterprises, and (*ii*) where necessary to avoid distorting the conditions of competition between the new investment and the established enterprises. Any TRIM so applied to a new investment shall be notified to the Council for Trade in Goods. The terms of such a TRIM shall be equivalent in their competitive effect to those applicable to the established enterprises, and it shall be terminated at the same time.

Article 6
Transparency

1. Members reaffirm, with respect to TRIMs, their commitment to obligations on transparency and notification in Article X of GATT 1994, in the undertaking on "Notification" contained in the Understanding Regarding Notification, Consultation, Dispute Settlement and Surveillance adopted on 28 November 1979 and in the Ministerial Decision on Notification Procedures adopted on 15 April 1994.

2. Each Member shall notify the Secretariat of the publications in which TRIMs may be found, including those applied by regional and local governments and authorities within their territories.

3. Each Member shall accord sympathetic consideration to requests for information, and afford adequate opportunity for consultation, on any matter arising from this Agreement raised by another Member. In conformity with Article X of GATT 1994 no Member is required to disclose information the disclosure of which would impede law enforcement or otherwise be contrary to the public interest or would prejudice the legitimate commercial interests of particular enterprises, public or private.

Article 7
Committee on Trade-Related Investment Measures

1. A Committee on Trade-Related Investment Measures (referred to in this Agreement as the "Committee") is hereby established, and shall be open to all Members. The Committee shall elect its own Chairman and Vice-Chairman, and shall meet not less than once a year and otherwise at the request of any Member.

2. The Committee shall carry out responsibilities assigned to it by the Council for Trade in Goods and shall afford Members the opportunity to consult on any matters relating to the operation and implementation of this Agreement.

3. The Committee shall monitor the operation and implementation of this Agreement and shall report thereon annually to the Council for Trade in Goods.

Article 8
Consultation and Dispute Settlement

The provisions of Articles XXII and XXIII of GATT 1994, as elaborated and applied by the Dispute Settlement Understanding, shall apply to consultations and the settlement of disputes under this Agreement.

Article 9
Review by the Council for Trade in Goods

Not later than five years after the date of entry into force of the WTO Agreement, the Council for Trade in Goods shall review the operation of this Agreement and, as appropriate, propose to the Ministerial Conference amendments to its text. In the course of this review, the Council for Trade in Goods shall consider whether the Agreement should be complemented with provisions on investment policy and competition policy.

ANNEX
Illustrative List

1. TRIMs that are inconsistent with the obligation of national treatment provided for in paragraph 4 of Article III of GATT 1994 include those which are mandatory or enforceable under domestic law or under administrative rulings, or compliance with which is necessary to obtain an advantage, and which require:

(a) the purchase or use by an enterprise of products of domestic origin or from any domestic source, whether specified in terms of particular products, in terms of volume or value of products, or in terms of a proportion of volume or value of its local production; or

(b) that an enterprise's purchases or use of imported products be limited to an amount related to the volume or value of local products that it exports.

2. TRIMs that are inconsistent with the obligation of general elimination of quantitative restrictions provided for in paragraph 1 of Article XI of GATT 1994 include those which are mandatory or enforceable under domestic law or under administrative rulings, or compliance with which is necessary to obtain an advantage, and which restrict:

(a) the importation by an enterprise of products used in or related to its local production, generally or to an amount related to the volume or value of local production that it exports;

(b) the importation by an enterprise of products used in or related to its local production by restricting its access to foreign exchange to an amount related to the foreign exchange inflows attributable to the enterprise; or

(c) the exportation or sale for export by an enterprise of products, whether specified in terms of particular products, in terms of volume or value of products, or in terms of a proportion of volume or value of its local production.

* * *

MARRAKESH AGREEMENT ESTABLISHING THE WORLD TRADE ORGANIZATION

ANNEX 1B: GENERAL AGREEMENT ON TRADE IN SERVICES

AND

MINISTERIAL DECISIONS RELATING TO THE GENERAL AGREEMENT ON TRADE IN SERVICES*

The General Agreement on Trade in Services is an integral part of the Marrakesh Agreement Establishing the World Trade Organization (Annex 1B) which was signed on 15 April 1994 by the participants in the Uruguay Round of Multilateral Trade Negotiations held under the auspices of GATT. The Agreement came into force on 1 January 1995 and had been ratified by 105 States as of 5 July 1995. The Ministerial Decisions relating to the General Agreement on Trade in Services were adopted by the Trade Negotiations Committee on 15 December 1993.

PART I SCOPE AND DEFINITION

Article I	Scope and Definition

PART II GENERAL OBLIGATIONS AND DISCIPLINES

Article II	Most-Favoured-Nation Treatment
Article III	Transparency
Article III *bis*	Disclosure of Confidential Information
Article IV	Increasing Participation of Developing Countries
Article V	Economic Integration
Article V *bis*	Labour Markets Integration Agreements
Article VI	Domestic Regulation
Article VII	Recognition
Article VIII	Monopolies and Exclusive Service Suppliers
Article IX	Business Practices
Article X	Emergency Safeguard Measures
Article XI	Payments and Transfers
Article XII	Restrictions to Safeguard the Balance of Payments
Article XIII	Government Procurement

*Source: World Trade Organization (1995). "Marrakesh Agreement Establishing the World Trade Organization. Annex 1B: General Agreement on Trade in Services" and "Ministerial Decisions and Declarations adopted by the Trade Negotiations Committee on 15 December 1993". *The Results of the Uruguay Round of Multilateral Trade Negotiations: The Legal Texts* (Geneva: World Trade Organization), pp. 325-364 and 456-463 [Note added by the editor].

Article XIV General Exceptions
Article XIV *bis* Security Exceptions
Article XV Subsidies

PART III SPECIFIC COMMITMENTS

Article XVI Market Access
Article XVII National Treatment
Article XVIII Additional Commitments

PART IV PROGRESSIVE LIBERALIZATION

Article XIX Negotiation of Specific Commitments
Article XX Schedules of Specific Commitments
Article XXI Modification of Schedules

PART V INSTITUTIONAL PROVISIONS

Article XXII Consultation
Article XXIII Dispute Settlement and Enforcement
Article XXIV Council for Trade in Services
Article XXV Technical Cooperation
Article XXVI Relationship with Other International Organizations

PART VI FINAL PROVISIONS

Article XXVII Denial of Benefits
Article XXVIII Definitions
Article XXIX Annexes

ANNEXES

Annex on Article II Exemptions
Annex on Movement of Natural Persons Supplying Services under the Agreement
Annex on Air Transport Services
Annex on Financial Services
Second Annex on Financial Services
Annex on Negotiations on Maritime Transport Services
Annex on Telecommunications
Annex on Negotiations on Basic Telecommunications

MINISTERIAL DECISIONS RELATING TO THE GENERAL AGREEMENT ON TRADE IN SERVICES

Decision on Institutional Arrangements for the General Agreement on Trade in Services

Decision on Certain Dispute Settlement Procedures for the General Agreement on Trade in Services
Decision on Trade in Services and the Environment
Decision on Negotiations on Movement of Natural Persons
Decision on Financial Services
Decision on Negotiations on Maritime Transport Services
Decision on Negotiations on Basic Telecommunications
Decision on Professional Services

UNDERSTANDING ON COMMITMENTS IN FINANCIAL SERVICES

* * *

GENERAL AGREEMENT ON TRADE IN SERVICES

Members,

Recognizing the growing importance of trade in services for the growth and development of the world economy;

Wishing to establish a multilateral framework of principles and rules for trade in services with a view to the expansion of such trade under conditions of transparency and progressive liberalization and as a means of promoting the economic growth of all trading partners and the development of developing countries;

Desiring the early achievement of progressively higher levels of liberalization of trade in services through successive rounds of multilateral negotiations aimed at promoting the interests of all participants on a mutually advantageous basis and at securing an overall balance of rights and obligations, while giving due respect to national policy objectives;

Recognizing the right of Members to regulate, and to introduce new regulations, on the supply of services within their territories in order to meet national policy objectives and, given asymmetries existing with respect to the degree of development of services regulations in different countries, the particular need of developing countries to exercise this right;

Desiring to facilitate the increasing participation of developing countries in trade in services and the expansion of their service exports including, *inter alia*, through the strengthening of their domestic services capacity and its efficiency and competitiveness;

Taking particular account of the serious difficulty of the least-developed countries in view of their special economic situation and their development, trade and financial needs;

Hereby *agree* as follows:

PART I
SCOPE AND DEFINITION

Article I
Scope and Definition

1. This Agreement applies to measures by Members affecting trade in services.

2. For the purposes of this Agreement, trade in services is defined as the supply of a service:

   (a) from the territory of one Member into the territory of any other Member;

   (b) in the territory of one Member to the service consumer of any other Member;

   (c) by a service supplier of one Member, through commercial presence in the territory of any other Member;

   (d) by a service supplier of one Member, through presence of natural persons of a Member in the territory of any other Member.

3. For the purposes of this Agreement:

   (a) "measures by Members" means measures taken by:

      (i) central, regional or local governments and authorities; and

      (ii) non-governmental bodies in the exercise of powers delegated by central, regional or local governments or authorities;

   In fulfilling its obligations and commitments under the Agreement, each Member shall take such reasonable measures as may be available to it to ensure their observance by regional and local governments and authorities and non-governmental bodies within its territory;

   (b) "services" includes any service in any sector except services supplied in the exercise of governmental authority;

   (c) "a service supplied in the exercise of governmental authority" means any service which is supplied neither on a commercial basis nor in competition with one or more service suppliers.

PART II
GENERAL OBLIGATIONS AND DISCIPLINES

Article II
Most-Favoured-Nation Treatment

1. With respect to any measure covered by this Agreement, each Member shall accord immediately and unconditionally to services and service suppliers of any other Member treatment no less favourable than that it accords to like services and service suppliers of any other country.

2. A Member may maintain a measure inconsistent with paragraph 1 provided that such a measure is listed in, and meets the conditions of, the Annex on Article II Exemptions.

3. The provisions of this Agreement shall not be so construed as to prevent any Member from conferring or according advantages to adjacent countries in order to facilitate exchanges limited to contiguous frontier zones of services that are both locally produced and consumed.

Article III
Transparency

1. Each Member shall publish promptly and, except in emergency situations, at the latest by the time of their entry into force, all relevant measures of general application which pertain to or affect the operation of this Agreement. International agreements pertaining to or affecting trade in services to which a Member is a signatory shall also be published.

2. Where publication as referred to in paragraph 1 is not practicable, such information shall be made otherwise publicly available.

3. Each Member shall promptly and at least annually inform the Council for Trade in Services of the introduction of any new, or any changes to existing, laws, regulations or administrative guidelines which significantly affect trade in services covered by its specific commitments under this Agreement.

4. Each Member shall respond promptly to all requests by any other Member for specific information on any of its measures of general application or international agreements within the meaning of paragraph 1. Each Member shall also establish one or more enquiry points to provide specific information to other Members, upon request, on all such matters as well as those subject to the notification requirement in paragraph 3. Such enquiry points shall be established within two years from the date of entry into force of the Agreement Establishing the WTO (referred to in this Agreement as the "WTO Agreement"). Appropriate flexibility with respect to the time-limit within which such enquiry points are to be established may be agreed upon for individual developing country Members. Enquiry points need not be depositories of laws and regulations.

5. Any Member may notify to the Council for Trade in Services any measure, taken by any other Member, which it considers affects the operation of this Agreement.

Article III bis
Disclosure of Confidential Information

Nothing in this Agreement shall require any Member to provide confidential information, the disclosure of which would impede law enforcement, or otherwise be contrary to the public interest, or which would prejudice legitimate commercial interests of particular enterprises, public or private.

Article IV
Increasing Participation of Developing Countries

1. The increasing participation of developing country Members in world trade shall be facilitated through negotiated specific commitments, by different Members pursuant to Parts III and IV of this Agreement, relating to:

(a) the strengthening of their domestic services capacity and its efficiency and competitiveness, *inter alia* through access to technology on a commercial basis;

(b) the improvement of their access to distribution channels and information networks; and

(c) the liberalization of market access in sectors and modes of supply of export interest to them.

2. Developed country Members, and to the extent possible other Members, shall establish contact points within two years from the date of entry into force of the WTO Agreement to facilitate the access of developing country Members' service suppliers to information, related to their respective markets, concerning:

(a) commercial and technical aspects of the supply of services;

(b) registration, recognition and obtaining of professional qualifications; and

(c) the availability of services technology.

3. Special priority shall be given to the least-developed country Members in the implementation of paragraphs 1 and 2. Particular account shall be taken of the serious difficulty of the least-developed countries in accepting negotiated specific commitments in view of their special economic situation and their development, trade and financial needs.

Article V
Economic Integration

1. This Agreement shall not prevent any of its Members from being a party to or entering into an agreement liberalizing trade in services between or among the parties to such an agreement, provided that such an agreement:

(a) has substantial sectoral coverage[1], and

(b) provides for the absence or elimination of substantially all discrimination, in the sense of Article XVII, between or among the parties, in the sectors covered under subparagraph (a), through:

(i) elimination of existing discriminatory measures, and/or

(ii) prohibition of new or more discriminatory measures,

either at the entry into force of that agreement or on the basis of a reasonable time-frame, except for measures permitted under Articles XI, XII, XIV and XIV bis.

2. In evaluating whether the conditions under paragraph 1(b) are met, consideration may be given to the relationship of the agreement to a wider process of economic integration or trade liberalization among the countries concerned.

3. (a) Where developing countries are parties to an agreement of the type referred to in paragraph 1, flexibility shall be provided for regarding the conditions set out in paragraph 1, particularly with reference to subparagraph (b) thereof, in accordance with the level of development of the countries concerned, both overall and in individual sectors and subsectors.

(b) Notwithstanding paragraph 6, in the case of an agreement of the type referred to in paragraph 1 involving only developing countries, more favourable treatment may be granted to juridical persons owned or controlled by natural persons of the parties to such an agreement.

4. Any agreement referred to in paragraph 1 shall be designed to facilitate trade between the parties to the agreement and shall not in respect of any Member outside the agreement raise the overall level of barriers to trade in services within the respective sectors or subsectors compared to the level applicable prior to such an agreement.

5. If, in the conclusion, enlargement or any significant modification of any agreement under paragraph 1, a Member intends to withdraw or modify a specific commitment inconsistently with

[1]This condition is understood in terms of number of sectors, volume of trade affected and modes of supply. In order to meet this condition, agreements should not provide for the *a priori* exclusion of any mode of supply.

the terms and conditions set out in its Schedule, it shall provide at least 90 days advance notice of such modification or withdrawal and the procedure set forth in paragraphs 2, 3 and 4 of Article XXI shall apply.

6. A service supplier of any other Member that is a juridical person constituted under the laws of a party to an agreement referred to in paragraph 1 shall be entitled to treatment granted under such agreement, provided that it engages in substantive business operations in the territory of the parties to such agreement.

7. (a) Members which are parties to any agreement referred to in paragraph 1 shall promptly notify any such agreement and any enlargement or any significant modification of that agreement to the Council for Trade in Services. They shall also make available to the Council such relevant information as may be requested by it. The Council may establish a working party to examine such an agreement or enlargement or modification of that agreement and to report to the Council on its consistency with this Article.

(b) Members which are parties to any agreement referred to in paragraph 1 which is implemented on the basis of a time-frame shall report periodically to the Council for Trade in Services on its implementation. The Council may establish a working party to examine such reports if it deems such a working party necessary.

(c) Based on the reports of the working parties referred to in subparagraphs (a) and (b), the Council may make recommendations to the parties as it deems appropriate.

8. A Member which is a party to any agreement referred to in paragraph 1 may not seek compensation for trade benefits that may accrue to any other Member from such agreement.

Article V bis
Labour Markets Integration Agreements

This Agreement shall not prevent any of its Members from being a party to an agreement establishing full integration[2] of the labour markets between or among the parties to such an agreement, provided that such an agreement:

(a) exempts citizens of parties to the agreement from requirements concerning residency and work permits;

(b) is notified to the Council for Trade in Services.

[2]Typically, such integration provides citizens of the parties concerned with a right of free entry to the employment markets of the parties and includes measures concerning conditions of pay, other conditions of employment and social benefits.

Article VI
Domestic Regulation

1. In sectors where specific commitments are undertaken, each Member shall ensure that all measures of general application affecting trade in services are administered in a reasonable, objective and impartial manner.

2. (a) Each Member shall maintain or institute as soon as practicable judicial, arbitral or administrative tribunals or procedures which provide, at the request of an affected service supplier, for the prompt review of, and where justified, appropriate remedies for, administrative decisions affecting trade in services. Where such procedures are not independent of the agency entrusted with the administrative decision concerned, the Member shall ensure that the procedures in fact provide for an objective and impartial review.

(b) The provisions of subparagraph (a) shall not be construed to require a Member to institute such tribunals or procedures where this would be inconsistent with its constitutional structure or the nature of its legal system.

3. Where authorization is required for the supply of a service on which a specific commitment has been made, the competent authorities of a Member shall, within a reasonable period of time after the submission of an application considered complete under domestic laws and regulations, inform the applicant of the decision concerning the application. At the request of the applicant, the competent authorities of the Member shall provide, without undue delay, information concerning the status of the application.

4. With a view to ensuring that measures relating to qualification requirements and procedures, technical standards and licensing requirements do not constitute unnecessary barriers to trade in services, the Council for Trade in Services shall, through appropriate bodies it may establish, develop any necessary disciplines. Such disciplines shall aim to ensure that such requirements are, *inter alia*:

(a) based on objective and transparent criteria, such as competence and the ability to supply the service;

(b) not more burdensome than necessary to ensure the quality of the service;

(c) in the case of licensing procedures, not in themselves a restriction on the supply of the service.

5. (a) In sectors in which a Member has undertaken specific commitments, pending the entry into force of disciplines developed in these sectors pursuant to paragraph 4, the Member shall not apply licensing and qualification requirements and technical standards that nullify or impair such specific commitments in a manner which:

(i) does not comply with the criteria outlined in subparagraphs 4(a), (b) or (c); and

(ii) could not reasonably have been expected of that Member at the time the specific commitments in those sectors were made.

(b) In determining whether a Member is in conformity with the obligation under paragraph 5(a), account shall be taken of international standards of relevant international organizations[3] applied by that Member.

6. In sectors where specific commitments regarding professional services are undertaken, each Member shall provide for adequate procedures to verify the competence of professionals of any other Member.

Article VII
Recognition

1. For the purposes of the fulfilment, in whole or in part, of its standards or criteria for the authorization, licensing or certification of services suppliers, and subject to the requirements of paragraph 3, a Member may recognize the education or experience obtained, requirements met, or licenses or certifications granted in a particular country. Such recognition, which may be achieved through harmonization or otherwise, may be based upon an agreement or arrangement with the country concerned or may be accorded autonomously.

2. A Member that is a party to an agreement or arrangement of the type referred to in paragraph 1, whether existing or future, shall afford adequate opportunity for other interested Members to negotiate their accession to such an agreement or arrangement or to negotiate comparable ones with it. Where a Member accords recognition autonomously, it shall afford adequate opportunity for any other Member to demonstrate that education, experience, licenses, or certifications obtained or requirements met in that other Member's territory should be recognized.

3. A Member shall not accord recognition in a manner which would constitute a means of discrimination between countries in the application of its standards or criteria for the authorization, licensing or certification of services suppliers, or a disguised restriction on trade in services.

4. Each Member shall:

(a) within 12 months from the date on which the WTO Agreement takes effect for it, inform the Council for Trade in Services of its existing recognition measures

[3]The term "relevant international organizations" refers to international bodies whose membership is open to the relevant bodies of at least all Members of the WTO.

and state whether such measures are based on agreements or arrangements of the type referred to in paragraph 1;

(b) promptly inform the Council for Trade in Services as far in advance as possible of the opening of negotiations on an agreement or arrangement of the type referred to in paragraph 1 in order to provide adequate opportunity to any other Member to indicate their interest in participating in the negotiations before they enter a substantive phase;

(c) promptly inform the Council for Trade in Services when it adopts new recognition measures or significantly modifies existing ones and state whether the measures are based on an agreement or arrangement of the type referred to in paragraph 1.

5. Wherever appropriate, recognition should be based on multilaterally agreed criteria. In appropriate cases, Members shall work in cooperation with relevant intergovernmental and non-governmental organizations towards the establishment and adoption of common international standards and criteria for recognition and common international standards for the practice of relevant services trades and professions.

Article VIII
Monopolies and Exclusive Service Suppliers

1. Each Member shall ensure that any monopoly supplier of a service in its territory does not, in the supply of the monopoly service in the relevant market, act in a manner inconsistent with that Member's obligations under Article II and specific commitments.

2. Where a Member's monopoly supplier competes, either directly or through an affiliated company, in the supply of a service outside the scope of its monopoly rights and which is subject to that Member's specific commitments, the Member shall ensure that such a supplier does not abuse its monopoly position to act in its territory in a manner inconsistent with such commitments.

3. The Council for Trade in Services may, at the request of a Member which has a reason to believe that a monopoly supplier of a service of any other Member is acting in a manner inconsistent with paragraph 1 or 2, request the Member establishing, maintaining or authorizing such supplier to provide specific information concerning the relevant operations.

4. If, after the date of entry into force of the WTO Agreement, a Member grants monopoly rights regarding the supply of a service covered by its specific commitments, that Member shall notify the Council for Trade in Services no later than three months before the intended implementation of the grant of monopoly rights and the provisions of paragraphs 2, 3 and 4 of Article XXI shall apply.

5. The provisions of this Article shall also apply to cases of exclusive service suppliers, where a Member, formally or in effect, (*a*) authorizes or establishes a small number of service suppliers and (*b*) substantially prevents competition among those suppliers in its territory.

Article IX
Business Practices

1. Members recognize that certain business practices of service suppliers, other than those falling under Article VIII, may restrain competition and thereby restrict trade in services.

2. Each Member shall, at the request of any other Member, enter into consultations with a view to eliminating practices referred to in paragraph 1. The Member addressed shall accord full and sympathetic consideration to such a request and shall cooperate through the supply of publicly available non-confidential information of relevance to the matter in question. The Member addressed shall also provide other information available to the requesting Member, subject to its domestic law and to the conclusion of satisfactory agreement concerning the safeguarding of its confidentiality by the requesting Member.

Article X
Emergency Safeguard Measures

1. There shall be multilateral negotiations on the question of emergency safeguard measures based on the principle of non-discrimination. The results of such negotiations shall enter into effect on a date not later than three years from the date of entry into force of the WTO Agreement.

2. In the period before the entry into effect of the results of the negotiations referred to in paragraph 1, any Member may, notwithstanding the provisions of paragraph 1 of Article XXI, notify the Council on Trade in Services of its intention to modify or withdraw a specific commitment after a period of one year from the date on which the commitment enters into force; provided that the Member shows cause to the Council that the modification or withdrawal cannot await the lapse of the three-year period provided for in paragraph 1 of Article XXI.

3. The provisions of paragraph 2 shall cease to apply three years after the date of entry into force of the WTO Agreement.

Article XI
Payments and Transfers

1. Except under the circumstances envisaged in Article XII, a Member shall not apply restrictions on international transfers and payments for current transactions relating to its specific commitments.

2. Nothing in this Agreement shall affect the rights and obligations of the members of the International Monetary Fund under the Articles of Agreement of the Fund, including the use of

exchange actions which are in conformity with the Articles of Agreement, provided that a Member shall not impose restrictions on any capital transactions inconsistently with its specific commitments regarding such transactions, except under Article XII or at the request of the Fund.

Article XII
Restrictions to Safeguard the Balance of Payments

1. In the event of serious balance-of-payments and external financial difficulties or threat thereof, a Member may adopt or maintain restrictions on trade in services on which it has undertaken specific commitments, including on payments or transfers for transactions related to such commitments. It is recognized that particular pressures on the balance of payments of a Member in the process of economic development or economic transition may necessitate the use of restrictions to ensure, *inter alia,* the maintenance of a level of financial reserves adequate for the implementation of its programme of economic development or economic transition.

2. The restrictions referred to in paragraph 1:

(a) shall not discriminate among Members;

(b) shall be consistent with the Articles of Agreement of the International Monetary Fund;

(c) shall avoid unnecessary damage to the commercial, economic and financial interests of any other Member;

(d) shall not exceed those necessary to deal with the circumstances described in paragraph 1;

(e) shall be temporary and be phased out progressively as the situation specified in paragraph 1 improves.

3. In determining the incidence of such restrictions, Members may give priority to the supply of services which are more essential to their economic or development programmes. However, such restrictions shall not be adopted or maintained for the purpose of protecting a particular service sector.

4. Any restrictions adopted or maintained under paragraph 1, or any changes therein, shall be promptly notified to the General Council.

5. (a) Members applying the provisions of this Article shall consult promptly with the Committee on Balance-of-Payments Restrictions on restrictions adopted under this Article.

(b) The Ministerial Conference shall establish procedures[4] for periodic consultations with the objective of enabling such recommendations to be made to the Member concerned as it may deem appropriate.

(c) Such consultations shall assess the balance-of-payment situation of the Member concerned and the restrictions adopted or maintained under this Article, taking into account, *inter alia,* such factors as:

(i) the nature and extent of the balance-of-payments and the external financial difficulties;

(ii) the external economic and trading environment of the consulting Member;

(iii) alternative corrective measures which may be available.

(d) The consultations shall address the compliance of any restrictions with paragraph 2, in particular the progressive phase out of restrictions in accordance with paragraph 2(e).

(e) In such consultations, all findings of statistical and other facts presented by the International Monetary Fund relating to foreign exchange, monetary reserves and balance of payments, shall be accepted and conclusions shall be based on the assessment by the Fund of the balance-of-payments and the external financial situation of the consulting Member.

6. If a Member which is not a member of the International Monetary Fund wishes to apply the provisions of this Article, the Ministerial Conference shall establish a review procedure and any other procedures necessary.

Article XIII
Government Procurement

1. Articles II, XVI and XVII shall not apply to laws, regulations or requirements governing the procurement by governmental agencies of services purchased for governmental purposes and not with a view to commercial resale or with a view to use in the supply of services for commercial sale.

2. There shall be multilateral negotiations on government procurement in services under this Agreement within two years from the date of entry into force of the WTO Agreement.

[4]It is understood that the procedures under paragraph 5 shall be the same as the GATT 1994 procedures.

Article XIV
General Exceptions

Subject to the requirement that such measures are not applied in a manner which would constitute a means of arbitrary or unjustifiable discrimination between countries where like conditions prevail, or a disguised restriction on trade in services, nothing in this Agreement shall be construed to prevent the adoption or enforcement by any Member of measures:

(a) necessary to protect public morals or to maintain public order;[5]

(b) necessary to protect human, animal or plant life or health;

(c) necessary to secure compliance with laws or regulations which are not inconsistent with the provisions of this Agreement including those relating to:

(i) the prevention of deceptive and fraudulent practices or to deal with the effects of a default on services contracts;

(ii) the protection of the privacy of individuals in relation to the processing and dissemination of personal data and the protection of confidentiality of individual records and accounts;

(iii) safety;

(d) inconsistent with Article XVII, provided that the difference in treatment is aimed at ensuring the equitable or effective[6] imposition or collection of direct taxes in

[5]The public order exception may be invoked only where a genuine and sufficiently serious threat is posed to one of the fundamental interests of society.

[6]Measures that are aimed at ensuring the equitable or effective imposition or collection of direct taxes include measures taken by a Member under its taxation system which:

(i) apply to non-resident service suppliers in recognition of the fact that the tax obligation of non-residents is determined with respect to taxable items sourced or located in the Member's territory; or

(ii) apply to non-residents in order to ensure the imposition or collection of taxes in the Member's territory; or

(iii) apply to non-residents or residents in order to prevent the avoidance or evasion of taxes, including compliance measures; or

(iv) apply to consumers of services supplied in or from the territory of another Member in order to ensure the imposition or collection of taxes on such consumers derived from sources in the Member's territory; or

respect of services or service suppliers of other Members;

(e) inconsistent with Article II, provided that the difference in treatment is the result of an agreement on the avoidance of double taxation or provisions on the avoidance of double taxation in any other international agreement or arrangement by which the Member is bound.

Article XIV bis
Security Exceptions

1. Nothing in this Agreement shall be construed:

(a) to require any Member to furnish any information, the disclosure of which it considers contrary to its essential security interests; or

(b) to prevent any Member from taking any action which it considers necessary for the protection of its essential security interests:

(i) relating to the supply of services as carried out directly or indirectly for the purpose of provisioning a military establishment;

(ii) relating to fissionable and fusionable materials or the materials from which they are derived;

(iii) taken in time of war or other emergency in international relations; or

(c) to prevent any Member from taking any action in pursuance of its obligations under the United Nations Charter for the maintenance of international peace and security.

2. The Council for Trade in Services shall be informed to the fullest extent possible of measures taken under paragraphs 1(b) and (c) and of their termination.

(v) distinguish service suppliers subject to tax on worldwide taxable items from other service suppliers, in recognition of the difference in the nature of the tax base between them; or

(vi) determine, allocate or apportion income, profit, gain, loss, deduction or credit of resident persons or branches, or between related persons or branches of the same person, in order to safeguard the Member's tax base.

Tax terms or concepts in paragraph (d) of Article XIV and in this footnote are determined according to tax definitions and concepts, or equivalent or similar definitions and concepts, under the domestic law of the Member taking the measure.

Article XV
Subsidies

1. Members recognize that, in certain circumstances, subsidies may have distortive effects on trade in services. Members shall enter into negotiations with a view to developing the necessary multilateral disciplines to avoid such trade-distortive effects.[7] The negotiations shall also address the appropriateness of countervailing procedures. Such negotiations shall recognize the role of subsidies in relation to the development programmes of developing countries and take into account the needs of Members, particularly developing country Members, for flexibility in this area. For the purpose of such negotiations, Members shall exchange information concerning all subsidies related to trade in services that they provide to their domestic service suppliers.

2. Any Member which considers that it is adversely affected by a subsidy of another Member may request consultations with that Member on such matters. Such requests shall be accorded sympathetic consideration.

PART III
SPECIFIC COMMITMENTS

Article XVI
Market Access

1. With respect to market access through the modes of supply identified in Article I, each Member shall accord services and service suppliers of any other Member treatment no less favourable than that provided for under the terms, limitations and conditions agreed and specified in its Schedule.[8]

2. In sectors where market-access commitments are undertaken, the measures which a Member shall not maintain or adopt either on the basis of a regional subdivision or on the basis of its entire territory, unless otherwise specified in its Schedule, are defined as:

(a) limitations on the number of service suppliers whether in the form of numerical quotas, monopolies, exclusive service suppliers or the requirements of an economic needs test;

(b) limitations on the total value of service transactions or assets in the form of

[7]A future work programme shall determine how, and in what time-frame, negotiations on such multilateral disciplines will be conducted.

[8]If a Member undertakes a market-access commitment in relation to the supply of a service through the mode of supply referred to in subparagraph 2(a) of Article I and if the cross-border movement of capital is an essential part of the service itself, that Member is thereby committed to allow such movement of capital. If a Member undertakes a market-access commitment in relation to the supply of a service through the mode of supply referred to in subparagraph 2(c) of Article I, it is thereby committed to allow related transfers of capital into its territory.

numerical quotas or the requirement of an economic needs test;

(c) limitations on the total number of service operations or on the total quantity of service output expressed in terms of designated numerical units in the form of quotas or the requirement of an economic needs test;[9]

(d) limitations on the total number of natural persons that may be employed in a particular service sector or that a service supplier may employ and who are necessary for, and directly related to, the supply of a specific service in the form of numerical quotas or the requirement of an economic needs test;

(e) measures which restrict or require specific types of legal entity or joint venture through which a service supplier may supply a service; and

(f) limitations on the participation of foreign capital in terms of maximum percentage limit on foreign share holding or the total value of individual or aggregate foreign investment.

Article XVII
National Treatment

1. In the sectors inscribed in its Schedule, and subject to any conditions and qualifications set out therein, each Member shall accord to services and service suppliers of any other Member, in respect of all measures affecting the supply of services, treatment no less favourable than that it accords to its own like services and service suppliers.[10]

2. A Member may meet the requirement of paragraph 1 by according to services and service suppliers of any other Member, either formally identical treatment or formally different treatment to that it accords to its own like services and service suppliers.

3. Formally identical or formally different treatment shall be considered to be less favourable if it modifies the conditions of competition in favour of services or service suppliers of the Member compared to like services or service suppliers of any other Member.

Article XVIII
Additional Commitments

Members may negotiate commitments with respect to measures affecting trade in services not subject to scheduling under Articles XVI or XVII, including those regarding qualifications,

---

[9]Subparagraph 2(c) does not cover measures of a Member which limit inputs for the supply of services.

[10]Specific commitments assumed under this Article shall not be construed to require any Member to compensate for any inherent competitive disadvantages which result from the foreign character of the relevant services or service suppliers.

standards or licensing matters. Such commitments shall be inscribed in a Member's Schedule.

PART IV
PROGRESSIVE LIBERALIZATION

Article XIX
Negotiation of Specific Commitments

1. In pursuance of the objectives of this Agreement, Members shall enter into successive rounds of negotiations, beginning not later than five years from the date of entry into force of the WTO Agreement and periodically thereafter, with a view to achieving a progressively higher level of liberalization. Such negotiations shall be directed to the reduction or elimination of the adverse effects on trade in services of measures as a means of providing effective market access. This process shall take place with a view to promoting the interests of all participants on a mutually advantageous basis and to securing an overall balance of rights and obligations.

2. The process of liberalization shall take place with due respect for national policy objectives and the level of development of individual Members, both overall and in individual sectors. There shall be appropriate flexibility for individual developing country Members for opening fewer sectors, liberalizing fewer types of transactions, progressively extending market access in line with their development situation and, when making access to their markets available to foreign service suppliers, attaching to such access conditions aimed at achieving the objectives referred to in Article IV.

3. For each round, negotiating guidelines and procedures shall be established. For the purposes of establishing such guidelines, the Council for Trade in Services shall carry out an assessment of trade in services in overall terms and on a sectoral basis with reference to the objectives of this Agreement, including those set out in paragraph 1 of Article IV. Negotiating guidelines shall establish modalities for the treatment of liberalization undertaken autonomously by Members since previous negotiations, as well as for the special treatment for least-developed country Members under the provisions of paragraph 3 of Article IV.

4. The process of progressive liberalization shall be advanced in each such round through bilateral, plurilateral or multilateral negotiations directed towards increasing the general level of specific commitments undertaken by Members under this Agreement.

Article XX
Schedules of Specific Commitments

1. Each Member shall set out in a schedule the specific commitments it undertakes under Part III of this Agreement. With respect to sectors where such commitments are undertaken, each Schedule shall specify:

(a) terms, limitations and conditions on market access;

(b) conditions and qualifications on national treatment;

(c) undertakings relating to additional commitments;

(d) where appropriate the time-frame for implementation of such commitments; and

(e) the date of entry into force of such commitments.

2. Measures inconsistent with both Articles XVI and XVII shall be inscribed in the column relating to Article XVI. In this case the inscription will be considered to provide a condition or qualification to Article XVII as well.

3. Schedules of specific commitments shall be annexed to this Agreement and shall form an integral part thereof.

Article XXI
Modification of Schedules

1. (a) A Member (referred to in this Article as the "modifying Member") may modify or withdraw any commitment in its Schedule, at any time after three years have elapsed from the date on which that commitment entered into force, in accordance with the provisions of this Article.

(b) A modifying Member shall notify its intent to modify or withdraw a commitment pursuant to this Article to the Council for Trade in Services no later than three months before the intended date of implementation of the modification or withdrawal.

2. (a) At the request of any Member the benefits of which under this Agreement may be affected (referred to in this Article as an "affected Member") by a proposed modification or withdrawal notified under subparagraph 1(b), the modifying Member shall enter into negotiations with a view to reaching agreement on any necessary compensatory adjustment. In such negotiations and agreement, the Members concerned shall endeavour to maintain a general level of mutually advantageous commitments not less favourable to trade than that provided for in Schedules of specific commitments prior to such negotiations.

(b) Compensatory adjustments shall be made on a most-favoured-nation basis.

3. (a) If agreement is not reached between the modifying Member and any affected Member before the end of the period provided for negotiations, such affected Member may refer the matter to arbitration. Any affected Member that wishes to enforce a right that it may have to compensation must participate in the arbitration.

(b) If no affected Member has requested arbitration, the modifying Member shall be free to implement the proposed modification or withdrawal.

4. (a) The modifying Member may not modify or withdraw its commitment until it has made compensatory adjustments in conformity with the findings of the arbitration.

(b) If the modifying Member implements its proposed modification or withdrawal and does not comply with the findings of the arbitration, any affected Member that participated in the arbitration may modify or withdraw substantially equivalent benefits in conformity with those findings. Notwithstanding Article II, such a modification or withdrawal may be implemented solely with respect to the modifying Member.

5. The Council for Trade in Services shall establish procedures for rectification or modification of Schedules. Any Member which has modified or withdrawn scheduled commitments under this Article shall modify its Schedule according to such procedures.

PART V
INSTITUTIONAL PROVISIONS

Article XXII
Consultation

1. Each Member shall accord sympathetic consideration to, and shall afford adequate opportunity for, consultation regarding such representations as may be made by any other Member with respect to any matter affecting the operation of this Agreement. The Dispute Settlement Understanding (DSU) shall apply to such consultations.

2. The Council for Trade in Services or the Dispute Settlement Body (DSB) may, at the request of a Member, consult with any Member or Members in respect of any matter for which it has not been possible to find a satisfactory solution through consultation under paragraph 1.

3. A Member may not invoke Article XVII, either under this Article or Article XXIII, with respect to a measure of another Member that falls within the scope of an international agreement between them relating to the avoidance of double taxation. In case of disagreement between Members as to whether a measure falls within the scope of such an agreement between them, it shall be open to either Member to bring this matter before the Council for Trade in Services.[11] The Council shall refer the matter to arbitration. The decision of the arbitrator shall be final and binding on the Members.

Article XXIII
Dispute Settlement and Enforcement

1. If any Member should consider that any other Member fails to carry out its obligations

[11]With respect to agreements on the avoidance of double taxation which exist on the date of entry into force of the WTO Agreement, such a matter may be brought before the Council for Trade in Services only with the consent of both parties to such an agreement.

or specific commitments under this Agreement, it may with a view to reaching a mutually satisfactory resolution of the matter have recourse to the DSU.

2. If the DSB considers that the circumstances are serious enough to justify such action, it may authorize a Member or Members to suspend the application to any other Member or Members of obligations and specific commitments in accordance with Article 22 of the DSU.

3. If any Member considers that any benefit it could reasonably have expected to accrue to it under a specific commitment of another Member under Part III of this Agreement is being nullified or impaired as a result of the application of any measure which does not conflict with the provisions of this Agreement, it may have recourse to the DSU. If the measure is determined by the DSB to have nullified or impaired such a benefit, the Member affected shall be entitled to a mutually satisfactory adjustment on the basis of paragraph 2 of Article XXI, which may include the modification or withdrawal of the measure. In the event an agreement cannot be reached between the Members concerned, Article 22 of the DSU shall apply.

Article XXIV
Council for Trade in Services

1. The Council for Trade in Services shall carry out such functions as may be assigned to it to facilitate the operation of this Agreement and further its objectives. The Council may establish such subsidiary bodies as it considers appropriate for the effective discharge of its functions.

2. The Council and, unless the Council decides otherwise, its subsidiary bodies shall be open to participation by representatives of all Members.

3. The Chairman of the Council shall be elected by the Members.

Article XXV
Technical Cooperation

1. Service suppliers of Members which are in need of such assistance shall have access to the services of contact points referred to in paragraph 2 of Article IV.

2. Technical assistance to developing countries shall be provided at the multilateral level by the Secretariat and shall be decided upon by the Council for Trade in Services.

Article XXVI
Relationship with Other International Organizations

The General Council shall make appropriate arrangements for consultation and cooperation with the United Nations and its specialized agencies as well as with other intergovernmental organizations concerned with services.

PART VI
FINAL PROVISIONS

Article XXVII
Denial of Benefits

A Member may deny the benefits of this Agreement:

(a) to the supply of a service, if it establishes that the service is supplied from or in the territory of a non-Member or of a Member to which the denying Member does not apply the WTO Agreement;

(b) in the case of the supply of a maritime transport service, if it establishes that the service is supplied:

(i) by a vessel registered under the laws of a non-Member or of a Member to which the denying Member does not apply the WTO Agreement, and

(ii) by a person which operates and/or uses the vessel in whole or in part but which is of a non-Member or of a Member to which the denying Member does not apply the WTO Agreement;

(c) to a service supplier that is a juridical person, if it establishes that it is not a service supplier of another Member, or that it is a service supplier of a Member to which the denying Member does not apply the WTO Agreement.

Article XXVIII
Definitions

For the purpose of this Agreement:

(a) "measure" means any measure by a Member, whether in the form of a law, regulation, rule, procedure, decision, administrative action, or any other form;

(b) "supply of a service" includes the production, distribution, marketing, sale and delivery of a service;

(c) "measures by Members affecting trade in services" include measures in respect of

(i) the purchase, payment or use of a service;

(ii) the access to and use of, in connection with the supply of a service, services which are required by those Members to be offered to the public generally;

(iii) the presence, including commercial presence, of persons of a Member for the supply of a service in the territory of another Member;

(d) "commercial presence" means any type of business or professional establishment, including through

(i) the constitution, acquisition or maintenance of a juridical person, or

(ii) the creation or maintenance of a branch or a representative office,

within the territory of a Member for the purpose of supplying a service;

(e) "sector" of a service means,

(i) with reference to a specific commitment, one or more, or all, subsectors of that service, as specified in a Member's Schedule,

(ii) otherwise, the whole of that service sector, including all of its subsectors;

(f) "service of another Member" means a service which is supplied,

(i) from or in the territory of that other Member, or in the case of maritime transport, by a vessel registered under the laws of that other Member, or by a person of that other Member which supplies the service through the operation of a vessel and/or its use in whole or in part; or

(ii) in the case of the supply of a service through commercial presence or through the presence of natural persons, by a service supplier of that other Member;

(g) "service supplier" means any person that supplies a service;[12]

(h) "monopoly supplier of a service" means any person, public or private, which in the relevant market of the territory of a Member is authorized or established formally or in effect by that Member as the sole supplier of that service;

(i) "service consumer" means any person that receives or uses a service;

(j) "person" means either a natural person or a juridical person;

---

[12]Where the service is not supplied directly by a juridical person but through other forms of commercial presence such as a branch or a representative office, the service supplier (i.e. the juridical person) shall, nonetheless, through such presence be accorded the treatment provided for service suppliers under the Agreement. Such treatment shall be extended to the presence through which the service is supplied and need not be extended to any other parts of the supplier located outside the territory where the service is supplied.

(k) "natural person of another Member" means a natural person who resides in the territory of that other Member or any other Member, and who under the law of that other Member:

(i) is a national of that other Member; or

(ii) has the right of permanent residence in that other Member, in the case of a Member which:

1. does not have nationals; or

2. accords substantially the same treatment to its permanent residents as it does to its nationals in respect of measures affecting trade in services, as notified in its acceptance of or accession to the WTO Agreement, provided that no Member is obligated to accord to such permanent residents treatment more favourable than would be accorded by that other Member to such permanent residents. Such notification shall include the assurance to assume, with respect to those permanent residents, in accordance with its laws and regulations, the same responsibilities that other Member bears with respect to its nationals;

(l) "juridical person" means any legal entity duly constituted or otherwise organized under applicable law, whether for profit or otherwise, and whether privately-owned or governmentally-owned, including any corporation, trust, partnership, joint venture, sole proprietorship or association;

(m) "juridical person of another Member" means a juridical person which is either:

(i) constituted or otherwise organized under the law of that other Member, and is engaged in substantive business operations in the territory of that Member or any other Member; or

(ii) in the case of the supply of a service through commercial presence, owned or controlled by:

1. natural persons of that Member; or

2. juridical persons of that other Member identified under subparagraph (i);

(n) a juridical person is:

(i) "owned" by persons of a Member if more than 50 per cent of the equity interest in it is beneficially owned by persons of that Member;

(ii) "controlled" by persons of a Member if such persons have the power to name a majority of its directors or otherwise to legally direct its actions;

(iii) "affiliated" with another person when it controls, or is controlled by, that other person; or when it and the other person are both controlled by the same person; and

(o) "direct taxes" comprise all taxes on total income, on total capital or on elements of income or of capital, including taxes on gains from the alienation of property, taxes on estates, inheritances and gifts, and taxes on the total amounts of wages or salaries paid by enterprises, as well as taxes on capital appreciation.

Article XXIX
Annexes

The Annexes to this Agreement are an integral part of this Agreement.

* * *

ANNEXES

Annex on Article II Exemptions

Scope

1. This Annex specifies the conditions under which a Member, at the entry into force of this Agreement, is exempted from its obligations under paragraph 1 of Article II.

2. Any new exemptions applied for after the date of entry into force of the WTO Agreement shall be dealt with under paragraph 3 of Article IX of that Agreement.

Review

3. The Council for Trade in Services shall review all exemptions granted for a period of more than 5 years. The first such review shall take place no more than five years after the entry into force of the WTO Agreement.

4. The Council for Trade in Services in a review shall:

(a) examine whether the conditions which created the need for the exemption still prevail; and

(b) determine the date of any further review.

Termination

5. The exemption of a Member from its obligations under paragraph 1 of Article II of the Agreement with respect to a particular measure terminates on the date provided for in the exemption.

6. In principle, such exemptions should not exceed a period of 10 years. In any event, they shall be subject to negotiation in subsequent trade-liberalizing rounds.

7. A Member shall notify the Council for Trade in Services at the termination of the exemption period that the inconsistent measure has been brought into conformity with paragraph 1 of Article II of the Agreement.

Lists of Article II Exemptions

[The agreed lists of exemptions under paragraph 2 of Article II appear as part of this Annex in the treaty copy of the WTO Agreement.]

* * *

Annex on Movement of Natural Persons Supplying Services under the Agreement

1. This Annex applies to measures affecting natural persons who are service suppliers of a Member, and natural persons of a Member who are employed by a service supplier of a Member, in respect of the supply of a service.

2. The Agreement shall not apply to measures affecting natural persons seeking access to the employment market of a Member, nor shall it apply to measures regarding citizenship, residence or employment on a permanent basis.

3. In accordance with Parts III and IV of the Agreement, Members may negotiate specific commitments applying to the movement of all categories of natural persons supplying services under the Agreement. Natural persons covered by a specific commitment shall be allowed to supply the service in accordance with the terms of that commitment.

4. The Agreement shall not prevent a Member from applying measures to regulate the entry of natural persons into, or their temporary stay in, its territory, including those measures necessary to protect the integrity of, and to ensure the orderly movement of natural persons across, its borders, provided that such measures are not applied in such a manner as to nullify or impair the benefits accruing to any Member under the terms of a specific commitment.[13]

* * *

Annex on Air Transport Services

1. This Annex applies to measures affecting trade in air transport services, whether scheduled or non-scheduled, and ancillary services. It is confirmed that any specific commitment or obligation assumed under this Agreement shall not reduce or affect a Member's obligations under bilateral or multilateral agreements that are in effect on the date of entry into force of the WTO Agreement.

2. The Agreement, including its dispute settlement procedures, shall not apply to measures affecting:

(a) traffic rights, however granted; or

(b) services directly related to the exercise of traffic rights,

except as provided in paragraph 3 of this Annex.

3. The Agreement shall apply to measures affecting:

(a) aircraft repair and maintenance services;

(b) the selling and marketing of air transport services;

(c) computer reservation system (CRS) services.

4. The dispute settlement procedures of the Agreement may be invoked only where obligations or specific commitments have been assumed by the concerned Members and where

[13]The sole fact of requiring a visa for natural persons of certain Members and not for those of others shall not be regarded as nullifying or impairing benefits under a specific commitment.

dispute settlement procedures in bilateral and other multilateral agreements or arrangements have been exhausted.

5. The Council for Trade in Services shall review periodically, and at least every five years, developments in the air transport sector and the operation of this Annex with a view to considering the possible further application of the Agreement in this sector.

6. Definitions:

(a) "Aircraft repair and maintenance services" mean such activities when undertaken on an aircraft or a part thereof while it is withdrawn from service and do not include so-called line maintenance.

(b) "Selling and marketing of air transport services" mean opportunities for the air carrier concerned to sell and market freely its air transport services including all aspects of marketing such as market research, advertising and distribution. These activities do not include the pricing of air transport services nor the applicable conditions.

(c) "Computer reservation system (CRS) services" mean services provided by computerized systems that contain information about air carriers' schedules, availability, fares and fare rules, through which reservations can be made or tickets may be issued.

(d) "Traffic rights" mean the right for scheduled and non-scheduled services to operate and/or to carry passengers, cargo and mail for remuneration or hire from, to, within, or over the territory of a Member, including points to be served, routes to be operated, types of traffic to be carried, capacity to be provided, tariffs to be charged and their conditions, and criteria for designation of airlines, including such criteria as number, ownership, and control.

* * *

Annex on Financial Services

1. *Scope and Definition*

(a) This Annex applies to measures affecting the supply of financial services. Reference to the supply of a financial service in this Annex shall mean the supply of a service as defined in paragraph 2 of Article I of the Agreement.

(b) For the purposes of subparagraph 3(b) of Article I of the Agreement, "services supplied in the exercise of governmental authority" means the following:

(i) activities conducted by a central bank or monetary authority or by any other public entity in pursuit of monetary or exchange rate policies;

(ii) activities forming part of a statutory system of social security or public retirement plans; and

(iii) other activities conducted by a public entity for the account or with the guarantee or using the financial resources of the Government.

(c) For the purposes of subparagraph 3(b) of Article I of the Agreement, if a Member allows any of the activities referred to in subparagraphs (b)(ii) or (b)(iii) of this paragraph to be conducted by its financial service suppliers in competition with a public entity or a financial service supplier, "services" shall include such activities.

(d) Subparagraph 3(c) of Article I of the Agreement shall not apply to services covered by this Annex.

2. *Domestic Regulation*

(a) Notwithstanding any other provisions of the Agreement, a Member shall not be prevented from taking measures for prudential reasons, including for the protection of investors, depositors, policy holders or persons to whom a fiduciary duty is owed by a financial service supplier, or to ensure the integrity and stability of the financial system. Where such measures do not conform with the provisions of the Agreement, they shall not be used as a means of avoiding the Member's commitments or obligations under the Agreement.

(b) Nothing in the Agreement shall be construed to require a Member to disclose information relating to the affairs and accounts of individual customers or any confidential or proprietary information in the possession of public entities.

3. *Recognition*

(a) A Member may recognize prudential measures of any other country in determining how the Member's measures relating to financial services shall be applied. Such recognition, which may be achieved through harmonization or otherwise, may be based upon an agreement or arrangement with the country concerned or may be accorded autonomously.

(b) A Member that is a party to such an agreement or arrangement referred to in subparagraph (a), whether future or existing, shall afford adequate opportunity for other interested Members to negotiate their accession to such agreements or arrangements, or to negotiate comparable ones with it, under circumstances in which there would be equivalent regulation, oversight, implementation of such regulation, and, if appropriate, procedures concerning the sharing of information between the parties to the agreement or arrangement. Where a Member accords recognition autonomously, it shall afford adequate opportunity for any other Member to demonstrate that such circumstances exist.

(c) Where a Member is contemplating according recognition to prudential measures of any other country, paragraph 4(b) of Article VII shall not apply.

4. *Dispute Settlement*

Panels for disputes on prudential issues and other financial matters shall have the necessary expertise relevant to the specific financial service under dispute.

5. *Definitions*

For the purposes of this Annex:

(a) A financial service is any service of a financial nature offered by a financial service supplier of a Member. Financial services include all insurance and insurance-related services, and all banking and other financial services (excluding insurance). Financial services include the following activities:

Insurance and insurance-related services

(i) Direct insurance (including co-insurance):

(A) life
(B) non-life

(ii) Reinsurance and retrocession;

(iii) Insurance intermediation, such as brokerage and agency;

(iv) Services auxiliary to insurance, such as consultancy, actuarial, risk assessment and claim settlement services.

Banking and other financial services (excluding insurance)

(v) Acceptance of deposits and other repayable funds from the public;

(vi) Lending of all types, including consumer credit, mortgage credit, factoring and financing of commercial transaction;

(vii) Financial leasing;

(viii) All payment and money transmission services, including credit, charge and debit cards, travellers cheques and bankers drafts;

(ix) Guarantees and commitments;

(x) Trading for own account or for account of customers, whether on an exchange, in an over-the-counter market or otherwise, the following:

(A) money market instruments (including cheques, bills, certificates of deposits);
(B) foreign exchange;
(C) derivative products including, but not limited to, futures and options;
(D) exchange rate and interest rate instruments, including products such as swaps, forward rate agreements;
(E) transferable securities;
(F) other negotiable instruments and financial assets, including bullion.

(xi) Participation in issues of all kinds of securities, including underwriting and placement as agent (whether publicly or privately) and provision of services related to such issues;

(xii) Money broking;

(xiii) Asset management, such as cash or portfolio management, all forms of collective investment management, pension fund management, custodial, depository and trust services;

(xiv) Settlement and clearing services for financial assets, including securities, derivative products, and other negotiable instruments;

(xv) Provision and transfer of financial information, and financial data processing and related software by suppliers of other financial services;

(xvi) Advisory, intermediation and other auxiliary financial services on all the activities listed in subparagraphs (v) through (xv), including credit reference and analysis, investment and portfolio research and advice, advice on acquisitions and on corporate restructuring and strategy.

(b) A financial service supplier means any natural or juridical person of a Member wishing to supply or supplying financial services but the term "financial service supplier" does not include a public entity.

(c) "Public entity" means:

(i) a government, a central bank or a monetary authority, of a Member, or an entity owned or controlled by a Member, that is principally engaged in carrying out governmental functions or activities for governmental purposes, not including an entity principally engaged in supplying financial services on commercial terms; or

(ii) a private entity, performing functions normally performed by a central bank or monetary authority, when exercising those functions.

* * *

Second Annex on Financial Services

1. Notwithstanding Article II of the Agreement and paragraphs 1 and 2 of the Annex on Article II Exemptions, a Member may, during a period of 60 days beginning four months after the date of entry into force of the WTO Agreement, list in that Annex measures relating to financial services which are inconsistent with paragraph 1 of Article II of the Agreement.

2. Notwithstanding Article XXI of the Agreement, a Member may, during a period of 60 days beginning four months after the date of entry into force of the WTO Agreement, improve, modify or withdraw all or part of the specific commitments on financial services inscribed in its Schedule.

3. The Council for Trade in Services shall establish any procedures necessary for the application of paragraphs 1 and 2.

* * *

Annex on Negotiations on Maritime Transport Services

1. Article II and the Annex on Article II Exemptions, including the requirement to list in the Annex any measure inconsistent with most-favoured-nation treatment that a Member will maintain, shall enter into force for international shipping, auxiliary services and access to and use of port facilities only on:

(a) the implementation date to be determined under paragraph 4 of the Ministerial Decision on Negotiations on Maritime Transport Services; or,

(b) should the negotiations not succeed, the date of the final report of the Negotiating Group on Maritime Transport Services provided for in that Decision.

2. Paragraph 1 shall not apply to any specific commitment on maritime transport services which is inscribed in a Member's Schedule.

3. From the conclusion of the negotiations referred to in paragraph 1, and before the implementation date, a Member may improve, modify or withdraw all or part of its specific commitments in this sector without offering compensation, notwithstanding the provisions of Article XXI.

* * *

Annex on Telecommunications

1. *Objectives*

Recognizing the specificities of the telecommunications services sector and, in particular, its dual role as a distinct sector of economic activity and as the underlying transport means for other economic activities, the Members have agreed to the following Annex with the objective of elaborating upon the provisions of the Agreement with respect to measures affecting access to and use of public telecommunications transport networks and services. Accordingly, this Annex provides notes and supplementary provisions to the Agreement.

2. *Scope*

(a) This Annex shall apply to all measures of a Member that affect access to and use of public telecommunications transport networks and services.[14]

(b) This Annex shall not apply to measures affecting the cable or broadcast distribution of radio or television programming.

(c) Nothing in this Annex shall be construed:

(i) to require a Member to authorize a service supplier of any other Member to establish, construct, acquire, lease, operate, or supply telecommunications transport networks or services, other than as provided for in its Schedule; or

[14]This paragraph is understood to mean that each Member shall ensure that the obligations of this Annex are applied with respect to suppliers of public telecommunications transport networks and services by whatever measures are necessary.

(ii) to require a Member (or to require a Member to oblige service suppliers under its jurisdiction) to establish, construct, acquire, lease, operate or supply telecommunications transport networks or services not offered to the public generally.

3. *Definitions*

For the purposes of this Annex:

(a) "Telecommunications" means the transmission and reception of signals by any electromagnetic means.

(b) "Public telecommunications transport service" means any telecommunications transport service required, explicitly or in effect, by a Member to be offered to the public generally. Such services may include, *inter alia*, telegraph, telephone, telex, and data transmission typically involving the real-time transmission of customer-supplied information between two or more points without any end-to-end change in the form or content of the customer's information.

(c) "Public telecommunications transport network" means the public telecommunications infrastructure which permits telecommunications between and among defined network termination points.

(d) "Intra-corporate communications" means telecommunications through which a company communicates within the company or with or among its subsidiaries, branches and, subject to a Member's domestic laws and regulations, affiliates. For these purposes, "subsidiaries", "branches" and, where applicable, "affiliates" shall be as defined by each Member. "Intra-corporate communications" in this Annex excludes commercial or non-commercial services that are supplied to companies that are not related subsidiaries, branches or affiliates, or that are offered to customers or potential customers.

(e) Any reference to a paragraph or subparagraph of this Annex includes all subdivisions thereof.

4. *Transparency*

In the application of Article III of the Agreement, each Member shall ensure that relevant information on conditions affecting access to and use of public telecommunications transport networks and services is publicly available, including: tariffs and other terms and conditions of service; specifications of technical interfaces with such networks and services; information on bodies responsible for the preparation and adoption of standards affecting such access and use; conditions applying to attachment of terminal or other equipment; and notifications, registration or licensing requirements, if any.

5. *Access to and Use of Public Telecommunications Transport Networks and Services*

(a) Each Member shall ensure that any service supplier of any other Member is accorded access to and use of public telecommunications transport networks and services on reasonable and non-discriminatory terms and conditions, for the supply of a service included in its Schedule. This obligation shall be applied, *inter alia*, through paragraphs (b) through (f).[15]

(b) Each Member shall ensure that service suppliers of any other Member have access to and use of any public telecommunications transport network or service offered within or across the border of that Member, including private leased circuits, and to this end shall ensure, subject to paragraphs (e) and (f), that such suppliers are permitted:

(i) to purchase or lease and attach terminal or other equipment which interfaces with the network and which is necessary to supply a supplier's services;

(ii) to interconnect private leased or owned circuits with public telecommunications transport networks and services or with circuits leased or owned by another service supplier; and

(iii) to use operating protocols of the service supplier's choice in the supply of any service, other than as necessary to ensure the availability of telecommunications transport networks and services to the public generally.

(c) Each Member shall ensure that service suppliers of any other Member may use public telecommunications transport networks and services for the movement of information within and across borders, including for intra-corporate communications of such service suppliers, and for access to information contained in data bases or otherwise stored in machine-readable form in the territory of any Member. Any new or amended measures of a Member significantly affecting such use shall be notified and shall be subject to consultation, in accordance with relevant provisions of the Agreement.

(d) Notwithstanding the preceding paragraph, a Member may take such measures as are necessary to ensure the security and confidentiality of messages, subject to the requirement that such measures are not applied in a manner which would constitute a means of arbitrary or unjustifiable discrimination or a disguised restriction on trade in services.

(e) Each Member shall ensure that no condition is imposed on access to and use of public telecommunications transport networks and services other than as necessary:

[15]The term "non-discriminatory" is understood to refer to most-favoured-nation and national treatment as defined in the Agreement, as well as to reflect sector-specific usage of the term to mean "terms and conditions no less favourable than those accorded to any other user of like public telecommunications transport networks or services under like circumstances".

(i) to safeguard the public service responsibilities of suppliers of public telecommunications transport networks and services, in particular their ability to make their networks or services available to the public generally;

(ii) to protect the technical integrity of public telecommunications transport networks or services; or

(iii) to ensure that service suppliers of any other Member do not supply services unless permitted pursuant to commitments in the Member's Schedule.

(f) Provided that they satisfy the criteria set out in paragraph (e), conditions for access to and use of public telecommunications transport networks and services may include:

(i) restrictions on resale or shared use of such services;

(ii) a requirement to use specified technical interfaces, including interface protocols, for inter-connection with such networks and services;

(iii) requirements, where necessary, for the inter-operability of such services and to encourage the achievement of the goals set out in paragraph 7(a);

(iv) type approval of terminal or other equipment which interfaces with the network and technical requirements relating to the attachment of such equipment to such networks;

(v) restrictions on inter-connection of private leased or owned circuits with such networks or services or with circuits leased or owned by another service supplier; or

(vi) notification, registration and licensing.

(g) Notwithstanding the preceding paragraphs of this section, a developing country Member may, consistent with its level of development, place reasonable conditions on access to and use of public telecommunications transport networks and services necessary to strengthen its domestic telecommunications infrastructure and service capacity and to increase its participation in international trade in telecommunications services. Such conditions shall be specified in the Member's Schedule.

6. *Technical Cooperation*

(a) Members recognize that an efficient, advanced telecommunications infrastructure in countries, particularly developing countries, is essential to the expansion of their trade in services. To this end, Members endorse and encourage the participation, to the fullest extent practicable, of developed and developing countries and their suppliers of public telecommunications transport networks and services and other entities in the development programmes of international and regional organizations, including the International Telecommunication Union, the United Nations Development Programme, and the International Bank for Reconstruction and Development.

(b) Members shall encourage and support telecommunications cooperation among developing countries at the international, regional and sub-regional levels.

(c) In cooperation with relevant international organizations, Members shall make available, where practicable, to developing countries information with respect to telecommunications services and developments in telecommunications and information technology to assist in strengthening their domestic telecommunications services sector.

(d) Members shall give special consideration to opportunities for the least-developed countries to encourage foreign suppliers of telecommunications services to assist in the transfer of technology, training and other activities that support the development of their telecommunications infrastructure and expansion of their telecommunications services trade.

7. *Relation to International Organizations and Agreements*

(a) Members recognize the importance of international standards for global compatibility and inter-operability of telecommunication networks and services and undertake to promote such standards through the work of relevant international bodies, including the International Telecommunication Union and the International Organization for Standardization.

(b) Members recognize the role played by intergovernmental and non-governmental organizations and agreements in ensuring the efficient operation of domestic and global telecommunications services, in particular the International Telecommunication Union. Members shall make appropriate arrangements, where relevant, for consultation with such organizations on matters arising from the implementation of this Annex.

* * *

Annex on Negotiations on Basic Telecommunications

1. Article II and the Annex on Article II Exemptions, including the requirement to list in the Annex any measure inconsistent with most-favoured-nation treatment that a Member will maintain, shall enter into force for basic telecommunications only on:

(a) the implementation date to be determined under paragraph 5 of the Ministerial Decision on Negotiations on Basic Telecommunications; or,

(b) should the negotiations not succeed, the date of the final report of the Negotiating Group on Basic Telecommunications provided for in that Decision.

2. Paragraph 1 shall not apply to any specific commitment on basic telecommunications which is inscribed in a Member's Schedule.

* * *

MINISTERIAL DECISIONS RELATING TO THE GENERAL AGREEMENT ON TRADE IN SERVICES

Decision on Institutional Arrangements for the General Agreement on Trade in Services

Ministers,

Decide to recommend that the Council for Trade in Services at its first meeting adopt the decision on subsidiary bodies set out below.

The Council for Trade in Services,

Acting pursuant to Article XXIV with a view to facilitating the operation and furthering the objectives of the General Agreement on Trade in Services,

Decides as follows:

1. Any subsidiary bodies that the Council may establish shall report to the Council annually or more often as necessary. Each such body shall establish its own rules of procedure, and may set up its own subsidiary bodies as appropriate.

2. Any sectoral committee shall carry out responsibilities as assigned to it by the Council, and shall afford Members the opportunity to consult on any matters relating to trade in services in the sector concerned and the operation of the sectoral annex to which it may pertain. Such responsibilities shall include:

(a) to keep under continuous review and surveillance the application of the Agreement with respect to the sector concerned;

(b) to formulate proposals or recommendations for consideration by the Council in connection with any matter relating to trade in the sector concerned;

(c) if there is an annex pertaining to the sector, to consider proposals for amendment of that sectoral annex, and to make appropriate recommendations to the Council;

(d) to provide a forum for technical discussions, to conduct studies on measures of Members and to conduct examinations of any other technical matters affecting trade in services in the sector concerned;

(e) to provide technical assistance to developing country Members and developing countries negotiating accession to the Agreement Establishing the World Trade Organization in respect of the application of obligations or other matters affecting trade in services in the sector concerned; and

(f) to cooperate with any other subsidiary bodies established under the General Agreement on Trade in Services or any international organizations active in any sector concerned.

3. There is hereby established a Committee on Trade in Financial Services which will have the responsibilities listed in paragraph 2.

* * *

Decision on Certain Dispute Settlement Procedures for the General Agreement on Trade in Services

Ministers,

Decide to recommend that the Council for Trade in Services at its first meeting adopt the decision set out below.

The Council for Trade in Services,

Taking into account the specific nature of the obligations and specific commitments of the Agreement, and of trade in services, with respect to dispute settlement under Articles XXII and XXIII,

Decides as follows:

1. A roster of panelists shall be established to assist in the selection of panelists.

2. To this end, Members may suggest names of individuals possessing the qualifications referred to in paragraph 3 for inclusion on the roster, and shall provide a curriculum vitae of their qualifications including, if applicable, indication of sector-specific expertise.

3. Panels shall be composed of well-qualified governmental and/or non-governmental individuals who have experience in issues related to the General Agreement on Trade in Services and/or trade in services, including associated regulatory matters. Panelists shall serve in their individual capacities and not as representatives of any government or organisation.

4. Panels for disputes regarding sectoral matters shall have the necessary expertise relevant to the specific services sectors which the dispute concerns.

5. The Secretariat shall maintain the roster and shall develop procedures for its administration in consultation with the Chairman of the Council.

* * *

Decision on Trade in Services and the Environment

Ministers,

Decide to recommend that the Council for Trade in Services at its first meeting adopt the decision set out below.

The Council for Trade in Services,

Acknowledging that measures necessary to protect the environment may conflict with the provisions of the Agreement; and

Noting that since measures necessary to protect the environment typically have as their objective the protection of human, animal or plant life or health, it is not clear that there is a need to provide for more than is contained in paragraph (b) of Article XIV;

Decides as follows:

1. In order to determine whether any modification of Article XIV of the Agreement is required to take account of such measures, to request the Committee on Trade and Environment to examine and report, with recommendations if any, on the relationship between services trade and the environment including the issue of sustainable development. The Committee shall also examine the relevance of inter-governmental agreements on the environment and their relationship to the Agreement.

2. The Committee shall report the results of its work to the first biennial meeting of the Ministerial Conference after the entry into force of the Agreement Establishing the World Trade Organization.

* * *

Decision on Negotiations on Movement of Natural Persons

Ministers,

Noting the commitments resulting from the Uruguay Round negotiations on the movement of natural persons for the purpose of supplying services;

Mindful of the objectives of the General Agreement on Trade in Services, including the increasing participation of developing countries in trade in services and the expansion of their service exports;

Recognizing the importance of achieving higher levels of commitments on the movement of natural persons, in order to provide for a balance of benefits under the General Agreement on Trade in Services;

Decide as follows:

1. Negotiations on further liberalization of movement of natural persons for the purpose of supplying services shall continue beyond the conclusion of the Uruguay Round, with a view to allowing the achievement of higher levels of commitments by participants under the General Agreement on Trade in Services.

2. A Negotiating Group on Movement of Natural Persons is established to carry out the negotiations. The group shall establish its own procedures and shall report periodically to the Council on Trade in Services.

3. The negotiating group shall hold its first negotiating session no later than 16 May 1994. It shall conclude these negotiations and produce a final report no later than six months after the entry into force of the Agreement Establishing the World Trade Organization.

4. Commitments resulting from these negotiations shall be inscribed in Members' Schedules of specific commitments.

* * *

Decision on Financial Services

Ministers,

Noting that commitments scheduled by participants on financial services at the conclusion of the Uruguay Round shall enter into force on an MFN basis at the same time as the Agreement Establishing the World Trade Organization (hereinafter referred to as the "WTO Agreement"),

Decide as follows:

1. At the conclusion of a period ending no later than six months after the date of entry into force of the WTO Agreement, Members shall be free to improve, modify or withdraw all or part of their commitments in this sector without offering compensation, notwithstanding the provisions of Article XXI of the General Agreement on Trade in Services. At the same time Members shall finalize their positions relating to MFN exemptions in this sector, notwithstanding the provisions of the Annex on Article II Exemptions. From the date of entry into force of the WTO Agreement and until the end of the period referred to above, exemptions listed in the Annex on Article II Exemptions which are conditional upon the level of commitments undertaken by other participants or upon exemptions by other participants will not be applied.

2. The Committee on Trade in Financial Services shall monitor the progress of any negotiations undertaken under the terms of this Decision and shall report thereon to the Council for Trade in Services no later than four months after the date of entry into force of the WTO Agreement.

* * *

Decision on Negotiations on Maritime Transport Services

Ministers,

Noting that commitments scheduled by participants on maritime transport services at the conclusion of the Uruguay Round shall enter into force on an MFN basis at the same time as the Agreement Establishing the World Trade Organization (hereinafter referred to as the "WTO Agreement"),

Decide as follows:

1. Negotiations shall be entered into on a voluntary basis in the sector of maritime transport services within the framework of the General Agreement on Trade in Services. The negotiations shall be comprehensive in scope, aiming at commitments in international shipping, auxiliary services and access to and use of port facilities, leading to the elimination of restrictions within a fixed time scale.

2. A Negotiating Group on Maritime Transport Services (hereinafter referred to as the "NGMTS") is established to carry out this mandate. The NGMTS shall report periodically on the progress of these negotiations.

3. The negotiations in the NGMTS shall be open to all governments and the European Communities which announce their intention to participate. To date, the following have announced their intention to take part in the negotiations:

> Argentina, Canada, European Communities and their member States, Finland, Hong Kong, Iceland, Indonesia, Korea, Malaysia, Mexico, New Zealand, Norway, Philippines, Poland, Romania, Singapore, Sweden, Switzerland, Thailand, Turkey, United States.

Further notifications of intention to participate shall be addressed to the depositary of the WTO Agreement.

4. The NGMTS shall hold its first negotiating session no later than 16 May 1994. It shall conclude these negotiations and make a final report no later than June 1996. The final report of the NGMTS shall include a date for the implementation of results of these negotiations.

5. Until the conclusion of the negotiations Article II and paragraphs 1 and 2 of the Annex on Article II Exemptions are suspended in their application to this sector, and it is not necessary to list MFN exemptions. At the conclusion of the negotiations, Members shall be free to improve, modify or withdraw any commitments made in this sector during the Uruguay Round without offering compensation, notwithstanding the provisions of Article XXI of the Agreement. At the same time Members shall finalize their positions relating to MFN exemptions in this sector, notwithstanding the provisions of the Annex on Article II Exemptions. Should negotiations not succeed, the Council for Trade in Services shall decide whether to continue the negotiations in accordance with this mandate.

6. Any commitments resulting from the negotiations, including the date of their entry into force, shall be inscribed in the Schedules annexed to the General Agreement on Trade in Services and be subject to all the provisions of the Agreement.

7. Commencing immediately and continuing until the implementation date to be determined under paragraph 4, it is understood that participants shall not apply any measure affecting trade in maritime transport services except in response to measures applied by other countries and with a view to maintaining or improving the freedom of provision of maritime transport services, nor in such a manner as would improve their negotiating position and leverage.

8. The implementation of paragraph 7 shall be subject to surveillance in the NGMTS. Any participant may bring to the attention of the NGMTS any action or omission which it believes to be relevant to the fulfilment of paragraph 7. Such notifications shall be deemed to have been submitted to the NGMTS upon their receipt by the Secretariat.

* * *

Decision on Negotiations on Basic Telecommunications

Ministers,

Decide as follows:

1. Negotiations shall be entered into on a voluntary basis with a view to the progressive liberalization of trade in telecommunications transport networks and services (hereinafter referred to as "basic telecommunications") within the framework of the General Agreement on Trade in Services.

2. Without prejudice to their outcome, the negotiations shall be comprehensive in scope, with no basic telecommunications excluded *a priori.*

3. A Negotiating Group on Basic Telecommunications (hereinafter referred to as the "NGBT") is established to carry out this mandate. The NGBT shall report periodically on the progress of these negotiations.

4. The negotiations in the NGBT shall be open to all governments and the European Communities which announce their intention to participate. To date, the following have announced their intention to take part in the negotiations:

Australia, Austria, Canada, Chile, Cyprus, European Communities and their member States, Finland, Hong Kong, Hungary, Japan, Korea, Mexico, New Zealand, Norway, Slovak Republic, Sweden, Switzerland, Turkey, United States.

Further notifications of intention to participate shall be addressed to the Depositary of the Agreement Establishing the World Trade Organization.

5. The NGBT shall hold its first negotiating session no later than 16 May 1994. It shall conclude these negotiations and make a final report no later than 30 April 1996. The final report of the NGBT shall include a date for the implementation of results of these negotiations.

6. Any commitments resulting from the negotiations, including the date of their entry into force, shall be inscribed in the Schedules annexed to the General Agreement on Trade in Services and shall be subject to all the provisions of the Agreement.

7. Commencing immediately and continuing until the implementation date to be determined under paragraph 5, it is understood that no participant shall apply any measure affecting trade in basic telecommunications in such a manner as would improve its negotiating position and leverage. It is understood that this provision shall not prevent the pursuit of commercial and governmental arrangements regarding the provision of basic telecommunications services.

8. The implementation of paragraph 7 shall be subject to surveillance in the NGBT. Any participant may bring to the attention of the NGBT any action or omission which it believes to be relevant to the fulfilment of paragraph 7. Such notifications shall be deemed to have been submitted to the NGBT upon their receipt by the Secretariat.

* * *

Decision on Professional Services

Ministers,

Decide to recommend that the Council for Trade in Services at its first meeting adopt the decision set out below.

The Council for Trade in Services,

Recognizing the impact of regulatory measures relating to professional qualifications, technical standards and licensing on the expansion of trade in professional services;

Desiring to establish multilateral disciplines with a view to ensuring that, when specific commitments are undertaken, such regulatory measures do not constitute unnecessary barriers to the supply of professional services;

Decides as follows:

1. The work programme foreseen in paragraph 4 of Article VI on Domestic Regulation should be put into effect immediately. To this end, a Working Party on Professional Services shall be established to examine and report, with recommendations, on the disciplines necessary to ensure that measures relating to qualification requirements and procedures, technical standards and licensing requirements in the field of professional services do not constitute unnecessary barriers to trade.

2. As a matter of priority, the Working Party shall make recommendations for the elaboration of multilateral disciplines in the accountancy sector, so as to give operational effect to specific commitments. In making these recommendations, the Working Party shall concentrate on:

(a) developing multilateral disciplines relating to market access so as to ensure that domestic regulatory requirements are: (*i*) based on objective and transparent criteria, such as competence and the ability to supply the service; (*ii*) not more burdensome than necessary to ensure the quality of the service, thereby facilitating the effective liberalization of accountancy services;

(b) the use of international standards and, in doing so, it shall encourage the cooperation with the relevant international organizations as defined under paragraph 5(b) of Article VI, so as to give full effect to paragraph 5 of Article VII;

(c) facilitating the effective application of paragraph 6 of Article VI of the Agreement by establishing guidelines for the recognition of qualifications.

In elaborating these disciplines, the Working Party shall take account of the importance of the governmental and non-governmental bodies regulating professional services.

* * *

UNDERSTANDING ON COMMITMENTS IN FINANCIAL SERVICES

Participants in the Uruguay Round have been enabled to take on specific commitments with respect to financial services under the General Agreement on Trade in Services (hereinafter referred to as the "Agreement") on the basis of an alternative approach to that covered by the provisions of Part III of the Agreement. It was agreed that this approach could be applied subject to the following understanding:

(i) it does not conflict with the provisions of the Agreement;

(ii) it does not prejudice the right of any Member to schedule its specific commitments in accordance with the approach under Part III of the Agreement;

(iii) resulting specific commitments shall apply on a most-favoured-nation basis;

(iv) no presumption has been created as to the degree of liberalization to which a Member is committing itself under the Agreement.

Interested Members, on the basis of negotiations, and subject to conditions and qualifications where specified, have inscribed in their schedule specific commitments conforming to the approach set out below.

A. *Standstill*

Any conditions, limitations and qualifications to the commitments noted below shall be limited to existing non-conforming measures.

B. *Market Access*

Monopoly Rights

1. In addition to Article VIII of the Agreement, the following shall apply:

Each Member shall list in its schedule pertaining to financial services existing monopoly rights and shall endeavour to eliminate them or reduce their scope. Notwithstanding subparagraph 1(b) of the Annex on Financial Services, this paragraph applies to the activities referred to in subparagraph 1(b)(iii) of the Annex.

Financial Services purchased by Public Entities

2. Notwithstanding Article XIII of the Agreement, each Member shall ensure that financial service suppliers of any other Member established in its territory are accorded most-favoured-nation treatment and national treatment as regards the purchase or acquisition of financial services by public entities of the Member in its territory.

Cross-border Trade

3. Each Member shall permit non-resident suppliers of financial services to supply, as a principal, through an intermediary or as an intermediary, and under terms and conditions that accord national treatment, the following services:

(a) insurance of risks relating to:

(i) maritime shipping and commercial aviation and space launching and freight (including satellites), with such insurance to cover any or all of the following: the goods being transported, the vehicle transporting the goods and any liability arising therefrom; and

(ii) goods in international transit;

(b) reinsurance and retrocession and the services auxiliary to insurance as referred to in subparagraph 5(a)(iv) of the Annex;

(c) provision and transfer of financial information and financial data processing as referred to in subparagraph 5(a)(xv) of the Annex and advisory and other auxiliary services, excluding intermediation, relating to banking and other financial services as referred to in subparagraph 5(a)(xvi) of the Annex.

4. Each Member shall permit its residents to purchase in the territory of any other Member the financial services indicated in:

(a) subparagraph 3(a);

(b) subparagraph 3(b); and

(c) subparagraphs 5(a)(v) to (xvi) of the Annex.

Commercial Presence

5. Each Member shall grant financial service suppliers of any other Member the right to establish or expand within its territory, including through the acquisition of existing enterprises, a commercial presence.

6. A Member may impose terms, conditions and procedures for authorization of the establishment and expansion of a commercial presence in so far as they do not circumvent the Member's obligation under paragraph 5 and they are consistent with the other obligations of the Agreement.

New Financial Services

7. A Member shall permit financial service suppliers of any other Member established in its territory to offer in its territory any new financial service.

Transfers of Information and Processing of Information

8. No Member shall take measures that prevent transfers of information or the processing of financial information, including transfers of data by electronic means, or that, subject to importation rules consistent with international agreements, prevent transfers of equipment, where such transfers of information, processing of financial information or transfers of equipment are necessary for the conduct of the ordinary business of a financial service supplier. Nothing in this paragraph restricts the right of a Member to protect personal data, personal privacy and the confidentiality of individual records and accounts so long as such right is not used to circumvent the provisions of the Agreement.

Temporary Entry of Personnel

9. (a) Each Member shall permit temporary entry into its territory of the following personnel of a financial service supplier of any other Member that is establishing or has established a commercial presence in the territory of the Member:

(i) senior managerial personnel possessing proprietary information essential to the establishment, control and operation of the services of the financial service supplier; and

(ii) specialists in the operation of the financial service supplier.

(b) Each Member shall permit, subject to the availability of qualified personnel in its territory, temporary entry into its territory of the following personnel associated with a commercial presence of a financial service supplier of any other Member:

(i) specialists in computer services, telecommunication services and accounts of the financial service supplier; and

(ii) actuarial and legal specialists.

Non-discriminatory Measures

10. Each Member shall endeavour to remove or to limit any significant adverse effects on financial service suppliers of any other Member of:

(a) non-discriminatory measures that prevent financial service suppliers from offering in the Member's territory, in the form determined by the Member, all the financial services permitted by the Member;

(b) non-discriminatory measures that limit the expansion of the activities of financial service suppliers into the entire territory of the Member;

(c) measures of a Member, when such a Member applies the same measures to the supply of both banking and securities services, and a financial service supplier of any other Member concentrates its activities in the provision of securities services; and

(d) other measures that, although respecting the provisions of the Agreement, affect adversely the ability of financial service suppliers of any other Member to operate, compete or enter the Member's market;

provided that any action taken under this paragraph would not unfairly discriminate against financial service suppliers of the Member taking such action.

11. With respect to the non-discriminatory measures referred to in subparagraphs 10(a) and (b), a Member shall endeavour not to limit or restrict the present degree of market opportunities nor the benefits already enjoyed by financial service suppliers of all other Members as a class in the territory of the Member, provided that this commitment does not result in unfair discrimination against financial service suppliers of the Member applying such measures.

C. *National Treatment*

1. Under terms and conditions that accord national treatment, each Member shall grant to financial service suppliers of any other Member established in its territory access to payment and clearing systems operated by public entities, and to official funding and refinancing facilities available in the normal course of ordinary business. This paragraph is not intended to confer access to the Member's lender of last resort facilities.

2. When membership or participation in, or access to, any self-regulatory body, securities or futures exchange or market, clearing agency, or any other organization or association, is required by a Member in order for financial service suppliers of any other Member to supply financial services on an equal basis with financial service suppliers of the Member, or when the Member provides directly or indirectly such entities, privileges or advantages in supplying financial services, the Member shall ensure that such entities accord national treatment to financial service suppliers of any other Member resident in the territory of the Member.

D. *Definitions*

For the purposes of this approach:

1. A non-resident supplier of financial services is a financial service supplier of a Member which supplies a financial service into the territory of another Member from an establishment located in the territory of another Member, regardless of whether such a financial service supplier

has or has not a commercial presence in the territory of the Member in which the financial service is supplied.

2. "Commercial presence" means an enterprise within a Member's territory for the supply of financial services and includes wholly- or partly-owned subsidiaries, joint ventures, partnerships, sole proprietorships, franchising operations, branches, agencies, representative offices or other organizations.

3. A new financial service is a service of a financial nature, including services related to existing and new products or the manner in which a product is delivered, that is not supplied by any financial service supplier in the territory of a particular Member but which is supplied in the territory of another Member.

* * *

MARRAKESH AGREEMENT ESTABLISHING THE WORLD TRADE ORGANIZATION

ANNEX 1C: AGREEMENT ON TRADE-RELATED ASPECTS OF INTELLECTUAL PROPERTY RIGHTS*

The Agreement on Trade-Related Aspects of Intellectual Property Rights is an integral part of the Marrakesh Agreement Establishing the World Trade Organization (Annex 1C) which was signed on 15 April 1994 by the participants in the Uruguay Round of Multilateral Trade Negotiations held under the auspices of GATT. The Agreement came into force on 1 January 1995 and had been ratified by 105 States as of 5 July 1995.

PART I GENERAL PROVISIONS AND BASIC PRINCIPLES

PART II STANDARDS CONCERNING THE AVAILABILITY, SCOPE AND USE OF INTELLECTUAL PROPERTY RIGHTS

1. Copyright and Related Rights
2. Trademarks
3. Geographical Indications
4. Industrial Designs
5. Patents
6. Layout-Designs (Topographies) of Integrated Circuits
7. Protection of Undisclosed Information
8. Control of Anti-Competitive Practices in Contractual Licences

PART III ENFORCEMENT OF INTELLECTUAL PROPERTY RIGHTS

1. General Obligations
2. Civil and Administrative Procedures and Remedies
3. Provisional Measures
4. Special Requirements Related to Border Measures
5. Criminal Procedures

PART IV ACQUISITION AND MAINTENANCE OF INTELLECTUAL PROPERTY RIGHTS AND RELATED *INTER-PARTES* PROCEDURES

---

*Source: World Trade Organization (1995). "Marrakesh Agreement Establishing the World Trade Organization. Annex 1C: Agreement on Trade-Related Aspects of Intellectual Property Rights", *The Results of the Uruguay Round of Multilateral Trade Negotiations: The Legal Texts* (Geneva: World Trade Organization), pp. 365-403 [Note added by the editor].

PART V DISPUTE PREVENTION AND SETTLEMENT

PART VI TRANSITIONAL ARRANGEMENTS

PART VII INSTITUTIONAL ARRANGEMENTS; FINAL PROVISIONS

* * *

AGREEMENT ON TRADE-RELATED ASPECTS OF INTELLECTUAL PROPERTY RIGHTS

Members,

Desiring to reduce distortions and impediments to international trade, and taking into account the need to promote effective and adequate protection of intellectual property rights, and to ensure that measures and procedures to enforce intellectual property rights do not themselves become barriers to legitimate trade;

Recognizing, to this end, the need for new rules and disciplines concerning:

(a) the applicability of the basic principles of GATT 1994 and of relevant international intellectual property agreements or conventions;

(b) the provision of adequate standards and principles concerning the availability, scope and use of trade-related intellectual property rights;

(c) the provision of effective and appropriate means for the enforcement of trade-related intellectual property rights, taking into account differences in national legal systems;

(d) the provision of effective and expeditious procedures for the multilateral prevention and settlement of disputes between governments; and

(e) transitional arrangements aiming at the fullest participation in the results of the negotiations;

Recognizing the need for a multilateral framework of principles, rules and disciplines dealing with international trade in counterfeit goods;

Recognizing that intellectual property rights are private rights;

Recognizing the underlying public policy objectives of national systems for the protection of intellectual property, including developmental and technological objectives;

Recognizing also the special needs of the least-developed country Members in respect of maximum flexibility in the domestic implementation of laws and regulations in order to enable them to create a sound and viable technological base;

Emphasizing the importance of reducing tensions by reaching strengthened commitments to resolve disputes on trade-related intellectual property issues through multilateral procedures;

Desiring to establish a mutually supportive relationship between the WTO and the World Intellectual Property Organization (referred to in this Agreement as "WIPO") as well as other relevant international organizations;

Hereby agree as follows:

PART I
GENERAL PROVISIONS AND BASIC PRINCIPLES

Article 1
Nature and Scope of Obligations

1. Members shall give effect to the provisions of this Agreement. Members may, but shall not be obliged to, implement in their law more extensive protection than is required by this Agreement, provided that such protection does not contravene the provisions of this Agreement. Members shall be free to determine the appropriate method of implementing the provisions of this Agreement within their own legal system and practice.

2. For the purposes of this Agreement, the term "intellectual property" refers to all categories of intellectual property that are the subject of Sections 1 through 7 of Part II.

3. Members shall accord the treatment provided for in this Agreement to the nationals of other Members.[1] In respect of the relevant intellectual property right, the nationals of other Members shall be understood as those natural or legal persons that would meet the criteria for eligibility for protection provided for in the Paris Convention (1967), the Berne Convention (1971), the Rome Convention and the Treaty on Intellectual Property in Respect of Integrated Circuits, were all Members of the WTO members of those conventions.[2] Any Member availing

[1]When "nationals" are referred to in this Agreement, they shall be deemed, in the case of a separate customs territory Member of the WTO, to mean persons, natural or legal, who are domiciled or who have a real and effective industrial or commercial establishment in that customs territory.

[2]In this Agreement, "Paris Convention" refers to the Paris Convention for the Protection of Industrial Property; "Paris Convention (1967)" refers to the Stockholm Act of this Convention of 14 July 1967. "Berne Convention" refers to the Berne Convention for the Protection of Literary and Artistic Works; "Berne Convention (1971)" refers

itself of the possibilities provided in paragraph 3 of Article 5 or paragraph 2 of Article 6 of the Rome Convention shall make a notification as foreseen in those provisions to the Council for Trade-Related Aspects of Intellectual Property Rights (the "Council for TRIPS").

Article 2
Intellectual Property Conventions

1. In respect of Parts II, III and IV of this Agreement, Members shall comply with Articles 1 through 12, and Article 19, of the Paris Convention (1967).

2. Nothing in Parts I to IV of this Agreement shall derogate from existing obligations that Members may have to each other under the Paris Convention, the Berne Convention, the Rome Convention and the Treaty on Intellectual Property in Respect of Integrated Circuits.

Article 3
National Treatment

1. Each Member shall accord to the nationals of other Members treatment no less favourable than that it accords to its own nationals with regard to the protection[3] of intellectual property, subject to the exceptions already provided in, respectively, the Paris Convention (1967), the Berne Convention (1971), the Rome Convention or the Treaty on Intellectual Property in Respect of Integrated Circuits. In respect of performers, producers of phonograms and broadcasting organizations, this obligation only applies in respect of the rights provided under this Agreement. Any Member availing itself of the possibilities provided in Article 6 of the Berne Convention (1971) or paragraph 1(b) of Article 16 of the Rome Convention shall make a notification as foreseen in those provisions to the Council for TRIPS.

2. Members may avail themselves of the exceptions permitted under paragraph 1 in relation to judicial and administrative procedures, including the designation of an address for service or the appointment of an agent within the jurisdiction of a Member, only where such exceptions are necessary to secure compliance with laws and regulations which are not inconsistent with the provisions of this Agreement and where such practices are not applied in a manner which would constitute a disguised restriction on trade.

---

to the Paris Act of this Convention of 24 July 1971. "Rome Convention" refers to the International Convention for the Protection of Performers, Producers of Phonograms and Broadcasting Organizations, adopted at Rome on 26 October 1961. "Treaty on Intellectual Property in Respect of Integrated Circuits" (IPIC Treaty) refers to the Treaty on Intellectual Property in Respect of Integrated Circuits, adopted at Washington on 26 May 1989. "WTO Agreement" refers to the Agreement Establishing the WTO.

[3]For the purposes of Articles 3 and 4, "protection" shall include matters affecting the availability, acquisition, scope, maintenance and enforcement of intellectual property rights as well as those matters affecting the use of intellectual property rights specifically addressed in this Agreement.

Article 4
Most-Favoured-Nation Treatment

With regard to the protection of intellectual property, any advantage, favour, privilege or immunity granted by a Member to the nationals of any other country shall be accorded immediately and unconditionally to the nationals of all other Members. Exempted from this obligation are any advantage, favour, privilege or immunity accorded by a Member:

(a) deriving from international agreements on judicial assistance or law enforcement of a general nature and not particularly confined to the protection of intellectual property;

(b) granted in accordance with the provisions of the Berne Convention (1971) or the Rome Convention authorizing that the treatment accorded be a function not of national treatment but of the treatment accorded in another country;

(c) in respect of the rights of performers, producers of phonograms and broadcasting organizations not provided under this Agreement;

(d) deriving from international agreements related to the protection of intellectual property which entered into force prior to the entry into force of the WTO Agreement, provided that such agreements are notified to the Council for TRIPS and do not constitute an arbitrary or unjustifiable discrimination against nationals of other Members.

Article 5
Multilateral Agreements on Acquisition or Maintenance of Protection

The obligations under Articles 3 and 4 do not apply to procedures provided in multilateral agreements concluded under the auspices of WIPO relating to the acquisition or maintenance of intellectual property rights.

Article 6
Exhaustion

For the purposes of dispute settlement under this Agreement, subject to the provisions of Articles 3 and 4 nothing in this Agreement shall be used to address the issue of the exhaustion of intellectual property rights.

Article 7
Objectives

The protection and enforcement of intellectual property rights should contribute to the promotion of technological innovation and to the transfer and dissemination of technology, to the mutual advantage of producers and users of technological knowledge and in a manner conducive to social and economic welfare, and to a balance of rights and obligations.

Article 8
Principles

1. Members may, in formulating or amending their laws and regulations, adopt measures necessary to protect public health and nutrition, and to promote the public interest in sectors of vital importance to their socio-economic and technological development, provided that such measures are consistent with the provisions of this Agreement.

2. Appropriate measures, provided that they are consistent with the provisions of this Agreement, may be needed to prevent the abuse of intellectual property rights by right holders or the resort to practices which unreasonably restrain trade or adversely affect the international transfer of technology.

PART II
STANDARDS CONCERNING THE AVAILABILITY, SCOPE AND USE OF INTELLECTUAL PROPERTY RIGHTS

Section 1: Copyright and Related Rights

Article 9
Relation to the Berne Convention

1. Members shall comply with Articles 1 through 21 of the Berne Convention (1971) and the Appendix thereto. However, Members shall not have rights or obligations under this Agreement in respect of the rights conferred under Article 6*bis* of that Convention or of the rights derived therefrom.

2. Copyright protection shall extend to expressions and not to ideas, procedures, methods of operation or mathematical concepts as such.

Article 10
Computer Programs and Compilations of Data

1. Computer programs, whether in source or object code, shall be protected as literary works under the Berne Convention (1971).

2. Compilations of data or other material, whether in machine readable or other form, which by reason of the selection or arrangement of their contents constitute intellectual creations shall be protected as such. Such protection, which shall not extend to the data or material itself, shall be without prejudice to any copyright subsisting in the data or material itself.

Article 11
Rental Rights

In respect of at least computer programs and cinematographic works, a Member shall provide authors and their successors in title the right to authorize or to prohibit the commercial rental to the public of originals or copies of their copyright works. A Member shall be excepted from this obligation in respect of cinematographic works unless such rental has led to widespread copying of such works which is materially impairing the exclusive right of reproduction conferred in that Member on authors and their successors in title. In respect of computer programs, this obligation does not apply to rentals where the program itself is not the essential object of the rental.

Article 12
Term of Protection

Whenever the term of protection of a work, other than a photographic work or a work of applied art, is calculated on a basis other than the life of a natural person, such term shall be no less than 50 years from the end of the calendar year of authorized publication, or, failing such authorized publication within 50 years from the making of the work, 50 years from the end of the calendar year of making.

Article 13
Limitations and Exceptions

Members shall confine limitations or exceptions to exclusive rights to certain special cases which do not conflict with a normal exploitation of the work and do not unreasonably prejudice the legitimate interests of the right holder.

Article 14
Protection of Performers, Producers of Phonograms (Sound Recordings) and Broadcasting Organizations

1. In respect of a fixation of their performance on a phonogram, performers shall have the possibility of preventing the following acts when undertaken without their authorization: the fixation of their unfixed performance and the reproduction of such fixation. Performers shall also have the possibility of preventing the following acts when undertaken without their authorization: the broadcasting by wireless means and the communication to the public of their live performance.

2. Producers of phonograms shall enjoy the right to authorize or prohibit the direct or indirect reproduction of their phonograms.

3. Broadcasting organizations shall have the right to prohibit the following acts when undertaken without their authorization: the fixation, the reproduction of fixations, and the rebroadcasting by wireless means of broadcasts, as well as the communication to the public of

television broadcasts of the same. Where Members do not grant such rights to broadcasting organizations, they shall provide owners of copyright in the subject matter of broadcasts with the possibility of preventing the above acts, subject to the provisions of the Berne Convention (1971).

4. The provisions of Article 11 in respect of computer programs shall apply *mutatis mutandis* to producers of phonograms and any other right holders in phonograms as determined in a Member's law. If on 15 April 1994 a Member has in force a system of equitable remuneration of right holders in respect of the rental of phonograms, it may maintain such system provided that the commercial rental of phonograms is not giving rise to the material impairment of the exclusive rights of reproduction of right holders.

5. The term of the protection available under this Agreement to performers and producers of phonograms shall last at least until the end of a period of 50 years computed from the end of the calendar year in which the fixation was made or the performance took place. The term of protection granted pursuant to paragraph 3 shall last for at least 20 years from the end of the calendar year in which the broadcast took place.

6. Any Member may, in relation to the rights conferred under paragraphs 1, 2 and 3, provide for conditions, limitations, exceptions and reservations to the extent permitted by the Rome Convention. However, the provisions of Article 18 of the Berne Convention (1971) shall also apply, *mutatis mutandis*, to the rights of performers and producers of phonograms in phonograms.

Section 2: Trademarks

Article 15
Protectable Subject Matter

1. Any sign, or any combination of signs, capable of distinguishing the goods or services of one undertaking from those of other undertakings, shall be capable of constituting a trademark. Such signs, in particular words including personal names, letters, numerals, figurative elements and combinations of colours as well as any combination of such signs, shall be eligible for registration as trademarks. Where signs are not inherently capable of distinguishing the relevant goods or services, Members may make registrability depend on distinctiveness acquired through use. Members may require, as a condition of registration, that signs be visually perceptible.

2. Paragraph 1 shall not be understood to prevent a Member from denying registration of a trademark on other grounds, provided that they do not derogate from the provisions of the Paris Convention (1967).

3. Members may make registrability depend on use. However, actual use of a trademark shall not be a condition for filing an application for registration. An application shall not be refused solely on the ground that intended use has not taken place before the expiry of a period of three years from the date of application.

4. The nature of the goods or services to which a trademark is to be applied shall in no case form an obstacle to registration of the trademark.

5. Members shall publish each trademark either before it is registered or promptly after it is registered and shall afford a reasonable opportunity for petitions to cancel the registration. In addition, Members may afford an opportunity for the registration of a trademark to be opposed.

Article 16
Rights Conferred

1. The owner of a registered trademark shall have the exclusive right to prevent all third parties not having the owner's consent from using in the course of trade identical or similar signs for goods or services which are identical or similar to those in respect of which the trademark is registered where such use would result in a likelihood of confusion. In case of the use of an identical sign for identical goods or services, a likelihood of confusion shall be presumed. The rights described above shall not prejudice any existing prior rights, nor shall they affect the possibility of Members making rights available on the basis of use.

2. Article 6*bis* of the Paris Convention (1967) shall apply, *mutatis mutandis*, to services. In determining whether a trademark is well known, Members shall take account of the knowledge of the trademark in the relevant sector of the public, including knowledge in the Member concerned which has been obtained as a result of the promotion of the trademark.

3. Article 6*bis* of the Paris Convention (1967) shall apply, *mutatis mutandis*, to goods or services which are not similar to those in respect of which a trademark is registered, provided that use of that trademark in relation to those goods or services would indicate a connection between those goods or services and the owner of the registered trademark and provided that the interests of the owner of the registered trademark are likely to be damaged by such use.

Article 17
Exceptions

Members may provide limited exceptions to the rights conferred by a trademark, such as fair use of descriptive terms, provided that such exceptions take account of the legitimate interests of the owner of the trademark and of third parties.

Article 18
Term of Protection

Initial registration, and each renewal of registration, of a trademark shall be for a term of no less than seven years. The registration of a trademark shall be renewable indefinitely.

Article 19
Requirement of Use

1. If use is required to maintain a registration, the registration may be cancelled only after an uninterrupted period of at least three years of non-use, unless valid reasons based on the existence of obstacles to such use are shown by the trademark owner. Circumstances arising independently of the will of the owner of the trademark which constitute an obstacle to the use of the trademark, such as import restrictions on or other government requirements for goods or services protected by the trademark, shall be recognized as valid reasons for non-use.

2. When subject to the control of its owner, use of a trademark by another person shall be recognized as use of the trademark for the purpose of maintaining the registration.

Article 20
Other Requirements

The use of a trademark in the course of trade shall not be unjustifiably encumbered by special requirements, such as use with another trademark, use in a special form or use in a manner detrimental to its capability to distinguish the goods or services of one undertaking from those of other undertakings. This will not preclude a requirement prescribing the use of the trademark identifying the undertaking producing the goods or services along with, but without linking it to, the trademark distinguishing the specific goods or services in question of that undertaking.

Article 21
Licensing and Assignment

Members may determine conditions on the licensing and assignment of trademarks, it being understood that the compulsory licensing of trademarks shall not be permitted and that the owner of a registered trademark shall have the right to assign the trademark with or without the transfer of the business to which the trademark belongs.

Section 3: Geographical Indications

Article 22
Protection of Geographical Indications

1. Geographical indications are, for the purposes of this Agreement, indications which identify a good as originating in the territory of a Member, or a region or locality in that territory, where a given quality, reputation or other characteristic of the good is essentially attributable to its geographical origin.

2. In respect of geographical indications, Members shall provide the legal means for interested parties to prevent:

(a) the use of any means in the designation or presentation of a good that indicates or suggests that the good in question originates in a geographical area other than the true place of origin in a manner which misleads the public as to the geographical origin of the good;

(b) any use which constitutes an act of unfair competition within the meaning of Article 10*bis* of the Paris Convention (1967).

3. A Member shall, *ex officio* if its legislation so permits or at the request of an interested party, refuse or invalidate the registration of a trademark which contains or consists of a geographical indication with respect to goods not originating in the territory indicated, if use of the indication in the trademark for such goods in that Member is of such a nature as to mislead the public as to the true place of origin.

4. The protection under paragraphs 1, 2 and 3 shall be applicable against a geographical indication which, although literally true as to the territory, region or locality in which the goods originate, falsely represents to the public that the goods originate in another territory.

Article 23
Additional Protection for Geographical Indications for Wines and Spirits

1. Each Member shall provide the legal means for interested parties to prevent use of a geographical indication identifying wines for wines not originating in the place indicated by the geographical indication in question or identifying spirits for spirits not originating in the place indicated by the geographical indication in question, even where the true origin of the goods is indicated or the geographical indication is used in translation or accompanied by expressions such as "kind", "type", "style", "imitation" or the like.[4]

2. The registration of a trademark for wines which contains or consists of a geographical indication identifying wines or for spirits which contains or consists of a geographical indication identifying spirits shall be refused or invalidated, *ex officio* if a Member's legislation so permits or at the request of an interested party, with respect to such wines or spirits not having this origin.

3. In the case of homonymous geographical indications for wines, protection shall be accorded to each indication, subject to the provisions of paragraph 4 of Article 22. Each Member shall determine the practical conditions under which the homonymous indications in question will be differentiated from each other, taking into account the need to ensure equitable treatment of the producers concerned and that consumers are not misled.

---

[4]Notwithstanding the first sentence of Article 42, Members may, with respect to these obligations, instead provide for enforcement by administrative action.

4. In order to facilitate the protection of geographical indications for wines, negotiations shall be undertaken in the Council for TRIPS concerning the establishment of a multilateral system of notification and registration of geographical indications for wines eligible for protection in those Members participating in the system.

Article 24
International Negotiations: Exceptions

1. Members agree to enter into negotiations aimed at increasing the protection of individual geographical indications under Article 23. The provisions of paragraphs 4 through 8 below shall not be used by a Member to refuse to conduct negotiations or to conclude bilateral or multilateral agreements. In the context of such negotiations, Members shall be willing to consider the continued applicability of these provisions to individual geographical indications whose use was the subject of such negotiations.

2. The Council for TRIPS shall keep under review the application of the provisions of this Section; the first such review shall take place within two years of the entry into force of the WTO Agreement. Any matter affecting the compliance with the obligations under these provisions may be drawn to the attention of the Council, which, at the request of a Member, shall consult with any Member or Members in respect of such matter in respect of which it has not been possible to find a satisfactory solution through bilateral or plurilateral consultations between the Members concerned. The Council shall take such action as may be agreed to facilitate the operation and further the objectives of this Section.

3. In implementing this Section, a Member shall not diminish the protection of geographical indications that existed in that Member immediately prior to the date of entry into force of the WTO Agreement.

4. Nothing in this Section shall require a Member to prevent continued and similar use of a particular geographical indication of another Member identifying wines or spirits in connection with goods or services by any of its nationals or domiciliaries who have used that geographical indication in a continuous manner with regard to the same or related goods or services in the territory of that Member either (*a*) for at least 10 years preceding 15 April 1994 or (*b*) in good faith preceding that date.

5. Where a trademark has been applied for or registered in good faith, or where rights to a trademark have been acquired through use in good faith either:

(a) before the date of application of these provisions in that Member as defined in Part VI: or

(b) before the geographical indication is protected in its country of origin;

measures adopted to implement this Section shall not prejudice eligibility for or the validity of the registration of a trademark, or the right to use a trademark, on the basis that such a trademark is identical with, or similar to, a geographical indication.

6. Nothing in this Section shall require a Member to apply its provisions in respect of a geographical indication of any other Member with respect to goods or services for which the relevant indication is identical with the term customary in common language as the common name for such goods or services in the territory of that Member. Nothing in this Section shall require a Member to apply its provisions in respect of a geographical indication of any other Member with respect to products of the vine for which the relevant indication is identical with the customary name of a grape variety existing in the territory of that Member as of the date of entry into force of the WTO Agreement.

7. A Member may provide that any request made under this Section in connection with the use or registration of a trademark must be presented within five years after the adverse use of the protected indication has become generally known in that Member or after the date of registration of the trademark in that Member provided that the trademark has been published by that date, if such date is earlier than the date on which the adverse use became generally known in that Member, provided that the geographical indication is not used or registered in bad faith.

8. The provisions of this Section shall in no way prejudice the right of any person to use, in the course of trade, that person's name or the name of that person's predecessor in business, except where such name is used in such a manner as to mislead the public.

9. There shall be no obligation under this Agreement to protect geographical indications which are not or cease to be protected in their country of origin, or which have fallen into disuse in that country.

Section 4: Industrial Designs

Article 25

Requirements for Protection

1. Members shall provide for the protection of independently created industrial designs that are new or original. Members may provide that designs are not new or original if they do not significantly differ from known designs or combinations of known design features. Members may provide that such protection shall not extend to designs dictated essentially by technical or functional considerations.

2. Each Member shall ensure that requirements for securing protection for textile designs, in particular in regard to any cost, examination or publication, do not unreasonably impair the opportunity to seek and obtain such protection. Members shall be free to meet this obligation through industrial design law or through copyright law.

Article 26
Protection

1. The owner of a protected industrial design shall have the right to prevent third parties not having the owner's consent from making, selling or importing articles bearing or embodying a design which is a copy, or substantially a copy, of the protected design, when such acts are undertaken for commercial purposes.

2. Members may provide limited exceptions to the protection of industrial designs, provided that such exceptions do not unreasonably conflict with the normal exploitation of protected industrial designs and do not unreasonably prejudice the legitimate interests of the owner of the protected design, taking account of the legitimate interests of third parties.

3. The duration of protection available shall amount to at least 10 years.

Section 5: Patents

Article 27
Patentable Subject Matter

1. Subject to the provisions of paragraphs 2 and 3, patents shall be available for any inventions, whether products or processes, in all fields of technology, provided that they are new, involve an inventive step and are capable of industrial application.[5] Subject to paragraph 4 of Article 65, paragraph 8 of Article 70 and paragraph 3 of this Article, patents shall be available and patent rights enjoyable without discrimination as to the place of invention, the field of technology and whether products are imported or locally produced.

2. Members may exclude from patentability inventions, the prevention within their territory of the commercial exploitation of which is necessary to protect *ordre public* or morality, including to protect human, animal or plant life or health or to avoid serious prejudice to the environment, provided that such exclusion is not made merely because the exploitation is prohibited by their law.

3. Members may also exclude from patentability:

(a) diagnostic, therapeutic and surgical methods for the treatment of humans or animals;

(b) plants and animals other than micro-organisms, and essentially biological processes for the production of plants or animals other than non-biological and microbiological processes. However, Members shall provide for the protection

---

[5]For the purposes of this Article, the terms "inventive step" and "capable of industrial application" may be deemed by a Member to be synonymous with the terms "non-obvious" and "useful" respectively.

of plant varieties either by patents or by an effective *sui generis* system or by any combination thereof. The provisions of this subparagraph shall be reviewed four years after the date of entry into force of the WTO Agreement.

Article 28
Rights Conferred

1. A patent shall confer on its owner the following exclusive rights:

(a) where the subject matter of a patent is a product, to prevent third parties not having the owner's consent from the acts of: making, using, offering for sale, selling, or importing[6] for these purposes that product;

(b) where the subject matter of a patent is a process, to prevent third parties not having the owner's consent from the act of using the process, and from the acts of: using, offering for sale, selling, or importing for these purposes at least the product obtained directly by that process.

2. Patent owners shall also have the right to assign, or transfer by succession, the patent and to conclude licensing contracts.

Article 29
Conditions on Patent Applicants

1. Members shall require that an applicant for a patent shall disclose the invention in a manner sufficiently clear and complete for the invention to be carried out by a person skilled in the art and may require the applicant to indicate the best mode for carrying out the invention known to the inventor at the filing date or, where priority is claimed, at the priority date of the application.

2. Members may require an applicant for a patent to provide information concerning the applicant's corresponding foreign applications and grants.

Article 30
Exceptions to Rights Conferred

Members may provide limited exceptions to the exclusive rights conferred by a patent, provided that such exceptions do not unreasonably conflict with a normal exploitation of the patent and do not unreasonably prejudice the legitimate interests of the patent owner, taking account of the legitimate interests of third parties.

---

[6]This right, like all other rights conferred under this Agreement in respect of the use, sale, importation or other distribution of goods, is subject to the provisions of Article 6.

Article 31
Other Use Without Authorization of the Right Holder

Where the law of a Member allows for other use[7] of the subject matter of a patent without the authorization of the right holder, including use by the government or third parties authorized by the government, the following provisions shall be respected:

(a) authorization of such use shall be considered on its individual merits;

(b) such use may only be permitted if, prior to such use, the proposed user has made efforts to obtain authorization from the right holder on reasonable commercial terms and conditions and that such efforts have not been successful within a reasonable period of time. This requirement may be waived by a Member in the case of a national emergency or other circumstances of extreme urgency or in cases of public non-commercial use. In situations of national emergency or other circumstances of extreme urgency, the right holder shall, nevertheless, be notified as soon as reasonably practicable. In the case of public non-commercial use, where the government or contractor, without making a patent search, knows or has demonstrable grounds to know that a valid patent is or will be used by or for the government, the right holder shall be informed promptly;

(c) the scope and duration of such use shall be limited to the purpose for which it was authorized, and in the case of semi-conductor technology shall only be for public non-commercial use or to remedy a practice determined after judicial or administrative process to be anti-competitive;

(d) such use shall be non-exclusive;

(e) such use shall be non-assignable, except with that part of the enterprise or goodwill which enjoys such use;

(f) any such use shall be authorized predominantly for the supply of the domestic market of the Member authorizing such use;

(g) authorization for such use shall be liable, subject to adequate protection of the legitimate interests of the persons so authorized, to be terminated if and when the circumstances which led to it cease to exist and are unlikely to recur. The competent authority shall have the authority to review, upon motivated request, the continued existence of these circumstances;

(h) the right holder shall be paid adequate remuneration in the circumstances of each case, taking into account the economic value of the authorization;

[7]"Other use" refers to use other than that allowed under Article 30.

(i) the legal validity of any decision relating to the authorization of such use shall be subject to judicial review or other independent review by a distinct higher authority in that Member;

(j) any decision relating to the remuneration provided in respect of such use shall be subject to judicial review or other independent review by a distinct higher authority in that Member;

(k) Members are not obliged to apply the conditions set forth in subparagraphs (b) and (f) where such use is permitted to remedy a practice determined after judicial or administrative process to be anti-competitive. The need to correct anti-competitive practices may be taken into account in determining the amount of remuneration in such cases. Competent authorities shall have the authority to refuse termination of authorization if and when the conditions which led to such authorization are likely to recur;

(l) where such use is authorized to permit the exploitation of a patent ("the second patent") which cannot be exploited without infringing another patent ("the first patent"), the following additional conditions shall apply:

  (i) the invention claimed in the second patent shall involve an important technical advance of considerable economic significance in relation to the invention claimed in the first patent;

  (ii) the owner of the first patent shall be entitled to a cross-licence on reasonable terms to use the invention claimed in the second patent; and

  (iii) the use authorized in respect of the first patent shall be non-assignable except with the assignment of the second patent.

Article 32
Revocation/Forfeiture

An opportunity for judicial review of any decision to revoke or forfeit a patent shall be available.

Article 33
Term of Protection

The term of protection available shall not end before the expiration of a period of twenty years counted from the filing date.[8]

[8]It is understood that those Members which do not have a system of original grant may provide that the term of protection shall be computed from the filing date in the system of original grant.

Article 34
Process Patents: Burden of Proof

1. For the purposes of civil proceedings in respect of the infringement of the rights of the owner referred to in paragraph 1(b) of Article 28, if the subject matter of a patent is a process for obtaining a product, the judicial authorities shall have the authority to order the defendant to prove that the process to obtain an identical product is different from the patented process. Therefore, Members shall provide, in at least one of the following circumstances, that any identical product when produced without the consent of the patent owner shall, in the absence of proof to the contrary, be deemed to have been obtained by the patented process:

(a) if the product obtained by the patented process is new;

(b) if there is a substantial likelihood that the identical product was made by the process and the owner of the patent has been unable through reasonable efforts to determine the process actually used.

2. Any Member shall be free to provide that the burden of proof indicated in paragraph 1 shall be on the alleged infringer only if the condition referred to in subparagraph (a) is fulfilled or only if the condition referred to in subparagraph (b) is fulfilled.

3. In the adduction of proof to the contrary, the legitimate interests of defendants in protecting their manufacturing and business secrets shall be taken into account.

Section 6: Layout-designs (Topographies) of Integrated Circuits

Article 35
Relation to the IPIC Treaty

Members agree to provide protection to the layout-designs (topographies) of integrated circuits (referred to in this Agreement as "layout-designs") in accordance with Articles 2 through 7 (other than paragraph 3 of Article 6), Article 12 and paragraph 3 of Article 16 of the Treaty on Intellectual Property in Respect of Integrated Circuits and, in addition, to comply with the following provisions.

Article 36
Scope of the Protection

Subject to the provisions of paragraph 1 of Article 37, Members shall consider unlawful the following acts if performed without the authorization of the right holder:[9] importing, selling, or otherwise distributing for commercial purposes a protected layout-design, an integrated circuit

[9] The term "right holder" in this Section shall be understood as having the same meaning as the term "holder of the right" in the IPIC Treaty.

in which a protected layout-design is incorporated, or an article incorporating such an integrated circuit only in so far as it continues to contain an unlawfully reproduced layout-design.

Article 37

Acts Not Requiring the Authorization of the Right Holder

1. Notwithstanding Article 36, no Member shall consider unlawful the performance of any of the acts referred to in that Article in respect of an integrated circuit incorporating an unlawfully reproduced layout-design or any article incorporating such an integrated circuit where the person performing or ordering such acts did not know and had no reasonable ground to know, when acquiring the integrated circuit or article incorporating such an integrated circuit, that it incorporated an unlawfully reproduced layout-design. Members shall provide that, after the time that such person has received sufficient notice that the layout-design was unlawfully reproduced, that person may perform any of the acts with respect to the stock on hand or ordered before such time, but shall be liable to pay to the right holder a sum equivalent to a reasonable royalty such as would be payable under a freely negotiated licence in respect of such a layout-design.

2. The conditions set out in subparagraphs (a) through (k) of Article 31 shall apply *mutatis mutandis* in the event of any non-voluntary licensing of a layout-design or of its use by or for the government without the authorization of the right holder.

Article 38

Term of Protection

1. In Members requiring registration as a condition of protection, the term of protection of layout-designs shall not end before the expiration of a period of 10 years counted from the date of filing an application for registration or from the first commercial exploitation wherever in the world it occurs.

2. In Members not requiring registration as a condition for protection, layout-designs shall be protected for a term of no less than 10 years from the date of the first commercial exploitation wherever in the world it occurs.

3. Notwithstanding paragraphs 1 and 2, a Member may provide that protection shall lapse 15 years after the creation of the layout-design.

Section 7: Protection of Undisclosed Information

Article 39

1. In the course of ensuring effective protection against unfair competition as provided in Article 10*bis* of the Paris Convention (1967), Members shall protect undisclosed information in accordance with paragraph 2 and data submitted to governments or governmental agencies in accordance with paragraph 3.

2. Natural and legal persons shall have the possibility of preventing information lawfully within their control from being disclosed to, acquired by, or used by others without their consent in a manner contrary to honest commercial practices[10] so long as such information:

(a) is secret in the sense that it is not, as a body or in the precise configuration and assembly of its components, generally known among or readily accessible to persons within the circles that normally deal with the kind of information in question;

(b) has commercial value because it is secret; and

(c) has been subject to reasonable steps under the circumstances, by the person lawfully in control of the information, to keep it secret.

3. Members, when requiring, as a condition of approving the marketing of pharmaceutical or of agricultural chemical products which utilize new chemical entities, the submission of undisclosed test or other data, the origination of which involves a considerable effort, shall protect such data against unfair commercial use. In addition, Members shall protect such data against disclosure, except where necessary to protect the public, or unless steps are taken to ensure that the data are protected against unfair commercial use.

Section 8: Control of Anti-competitive Practices in Contractual Licences

Article 40

1. Members agree that some licensing practices or conditions pertaining to intellectual property rights which restrain competition may have adverse effects on trade and may impede the transfer and dissemination of technology.

2. Nothing in this Agreement shall prevent Members from specifying in their legislation licensing practices or conditions that may in particular cases constitute an abuse of intellectual property rights having an adverse effect on competition in the relevant market. As provided above, a Member may adopt, consistently with the other provisions of this Agreement, appropriate measures to prevent or control such practices, which may include for example exclusive grantback conditions, conditions preventing challenges to validity and coercive package licensing, in the light of the relevant laws and regulations of that Member.

3. Each Member shall enter, upon request, into consultations with any other Member which has cause to believe that an intellectual property right owner that is a national or domiciliary of

[10]For the purpose of this provision, "a manner contrary to honest commercial practices" shall mean at least practices such as breach of contract, breach of confidence and inducement to breach, and includes the acquisition of undisclosed information by third parties who knew, or were grossly negligent in failing to know, that such practices were involved in the acquisition.

the Member to which the request for consultations has been addressed is undertaking practices in violation of the requesting Member's laws and regulations on the subject matter of this Section, and which wishes to secure compliance with such legislation, without prejudice to any action under the law and to the full freedom of an ultimate decision of either Member. The Member addressed shall accord full and sympathetic consideration to, and shall afford adequate opportunity for, consultations with the requesting Member, and shall cooperate through supply of publicly available non-confidential information of relevance to the matter in question and of other information available to the Member, subject to domestic law and to the conclusion of mutually satisfactory agreements concerning the safeguarding of its confidentiality by the requesting Member.

4. A Member whose nationals or domiciliaries are subject to proceedings in another Member concerning alleged violation of that other Member's laws and regulations on the subject matter of this Section shall, upon request, be granted an opportunity for consultations by the other Member under the same conditions as those foreseen in paragraph 3.

PART III

ENFORCEMENT OF INTELLECTUAL PROPERTY RIGHTS

Section 1: General Obligations

Article 41

1. Members shall ensure that enforcement procedures as specified in this Part are available under their law so as to permit effective action against any act of infringement of intellectual property rights covered by this Agreement, including expeditious remedies to prevent infringements and remedies which constitute a deterrent to further infringements. These procedures shall be applied in such a manner as to avoid the creation of barriers to legitimate trade and to provide for safeguards against their abuse.

2. Procedures concerning the enforcement of intellectual property rights shall be fair and equitable. They shall not be unnecessarily complicated or costly, or entail unreasonable time-limits or unwarranted delays.

3. Decisions on the merits of a case shall preferably be in writing and reasoned. They shall be made available at least to the parties to the proceeding without undue delay. Decisions on the merits of a case shall be based only on evidence in respect of which parties were offered the opportunity to be heard.

4. Parties to a proceeding shall have an opportunity for review by a judicial authority of final administrative decisions and, subject to jurisdictional provisions in a Member's law concerning the importance of a case, of at least the legal aspects of initial judicial decisions on the merits of a case. However, there shall be no obligation to provide an opportunity for review of acquittals in criminal cases.

5. It is understood that this Part does not create any obligation to put in place a judicial system for the enforcement of intellectual property rights distinct from that for the enforcement of law in general, nor does it affect the capacity of Members to enforce their law in general. Nothing in this Part creates any obligation with respect to the distribution of resources as between enforcement of intellectual property rights and the enforcement of law in general.

Section 2: Civil and Administrative Procedures and Remedies

Article 42
Fair and Equitable Procedures

Members shall make available to right holders[11] civil judicial procedures concerning the enforcement of any intellectual property right covered by this Agreement. Defendants shall have the right to written notice which is timely and contains sufficient detail, including the basis of the claims. Parties shall be allowed to be represented by independent legal counsel, and procedures shall not impose overly burdensome requirements concerning mandatory personal appearances. All parties to such procedures shall be duly entitled to substantiate their claims and to present all relevant evidence. The procedure shall provide a means to identify and protect confidential information, unless this would be contrary to existing constitutional requirements.

Article 43
Evidence

1. The judicial authorities shall have the authority, where a party has presented reasonably available evidence sufficient to support its claims and has specified evidence relevant to substantiation of its claims which lies in the control of the opposing party, to order that this evidence be produced by the opposing party, subject in appropriate cases to conditions which ensure the protection of confidential information.

2. In cases in which a party to a proceeding voluntarily and without good reason refuses access to, or otherwise does not provide necessary information within a reasonable period, or significantly impedes a procedure relating to an enforcement action, a Member may accord judicial authorities the authority to make preliminary and final determinations, affirmative or negative, on the basis of the information presented to them, including the complaint or the allegation presented by the party adversely affected by the denial of access to information, subject to providing the parties an opportunity to be heard on the allegations or evidence.

Article 44
Injunctions

1. The judicial authorities shall have the authority to order a party to desist from an

[11]For the purpose of this Part, the term "right holder" includes federations and associations having legal standing to assert such rights.

infringement, *inter alia* to prevent the entry into the channels of commerce in their jurisdiction of imported goods that involve the infringement of an intellectual property right, immediately after customs clearance of such goods. Members are not obliged to accord such authority in respect of protected subject matter acquired or ordered by a person prior to knowing or having reasonable grounds to know that dealing in such subject matter would entail the infringement of an intellectual property right.

2. Notwithstanding the other provisions of this Part and provided that the provisions of Part II specifically addressing use by governments, or by third parties authorized by a government, without the authorization of the right holder are complied with, Members may limit the remedies available against such use to payment of remuneration in accordance with subparagraph (h) of Article 31. In other cases, the remedies under this Part shall apply or, where these remedies are inconsistent with a Member's law, declaratory judgments and adequate compensation shall be available.

Article 45
Damages

1. The judicial authorities shall have the authority to order the infringer to pay the right holder damages adequate to compensate for the injury the right holder has suffered because of an infringement of that person's intellectual property right by an infringer who knowingly, or with reasonable grounds to know, engaged in infringing activity.

2. The judicial authorities shall also have the authority to order the infringer to pay the right holder expenses, which may include appropriate attorney's fees. In appropriate cases, Members may authorize the judicial authorities to order recovery of profits and/or payment of pre-established damages even where the infringer did not knowingly, or with reasonable grounds to know, engage in infringing activity.

Article 46
Other Remedies

In order to create an effective deterrent to infringement, the judicial authorities shall have the authority to order that goods that they have found to be infringing be, without compensation of any sort, disposed of outside the channels of commerce in such a manner as to avoid any harm caused to the right holder, or, unless this would be contrary to existing constitutional requirements, destroyed. The judicial authorities shall also have the authority to order that materials and implements the predominant use of which has been in the creation of the infringing goods be, without compensation of any sort, disposed of outside the channels of commerce in such a manner as to minimize the risks of further infringements. In considering such requests, the need for proportionality between the seriousness of the infringement and the remedies ordered as well as the interests of third parties shall be taken into account. In regard to counterfeit trademark goods, the simple removal of the trademark unlawfully affixed shall not be sufficient, other than in exceptional cases, to permit release of the goods into the channels of commerce.

Article 47
Right of Information

Members may provide that the judicial authorities shall have the authority, unless this would be out of proportion to the seriousness of the infringement, to order the infringer to inform the right holder of the identity of third persons involved in the production and distribution of the infringing goods or services and of their channels of distribution.

Article 48
Indemnification of the Defendant

1. The judicial authorities shall have the authority to order a party at whose request measures were taken and who has abused enforcement procedures to provide to a party wrongfully enjoined or restrained adequate compensation for the injury suffered because of such abuse. The judicial authorities shall also have the authority to order the applicant to pay the defendant expenses, which may include appropriate attorney's fees.

2. In respect of the administration of any law pertaining to the protection or enforcement of intellectual property rights, Members shall only exempt both public authorities and officials from liability to appropriate remedial measures where actions are taken or intended in good faith in the course of the administration of that law.

Article 49
Administrative Procedures

To the extent that any civil remedy can be ordered as a result of administrative procedures on the merits of a case, such procedures shall conform to principles equivalent in substance to those set forth in this Section.

Section 3: Provisional Measures

Article 50

1. The judicial authorities shall have the authority to order prompt and effective provisional measures:

   (a) to prevent an infringement of any intellectual property right from occurring, and in particular to prevent the entry into the channels of commerce in their jurisdiction of goods, including imported goods immediately after customs clearance;

   (b) to preserve relevant evidence in regard to the alleged infringement.

2. The judicial authorities shall have the authority to adopt provisional measures *inaudita altera parte* where appropriate, in particular where any delay is likely to cause irreparable harm

to the right holder, or where there is a demonstrable risk of evidence being destroyed.

3. The judicial authorities shall have the authority to require the applicant to provide any reasonably available evidence in order to satisfy themselves with a sufficient degree of certainty that the applicant is the right holder and that the applicant's right is being infringed or that such infringement is imminent, and to order the applicant to provide a security or equivalent assurance sufficient to protect the defendant and to prevent abuse.

4. Where provisional measures have been adopted *inaudita altera parte*, the parties affected shall be given notice, without delay after the execution of the measures at the latest. A review, including a right to be heard, shall take place upon request of the defendant with a view to deciding, within a reasonable period after the notification of the measures, whether these measures shall be modified, revoked or confirmed.

5. The applicant may be required to supply other information necessary for the identification of the goods concerned by the authority that will execute the provisional measures.

6. Without prejudice to paragraph 4, provisional measures taken on the basis of paragraphs 1 and 2 shall, upon request by the defendant, be revoked or otherwise cease to have effect, if proceedings leading to a decision on the merits of the case are not initiated within a reasonable period, to be determined by the judicial authority ordering the measures where a Member's law so permits or, in the absence of such a determination, not to exceed 20 working days or 31 calendar days, whichever is the longer.

7. Where the provisional measures are revoked or where they lapse due to any act or omission by the applicant, or where it is subsequently found that there has been no infringement or threat of infringement of an intellectual property right, the judicial authorities shall have the authority to order the applicant, upon request of the defendant, to provide the defendant appropriate compensation for any injury caused by these measures.

8. To the extent that any provisional measure can be ordered as a result of administrative procedures, such procedures shall conform to principles equivalent in substance to those set forth in this Section.

Section 4: Special Requirements Related to Border Measures[12]

Article 51
Suspension of Release by Customs Authorities

Members shall, in conformity with the provisions set out below, adopt procedures[13] to enable a right holder, who has valid grounds for suspecting that the importation of counterfeit trademark or pirated copyright goods[14] may take place, to lodge an application in writing with competent authorities, administrative or judicial, for the suspension by the customs authorities of the release into free circulation of such goods. Members may enable such an application to be made in respect of goods which involve other infringements of intellectual property rights, provided that the requirements of this Section are met. Members may also provide for corresponding procedures concerning the suspension by the customs authorities of the release of infringing goods destined for exportation from their territories.

Article 52
Application

Any right holder initiating the procedures under Article 51 shall be required to provide adequate evidence to satisfy the competent authorities that, under the laws of the country of importation, there is *prima facie* an infringement of the right holder's intellectual property right and to supply a sufficiently detailed description of the goods to make them readily recognizable by the customs authorities. The competent authorities shall inform the applicant within a reasonable period whether they have accepted the application and, where determined by the competent authorities, the period for which the customs authorities will take action.

---

[12] Where a Member has dismantled substantially all controls over movement of goods across its border with another Member with which it forms part of a customs union, it shall not be required to apply the provisions of this Section at that border.

[13] It is understood that there shall be no obligation to apply such procedures to imports of goods put on the market in another country by or with the consent of the right holder, or to goods in transit.

[14] For the purposes of this Agreement:

(a) "counterfeit trademark goods" shall mean any goods, including packaging, bearing without authorization a trademark which is identical to the trademark validly registered in respect of such goods, or which cannot be distinguished in its essential aspects from such a trademark, and which thereby infringes the rights of the owner of the trademark in question under the law of the country of importation;

(b) "pirated copyright goods" shall mean any goods which are copies made without the consent of the right holder or person duly authorized by the right holder in the country of production and which are made directly or indirectly from an article where the making of that copy would have constituted an infringement of a copyright or a related right under the law of the country of importation.

Article 53
Security or Equivalent Assurance

1. The competent authorities shall have the authority to require an applicant to provide a security or equivalent assurance sufficient to protect the defendant and the competent authorities and to prevent abuse. Such security or equivalent assurance shall not unreasonably deter recourse to these procedures.

2. Where pursuant to an application under this Section the release of goods involving industrial designs, patents, layout-designs or undisclosed information into free circulation has been suspended by customs authorities on the basis of a decision other than by a judicial or other independent authority, and the period provided for in Article 55 has expired without the granting of provisional relief by the duly empowered authority, and provided that all other conditions for importation have been complied with, the owner, importer, or consignee of such goods shall be entitled to their release on the posting of a security in an amount sufficient to protect the right holder for any infringement. Payment of such security shall not prejudice any other remedy available to the right holder, it being understood that the security shall be released if the right holder fails to pursue the right of action within a reasonable period of time.

Article 54
Notice of Suspension

The importer and the applicant shall be promptly notified of the suspension of the release of goods according to Article 51.

Article 55
Duration of Suspension

If, within a period not exceeding 10 working days after the applicant has been served notice of the suspension, the customs authorities have not been informed that proceedings leading to a decision on the merits of the case have been initiated by a party other than the defendant, or that the duly empowered authority has taken provisional measures prolonging the suspension of the release of the goods, the goods shall be released, provided that all other conditions for importation or exportation have been complied with; in appropriate cases, this time-limit may be extended by another 10 working days. If proceedings leading to a decision on the merits of the case have been initiated, a review, including a right to be heard, shall take place upon request of the defendant with a view to deciding, within a reasonable period, whether these measures shall be modified, revoked or confirmed. Notwithstanding the above, where the suspension of the release of goods is carried out or continued in accordance with a provisional judicial measure, the provisions of paragraph 6 of Article 50 shall apply.

Article 56
Indemnification of the Importer and of the Owner of the Goods

Relevant authorities shall have the authority to order the applicant to pay the importer, the consignee and the owner of the goods appropriate compensation for any injury caused to them through the wrongful detention of goods or through the detention of goods released pursuant to Article 55.

Article 57
Right of Inspection and Information

Without prejudice to the protection of confidential information, Members shall provide the competent authorities the authority to give the right holder sufficient opportunity to have any goods detained by the customs authorities inspected in order to substantiate the right holder's claims. The competent authorities shall also have authority to give the importer an equivalent opportunity to have any such goods inspected. Where a positive determination has been made on the merits of a case, Members may provide the competent authorities the authority to inform the right holder of the names and addresses of the consignor, the importer and the consignee and of the quantity of the goods in question.

Article 58
Ex Officio Action

Where Members require competent authorities to act upon their own initiative and to suspend the release of goods in respect of which they have acquired *prima facie* evidence that an intellectual property right is being infringed:

(a) the competent authorities may at any time seek from the right holder any information that may assist them to exercise these powers;

(b) the importer and the right holder shall be promptly notified of the suspension. Where the importer has lodged an appeal against the suspension with the competent authorities, the suspension shall be subject to the conditions, *mutatis mutandis*, set out at Article 55;

(c) Members shall only exempt both public authorities and officials from liability to appropriate remedial measures where actions are taken or intended in good faith.

Article 59
Remedies

Without prejudice to other rights of action open to the right holder and subject to the right of the defendant to seek review by a judicial authority, competent authorities shall have the authority to order the destruction or disposal of infringing goods in accordance with the principles set out in Article 46. In regard to counterfeit trademark goods, the authorities shall not allow the re-exportation of the infringing goods in an unaltered state or subject them to a different customs procedure, other than in exceptional circumstances.

Article 60
De Minimis Imports

Members may exclude from the application of the above provisions small quantities of goods of a non-commercial nature contained in travellers' personal luggage or sent in small consignments.

Section 5: Criminal Procedures

Article 61

Members shall provide for criminal procedures and penalties to be applied at least in cases of wilful trademark counterfeiting or copyright piracy on a commercial scale. Remedies available shall include imprisonment and/or monetary fines sufficient to provide a deterrent, consistently with the level of penalties applied for crimes of a corresponding gravity. In appropriate cases, remedies available shall also include the seizure, forfeiture and destruction of the infringing goods and of any materials and implements the predominant use of which has been in the commission of the offence. Members may provide for criminal procedures and penalties to be applied in other cases of infringement of intellectual property rights, in particular where they are committed wilfully and on a commercial scale.

PART IV

ACQUISITION AND MAINTENANCE OF INTELLECTUAL PROPERTY RIGHTS AND RELATED *INTER-PARTES* PROCEDURES

Article 62

1. Members may require, as a condition of the acquisition or maintenance of the intellectual property rights provided for under Sections 2 through 6 of Part II, compliance with reasonable procedures and formalities. Such procedures and formalities shall be consistent with the provisions of this Agreement.

2. Where the acquisition of an intellectual property right is subject to the right being granted or registered, Members shall ensure that the procedures for grant or registration, subject to compliance with the substantive conditions for acquisition of the right, permit the granting or registration of the right within a reasonable period of time so as to avoid unwarranted curtailment of the period of protection.

3. Article 4 of the Paris Convention (1967) shall apply *mutatis mutandis* to service marks.

4. Procedures concerning the acquisition or maintenance of intellectual property rights and, where a Member's law provides for such procedures, administrative revocation and *inter partes* procedures such as opposition, revocation and cancellation, shall be governed by the general principles set out in paragraphs 2 and 3 of Article 41.

5. Final administrative decisions in any of the procedures referred to under paragraph 4 shall be subject to review by a judicial or quasi-judicial authority. However, there shall be no obligation to provide an opportunity for such review of decisions in cases of unsuccessful opposition or administrative revocation, provided that the grounds for such procedures can be the subject of invalidation procedures.

PART V

DISPUTE PREVENTION AND SETTLEMENT

Article 63
Transparency

1. Laws and regulations, and final judicial decisions and administrative rulings of general application, made effective by a Member pertaining to the subject matter of this Agreement (the availability, scope, acquisition, enforcement and prevention of the abuse of intellectual property rights) shall be published, or where such publication is not practicable made publicly available, in a national language, in such a manner as to enable governments and right holders to become acquainted with them. Agreements concerning the subject matter of this Agreement which are in force between the government or a governmental agency of a Member and the government or a governmental agency of another Member shall also be published.

2. Members shall notify the laws and regulations referred to in paragraph 1 to the Council for TRIPS in order to assist that Council in its review of the operation of this Agreement. The Council shall attempt to minimize the burden on Members in carrying out this obligation and may decide to waive the obligation to notify such laws and regulations directly to the Council if consultations with WIPO on the establishment of a common register containing these laws and regulations are successful. The Council shall also consider in this connection any action required regarding notifications pursuant to the obligations under this Agreement stemming from the provisions of Article 6*ter* of the Paris Convention (1967).

3. Each Member shall be prepared to supply, in response to a written request from another Member, information of the sort referred to in paragraph 1. A Member, having reason to believe that a specific judicial decision or administrative ruling or bilateral agreement in the area of intellectual property rights affects its rights under this Agreement, may also request in writing to be given access to or be informed in sufficient detail of such specific judicial decisions or administrative rulings or bilateral agreements.

4. Nothing in paragraphs 1, 2 and 3 shall require Members to disclose confidential information which would impede law enforcement or otherwise be contrary to the public interest

or would prejudice the legitimate commercial interests of particular enterprises, public or private.

Article 64
Dispute Settlement

1. The provisions of Articles XXII and XXIII of GATT 1994 as elaborated and applied by the Dispute Settlement Understanding shall apply to consultations and the settlement of disputes under this Agreement except as otherwise specifically provided herein.

2. Subparagraphs 1(b) and 1(c) of Article XXIII of GATT 1994 shall not apply to the settlement of disputes under this Agreement for a period of five years from the date of entry into force of the WTO Agreement.

3. During the time period referred to in paragraph 2, the Council for TRIPS shall examine the scope and modalities for complaints of the type provided for under subparagraphs 1(b) and 1(c) of Article XXIII of GATT 1994 made pursuant to this Agreement, and submit its recommendations to the Ministerial Conference for approval. Any decision of the Ministerial Conference to approve such recommendations or to extend the period in paragraph 2 shall be made only by consensus, and approved recommendations shall be effective for all Members without further formal acceptance process.

PART VI

TRANSITIONAL ARRANGEMENTS

Article 65
Transitional Arrangements

1. Subject to the provisions of paragraphs 2, 3 and 4, no Member shall be obliged to apply the provisions of this Agreement before the expiry of a general period of one year following the date of entry into force of the WTO Agreement.

2. A developing country Member is entitled to delay for a further period of four years the date of application, as defined in paragraph 1, of the provisions of this Agreement other than Articles 3, 4 and 5.

3. Any other Member which is in the process of transformation from a centrally-planned into a market, free-enterprise economy and which is undertaking structural reform of its intellectual property system and facing special problems in the preparation and implementation of intellectual property laws and regulations, may also benefit from a period of delay as foreseen in paragraph 2.

4. To the extent that a developing country Member is obliged by this Agreement to extend product patent protection to areas of technology not so protectable in its territory on the general date of application of this Agreement for that Member, as defined in paragraph 2, it may delay

the application of the provisions on product patents of Section 5 of Part II to such areas of technology for an additional period of five years.

5. A Member availing itself of a transitional period under paragraphs 1, 2, 3 or 4 shall ensure that any changes in its laws, regulations and practice made during that period do not result in a lesser degree of consistency with the provisions of this Agreement.

Article 66

Least-Developed Country Members

1. In view of the special needs and requirements of least-developed country Members, their economic, financial and administrative constraints, and their need for flexibility to create a viable technological base, such Members shall not be required to apply the provisions of this Agreement, other than Articles 3, 4 and 5, for a period of 10 years from the date of application as defined under paragraph 1 of Article 65. The Council for TRIPS shall, upon duly motivated request by a least-developed country Member, accord extensions of this period.

2. Developed country Members shall provide incentives to enterprises and institutions in their territories for the purpose of promoting and encouraging technology transfer to least-developed country Members in order to enable them to create a sound and viable technological base.

Article 67

Technical Cooperation

In order to facilitate the implementation of this Agreement, developed country Members shall provide, on request and on mutually agreed terms and conditions, technical and financial cooperation in favour of developing and least-developed country Members. Such cooperation shall include assistance in the preparation of laws and regulations on the protection and enforcement of intellectual property rights as well as on the prevention of their abuse, and shall include support regarding the establishment or reinforcement of domestic offices and agencies relevant to these matters, including the training of personnel.

PART VII

INSTITUTIONAL ARRANGEMENTS: FINAL PROVISIONS

Article 68

Council for Trade-Related Aspects of Intellectual Property Rights

The Council for TRIPS shall monitor the operation of this Agreement and, in particular, Members' compliance with their obligations hereunder, and shall afford Members the opportunity of consulting on matters relating to the trade-related aspects of intellectual property rights. It shall carry out such other responsibilities as assigned to it by the Members, and it shall, in particular, provide any assistance requested by them in the context of dispute settlement procedures. In carrying out its functions, the Council for TRIPS may consult with and seek information from any source it deems appropriate. In consultation with WIPO, the Council shall seek to establish, within one year of its first meeting, appropriate arrangements for cooperation with bodies of that Organization.

Article 69
International Cooperation

Members agree to cooperate with each other with a view to eliminating international trade in goods infringing intellectual property rights. For this purpose, they shall establish and notify contact points in their administrations and be ready to exchange information on trade in infringing goods. They shall, in particular, promote the exchange of information and cooperation between customs authorities with regard to trade in counterfeit trademark goods and pirated copyright goods.

Article 70
Protection of Existing Subject Matter

1. This Agreement does not give rise to obligations in respect of acts which occurred before the date of application of the Agreement for the Member in question.

2. Except as otherwise provided for in this Agreement, this Agreement gives rise to obligations in respect of all subject matter existing at the date of application of this Agreement for the Member in question, and which is protected in that Member on the said date, or which meets or comes subsequently to meet the criteria for protection under the terms of this Agreement. In respect of this paragraph and paragraphs 3 and 4, copyright obligations with respect to existing works shall be solely determined under Article 18 of the Berne Convention (1971), and obligations with respect to the rights of producers of phonograms and performers in existing phonograms shall be determined solely under Article 18 of the Berne Convention (1971) as made applicable under paragraph 6 of Article 14 of this Agreement.

3. There shall be no obligation to restore protection to subject matter which on the date of application of this Agreement for the Member in question has fallen into the public domain.

4. In respect of any acts in respect of specific objects embodying protected subject matter which become infringing under the terms of legislation in conformity with this Agreement, and which were commenced, or in respect of which a significant investment was made, before the date of acceptance of the WTO Agreement by that Member, any Member may provide for a limitation of the remedies available to the right holder as to the continued performance of such acts after the date of application of this Agreement for that Member. In such cases the Member shall, however, at least provide for the payment of equitable remuneration.

5. A Member is not obliged to apply the provisions of Article 11 and of paragraph 4 of Article 14 with respect to originals or copies purchased prior to the date of application of this

Agreement for that Member.

6. Members shall not be required to apply Article 31, or the requirement in paragraph 1 of Article 27 that patent rights shall be enjoyable without discrimination as to the field of technology, to use without the authorization of the right holder where authorization for such use was granted by the government before the date this Agreement became known.

7. In the case of intellectual property rights for which protection is conditional upon registration, applications for protection which are pending on the date of application of this Agreement for the Member in question shall be permitted to be amended to claim any enhanced protection provided under the provisions of this Agreement. Such amendments shall not include new matter.

8. Where a Member does not make available as of the date of entry into force of the WTO Agreement patent protection for pharmaceutical and agricultural chemical products commensurate with its obligations under Article 27, that Member shall:

(a) notwithstanding the provisions of Part VI, provide as from the date of entry into force of the WTO Agreement a means by which applications for patents for such inventions can be filed;

(b) apply to these applications, as of the date of application of this Agreement, the criteria for patentability as laid down in this Agreement as if those criteria were being applied on the date of filing in that Member or, where priority is available and claimed, the priority date of the application; and

(c) provide patent protection in accordance with this Agreement as from the grant of the patent and for the remainder of the patent term, counted from the filing date in accordance with Article 33 of this Agreement, for those of these applications that meet the criteria for protection referred to in subparagraph (b).

9. Where a product is the subject of a patent application in a Member in accordance with paragraph 8(a), exclusive marketing rights shall be granted, notwithstanding the provisions of Part VI, for a period of five years after obtaining marketing approval in that Member or until a product patent is granted or rejected in that Member, whichever period is shorter, provided that, subsequent to the entry into force of the WTO Agreement, a patent application has been filed and a patent granted for that product in another Member and marketing approval obtained in such other Member.

Article 71
Review and Amendment

1. The Council for TRIPS shall review the implementation of this Agreement after the expiration of the transitional period referred to in paragraph 2 of Article 65. The Council shall, having regard to the experience gained in its implementation, review it two years after that date,

and at identical intervals thereafter. The Council may also undertake reviews in the light of any relevant new developments which might warrant modification or amendment of this Agreement.

2. Amendments merely serving the purpose of adjusting to higher levels of protection of intellectual property rights achieved, and in force, in other multilateral agreements and accepted under those agreements by all Members of the WTO may be referred to the Ministerial Conference for action in accordance with paragraph 6 of Article X of the WTO Agreement on the basis of a consensus proposal from the Council for TRIPS.

Article 72
Reservations

Reservations may not be entered in respect of any of the provisions of this Agreement without the consent of the other Members.

Article 73
Security Exceptions

Nothing in this Agreement shall be construed:

(a) to require a Member to furnish any information the disclosure of which it considers contrary to its essential security interests; or

(b) to prevent a Member from taking any action which it considers necessary for the protection of its essential security interests;

(i) relating to fissionable materials or the materials from which they are derived;

(ii) relating to the traffic in arms, ammunition and implements of war and to such traffic in other goods and materials as is carried on directly or indirectly for the purpose of supplying a military establishment;

(iii) taken in time of war or other emergency in international relations; or

(c) to prevent a Member from taking any action in pursuance of its obligations under the United Nations Charter for the maintenance of international peace and security.

* * *